PUTIN'S LABOR DILEMMA

PUTIN'S LABOR DILEMMA

Russian Politics between Stability and Stagnation

Stephen Crowley

ILR PRESS

AN IMPRINT OF CORNELL UNIVERSITY PRESS   ITHACA AND LONDON

First published 2021 by Cornell University Press

Library of Congress Cataloging-in-Publication Data

Names: Crowley, Stephen, 1960– author.
Title: Putin's labor dilemma : Russian politics between stability and stagnation / Stephen Crowley.
Description: Ithaca [New York] : ILR Press, an imprint of Cornell University Press, 2021. | Includes bibliographical references and index.
Identifiers: LCCN 2020056468 (print) | LCCN 2020056469 (ebook) | ISBN 9781501756276 (hardcover) | ISBN 9781501756283 (paperback) | ISBN 9781501756290 (epub) | ISBN 9781501756306 (pdf)
Subjects: LCSH: Working class—Russia (Federation) | Industrial relations—Political aspects—Russia (Federation) | Business and politics—Russia (Federation) | Industrial policy—Russia (Federation) | Economic stabilization—Russia (Federation) | Political stability—Russia (Federation) | Social stability—Russia (Federation) | Russia (Federation)—Economic conditions—1991– | Russia (Federation)—Economic policy—1991–
Classification: LCC HD8530.2 .C76 2021 (print) | LCC HD8530.2 (ebook) | DDC 331.120947—dc23
LC record available at https://lccn.loc.gov/2020056468
LC ebook record available at https://lccn.loc.gov/2020056469

For Cynthia and Anna

Contents

Acknowledgments

This project benefited from a number of individuals and sources of support. I am grateful for a yearlong fellowship at the Woodrow Wilson Center for International Scholars. Many thanks to Robert Litwak, Blair Ruble, the Wilson Center staff, and, at the Wilson Center's Kennan Institute, to Will Pomeranz, Matt Rojansky, Izabella Tabarovsky, and to my co-fellows, especially Volodymyr Kulikov, Sergey Parkhomenko, and Igor Zevelev.

I also benefited from a semester spent as a visiting research scholar at George Washington University's Institute for European, Russian, and Eurasian Studies, and from the workshop on postcommunist politics there organized by Henry Hale. In addition to Henry, I am grateful for comments in particular from Stas Gorelik, Bob Orttung, Peter Rollbert, David Szakonyi, and Yuval Weber.

I profited as well from a monthlong stay as visiting scholar at the Aleksanteri Institute / Finnish Center for Russian and Eastern European Studies at the University of Helsinki. There I am especially thankful for the comments and assistance from Alla Bolotova, Marina Khmelnitskaya, Markku Kivinen, and Eeva Korteniemi.

Oberlin College granted me a yearlong Thomas J. Klutznick Research Fellowship. There I am very grateful to a number of colleagues for advice and support, including Matt Berkman, Marc Blecher, Sarah El-Kazaz, Chris Howell, Pam Snyder, Maia Solovieva, and Veljko Vujacic.

Able research assistance was given to me by Christina Sorensen and Dimitar Nikolov at the Wilson Center, and at Oberlin by Roman Broszkowski, Paul Kleiman, Patrick Powers, and Meredith Walker—impressive students all.

At Cornell University Press, I'm grateful for the strong support of this project from Fran Benson, and the incisive input and shepherding from Ellen Labbate, Jennifer Savran Kelly, Glenn Novak, and Brock Schnoke.

I greatly benefited from a number of individuals who gave indispensable suggestions along the way. While I will no doubt miss some, I would like to acknowledge the comments of Petr Bizyukov, Carine Clement, Irina Denisova, Allison Evans, Cliff Gaddy, Vladimir Gimpelson, Aleksandr Golts, Vladislav Inozemtsev, Irina Ivakhnyuk, Tatiana Mikhailova, Jeremy Morris, Tom Remington, Andrey Semenev, Lewis Siegelbaum, Rudy Sil, and Regina Smyth, and Ryan James Tutak.

I would like to give special thanks to Irina Olimpieva, who greatly helped my understanding of contemporary labor politics in Russia. Chapter 5 draws quite a bit from our joint article, "Labor Protests and Their Consequences in Putin's Russia," in *Problems of Post-Communism*.

Above all, thanks to Cynthia and Anna. They know why.

Abbreviations

CPRF	Communist Party of the Russian Federation
CSLR	Center for Social and Labor Rights
DIA	Defense Intelligence Agency
EBRD	European Bank of Reconstruction and Development
FAS	Federal Antimonopoly Service
FNPR	Federation of Independent Trade Unions of Russia
FPU	Federation of Trade Unions of Ukraine
FSO	Federal Protective Service
FTUK	Federation of Trade Unions of Kazakhstan
GAZ	Gorky Automobile Plant
GTA	Global Trade Alert
G20	Group of Twenty
IMF	International Monetary Fund
MPRA	Interregional Labor Union of Automobile Workers (later Interregional Trade Union Workers Association)
MPVP	Interregional Trade Union of Professional Drivers
NGO	nongovernmental organization
OECD	Organisation for Economic Co-operation and Development
OPR	Association of Russian Carriers
TOR or TOSER	Territories of Advanced Social and Economic Development
WTO	World Trade Organization

Note on Transliteration and Currency

I have used the Library of Congress transliteration scheme, except for names that have appeared prominently in Western publications. Currency equivalents are given in US dollars.

PUTIN'S LABOR DILEMMA

THE POLITICAL CONSEQUENCES OF RUSSIAN DEINDUSTRIALIZATION

What is the relationship between Russia's political leaders and the country's working class? As a first take on that question, consider two contrasting anecdotes. In December 2011, when ostensibly cosmopolitan and middle-class protesters were denouncing President Vladimir Putin in the streets in Moscow and St. Petersburg, Igor Kholmanskikh, a factory foreman at the Ural Tank Factory in Nizhniy Tagil, told Putin on national television that "if the militia . . . can't handle it, then me and the guys [*muzhiki*] are ready to come out and defend stability." Putin's administration played up this event considerably, with Putin later appointing Kholmanskikh, despite his lack of relevant credentials, as the presidential representative for the Urals Federal Region, a human symbol of Putin's working-class support.[1] Yet a few years later, in December 2015, a slight increase in a road tax for tractor-trailers united truck drivers across Russia in protest. While initially they raised only economic demands—and even pleaded, "President, help us!"—in little over a year they became politicized, calling for the resignation of the government and no-confidence in the president, and a leader of the truckers' movement announced his intention to run for president against Putin.

While some commentators have argued that Putin has survived the protests of liberals in Moscow by pitting "rural and Rust Belt Russia against urban and modernizing Russia," others have argued that the country's industrial centers are struggling, and its many "monotowns"—one-industry working-class towns left from the Soviet era—are a "time bomb" for Russian politics.[2] So, which is it? Is Russia's working class the ballast of stability for the Putin regime, or combustible material that might sink the ship of state? This book is not about Putin, not centrally anyway. Rather it is about the dilemmas that arise in Russia's many industrial regions and centers, or what Natalia Zubarevich has called—in contrast to Moscow and St. Petersburg—"second Russia," as well as a range of "social concerns" about public expectations for the provision of a minimal level of social benefits, expectations that constrain the seemingly invincible Russian leadership.[3]

Russia's workers neither make up an unquestioning pillar of support for Putin, nor are they ready to explode in a mass movement demanding regime change. But their actions remain central to the question of social and ultimately political stability in Russia, a stability that becomes much harder to maintain in challenging economic times. So the central question is: How have the *fears* of social unrest placed limits on, constrained, and helped mold Russia's political and economic system? Indeed, the challenge for Russia's leaders is not only to prevent social instability, but to craft a legitimation strategy that allows for generating economic growth while also maintaining sufficient popular support. Such are the concerns for top Kremlin officials, as well as for oligarchs and various economic and political power holders seeking to maintain their wealth and authority. Though often less articulated, such concerns should also weigh on Russia's liberals: both economic liberals who seek greater market reforms but too often fail to comprehend the likely social and political consequences of those reforms, and political liberals who seek greater democracy but too often fail to reconcile their own desires with the wishes and preferences of much of the Russian population.

One might assume that a rather authoritarian state like Russia's should be able to push past the dilemmas mentioned above and any protest that might result. Indeed, the probability of labor and social protest directly leading to political instability in Russia is fairly low. That probability is not zero, however, and the stakes are high. Russian leaders have a palpable fear of a "color revolution" (such as Ukraine's 2014 "Maidan revolution") that might depose them, and the steep costs that losing power might entail. Quite clearly, that concern overrides all others, including building a more vibrant economy. In his study of "Putinomics," Chris Miller concludes that there is a hierarchy of goals at work in Russia's political economy: "first, political control; second, social stability; third, efficiency and profit."[4] Yet the contradictions in such a goal ranking soon become clear. Political control cannot rely indefinitely on repression and propaganda, especially if the third goal—an efficient economy that provides some public benefit—is not being met. Yet prioritizing that third goal, especially in contemporary Russian society, risks undermining the second goal, and ultimately the first.

Too often in discussion of nondemocratic regimes such as Russia's, "stability" is counterposed with "revolution," as if the alternatives were simply one or the other. Yet leaders seeking to remain in power must also be concerned with popular support and legitimacy, the absence of which might be perceived by rival elites and others as a sign of vulnerability. Hence Putin's well-known concern with his approval ratings (long famously high but now fluctuating) and his maneuvering to amend the constitution to potentially extend his time in office and avoid the dreaded "succession question." Such trepidation is deepened when the economy faces slow growth or even stagnation, and— particularly given dependence on global commodities markets—the potential threat of another economic crisis.

Indeed, beneath the façade of strength and stability, Russia's political economy faces a number of critical challenges. Not least among them is the continuing predicament of deindustrialization. During the economic collapse in the 1990s, amid fears of "social explosion," Russia's labor market took a peculiar form: rather than the expected mass unemployment and closure of large factories, it adjusted instead through very flexible and very low (often unpaid) wages (chapter 2). This reliance on adjusting to economic conditions through flexible wages rather than employment levels has contributed to a level of labor productivity— arguably the key driver of economic growth, and of crucial importance given Russia's demographic crunch—that is extremely low by comparative standards. This, if left unchanged, could consign Russia to the status of a middle-income country for the foreseeable future (chapter 3). The paths out of that trap soon run into the obstacle of the industrial infrastructure left behind by the old Soviet coal-and-steel economy, including many large yet inefficient industrial enterprises, not least those in Russia's "monotowns"—the large number of one-company towns where an entire population is dependent on a single, often struggling, factory (chapter 4). While Russia's state and society struggled to survive the tumultuous 1990s, such impasses appeared to fade from view with the oil boom of the 2000s. With the global economic crisis of 2008–9, however, and the drop in oil prices in 2014, the Russian economy has struggled again, and as of this writing appears to be stuck somewhere between slow growth and stagnation. While accurate predictions are difficult, current projections put Russian economic growth over the next decade at around 1–2 percent per year. This would have Russia lagging behind the world average, and while the economy would technically be growing, in terms of living standards it would almost certainly be experienced as stagnation.

Given such dilemmas, the obvious question would seem to be, why not reform? If such challenges were not resolved during the tumultuous changes of the 1990s, why not during the boom years of the 2000s, or any time since? A return to solid economic growth, and avoiding perpetual status as a middle-income country, would appear to be a goal all would welcome. Various explanations have been proposed as to why such reform steps have not been taken: some point to the dependence on oil and the "resource curse," others to the lack of political will for modernization, with the *siloviki* (security officials turned politicians) topping the liberal reformers in the Kremlin, and still others point to elites trapped in a system of self-enrichment.[5] While each of these explanations has some merit, here we will advance another explanation—the specter of labor and social protest looming over Russia's leadership. Russia's postcommunist economy has experienced only a partial transformation and remains faced with challenges that can only be resolved through high social—and ultimately political—costs.

Why might Russia's leadership, centered on President Putin, be concerned with labor protest? By all accounts, Putin, who has been in office (either as president or prime minister) for over two decades, has a solid grasp on power and has greatly strengthened the Russian state, not least its security services (or "power ministries," in the Russian parlance). Labor and related social protests have been relatively few and sporadic, especially compared with those under Putin's predecessor Boris Yeltsin. True, pensioners rose up in large numbers to protest the monetization of benefits in 2005, and protests erupted in 2018 over the raising of the pension age. Russia did experience a large-scale strike wave in the late 1990s. Yet as Graeme Robertson concluded about that earlier episode, "Despite all this evidence of protest mobilization, it is clear that the contention did not add up to a sustained challenge to the authorities." He adds, "Protests were very numerous but mostly isolated, mainly local in nature, and focused on very basic, bread-and-butter issues."[6]

Why then should we expect the situation to be any different now, especially since following that earlier strike wave, the Russian economy experienced close to a decade of wage hikes and economic growth? Moreover, the growth contributed to a huge rise in public support for President Putin—an almost complete contrast from the Yeltsin years—and was accompanied by significant constricting of the political space for protest from workers and society at large. Indeed, it would seem rather paradoxical to argue that a much smaller amount of protests in the current political and economic conditions could be potentially more destabilizing than a much larger amount of protest was in the 1990s.

Further still, the Kremlin's fear of a color revolution would hardly seem to center on workers, since the color revolutions that have removed leaders from power in postcommunist states have typically centered on allegations of electoral fraud, and rarely have workers played a central role.[7] The "Russia without Putin" protests that arose around the parliamentary and presidential elections of 2011–12, while not successful in removing Putin from power, underscored the fact that such large-scale protests were typically spurred not by labor or social protests but by charges of electoral deception. Moreover, these protests were said to be driven by the "middle class"—educated professionals in Russia's largest urban centers.[8] During the 2011–12 protests, Russia's workers appeared to be defenders of authoritarianism, as the case of Igor Kholmanskikh suggests.

Yet the Putin-era economic growth has wavered, and the downturns in 2008–9 and again after 2014 exposed the largely unchanged and potentially explosive nature of Russia's industrial and other workplaces, where loyalist unions refrain from disruption, and disruptive unions are marginalized. This leads to labor relations that are both rigidly controlled and yet paradoxically deinstitutionalized, with economic downturns prompting a return to the spontaneous direct actions (if on a smaller scale) that Russia witnessed in the 1990s. Thus, Simon Clarke's description of Russian labor relations, while made in very different economic and political conditions over twenty years ago, remains remarkably relevant today. He argued then that there were "no established institutional channels through which workers can express their grievances," with the result that "grievances build up until they reach the point of explosion." He predicted, rather presciently, that "worker opposition is likely to take primarily negative and destructive forms, with workers increasingly looking to populist and extremist politicians for their salvation."[9]

More troubling for the Kremlin, the trepidations over a possible Russian color revolution were heightened considerably by the uprising in Belarus in mid-2020 (chapter 9). Once again, the protests were generated by charges of fraudulent elections; but given worsening economic conditions, the protests were soon joined by workers in a number of major industrial enterprises, amid calls for a general strike. More so than the protests in Minsk and other major cities, the worker protests clearly unnerved Belarus's long-standing president Alexander Lukashenko. He went directly to the protesting factories, telling the workers that they were betraying his trust, and that their protests were to him like a knife in the back (*udar v spinu*).[10] Once seen as Lukashenko's traditional constituency, the workers responded, "It's time for you to go!" and "The people are tired [of you]!"[11] While as of this writing Lukashenko has remained in power thanks to the backing of Russia, the image of workers at major factories calling for the leader's removal provides a stark warning for Russia's leaders. Protests by students and middle-class professionals might be challenging, but for reasons that will become clear, strikes and protests by Russia's workers could become crippling to the country's leadership.

Most studies of Russian politics focus attention on the country's elites, and understandably so. Putin is clearly in charge, and from him extend a number of concentric circles: to Kremlin insiders; to various oligarchs; to government officials on various levels; and so on. Discussions about the possibility for political change in Russia tend to revolve around debates between liberal economists and statist officials, or struggles between various government factions, and from there extend to the political opposition. By comparison, beyond survey data, much less attention has been placed on what major segments of the Russian people want, such as better lives for themselves and their families, and how this might impact the possibilities (and limitations) for political change. On one hand, there is little wonder in this—at most Russia is a political hybrid of democracy and dictatorship, increasingly weighted toward the latter. Thus, an assumption is often made that preferences of the bulk of the population matter little or are easily manipulated. And yet when social or economic policy changes are debated inside Russia, the question of their social consequences—a euphemism for the potential for protest—is never far from the surface. In short, to what extent do even seemingly powerful leaders, with high approval ratings and a firm grip on state power, have to contemplate taking a step too far, a step that might cross the threshold of a population's breaking point?

All states face the dilemma of seeking to extract resources from society (such as through taxation) without provoking rebellion.[12] In a very different context from Russia, the German sociologist Claus Offe characterized the challenges facing advanced capitalist societies as a contradiction between accumulation and legitimation—that is, of accumulating wealth and capital on the one hand while maintaining political legitimacy on the other.[13] Yet when we look at Russia, we see a society that has, within twenty-five years, been transformed from (whatever its other faults) a relatively egalitarian and self-described "workers' state" to one with—at least by some accounts—the most unequal distribution of wealth in the world.[14] However, despite some scattered protests, in Russia today there would appear to be little conflict, let alone contradiction, between accumulation and legitimation.

Indeed, however counterintuitively, much research in the field of comparative political economy suggests only a weak relationship between inequality and political conflict.[15] Yet the challenge for Russian leaders may stem less from legitimating the inequitable accumulation of wealth and assets than from maintaining economic growth sufficient to satisfy oligarchs and other elites while also preventing unrest from a disgruntled population. This was fairly easily done during the oil boom, but much less so in the absence of high oil and gas prices. Given the latter, the challenge increasingly becomes finding other sources of growth. Once again, the question that then typically gets posed is, why not reform? What prevents Russia, as some put it, from "modernizing"?[16]

According to Haggard and Kaufman, "one of the most heated and long-standing debates" in the literature on political economy centers on the following: "Do

authoritarian regimes have greater capacity than political democracies to insu-
late technocrats, 'manage' opposition, and reorient economic policy?"[17] Some
prominent historical examples, from Pinochet's Chile to the military dictatorships in South Korea and Taiwan, to the more recent case of China, suggest they
do.[18] Yet, as Haggard and Kaufman also note, "authoritarian regimes do not necessarily guarantee the executive the autonomy required to impose unpopular
adjustment programs."[19]

   In *The Politics of Authoritarian Rule*, Milan Svolik argues that authoritarians
face two central problems: the "problem of authoritarian power-sharing," that is,
horizontal threats from rival elites, and the "problem of authoritarian control,"
or vertical threats stemming from unrest from below.[20] Given the relative lack of
protest in Russia, and the durability of its nondemocratic regime (as well as those
in a number of other post-Soviet states), much attention has been placed on elite-
focused accounts of political stability and transformation, whereby generating
patronage, or the ability to buy off significant allies and opponents, is essential.[21] Yet such a goal must be balanced with the capacity to provide an acceptable
(if minimal) level of economic benefits and public goods to the population.
Should the state seek "to impose unpopular adjustment programs," it must also
contend with the potential for destabilizing protest from below.[22] All of this
makes the challenge of generating economic growth while maintaining political
stability a core test for state leaders.

   While a number of studies have pointed to the working class as the core
driving force pushing societies from authoritarianism to democracy, at least in
certain periods, others argue that in a postindustrial era, educated professionals
or the "middle class" are often the driving force for democratization.[23] In Russia, the latter view has predominated: workers are most often seen as supporters of stability, while the middle class is seen as the agent of change.[24] Indeed,
as the Kholmanskikh episode illustrates, Russia's workers are assumed to be a
core part of Putin's political base (this assumption will be critically explored in
chapter 7).

   However, to the extent that the Putin regime's legitimacy and electoral success rely significantly on working-class support, this poses serious challenges to
Russia's ability to escape from the middle-income trap. The pathologies generally
associated with that trap are well known to Russia: low productivity, low-skilled
and low-paid work, inequality, and informality. Economists argue that there
is a pathway out of that trap: the key is to boost productivity growth through
investment, especially in higher and technical education and research and development. In Russia, liberal economic advisers such as Alexei Kudrin have long
pushed for such policies (chapter 4). Yet, as Doner and Schneider argue, the central challenge to escaping the trap is "more politics than economics": it requires

the formation of a "growth coalition" that can support and defend such policies. As they survey the formation of such coalitions, Doner and Schneider focus on key groups, "especially business and labor, which are the core potential constituencies for a coalition that could take the big leap."[25] For Russia to escape from the middle-income trap, it must politically manage the shifting of substantial resources not only from certain oligarchs and state-owned enterprises, but also from struggling working-class communities and public-sector workers that are also a central element in the regime's political coalition.

Moreover, escaping the middle-income trap, and even the prospect of prolonged economic stagnation, are not the only challenges Russia faces. While economic hardship does not lead axiomatically to protest, "economic performance" is often a driver of political protest and instability, and a number of studies have demonstrated that authoritarian leaders are more likely to be deposed during economic downturns.[26] In a comprehensive analysis of "democracy protests" worldwide between 1989 and 2011, Dawn Brancati finds that economic crises are a central factor in triggering those protests, especially against authoritarianism. Such crises tend to increase support for opposition candidates, especially around elections, suggesting that demands for political change are hardly independent of economic conditions. She finds that when crises are severe enough and protests resultingly large, governments are more likely to make accommodations with protesters, though doing so can increase the risk of losing office.[27] Such a connection between economic crisis and political stability should be especially troubling for Russia's leadership, given the volatile nature of global commodity markets on which the Russian economy largely depends.

Economic crises don't necessarily spell the end of authoritarian regimes, which typically have many tools at their disposal to prevent such an outcome. But economic crises often induce those regimes to transform their legitimation strategies, to revise their tactics and ruling coalitions.[28] In Russia, there are clear "popularity costs" from economic crisis, as citizens are able to weigh their personal experience and local conditions against state propaganda.[29] As we shall see in chapter 7, the economic crises of 2008 and then 2014 pushed the Kremlin to substantially shift its legitimation strategy, in the process making it more difficult to form the liberal-minded "growth coalition" that might avoid continued stagnation.

For Russia, such dilemmas are not new. Throughout Russian history there has been a contradiction in discussions about the "popular classes" and the likelihood of protest from below. Common cultural tropes—heard inside Russia as well as out—often characterize the Russian people (almost always meaning the less educated) as patient and "long-suffering" (*mnogostradal'nyi, dolgoterpelivyi*). As some have put it, coping with hardship is in the Russians' "genetic code."[30] During the catastrophic conditions of Russia in the 1990s, workers were said to be hampered by a mentality of "paternalism" that explained their quiescence, patience, and passivity.[31] In some contemporary characterizations, working-class Russians in particular have narrow economic concerns and will refrain from protest as long as they are provided with potatoes and vodka.[32] More sympathetically, during times of economic hardship Russian workers and others are said to rely on time-honored survival strategies.[33] Not surprisingly, given a long history of autocracy, many Russian peasant and workers were said to believe in the notion of "the good tsar," that their miserable conditions would be improved "if only the tsar knew," a belief that, as we shall see, finds a contemporary echo in the direct appeal to Putin over issues like unpaid wages ("President, help us!").

Yet there is also in Russian history the tradition of the spontaneous protest—the *bunt*—and the corresponding fear on the part of those in power that such protest might lead to a broader revolt (unless it was channeled toward a different target, as in a pogrom).[34] Beyond the tradition of peasant revolts and rebellions (and pogroms) there is, one hardly needs to add, the Russian Revolution of 1917, when workers, soldiers, and peasants rose up in one of the greatest social insurrections in history. Needless to say, the Russian Revolution remains a core part of Russia's historical memory.

Yet, particularly with the rise of Stalinism, revolutionary symbolism and rhetoric were juxtaposed with authoritarianism. Workers as a class may have been lionized—their image often literally placed on a pedestal—and with rapid industrialization they became a major social force; but workers themselves were hardly the drivers of history. Workers were central to the Soviet industrial economy, but their work and lives were directed from above, and their only recourse was through largely individual resistance or small work-group rebellions. Yet the specter of the *bunt* remained, for example during the worker uprising in Novocherkassk in 1962. The name "Novocherkassk" remains synonymous with spontaneous worker unrest—and bloody repression—to this day (chapter 4).

Only with Mikhail Gorbachev's perestroika was independent organizing by workers and others possible. Soviet coal miners burst on the scene in 1989 with a nationwide strike. In an indication of the degree to which workers remained central to the Soviet system, both economically and ideologically, Gorbachev reflected in his memoirs that "the rapid destruction of the social order that existed for seventy years began with the miners' [strike] wave."[35] Two years later the miners struck again, in a self-described "political strike" that backed Yeltsin and other radical reformers and helped bring about the end of the Soviet Union.[36] Thus, while workers and other segments of Russian society may have been "long-suffering," they also participated in two major revolutions in the twentieth century.

Given the miners' example, following that of Poland's Solidarity movement, in the immediate wake of the communist collapse the fear most often expressed by reformers (whether neoliberals or those opposed to "shock therapy") was that workers, marked as the clear losers of postcommunism, would rise up to prevent the "transition to the market."[37] In the event, the response by workers throughout postcommunist societies was quite limited, with most observers characterizing workers in these societies as "quiescent" and labor unions as "weak."[38] Rather than undergoing the predicted backlash by workers and others, postcommunist political economies settled into a "low-level equilibrium," where capitalist institutions were weakly embedded and political democracy was not fully achieved.[39]

Russia of course is hardly alone in experiencing the decline of industrial labor as an economic and political force; beyond postcommunist societies, this phenomenon is a core challenge faced throughout the developed capitalist world. To be sure, within global capitalism, while industrial labor has declined in some world regions, it has risen in others. Thus, the waning of rust belt regions is only possible alongside the rise of industrial production in countries like China, which within a few decades became "the workshop of the world."[40] Yet while Russia is often lumped with China, India, and Brazil into the so-called BRICs category, Russia is not an industrializing economy driven by a growing share of manufacturing exports. In developing economies, industrial production grows faster than GDP; in Russia it is the opposite. In fact, Russia is a unique hybrid, both an "emerging market" in the sense of being relatively new to global capitalism, and yet one where the challenge has been too much industry, rather than too little. As Susanne Wengle notes, "post-Soviet development strategies were devised in the context of large-scale *de*industrialization rather than as a strategy to industrialize a rural economy."[41] Put differently, in Russia, industrial labor is not viewed as a source of economic growth but rather as a residual category, often seen as an obstacle in the way of progress toward a postindustrial society.

As some have argued, perhaps with a different economic strategy, rather than rapidly opening to capitalist markets following the Soviet collapse, Russia could have protected certain industrial sectors and restructured, taking advantage of its highly skilled and relatively low-wage labor force to create a comparative advantage on global markets. However, Russia was not inserted into the global capitalist economy as an exporter of industrial goods, low-wage or otherwise; rather it became primarily an exporter of energy and commodities.

Russia's trajectory from communism to capitalism is perhaps best character-ized by Timothy Mitchell's notion of "carbon democracy."[42] Mitchell's argument, in brief, is that coal production required a massive and geographically dispersed labor force, one that was capable of shutting down the entire economies on which coal depended. Coal miners, prone to radicalism, exploited that dependence to push for changes that led to democratization in Europe and elsewhere during the coal-fueled age of industrialization. Oil production, on the other hand, tends to be centralized and requires a much smaller labor force, which contributes to the well-known "resource curse" and the correlation of oil-producing economies and authoritarianism.

While oil and gas exports became important to the overall fate of the Soviet economy in the 1970s, internally the Soviet Union remained primarily a coal and steel economy. Coal remained so central to the economy that the shutting down of coal production with the 1989 and 1991 miner strikes threatened (through the lack of coking coal) the ruination of blast furnaces in steel mills, as well as the generation of electricity. The coal miners' radicalization, including their demands in their subsequent strike for an end to Communist Party hegemony and a rapid transition to democracy, fits well with Mitchell's argument about the connection between coal miners' structural power and democratization. Thus Gorbachev's later rumination about the coal strikes leading to the end of Soviet power.

But in contrast to the advanced capitalist societies of the West, where a reliance on coal in an earlier era was replaced by the importation of oil from abroad—and the exporting of the "resource curse" to authoritarian regimes elsewhere—oil and gas production largely replaced the production of coal as central to the Rus-sian domestic economy, as well as to its comparative advantage within global capitalism. Following Mitchell, this transformation can help explain the paradox of why—if only in its final years—the Soviet Union appeared more democratic (or certainly more pluralistic) under the communist leader Gorbachev than under the capitalist and nominally democratic system led by Vladimir Putin. This political transformation was closely connected to the weakened strategic position of industrial workers, where in contrast to the full employment (and overmanning) of the Soviet era, by 2012 the oil and gas sector accounted for 25 percent of the nominal value added to Russia's GDP, but only 4.5 percent of the total hours worked across all sectors.[43]

Yet this weakened structural position for Russia's workers is not unique to Russia. In examining the changing nature of social and labor protest in capi-talist societies over time, Joshua Clover describes the historical arc of what he terms "riot, strike, riot."[44] The notion of the preindustrial riot fits quite closely with the Russian experience of the peasant *bunt*. The strikes preceding the revolution of 1917, and that of coal miners and others at the end of the Soviet period—the intervening period clearly interrupted by state repression—reflect the structural power of workers in the industrial era. What power then remains with workers in an era of deindustrialization? In that context, the power to threaten the closure of a failing mine or factory lies less with workers and more with employers: private owners or the state. As Clover would predict, the most impactful worker protests in the postcommunist era have been less aimed at stopping the production of goods and more at halting their circulation, such as through blockading highways and rail lines. Yet while not riots per se, worker protests retain considerable symbolic (and ultimately political) power in the post-Soviet era. At times, the fear has been that they might culminate in a dreaded "social explosion."

By one important measure at least, Russia has successfully deindustrialized: a substantial portion of the labor force has shifted from the industrial to the service sector. Yet in doing so, Russia created a very peculiar labor market: defying predictions to the contrary, the steep decline of the Russian economy of the 1990s, rather than leading to mass unemployment, resulted in extreme flexibility in wages, which declined dramatically.

Following the collapse of the Soviet Union, the Russian government took a number of very large steps along the road of radical economic reform. It liberalized prices, dismantled central planning, opened up to the global market, and privatized enterprises, all in rapid fashion. Yet the Russian government could not get past the step—so crucial for a capitalist economy—of shutting down large but noncompetitive and unprofitable enterprises. While there were a number of reasons for not doing so, one stands out: the fear on the part of elites about the possibility of a "social explosion." As Pavel Romanov summarized this view in 1996, "The fear of social explosion is constantly visible in many public statements of both local and national leaders."[45]

The likelihood that the fear of social unrest might prevent the closure of large (even if largely unprofitable) enterprises has to do with the peculiar nature of Soviet industrialization, and how work and community were often intertwined in the Soviet experience. In the Soviet Union, industrialization preceded urbanization, both happening in compressed fashion, with the needs of industry greatly shaping the location and the form of the country's new urban areas. More than one thousand new cities were built in the early decades of the Soviet Union, the majority in the 1930s, many of which were "born and raised as Soviet-style company towns, in the shadow of one industrial establishment or with several establishments dividing responsibility or competing for control." These enterprises provided "housing and whatever meager services" there were.[46] These cities—built around industrial enterprises (sometimes called *gradoobrazuyush-chie predpriyatiya*, or "city-forming enterprises") and created to meet the needs of a planned economic system that no longer exists—remain a sizable legacy from the Soviet past.[47]

During the Soviet period, few industrial enterprises were closed, even if they were grossly inefficient. One reason was that, in many cases, the factories provided a number of essential services to the cities in which they were located.[48] Even with the steep drop in output in the post-Soviet 1990s, closing large factories in many cases would have been devastating not only to the workers, but to entire communities. That hardly meant that workers and others did not suffer. While large-scale unemployment was avoided, wages declined so substantially that often they went unpaid: by the end of the decade there was a substantial crisis of wage arrears. As we shall see, while nonpayment of wages didn't lead to a social explosion exactly, it came close, spurring a substantial wave of strikes and labor protests.

That strike wave peaked just as Putin was coming to power, initially as prime minister, and considerably shaped the initial steps he took to consolidate his power as president. Yet Putin's rise also fortuitously coincided with the end of Russia's deep economic crisis, and with it wage arrears were soon replaced by substantial wage increases. During the oil boom years of the 2000s, labor protest began to recede from view, and with it the fear of social explosion. While labor conflicts hardly disappeared (and in some sectors workers became emboldened), such concerns largely dropped off the agenda of Russian policy makers, as well as disappearing from the view of all but a handful of academic specialists.

However, the path taken in dealing with Russia's deep economic crisis of the 1990s, stemming in no small part from the Soviet model of industrialization, while successfully avoiding large-scale unemployment and social explosion, led to profound consequences nonetheless. Not least of these (as explored in chapter 3) is the challenge of very low labor productivity—measured by the amount that one worker working one hour contributes to the economy's GDP. While the term "labor productivity" may sound like a piece of economic jargon, productivity is a key driver—some would say *the* key driver—of economic growth. Without the return of the high oil and gas revenues of the 2000s, future economic growth will almost certainly depend on increasing labor productivity, a concern made more compelling by the significant demographic decline in Russia's working-age cohort. And yet, Russian labor productivity is unusually low by comparative standards. In fact, the Russian economy appears to be stuck in a low-productivity trap and, as a consequence, in a middle-income trap.

Why does labor productivity remain so low, thirty years after Russia entered the global capitalist economy? Through the years of bust, and then boom, a couple of factors have remained constant. The first is that while small and medium-size enterprises have closed and opened, there have been very few closures of large enterprises. While closures have been avoided, workers are often pressured to leave, by low wages and poor working conditions; yet those that remain may simply have fewer options. Given the high levels of inequality between regions, internal migration in Russia has been surprisingly limited. Workers who do depart often do so into the even less productive informal economy.[49]

Further, well beyond the 1990s, the labor market is still adjusting not through the number of jobs, but rather the amount of pay. In Russia's second postcommunist decade, as the economy surged, wages increased substantially. Now that Russia is faced with a slow-growth economy, Russian employers have responded once again with low wages. To take one indication, despite promises going back to the year 2000, Russia's legally defined minimum wage has only just been raised to meet the officially determined "minimum subsistence wage," below which an individual is said to be in danger of not consuming enough calories to maintain his or her body weight.

Low wages, however brutal for workers, can become a country's comparative advantage, provided that the economy is centered on the export of labor-intensive products. However, this is simply not the case in Russia, where outside of certain firms in the metals sector and military industry, Russian manufacturing exports are noncompetitive. Yet if wages are so low, as they have been in Russia, there is less incentive to invest in education and technology (which could boost productivity).

One path for escaping low productivity and middle-income status has recently been proposed: focusing on the growth of major metropolitan cities as centers of innovation in a global capitalist economy. As urban economists elsewhere have argued, large "global cities" are the engines of technological change, receive a disproportionate share of capital investment, and house the world's leading-edge companies and talent.[50]

Following this line of reasoning, liberal economist and Kremlin adviser Alexei Kudrin has argued that the Russian government should focus its attention and investment on a small handful of major cities, as well as Moscow and St. Petersburg, to become engines of economic growth. These priorities have been explicitly endorsed by Putin and have now become part of the Russian government's strategic plans. Yet Russia's built urban geography stands in stark contrast to the vision of global cities: almost uniquely, rather than a small number of large metropolitan centers, Russia contains hundreds of small and medium-size cities, many formed during Stalinist and post-Stalinist industrialization, many of those distributed across Russia's vast territory, far from other metropolitan agglomerations. These include the officially designated monotowns, whose fate is dependent on a single industry, and which the government ranks according to the severity of their "socioeconomic conditions" (chapter 4).

Thus, in seeking to explain why Russia remains "stuck in the middle-income trap," one outside observer of Russia's economy put it bluntly, with only slight overstatement: "The problem the Kremlin faces is that to really make a difference it needs to basically sack half the workforce and tell them to find a better job— and in most regions these private sector jobs simply don't exist."[51]

Yet the Russian government has proved consistently unwilling to close large industrial enterprises, let alone compel the resettlement of sizable centers of population. Hence the dilemma: the need for new sources of growth—or, in Kudrin's phrase, "cities instead of oil"—is compelling, and yet Russia's existing human geography, and the regime's clear desire for political stability, suggest that such a policy of urban transformation faces overwhelming obstacles.

The actual likelihood that Russia's monotowns or other industrial regions would erupt in destabilizing social unrest can be questioned. Indeed, while monotown residents—as well as those in other Russian working-class communities—do engage in collective protest, most often they employ individual strategies to adapt to challenging conditions. In doing so, they resist following simple economic logic, say by migrating to better economic conditions, and instead refuse to abandon place, engaging in what Sam Greene has termed "aggressive immobility," while they make their struggling communities, in Jeremy Morris's apt term, "habitable."[52]

Yet, as Mischa Gabowitsch has argued, protests in Russia often erupt precisely over "place."[53] Despite the fact that monotowns are by definition isolated communities, where the potential for protest to spread from one to another would appear to be limited, the Russian authorities have demonstrated a palpable fear of social unrest stemming from these particularly vulnerable cities and towns. Such fear places a sizable barrier in front of any attempt to increase economic growth by shifting capital and state resources from declining regions to more dynamic urban centers.

Still, how realistic is it for the Russian leadership to fear labor protest? When labor has led efforts to democratize authoritarian governments elsewhere in recent decades, labor-based parties and trade unions have typically played a crucial role.[54] Yet the former are essentially nonexistent in Russia; and as for the latter, as we shall see (in chapter 5), Russia's main union is a "legacy union"—a holdover from the communist era and one allied with the Kremlin and United Russia, the Kremlin-backed party that dominates Russia's parliament.[55] Alternative unions, while combative, are small and have often been marginalized. Strikes are severely restricted by law, and labor protests, when they do happen, are largely—though not always—isolated events.

In a classic work of political sociology, Charles Tilly argued that the ability of aggrieved groups to mobilize from isolated protests to broader movements was dependent on two factors, the first of which he termed "netness."[56] Netness refers to networks, or the ability of groups to organize beyond single nodes of contention; for workers that means unions above all.

In Russia, the preempting of the "netness" power of unions helps ensure that labor protests, when they do happen, are typically isolated in a single workplace, particularly when conflict arises with a private employer. However, such preventive measures come with their own costs. Research in a number of comparative settings has shown how blocking avenues for the expression of grievances and negotiation increases the likelihood of wildcat strikes—that is, the strikes take place with little to no union participation.[57] But for that very reason they represent a potential threat, since whatever is uncontrolled is potentially uncontrollable. Since workers lack an institutional channel to express their grievances, those grievances can simmer until they boil over, in unexpected and dramatic fashion. For example, in the 1990s and again today, workers at times revert to "extreme measures" in order to be heard—such as public threats of dramatic self-harm.

While there may not appear to be an immediate threat from worker protests, Putin and his team are clearly obsessed with the possibility of a "color revolution" of the sort that drove out the leaders in the neighboring countries of Georgia (2003) and Ukraine (in 2004 and 2014) and threatened Lukashenko's hold on power in Belarus (2020). Just how vulnerable Russia is to a color revolution is debatable. Yet those in the Kremlin are no doubt aware that there is a paradox at the heart of authoritarian power: in such a system, the sense of a leader's invulnerability—the "illusion of invincibility"—can change quickly. Leaders can become vulnerable to even small signs that their hold on power is weakening.[58] To date, there has never been a revolution in a liberal democracy. The most likely explanation is also the simplest one: in a liberal democracy, there is always hope that even a despised leader can be removed from office through constitutional means. But in authoritarian systems there is no procedure for the people themselves to remove a leader except by revolution.[59]

Russia is not technically an authoritarian state, since it has at least the semblance of elections and a political opposition, and most political scientists characterize it instead as a hybrid regime, containing a mix of authoritarian and democratic elements. But a hybrid political system contains dilemmas of its own.[60] For instance, although Russia has not eliminated independent media entirely, it has pushed critical views to the periphery. And when sycophantic state media dominates, political leaders receive little feedback about how they are truly perceived by their citizens. Likewise, when political parties and other institutions that might represent social interests become instruments of top-down control, it becomes difficult for leaders to judge how close they are to reaching society's breaking point. That is why, as we shall see, so often the appearance and scale of various protests come as a surprise to Russia's leaders.

While the probability of a Russian color revolution for now remains fairly low, it is not zero, and the stakes are high. They are high because in the post-Soviet transition from communism to capitalism, virtually all valuable assets moved into private hands in a process shaped by those in power, leading to incredible gains in wealth for the well-connected in often illicit—and almost always illegitimate—fashion. The result was not only a huge rise in inequality, but a system in which political power is the only real guarantor of property rights.[61] After the Maidan revolution in 2014, when the Ukrainian president Viktor Yanukovych was chased from office, the absurdly lavish mansion he had built for himself (including a zoo, and a restaurant on a faux pirate ship) was turned into a museum, where citizens could gape at what their erstwhile leader had stolen. As Yanukovych's fate makes clear, whatever vast holdings Russian leaders currently enjoy, a fall from political heights can mean losing wealth as well as power. Given such threats, leaders might be tempted to rely even more on coercive measures, though these can potentially backfire, radicalizing the opposition (as they did in the case of Yanukovych) and increasing the possibility of subsequent jailing and prosecution.

One could make the argument that Russia's leadership is most afraid of explicitly political protests rather than those with socioeconomic demands. At least since the 2005 protests over the attempted monetization of benefits, the Kremlin has "sought to delineate a legitimate sphere of protest over economic demands from an illegitimate sphere of attempts to politicize the situation."[62] This has contributed to a sharp "discursive divide" in Russia between socioeconomic protests on the one hand and political protests on the other.[63] In short, outside of a major economic catastrophe such as Russia experienced in the 1990s, widespread labor protest leading to political destabilization would appear to be a low-probability event.

On closer inspection, however, and as explored in detail in chapter 8, the analytical distinction between political and economic protests and demands appears artificial. In cases such as Russia, where the state plays a dominant role in the economy, demands of a socioeconomic nature by themselves carry political implications, whether intended or not. In Russia, most worker demands include an appeal to government officials at some level, even when the conflict is between workers and a private employer. This is certainly part of what Graeme Robertson had in mind when he argued that "contemporary authoritarians not only need to find ways to defeat-proof elections; they also need to defeat-proof the streets."[64]

Such concerns prompt authoritarian leaders to engage in what Vitali Silitski called "pre-emptive authoritarianism," that is, eliminating threats before they arise, aiming at sources of potential opposition while they are still weak.[65] Such efforts at "pre-emptive authoritarianism" entail repressing those elements of civil society (such as trade unions) from which protest might arise, but also necessitate providing tangible benefits to key constituencies (such as public-sector workers) in an effort to maintain their loyalty. Yet such steps aimed at preemption come with inevitable tradeoffs, particularly in the economic realm. At the most fundamental level, attempts to maintain "stability" are likely to stifle innovation and economic dynamism.

In attempting to preempt wider protest, the Kremlin under Putin's leadership turned to a proven strategy: relying on class, regional, and other resentments to deflect grievances onto other groups. When Putin came to power at the end of the first postcommunist decade, Russians were exhausted by wrenching economic changes and social decline. As Vladislav Inozemtsev notes, Putin and his advisers "openly blame the reformers of the 1990s for neglecting the people's needs and conducting the reforms in a way that caused a 35 percent economic contraction, pushed close to a half of all citizens below the poverty line, and created an oligarchic economic structure. All this, they argue, produced a quest for a more 'organized' economic environment and made Mr. Putin's rhetoric welcomed by a huge portion of the population."[66]

Since Putin's rise coincided with economic recovery, it was not only his rhetoric but the accompanying high wages that were welcomed, even if the re-tightening of the political space left workers as largely passive beneficiaries of economic growth. The economic crisis of 2008 challenged that relationship, as it shook the foundations of Putin-era stability.[67] The Russian state, together with the now-threatened oligarchs, had to craft new methods of preempting social unrest, which included greater state intervention and support for threatened industries. While those efforts were largely successful in the short term, they led to unintended consequences that still persist (explored in chapters 4 and 6).

Such state support for industry appeared to pay dividends, when during the ostensibly middle-class protests of 2011–12 Putin positioned himself as a defender of working-class interests; yet that working-class backing appears based more on the promise of continued material support than on ongoing cultural affinity, and that support is now in question (chapter 7). The next challenge soon appeared in 2014, when the color revolution took place next door in Ukraine. Certainly, part of Russia's response to the Maidan revolution, such as the seizure of Crimea, was geopolitical. Yet the events in Ukraine coincided with a sudden drop in the global price of oil, leading to another recession, and more work was needed to preempt protest. Russian leaders and state-owned media pursued a further shift in their legitimation strategy with a campaign of hardened national-ism, and Putin's popularity soared with the seizure of Crimea. But that euphoria predictably waned with time, and with slower economic growth the battle then becomes (in the now-familiar Russian metaphor) one between the television and the refrigerator.

Social and economic protests in Russia tend to be local and isolated events. These include labor protests in monotowns and other industrial centers, but also protests over toxic garbage dumps, lethal fires in shopping malls, or gas explosions in apartment buildings, all of which have sent signals of state inca-pacity and weakness. Yet given the lack of civil-society-based network power, a galvanizing source for coalescing around socioeconomic demands often comes from "catness," Tilly's second mobilizing factor.[68] Catness refers to categories, and the process by which individuals can become suddenly united by poli-cies and other changes that impact them as a single category. This mobilizing impetus can be concrete—for example a policy that impacts individuals' mate-rial well-being—yet it can extend well beyond any specific place, and connect people even without existing networks. This was clear in the 2005 protests over the monetization of benefits, when protesters, mainly pensioners, rose up with little coordination in numerous cities across Russia. As we shall see in chapter 8, this was also true for Russia's truckers, who spontaneously coalesced in a protest movement across Russia's many regions over a simple road tax. While the eco-nomic logic behind raising taxes or cutting benefits might be compelling, par-ticularly during a period of economic stagnation, the political logic is another matter, and any such changes need to be carefully calibrated to prevent social unrest. Moreover, as with the truckers, once those previously isolated individu-als mobilize and begin to act collectively, they can begin to discuss Russia's "accursed questions": "Who is to blame?" and "What is to be done?" In doing so, they can transform their demands from the economic to the political very rapidly.

Putin's obsession with a Russian color revolution is quite likely misplaced; there is only limited evidence that labor or social protest in Russia might lead to "regime change," at least in the short run. Yet, for those in power, the great-est danger is that the social-economic protests from Russia's industrial regions will converge with political demands for a "Russia without Putin." Revolutions are almost always the result of coalitions of classes, and rarely if ever the prod-uct of one class of social actors.[69] Thus, for those seeking to remain in power, maintaining the "discursive divide" between economic and political protests is essential.

In the longer run a slow-growth economy with stagnant or declining stan-dards of living will make the convergence of political and economic demands more likely. One potential way to lower the risk of socioeconomic protest is to ensure that the economy grows rather than stagnates. But that would almost certainly entail substantial economic reforms. Liberal economists—both inside and outside Russia—often appear blind to the political implications of their policy proposals. Given the fear of protest from below, which in turn could threaten political stability, the further liberalization of Russia's economy—involving scaling back industrial subsidies, closing plants and laying off workers, increasing taxes and cutting social benefits and pensions—is a risky proposition for those in power.

While Putin has staked his legitimacy since coming to power on providing "stability" after the disastrous 1990s, without higher levels of economic growth, stability might come to be viewed as stagnation, and declining living standards can create their own threat to stability. In short, at some point, economic growth will depend on restructuring the country's industrial and social landscape, but doing so threatens social (and political) stability. Russia can continue with the status quo, but at the cost of slow or all but stagnant economic growth, which itself threatens stability.

Making an extended argument about the threat of labor and social protest in contemporary Russia might seem strange, since the last large-scale wave of such protests took place in the 1990s. That would explain why the last book-length study of Russian labor protest was Graeme Robertson's *The Politics of Protest in Hybrid Regimes*, published in 2011.[70] The relative lack of such protest since helps explain why some of the most trenchant studies of post-Soviet political economy and society—including those that this study relies on considerably—can almost ignore labor altogether. Susanne Wengle's otherwise excellent account of the Russian electrical power sector and its impact on the peculiar path of post-Soviet (de)industrialization examines the impact of oligarchs and central state and regional officials, and the complex bargains between them, but sees little need to place attention on the actions of those from below.[71] Thomas Remington's comprehensive study of Russian inequality examined how even the most entrepreneurial regions in Russia remain constrained by various legacies of the Soviet past, and includes probably the most comprehensive account of the social and political impact of the 2008–9 economic crisis.[72] However, given the weakness of Russian trade unions, he is able to summarily dismiss the impact of labor as a factor. In two of the most definitive studies of Russian civil society and protest in recent years, *Moscow in Movement* by Sam Greene, and Greene and Robertson's *Putin v. the People*, workers and trade unions barely merit a mention.[73] Again testifying to the perceived quiescence of Russia's workers, a substantial and thoughtful study titled *Protest in Putin's Russia* devotes only a few paragraphs to labor protest.[74] The present book thus seeks to fill a substantial gap and to demonstrate that workers do still matter, sometimes as rather passive constraints on Russian economic growth, but sometimes as actors with the potential to directly impact Russia's future.

This study has relied—perhaps to an unusual degree—on the works of others. Unlike previous research by the author, which relied on intensive fieldwork in Russia's industrial regions, the present study is the product of synthesizing a large amount of work carried out by fellow researchers. No doubt such an approach has its disadvantages. Yet a more synthetic or integrative approach also has its advantages. Most especially, it has the potential to be truly multidisciplinary, and that has been the path chosen here. This book is written by a political scientist, and the questions that it is interested in are ultimately political. Yet too often, in academic writing as well as popular discourse on Russia, too much attention gets concentrated on Kremlin-level politics, and particularly on one individual— Vladimir Putin. What follows here builds not only on the work done by other political scientists, but also on those looking at Russia through the disciplinary lenses of sociology, economics, geography, history, and anthropology. That such an approach would be necessary to understand a complex society such as Russia should be obvious, yet too often such multidisciplinary work is looked down upon as mere "area studies."

This book faces a further challenge, in that its main argument aims to explain why something didn't happen: namely, that the fear of labor and social protest inhibits substantial economic transformation. A number of questions, both conceptual and methodological, could be raised about such a research question. First, Russia has already undergone substantial—indeed dramatic—economic transformation, so how can one demonstrate where the line might lie beyond which (leaders might fear) the population might rise up in reaction? Second, inevitably whenever discussing policy actions (and especially inactions), one confronts a black box in which decisions are ultimately made, and this is particularly true when the political leadership is as cloistered as it is in contemporary Russia. Third, and relatedly, there are other possible explanations for why Russian leaders might opt not to take painful policy decisions. In seeking to explain Kremlin politics, much has been written about the importance of state officials and oligarchs seeking self-enrichment, the security forces (*siloviki*) gaining sway over liberal technocrats, and the need for a sizable state sector and large public enterprises to serve as vote-generating machines for those in power. While none of these factors precludes the possibility that Russian leaders are inhibited by the fear of social unrest, how might the significance of concerns over potential unrest possibly be demonstrated, let alone measured?

Such a contention is hard to prove (and probably impossible to measure). This is arguably a major reason why it has been understudied. In what follows we will proceed less through the standard methods of social science and more by building a forensic case, compiling a large amount of corroborating evidence that will hopefully build to a convincing conclusion. Whether that case is sufficiently compelling will be up to the reader to judge.

In chapter 2 we begin to build the case by answering the questions of how and why Russia adapted to capitalism and deindustrialization through a labor market that avoided mass unemployment, relying instead on extremely flexible wages, and why that system has persisted through subsequent cycles of boom and bust. Chapter 3 explores some of the consequences of such a labor market, namely low wages and struggling industrial enterprises, and especially low labor productivity, a crucial factor impinging on economic growth. Yet instead of tackling that problem head-on, the government has pursued industrial policies that reinforce it by maintaining employment.

In chapter 4 we explore the unique economic and industrial geography that Russia inherited from the Soviet past. This includes the large number of Russian monotowns, which have become flash points for real and anticipated labor protest, and has led to elaborate government programs to prevent that unrest. Yet government plans, announced in 2019, to shift investment toward a handful of major metropolitan centers could place Russia's monotowns in untenable conditions, with potentially dire consequences. Chapter 5 probes Russia's labor relations and labor protest. The avenues for resolving labor disputes have become so restricted under Putin that often the only recourse is spontaneous action taken out of desperation, resulting in a paradox of overcontrol. In chapter 6 we delve into the case of Tolyatti, the country's largest monotown, often referred to as "Russia's Detroit." While at first glance the city's auto giant AvtoVAZ looks like a successful case of massive downsizing, a closer view reveals sizable government efforts, often with unintended consequences, to prevent social upheaval. Chapter 7 directly confronts the question of how a state as strong as Putin's Russia could yet be afraid of its own population. We explore the fear of a Russian color revolution, the importance of stability and economic growth to Putin's legitimacy, and his use of class divisions and nationalist rhetoric to divide real and potential opponents. Then in chapter 8 we examine the potential for socioeconomic protests to combine with more radical political demands. We explore the protest by Russia's truck drivers, whose actions demonstrate how simple economic concerns can unite otherwise isolated individuals and quickly lead to demands for political transformation. We then look, in chapter 9, at the Russian example in comparative context, in particular addressing the question of how countries immediately to the west (other postcommunist countries, especially Ukraine and Belarus) and to the east (in particular China) have dealt with (de)industrialization and labor protest. A concluding chapter follows.

Is there really a fear of a "social explosion" in Russia? That might seem far-fetched, but we will begin with an exploration of the cataclysmic 1990s, when such a fear was palpable. While such an outcome was—if barely—avoided, the means of doing so laid the foundation for Russia's current labor dilemma. We turn to the building of that foundation in the next chapter.

RUSSIA'S PECULIAR LABOR MARKET AND THE FEAR OF SOCIAL EXPLOSION

Following the collapse of the Soviet Union, Russia experienced a depression longer and deeper than that of the United States during the Great Depression. Given that, I seek to answer three related questions: How did Russian workers survive the 1990s? Why did the Russian labor market respond with extreme flexibility in wages instead of massive unemployment? Why have these labor market practices persisted through the Putin era, beyond the oil boom of the 2000s and into the present?

The groundwork for such practices was laid during the Soviet period. The bulk of Soviet industrialization took place in the Stalinist 1930s, when a "revolution from above" turned peasants (then roughly 80 percent of the Soviet population) into workers, and created, in little more than a decade, an industrial society.[1] With the massive transfer of peasants to the new factory sites, new cities were created, many, as we have seen, built around industrial enterprises (*gradoobrazuyushchie predpriyatiya*, or "city-forming enterprises"). This rapid industrialization created the Soviet "coal and steel economy," centered on large enterprises.[2] Since planners saw no need for market competition, the Soviet economy was biased toward large enterprises, with some of the largest industrial projects described as being "pharaonic" or exhibiting "gigantomania." Beyond these were the thousands of new factories where a larger size was seen not as a detriment to profit making but a means to gain greater leverage and resources from ministries in Moscow (which would typically provide a greater wage bill to cover labor costs) as well as bring more prestige to the city and region. Whatever their inefficiencies, few of these industrial enterprises were closed during the Soviet period, in no small part because the factories provided a number of vital services to the cities in which they were located.

In some ways the Soviet Union was never truly a welfare state, since the vast (if often inadequate) Soviet welfare system was largely distributed through the workplace.[3] This was in large part due to what János Kornai described as the "shortage economy" in Soviet-type societies, whereby virtually all commodities, including labor, were in short supply.[4] In order to attract and retain (especially skilled) labor, Soviet industrial enterprises, in the face of shortages of consumer goods and services, as well as labor, developed a unique system for providing their workforces with services, from housing to food. If a worker in a capitalist society received a wage packet and various benefits, a worker in Soviet society received that and also housing, access to the enterprise hospital, to day care and other forms of education for one's children, often employment for one's spouse, trips to rest homes and vacation centers, and consumer goods ranging from automobiles to perishable food items.[5] Yet this enterprise paternalism was ultimately coercive in that the enterprise provided goods that were not available on the market and were distributed on a discretionary basis through personal ties to superiors.[6] Nevertheless, largely as a result, the enterprise became the central social unit of Soviet society.

With the dictatorship of the Communist Party ostensibly ruling in the interests of the working class, unions in the Soviet system functioned very differently from the typical unions found in a capitalist society. Especially in the post-Stalin era, Soviet trade unions were concerned primarily not with the protection of workers, but with the distribution of social benefits within the enterprise.[7] Functioning essentially as social welfare agencies, unions were responsible for distributing enterprise-owned and enterprise-controlled housing and consumer goods, as well as trips to the enterprise resort centers and children's camps, and for maintaining the enterprises' day care centers, "houses of culture," sports teams and musical groups, and the like. Unions also distributed the state's social insurance fund.[8]

Unions, at the behest of management, distributed scarce goods in an effort to retain skilled workers. This was critical, since given the shortage of labor, workers could and did take advantage of the ability to leave one job for another, seeking those with the best package of pay and in-kind benefits. This led to many complaints from economic officials and enterprise directors of the problem of labor turnover (*tekuchest' kadrov*).[9] In short, in Albert Hirschman's well-known metaphor, workers under the Soviet system lacked "voice," either through their unions or the political system, but they successfully used their power of "exit."[10]

Yet without voice—or more precisely, the lack of an institutional mechanism through which workers might channel their collective grievances—Soviet workers presented a potential challenge for the ruling Communist Party. A number of observers argued that there was an informal "social contract" between regime and society, especially blue-collar workers, who benefited from full employment, roughly egalitarian wages, and the toleration of slack work rules; in return, workers provided the social basis of support for the Soviet system.[11] Such an arrangement, however, meant that the system must continue to "deliver the goods," which led to a contradiction, given that workers often found little incentive to be productive, creating further shortages rather than the satisfaction of worker expectations. Particularly since this was a "contract" that was never negotiated, but one implemented from above, when the regime challenged social expectations, say by raising the prices of basic goods or revising pay rates downward, workers often rose up in spontaneous protest. This was particularly true in the Soviet bloc countries of eastern Europe, especially (though not only) in Poland. Such protests were quickly repressed, often with bloodshed. Though such incidents were fewer in the Soviet Union, the example of Novocherkassk in 1962, where twenty-five workers protesting price increases were shot and killed, with another seven later executed and many more injured and imprisoned, became infamous throughout Soviet society.[12] (As we shall see, Novocherkassk remains a historical touchstone for Russian society to this day.) In most every case, such protests were unanticipated by the authorities, who lacked adequate information and feedback to adequately judge where society's breaking point might lie—a concern that continues to resonate for Russia's leaders.

Thus, in Soviet times it was argued that simple price rises—say raising the price of bread, which remained unchanged from the Stalinist era through Gorbachev's rule—would be enough to set off spontaneous protest.[13] There would appear to be much irony in such beliefs, shared by top officials and those on bottom of society, since there was very little open protest in the Soviet Union from Stalin's time until Gorbachev's perestroika. Yet by 1980 the rise of Poland's Solidarity movement, led by workers amid growing shortages and quickly leading to radical demands such as the right to form an independent trade union, which could only be suppressed through martial law, clearly demonstrated to Soviet leaders that worker protests posed a direct challenge to Communist Party rule.

When Gorbachev, realizing that the Soviet economy could no longer "deliver the goods," began implementing radical changes to the Soviet system—promising to fundamentally revise the old social contract—he was faced with worker protests, most dramatically with the Soviet coal miners' strike of 1989. Four hundred thousand coal miners, from western Ukraine to Sakhalin in the

Far East, went on strike throughout the Soviet Union, occupied city squares, and articulated demands that ranged from the provision of more consumer goods to the deepening of political and economic reforms. As economic conditions worsened and the political space widened, the coal miners became radicalized, and struck again in the spring of 1991, this time allying with Yeltsin and other reformers, and called for a general strike demanding an end to the Soviet system.[14] Hence Gorbachev's later reflection that the miners' strike wave marked the beginning of the end.[15] Such a dramatic example of worker radicalization is one that Russians of a certain age would surely remember.

The Market Transition

The assessment of workers as powerful social actors in the old regime carried over into the new era. Since the postcommunist liberalization—nothing less than a full-scale transformation from communism to capitalism—would entail quite a bit more hardship than merely raising the price of bread, the specter of a "social explosion," led especially by labor, was raised repeatedly by political analysts, labor experts, and politicians in the region.

Such beliefs helped shape strategies of economic transformation throughout the former Soviet bloc. That workers were potentially powerful was implicit in the arguments for both radical and gradual economic reform plans.[16] Those pushing radical reform—especially rapid privatization—argued that workers had become the effective owners of state enterprises in the late communist period, and that profits were being consumed by wages. Labor was strong and had to be broken. Gradualists, on the other hand, argued that such actions would lead to a backlash from workers and others that would undercut reform.

Yet Russian president Yeltsin and his advisers not only chose the path of radical reform, but did so with initially few visible signs of resistance. Though Soviet leaders had long refrained from raising prices, the Russian government liberalized prices almost immediately on becoming an independent state, on January 2, 1992. Yet while there was much grumbling as inflation soon reached the heights of hyperinflation, at first there was little organized protest, at least from workers. Radical reform continued apace, including rapid privatization, so that by June 1994 around fifteen thousand enterprises, with about seventeen million employees, amounting to roughly two-thirds of the industrial workforce, were now under private ownership.[17]

Yet the manner as well as the pace of privatization sent Russia down a particular path. The new owners often acquired assets at very low prices. As well as the oil and metals firms obtained by the rising oligarchs, many large enterprises were obtained for a few million dollars each.[18] Since the very concept of privatization was immensely unpopular, the Yeltsin government worked to make it more palatable through the distribution of privatization vouchers to citizens, and the most widely adopted form of privatization was nominally to "insiders"—workers as well as managers. Yet in most cases such assets were typically quickly transferred to the powerful and well-connected.[19]

The oligarchs and regional barons who emerged had little incentive to invest in the industrial assets they had obtained, and typically sought to siphon off anything of monetary value, often for sale abroad. There was little attempt at the time to take advantage of Russia's vast industrial infrastructure and its qualified and relatively inexpensive labor force. While substantial restructuring would have been required to make many industrial sectors efficient, and many firms would have needed to find new product lines, such an option was closed off by the decision to open Russia's economy almost overnight to global competition.[20] With the exception of processed metals, Russia would from then on become an exporter of fuels and other raw materials, rather than of industrial products, with a profound impact on Russia's vast industrial labor force.

Economic Collapse and Russia's Labor Market

From the early 1930s until the end of the Soviet period, Russians had no experience at all with unemployment (not to mention bankruptcies). With the end of the communist period, Russian workers faced a dramatic shock in the rapid conversion of the labor market from one of labor shortage to labor surplus.[21] As Gimpelson and Kapeliushnikov recall, "most international and Russian experts strongly believed that a sharp jump in open unemployment would be unavoidable."[22] They point to a study jointly published by the IMF, the World Bank, the OECD, and the European Bank of Reconstruction and Development that predicted unemployment to range from twelve to fifteen million by 1992.[23] Russia's labor minister Alexander Shokhin predicted that thirty million Russian workers would lose jobs over the first year of reform, with half of them becoming unemployed for the long term.[24] Yet to the surprise of almost all observers, despite an economic decline much greater than had been anticipated, Russia avoided massive unemployment.

During the Great Depression in the United States, while real wages remained stable, unemployment rose to between 20 and 25 percent. In Russia, notwithstanding a downturn deeper and longer than the US experienced during the Great Depression, the result was the opposite: in what some have called the

"Russian model" of labor market adjustment, wages rather than the number of jobs became extremely flexible.[25] In the 1990s, according to official statistics, Russia's GDP declined by roughly 40 percent at its nadir; in terms of industrial output, Russia's factories produced about half the goods they did prior to the collapse of communism.[26] Yet Russian unemployment only exceeded 10 percent six years after the start of the economic decline, and reached a maximum of 13.3 percent only briefly in 2008 (see figure 2.1).[27]

What explains this strange phenomenon? Why did unemployment remain low when Russia's economy shrank almost in half? Moreover, why, despite such a dramatic drop in output, were there so few closures of large (and often inefficient Soviet-era) industrial enterprises?

One straightforward answer would appear to be a continuation of the paternalistic mentality and practices of the Soviet past. In human terms, the industrial enterprise was known as the "labor collective." As "both a real and symbolic community," the labor collective was central to the lives of the large number of Russian workers.[28] Given the centrality of the workplace as a social unit, with the economic crisis workers developed a contradictory relationship with managers: alongside their conflicting interests in the workplace, they had a common interest seeking the survival of their enterprise, resulting in a "supplicatory unity" of workers and managers before the Russian state, seeking support for their struggling workplaces and livelihoods.[29]

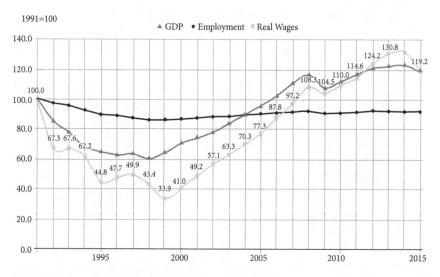

FIGURE 2.1.   Changes in GDP, employment, and real wages, 1991–2015

Sources: Gimpelson, Kapeliushnikov, and Roshchin 2017; Rosstat.

Especially in the first years following privatization, managers had an additional incentive to maintain this paternalistic relationship. The vast majority of enterprises chose the "second model" of privatization, where the majority of shares were at least nominally allotted to the "labor collective." In these conditions, enterprise directors still needed the tools that had worked for them in the past to keep the labor force quiescent, so as to keep themselves in office; and with ownership the ultimate goal, the stakes were higher than ever before. Even when property rights formally shifted to management, as they typically did, a strong stakeholder mentality remained among the workforce. The new owners often sought to provide benefits and other incentives to maintain a loyal workforce that secured them against possible predation. Should the employees succeed in striking, however remote the prospect, they might well force out the management team, signal the enterprise's vulnerability to outside takeover, or perhaps invite the renationalization of the firm by regional governments.[30]

In a case study of two very similar firms (in this case banks), one controlled by "insiders" and another by "outsiders," Veronika Kabalina found that paradoxically the insider firm performed better precisely because, in Russian conditions, some of the old (and more political) management methods were more effective than newer (and more economic) ones. She concluded that whereas the management style of the outside owners led to conflict, the common interests of insiders, both managers and workers, in preserving jobs served not as an obstacle but as a "stimulus to reconstruction" of the enterprise, and thus "such socially responsible behavior on the part of management is rational, for without it there would be a significant increase in the risk of social disintegration."[31]

Yet by itself paternalism cannot explain the phenomena of the flexibility of wages rather than jobs, let alone the lack of closures of large enterprises. In Soviet times the in-kind benefits distributed through the workplace were intended to recruit and retain workers given the labor shortage, by providing goods and services that were otherwise in short supply. In the post-Soviet context, both those conditions changed dramatically: the labor shortage ended abruptly, and the consumer market became quickly saturated. Rather surprisingly, however, given at least the threat of unemployment, workers, rather than becoming more dependent on their places of work, responded in ways they had in the past: the high rates of labor turnover continued, as skilled and younger workers left for better prospects. Firms, even in a period of economic crisis, continued to hire, if at lower rates.[32]

Besides the paternalistic mentality, the expectations of workers about preserving the "labor collective," and the need for managers as new owners to maintain social peace within the enterprise while consolidating their property holdings, the owners and managers of privatized enterprises had more direct incentives for making wages rather than jobs flexible. Even though labor laws were rarely enforced in the immediate and chaotic post-Soviet period, enterprises were legally obliged to pay three months of unemployment benefits to workers that had been let go.[33] Further, with the high rate of inflation that followed market liberalization, the government imposed an excess wage tax to prevent large increases in wages. Though this was later repealed in 1996, the law contributed to the enduring practice of employers paying their workers a low nominal wage, with supplemental pay being given as a bonus, often as cash "in the envelope" and thus free from taxation.[34]

One might assume that the ideal preference for Russian employers would have been to lay off their least desirable workers and redistribute their pay to their most skilled and desirable workers, employing the least number possible to meet demand for one's product.[35] Yet given the chaos of the 1990s, with the unpredictability and variable quality of supplies, the deterioration of equipment and infrastructure, and, not least, the difficulty of obtaining needed investment, managers relied on cheap labor to maintain production. As Gregory Schwartz argued, "what has saved many enterprises in such conditions [was] the existence of extremely low wages, providing the flexibility needed to cushion the effects of the crisis and to survive the transition without fundamentally restructuring."[36]

Reducing hours proved to be the simplest way to adjust labor costs, through forced or administrative leave (unpaid or partially paid) and part-time work. Wages could be cut simply by failing to adjust them for inflation. Moreover, since the nominal base wage was (and often remains) so low, "a considerable portion of total wage payments is variable and not fixed in labor contracts," often in the form of premiums and bonuses.[37] This meant that wages could also be quickly adjusted upward during economic growth. The flexible part of the wage bill could reach above 50 percent of total wages, as it did in the boom year of 2005 for the oil and gas and metallurgical industries.[38] But as a result, during an economic downturn, wage costs are cut almost automatically.

Thus, one reason for avoiding layoffs was simply that labor was cheap and wages were flexible. Paying through bonuses and often in cash gave managers additional leverage over their workforce, as real wage differentials within the firm could be quite high, and often depended on personalized relations with managers.

Regional Politics and Social Implosion

There was a further compelling reason to avoid mass layoffs, let alone the bankruptcy and closure of large industrial enterprises. Since Russia had not experienced unemployment since the 1920s, there were no institutions in place to cushion the blow of losing one's job, or deal with unemployment as a widespread social phenomenon. Unemployment benefits were (and, as we shall see, continue to be) paltry. With the Soviet welfare system being distributed through the enterprise, closing those workplaces could lead to social disaster. The Russian state, dealing with multiple crises, both economic and political, proved incapable of providing even minimal social welfare directly to its population. As Thomas Remington notes,

> The post-Soviet state was too weak to replace the Soviet model of income and social policy with one putting enterprises entirely on a market-oriented footing and providing universal, redistributive, and cash-based social protection. The central government, motivated by a mixture of ideological and purely practical considerations, off-loaded responsibility for many of the social obligations the Soviet state had managed to the regions. In assuming them, regional governments turned to the large enterprises to maintain and expand their traditional paternalistic role in providing for social welfare.[39]

By the mid-1990s, 85 percent of all social spending came from regional and local budgets. Yet "faced with devastating shortfalls in their budgets, regional and local governments became still more dependent on enterprises to supply social services," as they had done in Soviet times.[40] Western advisers as well as liberal Russian reformers were trying to convince steel factories that they should focus on their core business instead of providing social services, and before long many of these services were at least nominally transferred to the various municipalities. Yet quite often those local governments simply lacked the funds to provide the services, particularly if, given plummeting production, the dominant enterprise in the town was not able to pay its taxes. While the level and quality of the enterprise-provided services declined significantly, these services took on increased importance, given the struggle of so many people to escape immiseration.[41] As long as the enterprises continued to operate and provide employment, many local governments accepted the provision of essential services—such as housing, child care, and public transportation—as a form of in-kind taxation.[42]

Yet the challenge was not simply separating the provision of social services from firms now meant to be operating on the basis of profit. The dilemma was also the seeming impossibility of pursuing economic logic to its conclusion and closing loss-making firms when a town and often a region were dependent on that firm not only for employment, but so much more. As David Woodruff noted, "Local leaders were completely bereft of alternatives to the social and infrastructural services provided by enterprises that would be shut down." Among other dilemmas, "the sewage and heating of sections of major cities or entire smaller ones could be technologically inseparable from that of the industrial enterprises around which they were built. As a result, shutdown would mean massive and expensive problems for which there were no funds."[43]

Given the collapse of the economy, however, a large number of firms faced potential bankruptcy and closure, particularly those in the military-industrial complex, whose funding was severely cut in the 1990s.[44] In September 1994, the deputy chief of the Samara region argued that the aircraft factory AO AVI.S could not be closed, despite being declared insolvent with a debt of 200 billion rubles, because doing so would create disastrous social consequences:

> First, the whole enormous social sphere of the enterprise (357 apartment blocks, 22 kindergartens and so on) would be left without a stable source of financing. Second, at least 8,000 workers would be laid off, adding to the ranks of the unemployed. Third, the *raion* [borough] and the city would lose ten billion rubles in taxes from their budgets. Fourth, if the factory changed its production over time, and made something else instead of airplanes, this would have a very bad impact on the regional economy, since 22 percent of the raw materials and parts are supplied by local enterprises, who would immediately lose their markets.[45]

While capitalist logic implied the need for "creative destruction," however painful, Russia's regional leaders faced a different set of incentives.[46] The "politics of economic transformation" suggests that the benefits of liberal economic reform, should they arrive, would be diffused broadly and sometime in the future, whereas the pain from the closure of a large industrial firm would be felt immediately by a very specific population.[47] Thus, as Woodruff notes, "for a local government, the failure of a single factory employing several thousand people seemed an unacceptable disaster."[48] While reformers in Moscow might seek to deepen market liberalization, "local authorities . . . must deal with the social consequences."[49]

This divergence of interests was deepened because of the relative weakness of the federal government during the Yeltsin era, with leaders in Russia's regions seeking greater autonomy. Thus, regional leaders pursued strategies very different from those of the central government, seeking to "prevent deindustrialization, unemployment, and labor migration that would turn provincial cities into ghost towns."[50] Since "regional governors' efforts to keep the factory doors open were a defining aspect of the state-business relationships" in the 1990s, governors created alliances with the large enterprise owners, including oligarchs, to enlist their help for broad social aims, in order to "rescue regions and towns from decline."[51] For example, to prevent deindustrialization, regional leaders often kept tariffs for electricity low for important industrial enterprises, with such privileges "usually reserved for companies with many employees."[52] Governors could dispense with such favors in a way to cement their alliances with owners of large firms, though doing so squeezed out smaller and newer firms. For their part, these owners came to view their control over social services as a form of strategic leverage, not only with their workforce but with regional and local governments as well.

Even new directors oriented toward the market maintained the enterprise's traditional paternalistic role for strategic regions. According to Remington, "the importance of the enterprise for providing not just employment and wages, but also essential public services meant that the relationship between enterprises and government at the federal level and at regional and local levels was the critical factor in determining whether the market transition succeeded or not."[53] In his comparative study of the differing strategies pursued by Russia's regions, Remington concludes that even the more democratic and market-oriented regional leaders avoided radical reforms and instead sought "subsidies to maintain production at often inefficient enterprises" and "worked actively to soften the impact for those (such as employees at the old state enterprises and workers in the budget sector) whose futures were threatened," even if doing so "sacrificed some economic efficiency for the stake of maintaining regional stability." In short, "even the most market-friendly of regions allowed inefficient enterprises to avoid direct competition in the global marketplace."[54]

With the collapse of the Soviet Union, the Russian government took a number of substantial steps along the road of radical economic reform. It liberalized prices, dismantled central planning, opened up to the global market, and privatized enterprises, all in rapid fashion. Yet the Russian government could not get past the step—so crucial for a capitalist economy—of shutting down large but noncompetitive and unprofitable enterprises. We have noted several reasons why Russian workplaces prevented mass layoffs and large enterprises largely avoided closure: the legacy of enterprise paternalism and the "labor collective," the path of insider privatization, the extreme flexibility in wages, the difficulty of untangling enterprises from vital social services, and the challenge of regional leaders in avoiding social catastrophe. While all these factors likely contributed, the last points to a crucial concern: the fear of elites about the possibility of a "social explosion." If workers had proven powerful in certain episodes in the Soviet period, how much more likely in the 1990s, when the fear of state repression had been removed and workers (and much of the population) faced catastrophic social conditions? The fear of social explosion was palpable and was often expressed in the statements of leaders on various levels.[55]

In short, there appears to have been an implicit deal between the regional (and at times central) government officials and industrial enterprises: enterprises might not pay their workers, pay their bills to creditors, or pay their taxes to the government, but they should continue to take care of the "collective."[56] The government thereby lost revenue, but it prevented social unrest, which would have been disastrous for regional leaders, and likely central ones as well. Beyond the loss of revenue, the cost included the rise of a "virtual economy" based on barter, but that was preferable to social and political unrest.[57]

The Crisis of Wage Arrears

As it turned out, the expected backlash from workers did not happen, at least on the scale that had been predicted. Indeed, most observers of the period discussed the relative weakness of labor and sought to explain why a greater level of protest did not take place.[58] Some, such as Anders Åslund, an economic adviser to then-president Yeltsin, argued at the time that "it is important to note that there has been little to no labor unrest in Russia, which may be proof that the situation is not so dire."[59] Yet as we shall see in chapter 5, workers were hardly quiescent, and a significant (if peculiar) strike wave did take place.[60] Indeed, by the end of the 1990s, while mass unemployment and the closures of large enterprises had been avoided, conditions became so truly catastrophic that some kind of "explosion" certainly seemed possible, even likely.

The pain of Russia's economic shock was cushioned to a degree through low wages spread throughout Russia's working population, rather than being concentrated on the unemployed, who would have nevertheless been a large portion of the population. As Gimpelson and Kapeliushnikov note, "It's hard to imagine what turmoil would have resulted during the transitional crisis of the 1990s had wage levels in Russia been as rigid as they are in most developed countries."[61] Unemployment rates at Great Depression levels, in a country without any history or provisions for unemployment, could well have been a humanitarian disaster.

Yet the low wages that resulted were difficult for many to endure. Writing in 1996, Sergei Alasheev and Marina Kiblitskaia addressed the question of "how to survive on a Russian's wage." Their answer was through second jobs in the informal economy, the help of family and friends, and above all lowered expectations.[62] But the situation continued downward. By 1999, according to the government's accounting, some 35 percent of the population lived below the poverty line, with most of these people considered "working poor."[63] One study of Russian social mobility—comparing class origins with class destinations—found that from

1990 to 1998, "downward mobility exceeded upward mobility by 30 percent," and that such a downward shift, especially of that magnitude, was highly unusual among mature economies.[64]

Indeed, wage flexibility had reached such extremes that wages went unpaid altogether. Often workers would not get paid in rubles but rather would be paid in kind—in products the enterprise had obtained by barter, or consumer goods the plant produced but was unable to sell, including matches, bras, coffins, and in one case, manure.[65] Most dramatically, at its height in late 1998, the crisis of "wage arrears" meant that approximately two-thirds of Russian workers reported overdue wages, with those affected reporting close to five months' pay in arrears on average.[66]

With the financial crisis of 1998, the amount of wages held in arrears declined, but given the devaluation of the ruble, the value of wages that were paid declined as well, and real wages plunged to less than half of their level in 1991, the last year of the Soviet Union.[67] According to one source, in dollar terms Russia's average hourly labor costs, including benefits, as of March 1999 were fifty-six cents an hour—less than one-half of the labor costs in Guatemala.[68]

According to the Russian government's human rights commissioner's report for 1999, Russia was "among the bottom 20 percent of the world's nations in terms of the 33 indicators the United Nations uses to determine the standard of living." The report also noted that "the payment of wages in the form of enterprise credit cards and vouchers is becoming a common practice, putting Russia in the same position as countries with the most primitive distribution systems." The report charged that the chronic delays in the payment of wages were a violation of basic human rights.[69]

While it was true that the amount of labor unrest was much lower than had been expected, it was hard to argue that the situation was not dire. The very quiescence of workers in such conditions, some argued, directly contributed to "increased rates of alcoholism, suicide, malnutrition, depression, and mortality."[70] As Guy Standing noted, one factor concealing the extent of unemployment was "the real disappearance of workers—in premature death," with life expectancy for males declining from about 65 years in 1987 to 58 in 1995.[71]

Probably the closest Western observer of Russian labor through the 1990s was Simon Clarke, who led a team of Russian researchers reporting on conditions in workplaces in Russia's regions. As he summarized his findings in 1996, he emphasized "the apparent contradiction between the extremely high levels of discontent recorded at all levels of post-Soviet society and the relatively very low levels of industrial and political unrest, with very little organized resistance." Lacking effective unions and a functioning system of labor relations (about which more later), "grievances build up until they reach the point of explosion."[72]

Such concerns were widely discussed in the Russian media. As Russia's coal miners led a "rail war" (discussed in chapter 5), the newspaper *Nezavisimaya Gazeta* ran a headline that asked ominously, "On the Threshold of Revolution?" About the same time, Oleg Chernovets, a forty-year-old scientific researcher who had not been paid in six months, stated, "Russians are the world's most patient people. We put up with things that cause revolutions in other countries. But history tells you that even Russians have their breaking point. If things get much worse, there will be a revolution here too."[73] Russian officials themselves referred to "the alarmingly high social tensions in the country."[74] Yeltsin warned the internal affairs minister Sergei Stepashin that "the situation in the country could explode."[75]

Deindustrialization, Russian Style

Yet the situation did not explode. Moreover, and paradoxically, given the absence of massive layoffs or the closures of large industrial enterprises, Russia deindustrialized to a substantial degree. Once again, in a striking departure from Western experience, this took place with relatively low levels of unemployment. From 1991 to 2000, the percentage of those employed in industry dropped markedly, from 34.4 percent down to 28.4 percent, and by 2017 the percentage reached 26.8 percent. Meanwhile, from 1990 to 2015 the number of workers employed in Russia's service sector grew from 45 percent to 63.6 percent.[76] Thus, if Russia began its postcommunist transformation with almost as many industrial workers as service sector workers, employment has shifted dramatically so that there are now over two times as many service workers as industrial workers. By this measure Russia looks more "deindustrialized" than a number of postcommunist countries in eastern Europe that are now members of the EU.[77] Yet, while Russia has certainly headed down the path of deindustrialization, industrial employment there has decreased at a slower rate than it has in the postcommunist Visegrad-4 (Hungary, Poland, Slovakia, and the Czech Republic) or than the continued rate of decline in the older (pre-expansion) members of the EU (see figure 2.2).

The bulk of this shift in employment took place in the 1990s. Then, despite the low levels of unemployment, there were "very substantial redundancies [layoffs] from industrial enterprises with minimal opposition," with the vast majority taking the form of either early retirement, workers let go for disciplinary reasons, or ostensibly "voluntary" departures often stemming from low pay and poor work conditions, all of which occurred "with relatively very few compulsory redundancies."[78] New hiring continued but lagged behind (at least nominally) voluntary separations, with many workers taking jobs in the service sector or the informal labor market.[79]

Thus, while avoiding mass layoffs and high levels of unemployment, Russian industry has dramatically restructured, relying instead on labor market levers to prod workers individually to "exit" while avoiding the threshold that might provoke them to exercise collective "voice."

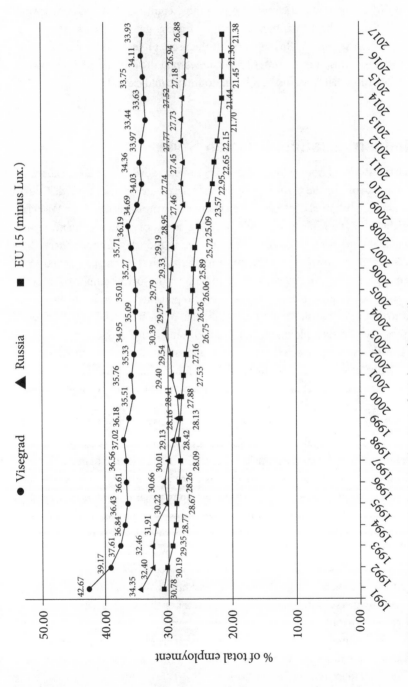

FIGURE 2.2. Employment in industry (percent of total employment)

Source: World Bank World Development Indicators.

While the liberal reformers in the Yeltsin administration looked to the examples of Ronald Reagan and Margaret Thatcher as inspiration for their radical reforms, their plan took a different form as the blueprints of economists met with the reality of post-Soviet society. Rather than attempting a frontal assault on Russia's working class, such as by firing striking air traffic controllers or coal miners, deindustrialization in Russia proceeded more like a war of attrition, or to use a historical metaphor that Russians would understand, akin to the siege of Leningrad. Enterprises in the 1990s were starved of cash and credit. Managers were implicitly permitted to use whatever means they could, legal or otherwise, to induce workers to quit without massive firings. Russia's reformers hoped these factories would not explode, but instead wither away, as workers eventually left of their own volition.

The Survival of Large Enterprises

By the end of the century, Russia's deep crisis had ended. Despite the steep drop in living standards due to the collapse of the ruble in 1998, the low price of the now-devalued currency led to an economic recovery, through an inadvertent form of import substitution. Putin's rise, first as prime minister and soon after as president, was extraordinarily well timed, as Russia's economy benefited from a steep rise in the price of oil.

Nevertheless, beyond the almost historically unprecedented collapse of the Russian economy in the 1990s, through the dramatic growth of the economy during the oil boom of the 2000s, and indeed, through the economic contractions of 2008–9 and 2014–16, Russia's labor market has remained surprisingly consistent. Despite the huge swings in the overall economy, wages remained highly flexible (during the boom years, flexible upward), employment levels remained largely fixed, and despite the substantial shift of workers out of industry, large industrial enterprises remained open.

Wages certainly increased. The economic recovery of the 2000s meant that wage arrears were replaced by extensive wage hikes: from 1999 to 2008 real wages increased each year between 10 and 20 percent.[80] Yet given the steep drop in wages during the previous decade, it was not until 2007 that average wages in Russia officially exceeded those of 1991, the last year of the Soviet Union.[81] Moreover, true to Russia's labor market model, while wages proved flexible upward, very few additional jobs were created. During the recovery of the 2000s, GDP almost doubled relative to 1998, but total employment gained by only 7 to 8 percent.[82] There is some evidence to suggest that the wage increases from 1999 to 2008 were overstated, since the gains may have reflected a greater share of wages paid through formal channels rather than as unreported cash "in the envelope."[83] Yet there is little doubt that the wage increases of the period were a substantial improvement for most of Russia's working population. Little wonder then that Putin became popular. Yet during the economic crisis of 2008–9, the Russian labor market responded in predictable fashion: while GDP declined by 7.9 percent in 2009, unemployment rose by only 2 percentage points. Instead, real wages declined by 3.5 percent overall, and 7.2 percent in manufacturing.[84] The labor market reacted similarly during the downturn of 2015, when the unemployment level (at approximately 5.5 percent) remained virtually unchanged from the previous year, and at a lower level than it was at the height of the boom years of the 2000s.[85] In short, Russia's labor market model has persisted, virtually unchanged, through over twenty-five years of dramatic booms and busts.

Further, despite the substantial shift of Russia's workforce from the industrial to the service sector, Russia hardly appears postindustrial. While Russia's largely passive approach to restructuring had maintained "social stability," it had done so while avoiding the closure of its large industrial enterprises.[86] To be sure, there have been closures of many firms in Russia, industrial as well as nonindustrial. One can walk through many industrial towns and regions in Russia and see the empty shells of former workplaces and warehouses.

Yet the vast majority of closures have been in small and medium firms, while with some important exceptions, large industrial enterprises with many employees have avoided closing their doors. In urging Russia to undertake further liberal reforms, the World Bank has complained that Russia has retained "a legacy of gigantic establishments. Compared to Western market economies, Russia has huge, over-staffed establishments of low productivity."[87] However, the survival of such firms stemmed not simply from a reticence to carry out further market liberalization. As Remington found in his comparative study of Russia's regions, "even the more democratic regimes featured high barriers to entry for small business owing to a policy emphasis on ensuring the survival of large, formerly state enterprises on which the survival of the region depends."[88] That large firms were privileged over small and medium firms is clear from looking at the composition of Russia's labor force by firm size: only 10 percent of Russia's workforce is employed by small and medium enterprises, whereas the corresponding figures in the EU and the US are 72 and 52 percent.[89] As of 2014, in Russia 80 percent of employment in manufacturing was in firms with over 250 employees. In this, Russia is a rather extreme outlier; in OECD comparator countries, only the US (at 63 percent) has much more than half of manufacturing employees in enterprises of that size (see figure 2.3).

Moreover, many of these large enterprises are a legacy from the Soviet past. As Russian economist Vladislav Inozemtsev has argued, as of 2015 "seventy-four of the largest 100 Russian firms by market capitalization work almost exclusively with fixed assets dating from the Soviet era." In contrast, roughly half of the thirty US companies that make up the Dow Jones Industrial Average were not part of it

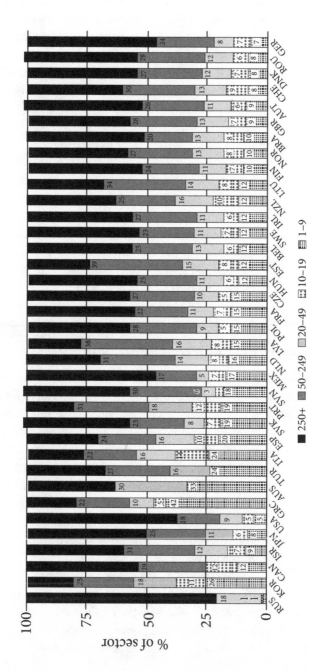

FIGURE 2.3. Manufacturing employment by enterprise size: percentage of total employment in the sector (2014 or latest available year)

Source: OECD.

in 1991, and only four of China's one hundred largest companies (by capitalization) were centrally dependent on productive capacity first brought online more than twenty-five years earlier.[90]

Without question, many large firms have become more competitive over the last two and a half decades, as market pressures have, among other things, pushed many workers in overstaffed factories to leave by attrition. As we shall see, beyond the oil and gas sector, a number of giant metallurgical firms have become successful on the global market through partial modernization, low wages, and competitive exchange rates. Yet as will become especially clear in discussing Russia's many monotowns (chapter 4), a large portion of Russia's large industrial enterprises continue to struggle as economically viable operations. A considerable number operate with obsolete technology, and others are poorly located in relation to markets. In short, rather than engaging in the painful process of closing unprofitable plants and relocating populations, Russia has instead opted, in the evocative phrase of Gaddy and Ickes, for the strategy of "keeping the lights on."[91] Indeed, as Gimpleson and Kapeliushnikov state, "a significant proportion of Russian firms remain loss-making so that their workforces continue to produce negative value-added. This is a vivid indication of unfinished restructuring. Even in the very successful year of 2007, after 9 years of buoyant growth, every fourth Russian enterprise reported zero or negative profits."[92] By 2016 the proportion of firms operating at a loss was close to one-third.[93]

Stability and the "Vertical of Power"

Viewed in hindsight, it hardly appears surprising that with the deep economic crisis of the 1990s and the weakness of the central state, regional leaders and new owners worked to prevent large-scale social unrest that might create further chaos and threaten their positions and property holdings. The response might not have been well thought out, but it was understandable, as an almost emergency-style response to a profound crisis.

What is more surprising, however, is that this response—a labor market where wages rather than jobs were extremely flexible, and the closing of large industrial firms was avoided—persisted through the boom of the 2000s, that is through conditions directly opposite of economic crisis. Just as wages had gone way down, they rose significantly during the boom, and then adjusted downward once again in 2008–9 and 2015. Moreover, not only did economic conditions change substantially from the 1990s to the 2000s, but the political context changed as least as dramatically, from the near state collapse of the Yeltsin years to the increasingly authoritarian leadership of Vladimir Putin. Hence one of the central puzzles that this book seeks to answer: What explains the persistence of Russia's peculiar labor market, and the persistence of its large industrial enterprises, across such wide-ranging variation in economic and political conditions?

Part of the explanation lies with path dependence: once enterprises had adjusted in a certain fashion, they found it cheaper and easier to continue to do so. For employers, while avoiding layoffs might not have been their first preference, they soon learned to regulate wage costs by keeping them extremely flexible. Yet continuity is also visible in the continued operation of large, inefficient firms. One prominent explanation for this phenomenon is the centrality of oil and gas to Russia's economy. At the World Economic Forum in Davos in 2003, Putin stated that while Russia above all sought "stability, both political and economic," he promised that this did not mean the country would "fall asleep under the warm blanket of petrodollars."[94] However, that appears to be just what happened. The assurances of not succumbing to the "oil curse" notwithstanding, the share of oil and gas in Soviet/Russian exports increased from 37 percent in 1989 to 66 percent in 2013.[95] Logically at least, Russia's economic rebound with the turn of the century, driven above all by the boom in world oil prices, could have provided an opportunity for a relatively costless restructuring of Russia's industrial landscape, for example by investing the oil profits into new areas of economic activity. Yet that is not typically how oil-rich countries operate, and Russia proved to be no exception. If closures of large workplaces were avoided despite the significant economic pressure of the 1990s, the boom of the 2000s largely removed the compulsion to make painful economic choices.

A number of observers have noted how this worked in practice. As Inozemtsev argued, "There was an unprecedented (and unspoken) deal: economic prosperity in exchange for political stability. . . . To bolster this stability, the government defends Russian industry with protectionist measures and allows tens of thousands of Russian companies to exercise a virtual monopoly on the markets. The rise in costs has pushed up prices . . . but in Russia it is offset by redistribution to the poorest of some of the country's oil profits."[96]

Gaddy and Ickes contend that during the oil-fueled boom of the 2000s, Russia "did worse than merely fail to dismantle this [industrial] structure. For the sake of job preservation and social stability, it used its windfall wealth to reinforce it."[97]

While dependence on oil exports can help explain the persistence of Russia's rather peculiar labor market and the survival of large industrial enterprises, as global commodity prices have varied considerably over the years so has the significance of oil and gas sales to the Russian economy. Thus, while arguments about the "oil curse" are helpful for explaining outcomes in the Putin years, they cannot account for the origin of Russia's labor market model, nor how that model has endured through various cycles of boom and bust.

Russia's labor policies have persisted through dramatically different political conditions as well. If the Russian state under Yeltsin could be considered weak, not so under Putin, especially over time. This was particularly true regarding the relative power of the federal state and Russia's regions, which had been transformed from the often-rebellious regional leadership of the Yeltsin years, with governors acting in their own interests in defiance of central authorities, to a recentralized "vertical of power" under the increasingly authoritarian control of Vladimir Putin. Though the locus of power has shifted, the crucial importance of "stability" remained throughout; whereas in the 1990s it was regional leaders who were most concerned with maintaining social stability in their regions during a calamitous period, Putin made the promise of stability a central tenet of his presidency, and judged regional leaders accordingly. Needless to say, such an emphasis on "stability" largely ruled out radical restructuring, let alone mass unemployment and the closure of large industrial enterprises.

While there was little alternative during the crisis years to ensuring that enterprises continued to provide the minimal guarantees of social survival, doing so allowed for some features of the system of enterprise provision of social benefits and services to survive beyond the 1990s into the 2000s.[98] Yet this was not simply a matter of path dependence. With the new millennium there was dramatic change not only in the degree of power consolidated by the federal state, but also its orientation, which roughly speaking veered over time from liberal to statist.

Liberal advisers to the Kremlin consistently argued that subsidies to keep former state enterprises open, and to maintain populations in the inhospitable climates of Siberia and the Far North, were economically unsustainable. Yet as "the site of regulation shifted from regions to Moscow, the efforts of liberal reformers to abolish old subsidies had mixed results."[99] Regional leaders, later joined by government proponents of a more statist orientation, were alarmed by the prospect of removing subsidies, which they saw as leading to mass migration and the creation of ghost towns. Instead, they sought a policy of transforming and modernizing existing population centers.[100] In the end, the Russian state followed something of a compromise strategy. It sharply reduced (and in some cases eliminated) state support for people living in Russia's remote regions. Mass migration from Russia's Arctic population that had begun in the 1990s, at times leading to abandoned villages or towns, continued, though at a reduced pace.[101] The "federal government remained committed, however, to supporting Soviet-era industrial enterprises, to both foster economic diversification and avoid turning provincial cities into ghost towns." Thus "while reasserting the center's authority over the regions, Putin still had to provide solutions to the problems that regional governors had been grappling with since the 1990s."[102]

In short, with the statist perspective dominant, considerable concessions were made to large industrial firms during the height of the oil boom from 2003 to 2008. The increasing amount of state intervention and ownership under Putin's leadership, a point that is fully consistent with arguments about the centrality of oil and gas exports to the economy, forms another part of the explanation for the persistence of Russia's industrial and labor policies. Under Putin, the freewheeling oligarchs of the Yeltsin era were brought under control or replaced by those who had direct ties to Kremlin leaders. Given this increasingly statist orientation, the concern of oligarchs over loss-making firms was replaced by the desire to remain in the good graces of the state, in order to retain control over assets and seek state intervention to avoid market competition. For Russia's business titans, part of remaining in those good graces entails ensuring social stability, or at least avoiding widespread social disruption in their economic enterprises and the localities in which they dominate.

Even with the reassertion of a "vertical of power" and an increasingly statist economic perspective, direct state intervention was the exception, and regional leaders were most often tasked with pursuing strategies that were, if nothing else, minimally disruptive. If regional authorities viewed a restructuring project as a potential political challenge for them, threatening social stability (at least in their perception), they would typically use their administrative levers to block it or slow it down. Indeed, the default position of the government on various levels has been to anticipate and prevent the mass downsizing of large enterprises, rather than offering targeted assistance to workers that might be let go.[103]

Whether governors were elected and thus (at least somewhat) accountable to their populations, or whether they were appointed by Putin, they were largely judged on their knack for maintaining stability. Stability in part meant being able to deliver winning results for Putin and his allied party United Russia come election time. Yet as the 2018 presidential elections approached, and in anticipation of such post-elections measures as raising the pension age, Putin appointed a round of new governors in various regions. As Pavel Baev noted, "These new governors' main task . . . amounts to ensuring that the cuts in the distribution of social expenditures produce no street protests."[104] Of course, the closure of large enterprises would hardly contribute to social peace or producing votes for the status quo. As Natalia Zubarevich, the leading expert on Russia's regions, put it, "life compels any governor to take into account the interests of various large corporations that exist in the region."[105]

Moreover, increasingly Kremlin-oriented oligarchs shared the same goal of economic and political "stability." Together these powerful actors had a considerable interest in ensuring that a significant part of the population remained dependent on the state—through the expansion of employment in the "budget sector" or in state-owned or state-dependent large enterprises—and thus that workforce would share a material interest in "stability" as well.[106] As we shall see, large and state-owned enterprises are increasingly called on to generate electoral support for Vladimir Putin and United Russia.

Postcommunist Russia inherited a substantial legacy regarding labor: large industrial enterprises, which in many communities formed the center of social life for
the working population. While workers were accustomed to a labor shortage,
immediately into the post-Soviet era the labor shortage was transformed into a
surplus of labor. Yet rather surprisingly, and contrary to the predictions of most
experts, the result was not mass unemployment but extremely flexible wages,
including at times their nonpayment.

There are several explanations for the rise of what became known as Russia's labor market model: the legacy of socialist paternalism and the mentality of
the working unit as a "labor collective"; the incentives privatization created for
managers and new owners; the motivations of regional leaders as they sought to
survive the crisis; and above all, the fear of many of a possible social explosion as
Russia suffered through an economic decline worse than the Great Depression.

While an explosion was avoided, Russia did experience a substantial strike
wave (explored in chapter 5), stemming in large part from a crisis of wage
arrears. Deindustrialization did indeed take place—a substantial portion of
Russia's workforce shifted from industry to the service sector and informal
employment—but without mass unemployment or the closure of most large
industrial enterprises.

Almost as surprising was the persistence of Russia's model of labor market
adjustment into the 2000s, under economic and political conditions that could
not have been more different. While arguments about the "resource curse" cannot explain how this model first arose, they can help account for why it persisted during the economic boom of the 2000s. This coincided with a more
statist economic approach of the new Russian government. Alongside the shift
in power from regional leaders to a "vertical of power" centered in Moscow,
Kremlin-aligned oligarchs and political leaders from the local to the federal level
shared an interest in promoting "stability," a watchword that was the antithesis
of radical restructuring.

Yet the promise of continued stability rested somewhat uneasily on the
assumption of continued economic growth. That assumption could be made
effortlessly during the years of high oil prices, but worsening economic conditions exposed underlying chronic challenges, much as a receding tide at the beach
reveals what had previously been submerged. We will explore a number of these
challenges in what follows, starting in the next chapter with an examination of
a trap of low labor productivity, and industrial policies that appear to have been
aimed less at resolving that predicament and more at continuing to prop up
employment.

RUSSIA'S LABOR PRODUCTIVITY TRAP

Though Russia avoided mass unemployment during the economic crisis of the 1990s, it did so at the cost of extremely flexible wages; further, steady employment levels combined with flexible pay persisted during the boom of the 2000s and through two subsequent economic recessions. Moreover, the Russian economy also avoided the closure of most large enterprises. In doing so Russia has, with some important exceptions, escaped widespread labor and social protest. But this has not come about without costs. This chapter explores two related questions: First, what are the economic consequences of Russia's labor market patterns and their potential impact on economic growth? Second, why, given that unemployment remains relatively low, has the Russian government pursued an industrial policy aimed at creating and maintaining jobs? These economic questions have important—in some cases vitally important—broader consequences. While the survival strategies of the 1990s prevented social catastrophe, they have left Russia ensnared with low productivity, low wages, and slow economic growth, all of which have considerable social and political impact.

Russia's Low Labor Productivity

The challenge of Russian industry is connected to an even larger problem, which we might call a trap of low labor productivity. As Paul Krugman has noted, "Productivity isn't everything, but in the long run it is almost everything. A country's ability to improve its standard of living over time depends almost entirely on its ability to raise its output per worker."[1] For Russia, productivity is particularly compelling, since without the high oil and gas revenues of the 2000s, future economic growth will almost certainly depend on increasing labor productivity.

Moreover, Russia faces a particularly serious demographic challenge. While it is not the only country confronted with an aging population, Russia will see a significant population decline, particularly in its working-age cohort. According to Kudrin and Gurvich, "the government should anticipate an 8% reduction in the labor force by 2030, a trend that could become a serious constraint on growth of the Russian economy."[2] Yet that decline in the working-age population would be less of a challenge if those that are working are able to produce more, making the question of productivity all the more crucial.[3]

Numerous statements by President Putin suggest that he understands the significance of productivity to Russia's economic growth. During his annual press conference in December 2019, Putin acknowledged, "Yes, we do have many unresolved issues in the economy, very many, and the key one is increasing labor productivity and on this base increasing the economic growth rate."[4]

Russian labor productivity is very low by comparative standards. According to the OECD, for every hour worked, a Russian worker contributes the equivalent of twenty-three US dollars to GDP, while the comparative figure for both the US and Germany is sixty-eight. Indeed, Russian labor productivity is lower than that of Chile and Turkey. Of OECD comparators, Russia outranks only Mexico and South Africa (see figure 3.1).

Why does labor productivity remain so low, thirty years after Russia entered the global capitalist economy? Certainly many factors affect labor productivity, such as the level of technology and investment, property rights, and a predictable legal environment. That is the capital side. But there is also the labor side. In the postwar Swedish model, for example (admittedly, one that is increasingly under threat), comprehensive wage agreements between unions and employers pushed the latter to increase productivity in order to meet wage commitments and remain globally competitive. In the US, Wall Street pushes corporations to cut labor costs, through offshoring or automation, in order to boost profits. In Russia, a central challenge has been how to shift labor from less productive (and often Soviet-oriented) sectors to more productive ones.

One cause of low productivity, and also of Russia's failure to become less reliant on the export of oil and gas and other commodities, is that it missed an opportunity following the Soviet collapse to develop a competitive industrial sector. Russia entered the postcommunist period with a highly educated population, especially in science and engineering, a skilled workforce with low wage demands, considerable industrial infrastructure, and relatively good access

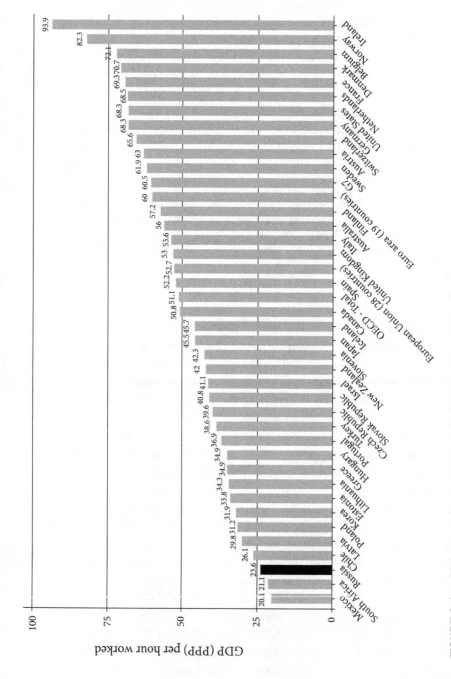

FIGURE 3.1. GDP per capita and productivity (GDP per hour worked)

Source: OECD. Data from 2016 or latest available year.

to markets in Europe. Yet rather than creating an industrial policy that might allow manufacturing firms to adapt and compete on world markets, much of that potential advantage was squandered in the headlong rush of "shock therapy" to open the economy to global competition.[5]

Nevertheless, for the reasons we have explored, the Yeltsin-era government proved unable to follow that free-market logic to its conclusion and compel the closure of loss-making large enterprises. Even by 2011, despite the oil-fueled growth of the 2000s, the World Bank complained that since "manufacturing industries are protected from foreign competition, inefficient firms are kept in business through state aid," and that "most sectors of Russian manufacturing are globally uncompetitive, suffering from low quality and low levels of innovation."[6]

One explanation for a country's uncompetitive manufacturing sector might be that wage increases have exceeded gains in productivity. Consistent with Russia's labor market model, with economic growth following the recovery of 1999, pay for Russian workers shot up dramatically. Indeed, from 1999 until the recession of 2008, real wages in Russia increased each year between 10 and 20 percent.[7]

This has led some liberal economists, such Kudrin and Gurvich, to argue that, far from suffering from low pay, the Russian economy has been hindered by wage gains that make Russian businesses unprofitable and noncompetitive.[8] They argue that "part of the windfall [from oil and gas exports] that remained with producers after taxation went to wage increases, not just in the oil, gas and metals branches, but across the entire economy. As a result, real wage growth far outstripped growth in labor productivity."[9] With this in mind, Kudrin and Gurvich call for stringent measures to curtail wage gains above productivity levels, such as "facilitating the movement of factors of production from less efficient to more efficient industries, i.e. to intensify what Schumpeter calls the process of 'creative destruction.'"[10]

Yet such an argument falls short on at least two grounds. First, Kudrin and Gurvich make 1999 the starting point of their comparison of wage levels, thus counting the years of wage increases but not the earlier years when wages collapsed. As we have noted, it was only in 2007 (the year before the global recession) that average wages in Russia officially exceeded those of 1991 (the year of the Soviet collapse).[11] Measured by cost per output, Russia's labor force was no more expensive in 2015 than it was in 1997.[12] Second, while wages overall increased dramatically from their low levels during the recovery, they did not do so universally. While unit labor costs were stable in Russia overall from 1997 to 2015, in industry there was a dramatic reduction in wage costs by roughly one-third, so that by 2015 industrial wage costs were at their lowest level since 1997. Thus,

Gimpelson and his colleagues conclude, "paradoxically, if the share of remuneration in the economy as a whole is currently near a historic high, in industry it is near a historic low."[13]

The precise level of wages in industry is difficult to calculate, given the value of hidden cash wages. Yet the argument of Kudrin and others that wage gains impede Russia's global competitiveness holds little water, since much of the gains in wages have taken place in the service industry and other "nontradable" sectors.[14] Indeed, despite the protectionist measures that the World Bank and others claim hold back Russian industry, competitive pressures have clearly led Russian manufacturers to squeeze labor costs. Moreover, despite the productivity challenges mentioned above, Russian industry has become more productive, in that productivity gains have greatly outpaced any increases in wage costs. As will become clear, there is little evidence that these gains in productivity have come from investment in new technology. Nor have the reductions in labor costs come from shedding labor: employment levels in industry have continued to shrink through voluntary departures, but not dramatically so. Instead, much of the gains in industrial productivity appear to have come from holding down wages. Such an approach might help explain a seeming paradox: while competitive pressures have pushed Russian industry to increase productivity, few manufacturing sectors in the country produce viable exports.

Russia's Minimal Minimum Wage

As we have noted, while wage levels have recovered somewhat during periods of growth, during economic downturns (as in 2009 and 2014) wages—but not the number of jobs—have gone down again. In May 2016, when Russia faced a slow-growth economy (following the end of the oil price boom), Russian employers continued to respond with low wages; according to Sberbank's chief analyst, Russia's average monthly pay, at $433, was lower than that of China.[15] Such comparisons make all the more puzzling the question of why Russia does not produce more competitive exports. Russia's low wages are also puzzling given demographic pressures, since the decline in the working-age population ought to mean greater demand for labor, pushing wages upward.[16]

A solution to the demographic challenges would be to allow for greater immigration of labor from abroad. As Caress Schenk argues, however, here the regime has had to balance competing demands: allowing enough migration to assist the economy and keep employers happy, while being seen by the broader public to be restricting migration perceived as a threat to the jobs of Russians.[17] Moreover, much of the labor migration from Central Asia involves unskilled workers, tending to push wages and productivity downward, particularly as migrants are especially vulnerable to violations of labor law.

One indication of Russia's endemic problem of low wages has been the chronic challenge of raising Russia's legally defined minimum wage to the level of the officially determined "minimum subsistence wage," below which individuals are said to be in danger of failing to consume enough calories to maintain their body weight. While poverty is a significant problem in Russia—indeed, government officials consider it to be a major factor preventing economic growth—widespread hunger is not.[18] As we shall see shortly, the informal economy is one explanation for why such a low minimum wage, and low wages generally, haven't led to hunger. Yet given low wages, some claim that one drag on labor productivity is the amount of time and energy that workers continue to devote to growing food on private plots.

The new labor code that Putin enacted in 2001 shortly after he took office (discussed in detail in chapter 5) promised to eliminate the discrepancy of a sub-subsistence minimum wage. At the time the minimum wage was notoriously low: while cross-national wage comparisons are difficult, one comparative study found that by November 2001 the minimum wage in Russia amounted to six cents an hour, lower than in Vietnam, where the minimum wage was twenty cents an hour.[19] Yet sixteen years later the discrepancy remained. In 2017 the minimum wage was 7,500 rubles ($131) per month, while the subsistence wage was 10,600 rubles ($185) per month. According to official statistics, one in ten workers in Russia were being paid subsistence wages or less.[20] Moreover, as Vice Premier Olga Golodets admitted, it was impossible to survive on the subsistence minimum alone.[21]

During his 2018 reelection campaign, President Putin promised to raise the minimum wage to the subsistence level, and the law doing so was enacted in January 2020.[22] In his address to the Federal Assembly that month, he proposed formalizing this arrangement in the constitution.[23] There were substantial obstacles to doing so earlier. The minimum wage is tied to various wage levels, especially public-sector wages. Further, given the high level of regional inequality in Russia, raising the minimum wage places pressure on economically weak regions, whose budgets get further burdened by increased public-sector pay increases.[24] This is a major reason why the minimum wage has served as such a weak floor for pay in Russia: while increasing it significantly would place undue burdens on economically weaker regions, even those increases would have only limited impact on most other regions.

Businesses in those weaker regions also come under pressure with a higher minimum wage, which perhaps helps explain a paradox: while one might expect wage increases to pull workers out of the underground economy, in Russia the reverse is true: since the mid-2000s at least, an increase in the minimum wage has led to a higher number of workers in the informal economy.[25] Work in Russia's informal economy can take several forms, such as working at an off-the-books (and often micro-size) enterprise, becoming self-employed, or moonlighting from one's formal sector job as, say, a gypsy cab driver. The total amount of jobs in the formal sector (that is, in all types of legal entities) is forty-five million, while Russia's Labor Force Survey finds there are seventy-three million employed people in Russia, a significant divergence.[26] But the informal economy also extends into formal-sector employment, since in many cases, as we have seen, a substantial portion of formal-sector pay comes from "bonuses" paid as cash "in the envelope," the amount of which can vary considerably, depending on economic conditions. According to official statistics, formal wages in Russia can account for only 38.3 percent of consumer expenditures—that is, what is actually consumed in the country—though this is partly because official statistics exclude wages from small firms.[27] Estimates of informal employment range from 25 percent (Rosstat) to 44.8 percent (RANEPA) of the country's employed population.[28] In any case, there is little doubt that the size of Russia's informal economy is substantial. While by the informal economy's very nature its exact scale is hard to capture, according to a 2017 study by the Association of Chartered Certified Accountants, Russia's informal sector makes up 39.4 percent of the country's GDP, making it the world's fourth-largest shadow economy, behind only Azerbaijan, Nigeria, and Ukraine.[29]

To be sure, the informal economy provides a substantial buffer for Russia's working population. As suggested, it prevents Russia's impoverished population from sliding into hunger. The fieldwork of Jeremy Morris and others makes clear that informal work can make Russia's rust belt communities—including its monotowns—"habitable," and can allow workers to escape from what they view as oppressive conditions of employment.[30] Yet such a reliance on the informal economy has several disadvantages. While workers in the formal sector might like to receive wages in cash (with no taxes withheld), such a payment system undercuts workers' power, rendering collective agreements meaningless. Informal bonus payments place workers in greater dependence on managers, who can raise and lower cash payments arbitrarily, rewarding or punishing individual workers as they see fit. In an indication of the arbitrariness of pay, one-third of Russian schoolteachers, despite being formally unionized and working in the public sector, are unaware of how their salaries are calculated or whether incentive payments and reimbursements are included in their paychecks.[31] Further, the cost advantages for firms that evade labor regulations over pay create incentives for other firms to do so, while providing little incentive to invest in worker training.[32] Outside the formal sector, workers find themselves with little to no employment benefits or labor protections. Moreover, informal-sector employment can become another source of low productivity, as workers might leave, say, a job in an aging machine-building plant, but for even less productive work in the informal economy.[33] Further still, the informal economy undercuts tax revenues and further restricts pension and other social funds that are already under strain.

A higher minimum wage, if properly enforced, would reduce the size of the informal economy. But it would also mean higher rates of unemployment, as some workers get pushed out.[34] By itself, higher unemployment would be one way to boost productivity, as the fear of losing one's job is certainly one way to make workers more productive, particularly if workers viewed as less efficient are laid off first. One challenge to raising unemployment levels, however, is that even after thirty years of capitalism, Russia still lacks an effective mechanism to cushion unemployment. Benefits for the unemployed are so low, and employment agencies and active labor market institutions so poorly functioning, that most unemployed workers don't even bother to register when losing their job. During the economic crisis of 2009, unemployment levels (as measured by surveys according to the ILO's methodology) reached 8.2 percent, but only 2.8 percent of the working population officially registered as unemployed. The ratio of average unemployment benefits to the average wage was under 10 percent before the crisis, thought it was later raised slightly.[35] Still, as with the minimum wage, unemployment benefits have long remained below subsistence living costs.[36]

Some speculate that, paradoxically, while the low level of benefits keeps the official unemployment rate quite low, by failing to provide a more substantial cushion for unemployment the Russian government has heightened its fear of the consequences of mass unemployment. Moreover, Russia's expenditures on labor market policies—both "passive" and "active"—are well below OECD levels, even after factoring in Russia's low unemployment levels. (Passive labor market programs include unemployment benefits; active programs can include job retraining and public works.) As of 2016, Russia's total spending on labor markets was only 0.08 percent of GDP, higher only than Mexico among OECD comparators (see figure 3.2).[37]

Since the Soviet Union had essentially never experienced unemployment from the early 1930s onward, one considerable task for post-Soviet Russia was creating new institutions to deal with unemployment. But an arguably even greater challenge was building popular acceptance of joblessness as a social phenomenon and as the inevitable byproduct of a capitalist economy. Russian workers faced a dramatic shock in moving from the conditions of labor shortage under communism to labor surplus under capitalism. A number of studies have reported

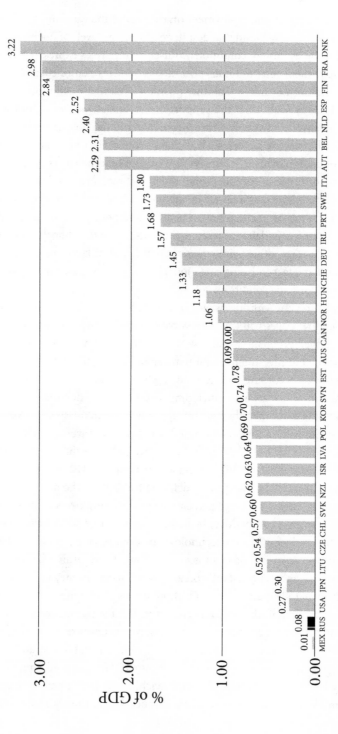

FIGURE 3.2. Total public spending on labor markets

Sources: OECD; Berglund. Data from 2016 or latest available year.

substantial fear of unemployment on the part of the Russian population.[38] One comparative study found that despite relatively low levels of unemployment (relative to the economic conditions), Russian employees express a greater fear of unemployment than those in most other countries examined, and, in the event of job loss, of not finding another position of similar quality. Survey data from 1994 to 2009 found that the proportion of Russian workers who feared losing their jobs was persistently above 50 percent and did not vary substantially over time with objective factors, such as changes in economic conditions or the actual level of unemployment.[39] Surveys also suggest that managers consider layoffs to be very costly and a "conflict prone adjustment measure."[40] While such fear might be partly explained as a legacy of the past, it is also almost certainly a result of very low levels of unemployment benefits and poorly functioning employment agencies and active labor market institutions. Taken together, the low levels of the minimum wage, of unemployment benefits, and of labor market expenditures, as well as the fear of losing one's job, place a very low floor on wages, especially in poor economic conditions.

One problem with low wages comes from a basic insight of Keynesian economics: low wages will lead to less consumer demand and thus slower growth. But another problem is that low wages can also downgrade the incentive for education and investment in human capital. This is true even for highly skilled professions. According to one report, when calculated as an hourly wage, the average monthly salaries (including overtime) for doctors in a number of regions was lower than the hourly wage of workers in Russia's McDonald's.[41] The Boston Consulting Group reported that in Russia the average doctor is paid only 20 percent more than the average for a driver, whereas the earnings gap for such professions in the US is 261 percent and in Germany 172 percent.[42]

In contrast to the Swedish model, where at least in the heyday of centralized bargaining, high-level wage agreements pushed employers to increase productivity to remain competitive, in Russia wages can be so low that there is little incentive to invest in new technology, or even basic equipment. The business newspaper *Vedomosti* gave an account of an electric utility in Ivanovo Oblast whose transformers constantly break down. Lacking money to replace them, the utility hires 130 repair workers, to whom it pays 20,000 rubles ($350) per month, a small fraction of what it would cost to replace the transformers.[43] According to the International Federation of Robotics, Russia has three industrial robots per ten thousand workers, whereas the world average is sixty-nine, and in advanced economies the number is more than a hundred.[44] In advanced capitalist societies, many fear the automation problem: machines replacing people. But in Russia, the problem is the reverse: people are cheaper than machines. Moreover, evidence suggests that Russia lags behind not only advanced capitalist countries in innovation, but is behind many so-called emerging market economies as well.[45]

The challenge is not merely technical, but social and political. As the *Financial Times* noted in discussing Russia's relative lack of technological upgrading, "such transformation has long proved disruptive, rendering massive numbers of workers obsolete. But in Russia, where years of under-investment mean equipment lags far behind that of the west, the vast leap required could shatter entire regions, many of which have changed little since the collapse of the USSR." The article notes further that "how to grapple with the social impact of this new industrial revolution is in many ways more difficult than deploying modern technology in Soviet-era factories."[46]

Low wages and low-quality work contribute to a high rate of labor turnover, as workers have little reason not to leave one job for another.[47] While high rates of turnover can be seen as a sign of a dynamic labor market, in Russia the employment shifts tend to be in the direction of lower-quality jobs in the informal sector.[48] Such movement gives both firms and workers little inducement to invest in firm-specific (or for workers, even industry-specific) skills training, further downgrading productivity.[49] Long decried as a chronic problem by Soviet officials, job turnover, even in the absence of the Soviet-era labor shortage, remains one of the tools Russian workers use to improve their lot. Given this, Gaddy and Ickes are certainly wrong to call workers "hostages" of large firms.[50] As Morris has demonstrated, many in Russia's working-class milieu see little reason to become more dutiful, better educated, and more productive workers. If stuck in a job with low wages and lousy conditions, they will leave, with abandon.[51] While informal-sector pay may be less dependable, it often involves working without a boss, at hours of one's own choosing. While the outcome might be lower productivity for the economy as a whole, given the options for individual workers, such choices are hardly irrational.

Again, particularly given Russia's demographic pressures, investing in Russia's workforce, in its pay, its training, and its work conditions, would appear imperative. A lower quantity of workers could be compensated by providing incentives and opportunities to improve their quality.[52] The other (and not exclusive) solution for a shrinking population is to increase the immigration of working-age adults; yet given the poor working conditions of the existing workforce, the introduction of low-skilled (and even less legally protected) immigrant workers will likely only worsen Russia's problem of low wages and productivity.

In sum, Russia has made a partial transformation toward a postindustrial economy, but at the cost of low productivity. It remains stuck, for the foreseeable future, in a low-productivity trap. That low productivity stems in large part from the Russian model of labor market adjustment, which entails low (though highly flexible) wages rather than high levels of unemployment. Indeed, Russia's unemployment levels remain relatively low by comparative standards. Thus, we return to a central puzzle: what explains the continued attempts to avoid mass layoffs and maintain employment in various industries? The rest of this chapter will begin to answer this question by exploring the steps the Russian state has taken to protect employment, including through bailouts and subsidies to industry, protectionist measures, efforts to create an industrial policy through import substitution, and support for and expansion of state-owned enterprises, in particular those in military industries and the automobile sector.

Russia's Industrial Policy

Low wages, however brutal for workers, can be beneficial for the economy overall. The low cost of labor can become a country's comparative advantage, provided that the economy is centered on the export of labor-intensive products. This was the path taken by the "tigers" of East Asia, such as South Korea and Taiwan, and was central to China's dramatic economic growth.[53] Those countries grew their economies by strategically building a competitive manufacturing sector. As Ruchir Sharma, the chief global strategist at Morgan Stanley Investment Management, put it, "no other sector has as much impact as manufacturing in generating the jobs and productivity gains that can make a nation rich."[54] Indeed, since the time of the Industrial Revolution, developing a competitive manufacturing industry has been the only proven path to joining the ranks of the advanced capitalist economies. Success in exporting manufacturing goods can provide a reliable stream of income for investment. Countries like Russia that concentrate on the export of raw materials such as oil and gas not only open themselves to the volatile fluctuations of global markets in commodities but also become mired in middle-income status. As Sharma notes, "among the leading oil exporters, 90 percent are no richer today relative to the United States than they were the year they started producing oil. Most are poorer."[55]

The inefficiencies of the Soviet legacy notwithstanding, Russian industry had several potential advantages at the start of the post-Soviet era. Yet instead of following the East Asian model and adopting a strategic approach to manufacturing exports, in the crucial initial period Russia implemented a much more laissez-faire attitude toward industry and its economy generally. Even during the Putin-era oil boom, as the economy generally became more statist in orientation, Russia lacked a sustained institutional framework or strategic plan to improve the prospects of its manufacturing sector, or even to reduce that sector's substantial challenges. Rather, government policy aimed, both implicitly and explicitly, at avoiding radical restructuring, relying instead on the passive approach of firms reducing employment levels by attrition. As a result, outside of certain firms in the metals sector and military industry, Russian manufacturing exports are noncompetitive and add relatively little to GDP. In the words of Vladislav Inozemtsev, "the Russian economy has developed and is still developing along relatively autarchic lines. It exports unprocessed raw materials and imports ready-made, high-tech goods. As such, industrialization is seen almost exclusively as a way of reducing Russia's dependence on foreign goods."[56] While Russia is hardly autarchic—indeed, it is fully intertwined with the global capitalist economy—Inozemtsev's comments point to the Russian leadership's policy of "import substitution," begun around the mid-2000s. While the East Asian economies adopted a similar approach, they did so as part of a strategy to exploit low-paid workers in order to export labor-intensive products at competitive prices and gradually increase the technological sophistication (and therefore profitability) of their industrial exports.[57] Even as the Russian government's approach became more statist, it has displayed little such strategic understanding to guide its global economic policy. For example, Inozemtsev points out that "Russia has the distinction of being the only country where 'free economic zones' were set up to increase the supply of goods on the internal market and not for export."[58]

With the conflict with Ukraine in 2014 and resulting Western sanctions, followed by Russian countersanctions, "import substitution" and "industrial policy" became explicit government aims, as Russia sought to boost certain sectors such as agricultural products and pharmaceuticals by restricting imports.[59] Yet even before the Ukraine conflict, the World Bank and other international organizations accused Russia of pursuing protectionist policies in international trade. Thus in 2013, a year before Ukraine's Maidan uprising and a year after Russia joined the World Trade Organization, the free-trade advocacy organization Global Trade Alert (GTA), which describes itself as a "leading independent trade monitoring service," charged that Russia was the world's most protectionist country, followed closely by its neighbor Belarus. According to a news report on the study, "Russia alone accounted for 20 percent of the protectionist policies identified worldwide," such as state support for the rare earth metals industry, agriculture, and aircraft makers. "With 78 such trade restrictions, Russia also accounted for almost a third of the protectionism imposed by G20 nations." The charges of protectionism extended to the Russian-backed Eurasian Economic Union, which, according to the GTA, accounted for one-third of worldwide trade protectionism in 2013. "The customs union was responsible for 15 times as many protectionist measures as China while having only an eighth of the population," said GTA's coordinator Simon Evenett, a professor at the Swiss Institute for International Economics. "Russia's policy of economic restructuring is nothing more than a potent mix of rampant subsidization and aggressive protectionism."[60]

Likewise the World Bank has claimed a "protectionist lobby" in Russia seeks to thwart competitive economic pressures from internal as well as international markets, with the result that "manufacturing industries are protected from foreign competition [and] inefficient firms are kept in business through state aid."[61] As Russia geared up for accession to the WTO (the negotiations for Russia's membership took eighteen years), the World Bank argued that Russia needed a "political strategy to facilitate trade reform." It pointed to the example of Australia in the 1980s, where according to the bank, trade liberalization exposed protected sectors to international competition, successfully pressuring them to boost their competitiveness. The World Bank claimed further that political support for the reforms was maintained in Australia because "measures were taken to compensate losers by subsidizing efficiency-enhancing measures in textiles and automobile assembly before exposing them to competition." With no hint of irony, however, in the next sentence the bank adds that "WTO strictures may no longer permit subsidizing the potential losers from reform."[62]

While what the World Bank terms Russia's "protectionist lobby" presumably refers to oligarchs and Kremlin-connected managers of state enterprises, the "losers" from a policy of free trade would certainly include those workers in industries exposed to heightened competition. Whatever protection those workers have received is questionable. They have suffered from poor work conditions and wages that have lagged considerably behind productivity, and large numbers of them have been pushed out of industry into the underground economy. Yet workers have thus far (despite Russia's WTO membership) been protected from high levels of unemployment and the closures of inefficient large enterprises. Rather than closing such loss-making firms, Russia continues to follow a policy of, again in Gaddy and Ickes's term, keeping the lights on.[63] Thus, despite the political restrictions and considerable power amassed by the Russian state, its leadership has not chosen to pursue the labor-repressive manufacturing policies of the East Asian tigers, or, despite the neoliberal nature of many of its other policies, the full-on austerity measures of a regime such as Pinochet's Chile.

Subsidizing Industrial Employment

In the Russian case, protections are not limited to explicit government expenditures and subsidies. The amount of overt subsidies the Russian government provides to industry from the federal budget is not dramatically high. Gaddy and Ickes have used the term "rent addiction" to characterize how rents from the oil and gas sector are transferred—in implicit and hidden fashion—to subsidize loss-making industries such as those in the machine-building sector.[64] These implicit subsidies move through a "rent distribution chain" whereby the oil and gas industry provides cheap inputs for industrial production down the line, and pays for orders from inefficient domestic producers. The low base wages paid to Russia's workers could be considered another form of hidden subsidy, in that, with the wage bill so flexible downward, this allows inefficient enterprises to stay open even when market pressures are extreme.[65]

The policies of protectionism and import substitution coincided with a related policy: the expansion of the state's role in the economy. Over 30 percent of Russia's labor force is employed in the public sector (including those working in state-owned firms), a high number by global standards.[66] According to Russia's Federal Antimonopoly Service (FAS), as of 2016 the public sector accounted for 70 percent of Russia's GDP.[67] Though the FAS's calculations include firms with partial state ownership, this is quite a turnaround from about twenty years earlier, when the Russian government was able to claim that the non-state sector accounted for 70 percent of GDP.[68] Kudrin and Gurvich, borrowing a phrase from the Soviet era, argue that because of the expanding state sector, the Russian economy operates once again under "soft budget constraints," meaning losses are simply endured.[69] These soft constraints, they claim, "arise from a willingness of the state to tolerate inefficient work in state companies, compensating for it with various forms of financial support (e.g. direct grants, tax breaks or preferential loans), as well as lax regulation of prices and tariffs, granting of privileges in the allocation of public procurement and licenses for the exploitation of mineral deposits, etc." Soft budget constraints, particularly through the ability to borrow funds at below-market interest rates, reduce incentives for state-owned companies to raise their productivity.[70]

State-owned enterprises aren't necessarily inefficient. In China, the world's most dynamic economy for many years now, state-owned firms still account for nearly one-third of the country's GDP.[71] The impact of such firms depends in large part on whose interests the state serves. But having state officials on the board of directors of economic firms allows for the possibility that political as well as economic goals might be pursued. Such goals could be expanding market power through political leverage, or avoiding excessive unemployment and preventing social unrest that might negatively impact state officials.

Considerable evidence suggests that in the Russian case, state enterprises have been able to drive out competitors and consolidate their own market power. The FAS, which is tasked with preventing just such a trend, argued in its 2016 annual report that the number of politically connected cartels had grown and spread across various economic sectors.[72] Meanwhile, the Russian government's Analytical Center survey of enterprises found that the portion of firms reporting that they faced "no competition" rose from 0.7 percent in 2013 to 13.9 percent in 2016.[73]

As David Szakonyi has argued, the "nearly continual state of economic crisis in Russia since 2008 has definitely contributed to consolidation in multiple sectors." As he notes, "Crises often lead to greater market concentration by exposing and ultimately killing off firms with more flimsy access to capital, weaker political connections, and thinner margins. Bankruptcy rates in Russia shot up following both the 2008 and 2014 crises, while small and medium-sized businesses felt the squeeze of skyrocketing interest rates, unsustainable tax burdens, and uncertain protection for their property rights. These crises helped clear the way for the larger Russian firms."[74]

Since monopolies tend to focus on protecting their dominant market position above all, they are less likely to seek ways to increase labor productivity, becoming an additional explanation for Russia's low productivity levels.

Under this consolidation, it is not the least competitive firms that were driven out by market forces, but smaller, less well-connected firms, and those with fewer employees. A 2007 joint study of the World Bank and the Higher School of Economics found in every branch of Russian industry a labor productivity gap of ten to twenty times between the top 20 percent of companies (in terms of productivity) and the bottom 20 percent.[75] This led Kudrin and Gurvich to argue that the least competitive enterprises, "while accounting for a small share of output, enjoy access to significant material resources and labor." They argue further that "this confirms the wide existence of soft budget constraints in the Russian economy. The use of a large set of tools to help all enterprises survive can be described as 'industrial paternalism.'"[76] Other like-minded economists complain that "the mechanism of 'creative destruction' doesn't work in Russia."[77]

While there is little doubt that this expansion of state-owned enterprises was driven by politically powerful and well-connected individuals seeking to profit financially, another factor cannot be excluded: the perceived importance of avoiding mass layoffs so as to prevent potentially destabilizing labor protest. As Szakonyi notes, during economic crises, as smaller firms get driven out, "subsidies find their way to large, inefficient state-owned enterprises at risk of laying off workers and sparking political unrest."[78]

Jobs and Russia's Military Industry

While critics claim that the Russian economy props up inefficient enterprises in paternalist fashion for the sake of employment, the issue of jobs is a core political concern for leaders like Putin. In one of his "May Decrees" during his 2012 presidential campaign, Putin called for the creation of twenty-five million high-productivity jobs by 2020, more than doubling the estimated number of such jobs. While in doing so Putin acknowledged Russia's endemic problem of low productivity, experts quickly pointed out such a goal was virtually impossible—as the subsequent years indeed proved—since it was unclear how the state could mandate the creating of highly productive employment.[79]

The Putin team did indicate one area for the creation of high-tech jobs, namely the military industry, a sector where Russia enjoyed some technological advantages. The Soviet Union created a military industry on a vast scale, employing more than eight million workers, which accounted for almost a fifth of all industrial employment in the country. The majority of the military industry was located in the Russian Republic: while Russia accounted for just over half (51.8 percent) of the population of the Soviet Union, by one estimate its share of employment in the Soviet military-industrial complex in 1985 was 71.2 percent.[80] Workers in Soviet military industries enjoyed top salaries and in-kind benefits. Yet by 1997 employment in the defense industry in Russia had fallen to 2.8 million, a reduction of more than half its previous amount.[81] This was indeed a major source of Russia's deindustrialization in the 1990s.

There are multiple explanations for Russia's military buildup under Putin, from simply stemming the steep decline of Russia's military in the 1990s to responding to the perception of threats from the West such as the expansion of NATO and the perceived shortcomings of the military following the 2008 war with Georgia. But Russia's domestic politics, in various ways, pushed in this direction as well.[82] There was the political significance of Putin's claim of getting Russia "to rise from its knees," as well as the symbolic support for Putin from the workers of the Uralvagonzavod tank factory during the 2012 protests (both topics are discussed in chapter 7). But there was also the political importance of the military industry as a source of employment.

Putin's rearmament campaign and sharp increase in military spending followed the war with Georgia, where the military was seen as lacking. Yet this also coincided with the need to consolidate support from his core electoral base, first following the 2008–9 economic crisis, and then in the wake of the so-called middle-class protests of 2011–12. By 2009 the government began canceling the debts of firms in the military industry and began to increase defense spending in what some termed "the militarization of the country's budget."[83]

The buildup was explicitly justified by the positive impact it would have on the economy and producing jobs. As Putin himself put it, "The huge resources invested in modernizing Russia's military-industrial complex and equipping the army shall serve as fuel to feed the engines of modernization of the economy, creating real growth and a situation where government expenditures fund new jobs, support market demand, and facilitate scientific research."[84]

Russia's 2015 National Security Strategy directly addressed the need to improve economic growth as a national security imperative, stating that it viewed "developing the country's defense industry complex as the motor for the modernization of industrial production."[85] In addition to subcontractors, the Ministry of Defense estimates that around four thousand enterprises are involved in fulfilling Russia's military contracts.[86] Military spending supports employment in monotowns, many of which are tied to the defense industry.[87] The deputy minister of defense Tatyana Shevtsova argued explicitly that Russia's increased level of military spending was driven more by goals for the economy than foreign policy. She stated that "the present level of Russian military expenditures do not reflect the costs of the army or the navy. The defense budget is an instrument for supporting domestic industry, in particular, the high-technological part."[88]

The claims of Shevstova, Putin, and others that Russia's military spending would help modernize industry through the adoption of high technology were undercut by comments made by the defense minister, Anatoly Serdyukov, shortly before he was fired. Serdyukov complained that in many cases Russia's military equipment was more expensive and less technologically sophisticated than material available for import. This was because, as *Nezavisimoe voennoe obozrenie* reported his remarks, "manufacturers begin to fold into their price all of their costs, including those of the social sector. If it takes the 'Sevmash' [plant] nine years to produce one ship, then all the costs, including for the pig farm, the children's and pioneer's camp, the workers' resort [*dom otdikha*], the medical clinic—all of this weighs down this one unfortunate ship."[89] Though Serdyukov was soon sacked, ostensibly on charges of corruption, others argue that he was let go for challenging the interests of Russia's military industrial complex.

According to Russian military analyst Aleksandr Golts, a large portion of Russia's military matériel is produced by monopolies, which worry little about price. While Russia's military industry is hardly unique in this regard, Golts argues that the Putin-era military industry has been rebuilt along Soviet lines, "where one more or less effective enterprise feeds a dozen half-bankrupt ones," with the cost of maintaining the latter simply folded into the final price the state pays for the military equipment. "The main thing," Golts argues, "is to have the maximal number of employees, allowing those running the firms to demand direct financing from the government, which fears a social explosion."[90]

The government's concern with a potential social explosion can be seen in its interventions in the military industrial sector during two recent economic crises. In 2008–9, sixty-four military firms were included in the list of enterprises eligible for state support "due to their status as a national or regional major employer or contributor to GDP."[91] In 2015 a comparable list included thirty-nine major defense enterprises, and large military contracts helped prop up a number of regions during that year's recession.[92]

Yet state support for the military industry did not prevent such firms from suffering from problems such as wage arrears and labor protests. For instance, workers in the Radiopribor factory in Primorskii Krai undertook several protest actions over a two-year period to demand payment of wage arrears. While their arrears were paid in part by regional reserve funds, by the end of December 2016 the deputy prime ministers Yuri Trutnev and Dmitry Rogozin instructed the Ministry of Defense to help the factory, and the factory soon signed a three-year contract with the ministry.[93] Golts named twenty different military enterprises in various regions that were undergoing wage arrears, shortened work weeks, compulsory leaves, and plans for layoffs; in his view, many of these firms were using threats of social unrest to extract more orders from the state.[94]

As the economy has continued to grow slowly and oil prices have remained relatively low, Russia's military industry has seen a decline in state orders. Putin has been pushing for defense plants to produce more for the civilian market, with part of the concern almost certainly to preserve jobs. Yet given the inefficiencies noted above, it is hard to see how those firms can produce consumer products at competitive prices, at least without substantially shedding labor. Indeed, at times the conversion of Russia's military industry and technology to civilian use has worked in reverse: for instance, Russia's once large aircraft industry today primarily exports military planes, with Russian civilian aircraft production less than 1 percent of the global total.[95] Meanwhile, Russia's domestic market for passenger airliners provides little consolation: some 80 percent of that market has been captured by Airbus and Boeing.[96]

Alternative Explanations

While state support for Russia's military industry as a means of job preservation is in some ways exceptional, we shall see similar efforts for Russia's auto industry in chapter 6. Nevertheless, job preservation, with its corollary of preventing social unrest, is far from the only explanation for Russia's statist approach to industry and the economy generally. Indeed, in most accounts, this statist approach is driven more by elite interests than concerns about popular backlash. As we have seen in the last chapter, Russia's governors have fought to keep factories with large workforces open in their region through the 1990s and into the 2000s. Gaddy and Ickes make the case that Russia—especially during the years of high oil prices—has suffered from "rent addiction," in which Putin, the oligarchs, and regional governors are all interdependent.[97] Putin maintains stability, while the oligarchs get to keep their property, provided they cooperate in the redistribution of oil and gas rents. Governors from the majority of regions, who don't directly benefit from export rents, push the rent-receiving regions to redistribute rents elsewhere. Gaddy and Ickes hypothesize that governors and other regional leaders need to keep labor in place in order to maintain the "fictitious capital" of loss-making enterprises on their territories. The closure of these enterprises, and the resulting loss in population, would greatly undercut whatever political power they have. It is more politically expedient (if not economically efficient) to "keep the lights on" in loss-making enterprises, including many monotowns.[98]

The power of governors, especially those in less economically dynamic regions, would appear to have been curtailed under Putin's policy of a "vertical of power," especially during the period from 2005 to 2012 when governors were appointed from the center rather than elected. Yet those changes did not make regional leaders more inclined to push for transforming their regions. Kudrin and Gurvich complain that a presidential decree from August 2012 makes the regional unemployment rate a part of the performance criteria for regional officials. They argue further that, "in practice, much blunter approaches are often used, such as imposing informal restrictions on firing workers. This is how many projects to modernize production are made unprofitable and in practice blocked."[99] As Harley Balzer argues, "under Putin, the incentive structure for Russian regional officials does not reward local development." He adds, "their calculations involve doing Moscow's bidding, turning out the vote for the ruling party, maintaining social stability, and lobbying for funds from the center."[100]

The importance of turning out votes provides another explanation for maintaining Russia's industrial structure, and this incentive has been emphasized in some important research. As Frye, Reuter, and Szakonyi have shown, subsidies to industrial enterprises and regions are exchanged for votes in clientelistic fashion.[101] In an analysis of the 2011–12 election cycle, they state, "our data clearly indicates that the primary locus for electoral intimidation in Russia is the workplace." They conclude that "it is quite common for Russian employers to threaten workers with dismissal or cuts in salary and benefits if they do not vote or vote [a] certain way."[102] Their findings are consistent with those of vote-monitoring groups such as GOLOS, which found that 83 percent of its crowd-sourced reports of electoral violations involved workplace intimidation. Even with secret ballots, Frye and colleagues found, 33 percent of workers thought that it was possible for employers to know how they voted.[103]

Most interesting for present purposes was the type of firms that were most likely to carry out election campaigning. In a study focused on the 2011 parliamentary elections, firm surveys revealed that large firms, those most dependent on state support (such as state-owned firms and those that sell to the state), and those in heavy industry and mining were most likely to engage in voter intimidation. Employee surveys found that while worker income had no impact on the amount of pressure received from employers, those who received significant nonwage benefits from their employers were more likely to report campaigning at the workplace. Interestingly, "respondents living in a monogorod [monotown] are twice as likely to have been mobilized than those living in other types of cities—(41.3 percent versus 20.2 percent)."[104] Frye and colleagues' subsequent study, covering the 2012 presidential elections as well as those for parliament in 2011, found an even higher divergence: 44 percent of employees in monotowns reported experiencing electoral intimidation, whereas only 17 percent of all employed respondents did so, and electoral intimidation was not statistically detectable among Russians who were not employed. The authors plausibly speculate that workers in monotown enterprises are particularly dependent on their employers, making them especially vulnerable to such intimidation.[105]

Yet such dependence cuts both ways. As another study concludes, "By incentivizing regional governors to use their political machines to win elections for the regime, the Kremlin effectively punishes those governors that are successfully developing their regional economies, with the effect being especially strong in regions where a high percentage of the population lives in Soviet-era single company towns."[106]

There was considerable evidence that such workplace voter mobilization continued in the 2016 parliamentary and the 2018 presidential elections.[107] State-owned enterprises were especially mobilized to support United Russia and President Putin's reelection.[108] To provide positive news during the campaign, large companies were directed to write stories that "say that state support helped lift them out of crisis, restored modern production, and reequipped them with new equipment and gave work to local residents."[109]

But besides spinning the news to the general public, state-owned enterprises were also being called on to provide accurate information to the authorities about the public mood ahead of the elections. Some Russian commentators speculated that given the lack of such information from state media in Russia's increasingly centralized political system, including the incentive for governors to report positive assessments about their regions, the Kremlin was turning to state-owned enterprises as a source of information. For example, Russia's nuclear power monopoly Rosatom was charged with assessing social sentiment and the potential for protest in Russia's closed atomic cities ahead of the 2018 presidential elections, and other state-owned enterprises were funding government-backed research organizations to carry out similar evaluations.[110] During the presidential campaign period, the Kremlin also tasked every large company in the oil and gas, metallurgical, and automobile industries to report monthly about the regional mood and, in the words of *Vedomosti*, "any events that might have a negative influence on the political and social-economic conditions in the regions." Such "risks" would include plans for mass layoffs or the nonpayment of salaries.[111]

The chapters that follow will emphasize the significance for the Russian state of maintaining the political backing of the working class. This effort to maintain working-class support was particularly evident following the ostensibly middle-class protests in Moscow and St. Petersburg in 2011–12. But increasing state intervention in the economy has also increased at least passive political support from important parts of Russia's middle class as well. As research by Bryn Rosenfeld has demonstrated, middle-class professionals employed in the state sector were much less likely to participate in the "Russia without Putin" protests of those years. Public-sector workers were more fearful than workers in the private sector of failing to find alternative employment should they lose their job. They also expressed more economic, as opposed to political, concerns.[112] This suggests yet another explanation for the expansion of the state sector under Putin's leadership.

Without question, each of these factors—"rent addiction" from high oil prices, the need for regional elites to promote stability, the importance of state-owned and large industrial enterprises (not least those in monotowns) for delivering votes for United Russia and Vladimir Putin, as well as the need for political support from state-sector workers—contributes significantly to the propping up of inefficient industrial centers. They also help explain the substantial shift in recent years toward a more statist orientation of Russia's economy. Yet each of these explanations stems from the Putin era. They can shed light on the persistence of Russia's peculiar labor market; they cannot explain its origins. Low unemployment with flexible wages and inefficient large enterprises (and resulting low productivity) have persisted across the rise and fall of economic growth and boom and bust of oil "rents," from a regional policy based on independent and assertive governors through the "vertical of power," and from a chaotic party and electoral system to one predictably under the control of the Kremlin. As Gimpelson and Oshchepkov note, Russia's "major labor market institutions were largely shaped in the early 1990s and with some modifications survived throughout the 2000s. The Russian authorities have never considered this policy area an explicit priority. Their implicit goal . . . was to prevent mass downsizing of the labor force which was considered a threat to political stability."[113]

Moreover, Russia's workers are not so easily manipulated. While their basic concerns might be more economic than political, they have their own interests and are able to act on them rather than simply being mobilized at election time.

That Russia's workers might be a threat to political stability, let alone lead a "social explosion," might seem an unfounded, even irrational, fear on the part of Russia's leaders. Yet as we shall see in the remaining chapters, the evidence suggests that Putin's reputed working-class support was not—or at least not simply— authentic and spontaneous support from below and instead required significant interventions from above.

Further still, the origins of Russia's labor market, its many large enterprises, and the fear of workers' unrest began not only before the Putin era or even the 1990s, but lie much earlier in the Soviet period, beginning with the Stalinist industrialization drive in the 1930s. Indeed, Russia's peculiar labor market is directly connected to Russia's unique urban geography, which remains substantially unchanged from Soviet days. Within that sprawling geography lie hundreds of monotowns—one-industry cities and towns that had been created to meet the needs of an entirely different economic system and historical era. This we will turn to next.

4

MONOTOWNS AND RUSSIA'S POST-SOVIET URBAN GEOGRAPHY

How might Russia escape its low-productivity and middle-income trap? As some have suggested, one clear path would be to focus on the growth of major metropolitan cities as centers of innovation in a global capitalist economy. Liberal economists look to large cities as creative environments and centers of innovation and entrepreneurship. Such thinking has been popularized by, among others, urbanist Richard Florida, who argues that "superstar" or "global" cities such as New York, London, and Tokyo are the engines of technological change, receive a disproportionate share of capital investment, and house the world's leading-edge companies and talent. Florida coined the term the "creative class" to describe the professionals who are drawn to such cities, a descriptor that was widely adopted to portray the anti-Putin protesters in Moscow and St. Petersburg in 2011–12.[1]

Others, writing from the perspective of "critical urban studies," tend to look at urban development through the lens of globalization and neoliberalism yet also see major cities as the nodes of global capitalist development.[2] As they point out, globalization remains rooted in place, and global cities provide the critical infrastructure for multinational corporations and house the world's richest people.[3] Such cities become centers of capital investment and accumulation through finance and real estate. Yet such a "spatial fix" for capital accumulation inevitably entails a reciprocal withdrawal of capital from, and the dispossession of, urban centers once considered vital to economic dynamism, a process with profound social, and at times political, consequences.[4] This crucial point is missed by some of the more breathless accounts of the rise of new "smart cities."[5]

Yet the economic logic behind investing in such cities appears compelling. As Carol Leonard has pointed out, "while accelerating globalization and the role of the information-driven knowledge economy may seem to reduce the importance of proximity for firm performance, it is now clear that the reverse is true; geographic proximity generates agglomerative advantage, and city regions surge forward as the locus of economic development."[6]

Picking up on such arguments, liberal economist and Kremlin adviser Alexei Kudrin argues that since global megalopolises are now the drivers of economic growth worldwide, Russia should concentrate on developing a handful of its largest cities, beyond the existing centers of Moscow and St. Petersburg. His Center for Strategic Research developed a policy strategy along these lines, which it claimed was "prepared on behalf of the Russian president." In an article titled "Cities Instead of Oil," Kudrin argued that while the structure of Russia's urban geography was laid down largely in the Soviet period, the situation actually worsened during the boom years of 2000–8. Then economic growth fueled by rising oil prices meant that the overall contribution of cities to the country's economy actually declined. "The urban economy was not the driver of the country's economic development, but the main recipient of the income from oil growth."[7]

Currently Moscow and St. Petersburg are Russia's only "global cities," with the rest of Russia's cities "barely noticeable on the map of the world." Russia's two

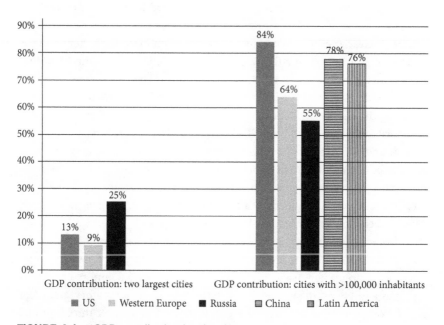

FIGURE 4.1.   GDP contribution by city size

Sources: *Vedomosti*; Tsentr strategicheskikh razrabotok.

largest cities account for more than 25 percent of the country's GDP, whereas in the US the corresponding number is 13 percent and in western Europe (on average) 9 percent. Meanwhile, cities with populations greater than one hundred thousand produce 84 percent of GDP in the US, and 64 percent in western Europe, while in Russia they account for only 55 percent, which is also substantially less than they do in China (78 percent) and Latin America (76 percent) (see figure 4.1). This, Kudrin contends, "is a huge gap, from which arises the sad and cynical mantra that it's impossible to secure a good quality of life outside the Moscow Ring Road."[8] Nevertheless, Kudrin claims that by 2035, Moscow and St. Petersburg will account for 40 percent of Russia's GDP.[9]

In sharp contrast to current government policy, Kudrin's plan would not seek to support Russia's struggling industrial centers and hundreds of monotowns, but rather to concentrate attention and resources on the country's most densely populated agglomerations, that is the roughly dozen urban centers that number a million or more in population. Doing so would boost economic growth by connecting infrastructure and intellectual potential and allowing business and the population to become more mobile. The goal is to create "smart cities" able to join the digital economy.[10] Other urban centers might be included, such as "multisectoral regional centers," a phrase that would appear to have been deliberately chosen to exclude monotowns.[11]

While such pronouncements might have appeared to be one more rhetorical attempt by the liberal side of Russia's establishment to influence policy, such arguments clearly found a sympathetic listener in Putin. In his annual Address to the Federal Assembly in 2018, Putin explicitly stated that "it is important that urban development becomes the driving force for the country," a statement that was repeated prominently in his campaign for reelection as president in 2018.[12] Following the election, the Russian government approved a 115-page "Strategy for Spatial Development through 2025," which envisions eighteen cities (besides Moscow and St. Petersburg) as "prospective centers of economic growth," most with the potential to become "world-class centers of science and education."[13] This strategy fits with the government's six-year infrastructure plan, where the bulk of investment is weighted toward building high-speed transportation links between such large urban centers.[14]

Such a strategy for Russia, however, runs directly against the facts on the ground: in stark contrast to almost the entire developed world, Russia's population is not concentrated in a few urban centers, but in several hundred medium-size cities and towns, many distributed across Russia's vast territory, and often far from other metropolitan agglomerations. These include over three hundred officially designated cities and towns whose fate is dependent on a single industry and thus are "monotowns" (*monoprofil'nye goroda*, or simply *monogoroda*) and which the government ranks according to the severity of their "socioeconomic conditions." While there has been migration from far-flung cities and towns to regional centers and major metropolises, few of the cities show any signs of disappearing.

Russia's economic geography, largely a product of Soviet industrialization, remains significantly unchanged close to three decades after the collapse of communism. This chapter focuses in particular on the challenge of Russia's monotowns, while examining them as an especially acute example of the dilemmas raised by Russia's industrial regions, or what Natalia Zubarevich has called—in contrast to Moscow and St. Petersburg—"second Russia."[15] Thus while monotowns are interesting in themselves, they represent in sharp form the overall challenges Russia faces in coming to terms with its depressed industrial regions and populations.

As we have seen, Russia survived its first two decades of postcommunist transformation while avoiding massive unemployment, and in doing so left much of its Soviet industrial infrastructure intact. Liberal economists inside Russia and out are urging its leaders to face the daunting task of modernizing, which often amounts to a thinly veiled euphemism for laying off and relocating large numbers of people. The monotowns represent a special test along these lines, since the closure of one plant threatens the entire town (or city) with economic and social collapse. Given the entanglement of industrial workplace and municipal services, even a significant drop in revenue for a monotown enterprise can mean the shutting off of heat and hot water to the entire city.[16]

The reason for not taking such steps should by now be obvious—the fear of social unrest and the potential threat to stability. Yet the likelihood that Russia's monotowns or other rust-belt regions would erupt in destabilizing social unrest can be questioned. Indeed, while monotown residents—as well as those in other Russian working-class communities—do engage in collective protest, most often they employ individual strategies to adapt to challenging conditions. In doing so, they resist following simple economic logic, say by migrating to better economic conditions, and instead refuse to abandon place, while making their struggling communities, in Jeremy Morris's apt phrase, "habitable."[17] As Samuel Greene put it, monotown residents are among those Russians who engage in "aggressive immobility."[18]

Still, as Mischa Gabowitsch has argued, protests in Russia often erupt precisely over "place."[19] While monotowns are by definition isolated communities, where the potential for protest to spread from one to another might be limited, Russian authorities have demonstrated a palpable fear of social unrest stemming from these particularly vulnerable cities and towns. Such fear places a sizable barrier in front of any attempt to increase economic growth by shifting capital and state resources from declining regions to more dynamic urban centers.

The Soviet Legacy of Large Enterprises

Soviet industrialization bequeathed to Russia a unique urban geography: in contrast to most other countries, where population is congregated in a few large cities, Russia has many small and dispersed industrial cities. According to the 2010 census, only eleven cities in Russia had more than a million people, though by 2020, Rosstat estimated, the number had grown to fifteen.[20] In 2010 over 66 percent of the urban population in the US lived in metropolitan areas of one million or more; in Russia only 31 percent did so. More than 30 percent of Russia's urban residents live in cities with fewer than one hundred thousand inhabitants, while only a small fraction of US urban residents do (see figure 4.2).[21]

One clear indication of Russia's unique urban geography is that it defies "Zipf's law for cities," a mathematical model that has proved able to predict city size in "in nearly every developed country across the world."[22] According to Zipf's law, Moscow, St. Petersburg, and other large Russian cities should be considerably

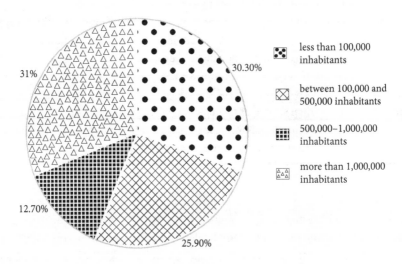

FIGURE 4.2.   Distribution of Russian urban population by city size

Sources: UN World Urbanization Prospects, 2018; Citypopulations.de; World Bank.

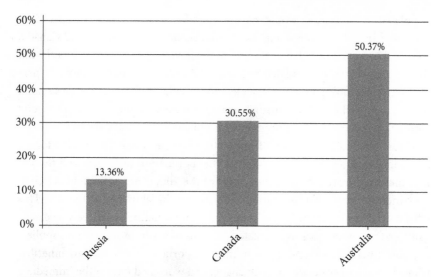

FIGURE 4.3.   Percentage of total population in three largest cities

Sources: Australian Bureau of Statistics; Statistics Canada; Citypopulations.de; World Bank.

larger. Yet Moscow, St. Petersburg, and Novosibirsk (the last at 1.6 million) are the only cities in Russia with populations larger than 1.5 million, while Japan, with less overall population, has five such cities, and Brazil (with a population 50 percent greater than Russia's) has eight.[23]

Moreover, Russia's cities are dispersed over the country's vast territory. Russia ranks first in the world in land area but is near the bottom of world rankings in terms of population density.[24] Russia lacks compact population centers even when compared with other large countries with sparse populations: while more than 30 percent of Canadians and 50 percent of Australians live in one of the three largest urban areas in their countries, only 13.4 percent of Russians live in Moscow, St. Petersburg, or Novosibirsk (see figure 4.3).[25]

Not only is Russia vast and relatively underpopulated, but the climate of much of its territory is quite harsh. In the Soviet period, Russia's industrial geography was established not to create greater market efficiencies—say by adding to existing urban agglomerations in order to lower transportation costs—but to meet the demands of military planners or to place production in close proximity to raw materials, even if labor there was scarce. The labor problem of harsh climates was overcome during Stalinist industrialization through the gulag system of prison camps, and in the post-Stalinist period by the positive inducement of wage supplements.[26]

Russia appears unique even in comparison with countries and regions with similarly harsh climates. For instance, by one estimate, if Alaska was as densely populated as Siberia, it would have a population of 13 million instead of 710,000.[27] In a study comparing the "spatial economies" of Russia and Canada, Irina Mikhailova found that at the end of the Soviet period, Russia's Siberia and the Far East were overpopulated by about 14.5 million people (or about 42 percent of the region's population) relative to Canada. Had Soviet Russia's spatial development followed the Canadian example, industrial employment in Siberia and the Far East would have been only one-third of its actual amount.[28]

Clearly such a distribution of population was not driven by market forces. According to the World Bank, "whereas the population of Siberia and the Far East increased forty-fold over the course of the 20th century, the region's GDP only increased five-fold, indicating a drastic fall in labor productivity."[29] This left a considerable part of Russia's industrial infrastructure at a three-way disadvantage: first, enterprises were isolated in terms of sheer distance from suppliers and consumers; second and relatedly, the transportation infrastructure inherited from the Soviet period was in poor shape, and worsened during the immediate post-Soviet period; and third, the placement of industries and populations in cold climates added considerable costs as well.[30]

Yet Soviet development was not only skewed toward the small and medium-size cities spread throughout its vast and cold space; as we have seen, it was also biased toward large enterprises. In the view of the World Bank, "the central planners' preoccupation with prescribing size has, ironically, bequeathed a double error: the size distribution of cities is skewed away from the large cities that generate agglomeration economies towards medium and small-sized population settlements, and firms and farms are skewed toward large units at the expense of mid-size and smaller production units."[31]

All of these Soviet-era development decisions—creating large industrial enterprises in relatively small and isolated cities, often in harsh climates, many geared toward the military—can be criticized on the grounds of market efficiency. Yet creating profit on global capitalist markets was not the goal of Soviet planners. As the World Bank put it, "the system 'worked' as long as relative prices were controlled to reflect domestic planning priorities rather than international relative scarcities."[32] Yet once exposed to global competition, these inefficiencies were quickly and often brutally exposed. To take one example, while industrial production had been placed in areas with little regard to transport costs, such factors are crucial to the profitability of manufacturing firms in market conditions. Once the costs of energy and inefficient transportation infrastructure became explicit, old production networks were faced with collapse.[33] Not surprisingly then, there were considerable struggles over the pricing of energy and transport, since for many enterprises market pricing would have led to disastrous outcomes.[34] In the estimates of some, the country's

greatest economic challenges "stem from the fact that today's Russian Federation has yet to overcome the nonmarket industrial structure it inherited from
the Soviet Union. . . . The structure of the Russian economy's industrial core,
along with its legacy of misdevelopment and mislocation for production and
population, remains intact."[35]

Russia's calamitous decade in the 1990s provided a significant impetus for
the restructuring of Soviet-era industrial enterprises, but as we have seen, many
of the largest struggled yet survived.[36] There was also little restructuring during
the oil boom years of the 2000s, when relative prosperity removed the impetus
to carry out painful reforms. This was true also for Russia's monotowns. The
World Bank's assessment is worth noting: "During the economic expansion of
the 2000s, many Russian monotowns benefited from high prices for resources
and semi-finished products, and the commodity price boom stimulated the local
economy. Rapid expansion of the construction sector created new demand for
metal and wood products. In these circumstances, most of the core enterprises
that survived the crash of the Soviet economy in the 1990s did well. Devolu-
tion of social assets was stopped or reversed, as the prosperous core enterprises
reverted to providing social services for their employees."[37]

Monotowns and the 2008 Economic Crisis

This complacency was abruptly shaken with the global economic crisis of 2008–9,
when a significant drop in industrial output led to fears of substantial unemployment and the specter of social unrest. Though initially little affected, Russia was hit
particularly hard. With the crisis, the term "monotown" grabbed the widespread
attention of Russian society and political observers. Given their narrow economic
base and, for many of them, a dependence on commodity prices, the monotowns
were directly impacted, especially those in the metals, chemicals, machine-building,
and wood and paper products industries. Social services provided by enterprises
were forced into a sudden decline, and city finances suffered as revenue dropped
from taxes on enterprises and on falling or nonexistent wages.[38]

It was in this atmosphere that in 2008 the Institute of Regional Policy, a Russian think tank, released a study commissioned by the Ministry of Regional
Development titled "The Monotowns of Russia: How to Survive the Crisis?" The
study—which was widely cited in the media and elsewhere—claimed that of the
many cities created during Soviet industrialization, 460 were dependent on a single industry and thus were monotowns. According to the study, the monotowns
represented 40 percent of all cities, with 25 percent of Russia's population, and
produced 40 percent of Russia's GDP.

PHOTO 4.1. Putin at Novocherkassk, February 1, 2008. Credit: kremlin.ru; Kremlin.ru/CC BY (https://creativecommons.org/licenses/by/3.0).

Soon thereafter, in November 2008, the economist (and former head of Russia's Department of Social Development) Yevgenii Gontmakher caused a sensation when he published an article in the newspaper *Vedomosti* about the potential for social unrest in monotowns, provocatively titled "Novocherkassk, 2009!"[39] Well into the postcommunist era, Novocherkassk remained synonymous with spontaneous labor uprising and state repression in Russia. In fact, just months earlier, in February 2008, President Putin had visited Novocherkassk and laid flowers at a memorial to the workers killed in 1962.

Gontmakher's article sketched out a hypothetical scenario where a labor protest in a single monotown quickly spread, leading to unrest and violence all the way to Moscow. Soon thereafter Russia's Federal Mass Media Inspection Service warned *Vedomosti*'s editor-in-chief that the article "could be considered an attempt to incite extremist activities" and thus in potential violation of Russia's antiterrorism law.[40]

Just five months later, in May 2009, protests erupted in Pikalyovo, a monotown in Leningrad Oblast. The town's three factories had shut down, with one-fifth of the city's population laid off, and many workers were owed back wages. Without revenue, the town was in debt to Gazprom for $4.5 million for its gas bill, and the town's heating plant was shut down, depriving the city's residents of hot water.

In response, residents stormed the mayor's office and then blockaded a major highway, creating a four-hundred-kilometer traffic jam, making the conflict difficult to ignore. Putin, then prime minister, soon arrived in the town by helicopter to personally intervene in the crisis, in large part by dressing down oligarch factory owner Oleg Deripaska. Putin forced Deripaska to accompany him on a tour of the town's cement factory, asking as the cameras rolled, "Why has your factory been so neglected?" before adding, "They've turned it into a rubbish dump. Why was everyone running around like cockroaches before my arrival? Why was no one capable of taking decisions?"[41] In an act of ritual humiliation shown on all the national television channels, Putin compelled Deripaska to sign a document promising that the town's factories would resume operation, in a scene that became known as the "bending of an oligarch" (see photos 4.2 and 4.3).[42] With a scathing look, Putin asked, "Oleg Vladimirovich, did you sign this? I don't see your signature." Once the disgraced Deripaska had signed the document, Putin gruffly demanded his pen back. For television viewers, the scene was a dramatic example of Putin acting as the nation's alpha male.[43]

According to Stephen Fortescue, "Putin's intervention was pure PR: a short-term solution had already been negotiated the day before Putin's dramatic visit to the town, one which was in fact generous to Deripaska," though without much

PHOTO 4.2.   Putin summons Oleg Deripaska. Credit: AFP/Getty.

PHOTO 4.3. The bending of an oligarch. Credit: AFP/Getty.

thought given to a long-term solution for the problems that led to the crisis.[44] The economic crisis had shrunk Deripaska's wealth dramatically, by one account from $28 billion to $3.5 billion. Yet one year before the Pikalyovo incident, his company Rusal had received a bailout of $4.5 billion from the state-owned Vnesheconombank (VEB).[45]

Given the mutual interest of the Kremlin and the oligarchs in stability—that is, in wanting to retain their positions of economic and political power—the Pikalyovo incident was more than a public relations stunt. It was also a demonstration of the ability of the Russian leadership to impose on oligarchs "levies of 'corporate responsibility' that extend to include support of towns and regions."[46] As Susanne Wengle notes, the public spectacle was a reminder to oligarchs of their social function; though in return for carrying out this function, they were given access to state resources and special provisions.[47] In the view of some critics, the name Pikalyovo became synonymous with an arrangement whereby the Russian state protected and subsidized major industries to prevent mass unemployment and social unrest, and the oligarchs leveraged the threat of social instability to extract more aid from federal and regional budgets, leading to what some described as a "post-Pikalyovo" political economy.[48]

In the wake of Pikalyovo, there was renewed talk of the potential for "social explosion" in Russia, particularly centered in the monotowns. During the crisis, labor protests took place in other monotowns as well.[49] Since Pikalyovo's long-suffering residents had appealed directly to both Deripaska and Putin several times, but gained redress only after blocking the highway, there was speculation of a possible "Pikalyovo syndrome" whereby other struggling monotowns would take dramatic action in order to be heard.[50] Outside of Russia, some Western analysts began describing such company towns as a potential "time bomb" for Russian society.[51]

Despite the considerable talk of mass layoffs during the 2008–9 crisis, rather than directly confront the problem of monotowns and unprofitable industries, the Russian government chose to avoid measures that might lead to social destabilization. In the words of Natalia Zubarevich, the fear of mass unemployment sharply increasing social tensions in the most worrisome monotowns led "Russian authorities to use all possible means to prevent this outcome, including regulating the price of raw materials (as in Pikalyovo), the transfer of enterprises to state control (as in the Baikalsk pulp and paper mill), strict prohibitions on layoffs including sanctions by prosecutors, etc."[52]

At the height of the crisis, the threat posed by the monotowns was almost certainly overstated, largely owing to a lack of clarity. First, the Institute of Regional Policy study was flawed: the number of monotowns it cited was taken from a study completed almost a decade earlier, with little to no updating or verification. Second and relatedly, the definition of the term "monotown" varied. For example, in 2009 the Ministry of Regional Development defined a monotown as any municipality where one enterprise or group of interconnected enterprises accounted for more than 50 percent of a city's industrial output, a list that included four hundred municipalities and 24 percent of Russia's urban population. Such a criterion, however, included a number of centers of oil and gas extraction, where the average wage greatly exceeds the Russian average.[53] While such industries might have labor and social problems of their own, they would hardly be of the same origin as those in, say, an unprofitable Soviet-era machine-building factory.

Thus, there remained confusion about the scope of the problem, since as Zubarevich remarked at the time, "no one knows how many Russian monotowns there are."[54] Zubarevich's institute, the Independent Institute for Social Policy, contended that there were fewer than 150 monotowns, representing about 8 percent of the country's population, or 11 percent of its urban populace. Nevertheless, in a clear signal of the Kremlin's concern, in the wake of the crisis the Russian government established a commission, still in operation, to monitor the country's monotowns. The official government list of Russian monotowns published in July 2014 by the Ministry of Economic Development included 313 municipalities, of which 229 are larger than "settlements."[55] The list was subsequently revised upward to a total of 319 monotowns. By that measure, fourteen million people, or roughly 10 percent of Russia's population, reside in monotowns.

There is an extensive Russian literature on monotowns, most of it written since the 2008 crisis, with the majority focused on various proposals for their transformation and survival.[56] Yet in what is arguably the most extensive Russian study of the monotown phenomenon, Zamyatina and Pilyasov argue that this literature is filled with "myths and fallacies."[57]

For one thing, Russia's monotowns vary on a number of dimensions, and thus it would be a mistake to characterize their problems and prospects as identical. For example, monotowns vary greatly in size. The largest monotown is Tolyatti, where until recently one out of every seven residents, in a city of seven hundred thousand, was directly employed at AvtoVAZ, a car factory producing the unprofitable Russian Lada, with many other residents employed in work dependent on the plant (Tolyatti is discussed in detail in chapter 6). Yet by one count, 48 out of a total of 335 monotowns were under five thousand in population. Most ranged anywhere from over five thousand to three hundred thousand in size.[58] Monotowns also vary in their level of isolation: some are located in areas with reasonable transportation to large cities, while others are quite remote.[59] Moreover, the industrial sector of the "city-forming enterprise" in each town can face very different prospects, with those prospects changing over time.[60]

Nevertheless, while the monotowns' conditions are far from identical, a significant proportion of them face difficult prospects. While Zubarevich has been skeptical of overdrawn fears of social unrest in monotowns, she still argues that "sooner or later the majority of them will become problematic."[61] She argues that the monotowns in the worst position include enterprises in the machine-building industry and those poorly positioned in other industries, such as older and unmodernized steel mills, chemical plants, and paper mills, where "mass layoffs would sharply strengthen social tensions." The World Bank has concluded that it "is likely that only a few of the enterprises can compete in international markets," since their "underlying problems are market unfriendly locations for enterprises which produce uncompetitive products."[62] Indeed, while a number of the monotowns are located relatively close to other urban agglomerations, Russia's enormous size, its low population density, and the decisions of Soviet planners have left many of Russia's monotowns vastly more isolated than "company towns" in other countries.[63]

The State's Response

For these reasons, as well as its clear concern for preventing social unrest, the Russian government's monotown list divides the cities into three categories, according to their "risk of worsening social-economic conditions." In the 2014 government list, seventy-five municipalities were included in "category 1" as having the "most complex [*slozhnyy*] social-economic conditions," with another 149 included in category 2 as being at risk of worsening social-economic conditions.[64] Those conditions are determined by such factors as the amount of actual or planned layoffs, the level of registered unemployment, and whether the local population judges the social-economic situation to be unfavorable (*neblagopoluchnaya*) "according to sociological surveys conducted by the Federal Protective Service" (FSO).[65] This last point was a further indication of the government's trepidation, as the entity put in charge of monitoring those conditions was not the Ministry of Economic Development or the Ministry of Regional Development, but rather the FSO, an organization that is the successor to the KGB's ninth directorate and charged with guarding Kremlin officials.[66]

Not surprisingly, the government has sought to maintain employment at relatively stable levels in Russia's monotowns. One indication comes from a study by Simon Commander and colleagues, relying on a database of Russian enterprises from 2003 to 2008. Using their own definition of "one-company towns," the authors find that the output of the dominant enterprises in such towns was 70 percent lower than that of their peers, after controlling for other factors. This lower level of labor productivity—which widened over time according to panel data—suggests significant labor hoarding.[67]

Yet not all Russian monotowns avoided closures. The Baikalsk pulp and paper mill—also owned by Oleg Deripaska—provides an interesting counterexample. Long a symbol of the environmental destructiveness of the Soviet economy (indeed, opposition to the mill sparked a Soviet environmental movement dating to the Brezhnev era) as it threatened the health of Lake Baikal, the largest freshwater lake in the world, Baikalsk is also a place where "the entire life of [the town]— the kindergartens, the schools, central heating and electricity—depended on the pulp mill."[68] Still, given its substantial environmental and economic costs, the mill was closed in 2008 and its thirteen hundred workers let go. As in Pikalyovo, the town's hot water supply was shut off for nonpayment. Some workers threatened to block the Trans-Siberian Railway, while others staged a hunger strike. Perhaps as a result, the mill was reopened in 2010. Yet the reopening itself led to competing protests, with two thousand people mobilizing against the reopening on environmental grounds and a comparable number rallying in support of the plant.[69] By 2013 (perhaps after the fears of the 2008–9 economic crisis had faded), Prime Minister Dmitry Medvedev called for the mill's closure once again. Acknowledging the "heated debates" over the plant's future, he argued that "it's time to muster up the courage and make responsible decisions." He pledged nearly $1 billion toward the development of the area and also hinted at providing tax breaks to boost local tourism, though it remains unclear how much of this promised assistance ever materialized.[70] The main income for some residents of Baikalsk after the closure of their town's main enterprise came from selling strawberries, first grown commercially by immigrants from war-torn Ukraine.[71]

Yet the Baikalsk plant appeared to be an exception, and large plant closures were avoided as a result of the 2008–9 crisis, which for Russia was deep but relatively short-lived. State spending, much of it from Russia's oil reserve funds, helped ensure a speedy recovery. The exact amount that was expended to support Russia's monotowns as a result of the crisis is difficult to determine. In 2010 the government allocated 25 billion rubles ($846 million) directly to twenty-seven monogorods. While this would appear to be a modest amount, according to the World Bank, applying the same amount to all monotowns would cost about 460 billion rubles, or 7 percent of Russia's 2010 federal revenue.[72]

Though the monotowns receded as a central focus of attention as the economy recovered after 2009, they reappeared again in 2014 with the drop in world oil prices. In April of that year, an official Kremlin session to discuss the problem of the monotowns was held in Petrozavodsk. Putin opened the session by stating that "today we have an important and very sensitive issue, a well-known and, I would even say, a painful one: the monotowns." While the cameras rolled, with Deripaska visibly seated directly across from Putin, the president acknowledged the scale of the problem. He added, "We well understand that . . . when the well-being of people depends on one or two city-forming enterprises, the situation is very dangerous, very dangerous."[73] As the latest crisis continued, the official government categorization of monotowns according to their risk was increasingly referred to by colors (green, yellow, and red), and commentators, including government officials, referred to the worst-off monotowns as the "red hundred."[74]

By 2015, the Russian press began to refer to the monotowns as "social dynamite."[75] In December 2016, the FSO reported that 60 percent of monotown inhabitants found their conditions to be either unbearable or "bearable with difficulty."[76] By 2017, Russia's Audit Chamber stated that that proportion had increased to 70 percent of monotown inhabitants.[77] Sergei Mykhortov, a mid-level tycoon who became the (unpaid) mayor of the city of Novoaltai in Altai Oblast, attended a government-sponsored meeting of officials from Russia's monotowns. Hearing stories from elsewhere, he realized his town was not so bad off. "There are monotowns with a yearly budget of 21 million rubles [$356,000 in 2017]. You wouldn't believe it. I myself was in shock." He added, "A yearly budget of 30–40 million rubles [$500,000 to $673,000] is far from rare. There are many towns where it is extremely difficult to live."[78]

Needless to say, such concerns refocused the government's attention on the problem. In addition to monitoring the conditions in Russia's monotowns, various ministries have been actively involved in various plans for their survival and further development. In 2014 the government created an official Fund for Monotown Development, with a number of government and quasi-government entities listed as partners, including two of the largest state-owned banks: VEB (said to be the most active supporter) and Sberbank.[79]

Earlier, the government's efforts were aimed at bailing out the monotowns that were in the direst shape, and also—especially through the oil boom years—at directing overt or implicit subsidies in order to keep the "city-forming enterprise" operating. This led to criticism from the World Bank and others that Russian officials should avoid arrangements that "encourage subsidies on nonviable enterprises in lagging regions."[80] Unless the investments were driven by market incentives, it was argued, efforts to modernize the monotown industries, or even to create new ones in towns with few prospects, "risk repeating the errors that created the monotowns in the first place."[81] Further questions were raised over the costs, especially over the long term, of trying to modernize, or simply revive, the central industry in various monotowns.

With these constraints in mind, the government has established various programs aimed at providing employment in the monotowns, with the focus now less on reviving the "city-forming" enterprises and more on creating new sources of jobs in other areas. Such an approach mimics what David Harvey has described as a shift in urban planning strategy elsewhere from "managerialism" to "entrepreneurialism."[82] For example, one program encouraged monotown governments to apply for competitive grants based on projects for economic development, such as turning certain monotowns into tourist centers. Some have pointed to the experience of places like Dawson, Canada—known from the days of the gold rush through the novels of Jack London—which transformed itself from a virtual ghost town into a "thematic tourist attraction."[83] Yet it is hard to envision more than a few Siberian monotowns successfully marketing themselves as tourist sites to commemorate former gulag camps or the heroic workers of the Soviet era. In the minds of critics, the various monotown schemes often resembled Soviet five-year plans and "wishes and dreams" (khotelki).[84]

Many proposals aimed at taking advantage of the existing infrastructure and workforce to create industrial parks or special economic zones (territorii operezhaiushchego razvitiia—TOR or TOSER in the Russian acronym). Originally proposed to spur investment in Russia's Far East, TORs provide tax breaks and other inducements for capital investment in a given zone. While economists have argued such zones have led to successful development elsewhere, as in China's coastal region, where they helped spur its economic boom, observers have been critical of Russia's experience with such zones. The World Bank argues that for such zones to be successful, they need to be near existing economic agglomerations, a problem almost by definition for most monotowns. Hence in Russia's experience "zones in underdeveloped regions with generally poorer infrastructure and thin labor markets have contributed to a low return on investment."[85] Zubarevich argues that, aside from a few exceptions, Russia's "zones are barely noticeable in the country's economy. The modest stimulus offered by law to these special zones does not allow them to overcome the barriers of unfavorable institutional circumstances." As a result, she contends, the zones have "barely influenced regional development."[86] Besides the geographical disadvantage such zones face, Russia's TORs miss the economic logic behind such zones elsewhere, which were geared toward producing competitive exports rather than boosting employment through production for the domestic market.[87] Yet such concerns have not stopped the Russian government from encouraging the development of TORs in monotowns, quite likely because of the low federal expenditures required, at least in the short run, for providing tax breaks as an incentive.

By no means are all the ideas being proposed for Russia's monotowns misguided. For example, the Fund for Monotown Development has collaborated with NGOs such as the Strelka Institute, which focuses on urban design and architecture, to create a sophisticated website that gathers ideas about monotown development.[88] One of their projects was called "5 steps to improvement!" where monotown residents could submit ideas for improving their communities, from cleaning up a park to installing a new promenade along a riverbank. The fund envisioned implementing the best of these ideas in each of the 319 monotowns. While such steps would appear to be small, they are in line with the emphasis many urban specialists place on getting the communities themselves involved in planning and shaping their cities and towns, rather than pursuing a centralized, top-down approach, which is especially ill-suited to Russia's diverse monotowns.[89]

Indeed, analyzing the diversity of monotowns would appear to be a more fruitful approach to seeking solutions. The Fund for Monotown Development has created its own categories for the cities, dividing them by their potential for diversification as well as their socioeconomic conditions. The fund concludes that while 134 of the 319 monotowns, and 57 out of the "red hundred," have limited prospects for diversification, these account for only 14 percent of the total population for Russia's monotowns. This suggests that the smallest towns are at the greatest risk, which makes sense in that one would expect smaller towns to have a harder time diversifying their economic base. According to the fund, 110 of the monotowns, and 32 of the "red hundred," accounting for 42 percent of monotown inhabitants, have difficult conditions but a greater potential for diversification.

This would suggest a more hopeful scenario for Russia's monotowns overall. The fund does not make clear, however, the criteria used to determine a city's potential for economic diversification. Nor does it specify the exact pathway for diversifying each town's economic base, beyond calling for the growth of small and micro-enterprises. While attempts to incubate small businesses and the service sector make sense, the Russian economy has had limited success in promoting such activity—beyond the informal economy—even in better-suited locations. Moreover, if the "city-forming enterprise" fails to provide steady employment, it is hard to see who will have the income to pay for such services.

In contrast to the fund's plans, the government has called for creating jobs directly. First Deputy Prime Minister Igor Shuvalov claimed that between 2015 and 2016, over two thousand new jobs were created in seventeen monotowns, yet that amounts to only 141 jobs per city or town.[90] Yet the fund itself estimates that solving the problems of "mono-dependence" (*monozavisimosti*) and unemployment in monotowns would have required the creation of 363,000 jobs by 2020.[91] A number of these jobs, Shuvalov conceded, would be temporary, which would hardly resolve a long-term and chronic problem—and, liberal critics contend, would provide incentives for people to remain in depressed communities rather than seeking employment elsewhere. Moreover, of the jobs to be created, only a small portion would be created directly by the Fund for Monotown Development; the bulk would come from private investment.[92] By 2018 the fund planned to invest 62.8 billion rubles (just over $1 billion) in monotowns, but it envisions, together with private investment (including "the co-financing of capital costs for investors"), 170 billion rubles (close to $3 billion) in outlays for monotowns to finance 150 investment projects.[93]

According to critics, the government's treatment of monotowns—the ranking of them by their conditions, and the direct government investment and tax breaks and special economic zones for those deemed worst off—creates perverse incentives. Similar to the allegations (as seen in chapter 3) that enterprises in the military industry inflate labor tensions in order to extract more state support, local officials can benefit by having their municipality officially designated a monotown, and then more so by having it recognized as a category 1 or "red" monotown. One monotown mayor claims there is a fight (*borba*) going on, involving the lobbying of (and by) governors and other officials, to point to bad conditions as a means of gaining government support.[94]

By 2019, the government was sending contradictory signals about the success of the Fund for Monotown Development. In August Vesti.ru headlined a report in dramatic language: "Dying Soviet "Monotowns" to Be Repurposed! The Era of Bleak Industrial Rust Cities Is Over!" The reporting, based on a segment broadcast on the state channel Rossiya-24, said that from 2016 to 2018 the program led to the creation of sixty-five TORs, which received a ten-year holiday on property and federal profit tax among other incentives, and zero-interest loans were available for other projects. As a result, the program generated over four hundred thousand "permanent and temporary jobs."[95]

Yet, in contrast to Vesti's spin, the Audit Chamber's review of the government's monotown program was rather scathing. Despite federal subsidies from 2014 to 2018 of just under 25 billion rubles ($400 million), the government was compelled to prepare a new program for monotowns, since "the previous one, designed for 2016–2025, was recognized as ineffective and terminated ahead of schedule." The auditors found that the subsidies did not have a significant impact on monotown development, and the program "had failed to achieve its primary goal: to improve the quality of life for monotown dwellers."[96]

The Audit Chamber—headed by Alexei Kudrin since May 2018—found that the program actually did have an impact on certain monotowns, just on the wrong ones: rather than targeted toward the "red hundred" or most depressed monotowns, funds went to monotowns that were better positioned and already more diversified. This would hardly seem surprising, since the federal subsidies—by themselves rather paltry, though supplemented by generous tax breaks—were intended, according to the fund's plans as described by first deputy prime minister Shuvalov, to be matched by a much greater amount of private investment.[97]

Regarding the fund's plan for job creation, economist Kirill Parfenov argues that "on the one hand, this ambitious plan to create a quarter of a million jobs is a frank admission of the impossibility of continuing direct support [for monotowns], and on the other hand it's an attempt to find a way out of a catastrophic situation." He called the plan largely "utopian." In more bureaucratic language, the state Audit Chamber claimed that its examination "showed that the social and economic situation of most single-industry towns, despite the measures taken by the state, is deteriorating, while budget expenditures are increasing."[98] Natalia Zubarevich, arguably the leading expert on Russia's regions, used a more colorful metaphor to question the government's hopes that private investors would solve the problem: "In a country with a disastrous investment climate, the last place to invest money will be monotowns lacking attractive industrial assets. Here's my question: Why would you choose a one-eyed, squint-eyed bride, when you can have a cute and long-legged one?"[99] Indeed, such plans appear to be as utopian as the government's earlier unmet goal, when in 2011 Prime Minister Putin proclaimed that two hundred thousand new jobs would be created in the monotowns by 2015.[100]

Global Cities and the Challenge of Migration

In the view of liberal economists including those at the World Bank, investing scarce government funds and capital to create jobs in depressed and isolated regions is not only ineffective, it is wasteful. According to the bank, "place-based

interventions such as providing subsidies to failing enterprises and local populations . . . perpetuate immobility, tying labor to a location where it is unproduc-
tive," acting as a drain on public resources. "The costs of keeping labor in the
wrong locations" include lower productivity, reduced GDP, and slower growth.[101]
"The alternative," according to the bank, "is to help people migrate from areas
of low economic opportunity to areas of rising opportunity and in so doing
prevent the fossilization of the economy." Further, "to become a dynamic economy, Russia will have to be more flexible—to constantly move human resources
and productive capital from low-value to high-value opportunities. This usually
entails shifts of labor and capital from declining regions to expanding regions."[102]
Indeed, the World Bank argues emphatically that Russia requires a "structural
transformation" so that the country "can shift its economic base from over-
reliance on natural resources toward productive manufacturing and services,"
but this "cannot take place without a facilitating geographic transformation
through increased mobility of labor."[103]

Not only foreign advisers are making arguments along these lines. As we have
seen, the policies promoted by Kudrin, now incorporated into the government's
"Strategy for Spatial Development through 2025," would, if fully implemented,
entail a substantial transformation. For one thing, even if state investment was
directed to the forty largest urban areas (rather than just the top twenty), that
would leave roughly half of Russia's population behind. As the commentator
Leonid Bershidsky pointed out, "Areas that aren't important for the government's
growth plans, transport corridors or geopolitics will suffer increasing neglect."[104]
The World Bank has acknowledged why Russian leaders were hesitant to adopt
the bank's proposals: "Russian policymakers worry that emerging production will
concentrate in some places of high economic opportunity and leave many workers trapped in less favored places. They worry that this will concentrate much of
the nation's wealth in a few cities and regions while leaving others with dispro-
portionately high poverty. Even if this situation were temporary, this would be
unfair and is unacceptable to many."[105]

The logic of Kudrin's proposals—aiming to make the population more
mobile—would suggest relocation as the preferred solution for the most troubled monotowns, an argument the World Bank makes explicit. Given Russia's
demographic dilemma—a shrinking population, especially of working-age
adults—a simple solution would appear to be transferring labor from less productive jobs and regions to more productive ones. This was of course the answer
for many Americans, who moved from Rust Belt cities to jobs in the Sun Belt.
Yet the American experience, where the average family is said to move six to seven
times over a lifetime, is exceptional; in Europe the average is twice, and in Russia
even less.[106]

To be sure, there has been substantial migration in Russia, especially in the 1990s and especially from the most inhospitable regions in the Far North and Siberia, when Soviet-era incentives for living there were reduced or eliminated altogether.[107] Yet significant outmigration from the most inhospitable locations slowed around 1999 with the economic recovery.[108] Overall, while more than 3 million Russians moved from one region to another in 1995, a decade later only 1.5 million had done so.[109]

Russian workers, including monotown residents, are quite flexible; as we have seen, labor turnover in Russia is fairly high. Migration within and between regions certainly does occur; while the data are imprecise, a comparison of the 2010 census with recent estimates from the official statistical agency Rosstat shows a clear decline of population in many small to medium-size cities, and considerable population gains in Moscow, St. Petersburg, and other large cities.[110] There is a general shift in the younger population, from small villages and towns to regional centers, if not Moscow and St. Petersburg, for university or work. As Jeremy Morris's fieldwork suggests, labor turnover not only takes place in major metropolitan areas but also in monotowns, as workers seek to make such localities "habitable" by eking out a living in the informal sector when the pay or work conditions in the town's city-forming enterprise becomes less than tolerable.[111] In many cases a family's major breadwinner travels for work, either daily or in a longer-term shift, even as the family unit maintains its primary residence in a monotown.[112] This is a variant of the old Russian tradition of *otkhodnichestvo*, of peasants temporarily leaving their villages to earn money elsewhere.[113] Such temporary labor migration is easier for residents in monotowns close to other urban centers, again underscoring the diversity of situations across different monotowns.

To be sure, there has been massive outmigration from some particularly troubled monotowns that have essentially gone bust. In Vorkuta, a coal-mining center above the Arctic Circle that was founded as a gulag labor site, the number of active mines shrank from nineteen to four in recent years, and the number of residents is said to have declined by close to half, from 110,000 to 60,000.[114] Yet the collapse of state support, private-sector investment, and weak institutions "opened the door to a broad-ranging informality" that has allowed those remaining to mitigate the boom-bust cycle.[115]

Overall interregional labor mobility in Russia remains low. This is puzzling, especially when one considers that Russia suffers from an extremely high level of regional inequality—in terms of wages, living standards, social benefits, and overall quality of life.[116] The Russian experience also stands in sharp contrast to many postcommunist countries in east central Europe, including the post-Soviet Baltic states, where many workers took advantage of the EU's provisions for the free mobility of labor to relocate to countries with higher wages and more dynamic economies.[117]

There are several reasons for Russia's low level of interregional migration. Part of the obstacle is cultural, since Soviet workplaces were not only a place of work but often a paternalistic enterprise providing for much of life's needs, and a "labor collective" that was almost a second family.[118] Yet the barriers are also structural and institutional. Russia's vast space increases the cost of searching for jobs, and of transportation and relocation.[119] There is a lack of a dynamic labor market in many regions. One of the consequences of an economy with a heavy reliance on oil and gas production is that while the economic return can be high, the number of jobs created is quite low.[120] There is limited available housing, and citizens in depressed regions can find themselves in a poverty trap, unable among other things to find buyers for their apartments in impoverished urban centers.[121] While in the past, wage arrears and the lack of available credit and mortgage markets were a hindrance, currently many poorer families are immobilized by debt.

Some in Russia and elsewhere have called for such radical solutions as the "liquidation or so-called 'controlled shrinking' of a town."[122] The World Bank contends that the government should "manag[e] the decline of settlements in remote regions that have lost their dominant industry and cannot be restructured." In these cases, it is argued, the government should facilitate the migration of younger and more able workers to regions with greater opportunities by such steps as paying any wage arrears and "compensating for abandoned accommodation," while also maintaining "adequate basic services for those unable or unwilling to move."[123]

The bank argues that "where the firms are inherently uneconomic and cannot be operated profitably, it would be better to close them than to subsidize or re-invest in them." Otherwise, such subsidies, which are location-based and not "spatially blind," immobilize workers and lock them in place, thereby penalizing workers by lowering their productivity and incomes. For the World Bank, "the overriding goal of reform is to create conditions *so that labor can redistribute itself* in line with emerging regional economic advantages rather than be trapped in lagging areas."[124] Yet the talk of "labor redistributing itself" treats Russia's population as if it were just another factor of production, or as if the life choices of the Russian people are shaped by economic incentives alone.

A similar if less economistic perspective is taken by some of Russia's top researchers into the phenomena of Russian monotowns. Zamyatina and Pilyasov argue that often several generations of a family have lived in a monotown and worked in its core enterprise.[125] Following Mark Granovetter, they speak of the population's "cultural embeddedness" in the local economy, leading to various "lock-in effects."[126] They hold that "the greatest challenges generally lie in overcoming *cognitive barriers*. These are primarily dependency mentalities fostered by a long experience of living in a context of social guarantees offered by a backbone enterprise during its prosperity phase. Such a mentality, on the one hand, stifles individual initiative, in particular that of small business. On the other hand, it decreases the perceived value of activities outside the single-industry town's specialization."[127] They argue further that monotown residents "are not usually keen to move to more dynamically developing regions" or even to "support obvious ways to overcome social tensions," such as accepting offers of work in nearby towns to offset downsizing in their city-forming enterprise.[128]

Yet Zamyatina and Pilyasov's contention that "cognitive barriers" and "dependence mentalities" are the main impediment to resolving the challenge of Russia's monotowns undercuts their earlier argument that any solution must be driven by the interests and concerns of residents themselves rather than imposed on them from above. Moreover, as we have seen, there is also much evidence that monotown residents are quite flexible. Indeed, as Zamyatina and Pilyasov's research shows, paradoxically the most isolated monotowns can become the most innovative, since they have little alternative. Conversely, the monotowns that are closer to an urban agglomeration can suffer from adverse effects not only on their core enterprise, as key workers seek employment elsewhere, but also from the service industries that might offer an alternative to that core industry, as consumers can seek better options.[129]

Whether or not one considers it the result of "cognitive barriers" and "dependence mentalities," there is a clear resistance among many monotown dwellers to relocate, a resistance that can seem puzzling to outsiders (perhaps especially to peripatetic Americans), given the challenging economic prospects in many such cities and towns. However difficult their current situation, many monotown dwellers retain strong attachments to place, to friends and communities, and to traditions. Thus, in a study of the monotown Sokol in Vologda Oblast, residents expressed significant dissatisfaction with social conditions but voiced a limited interest in migration, given a high level of rootedness (*ukorenennost'*).[130] While such attachments can exist in many settings, they can be especially strong in monotowns, where bonds were often formed during the Soviet period, when workplace and community were closely intertwined. What might appear to be a dependency mentality to some can seem quite rational: in the absence of robust formal institutions (such as a reliable job in the formal economy), the reliance on family, friends, and informal networks becomes especially crucial for survival.[131] While relocating to a new city might offer economic advantages, it is not clear that on balance such a move would be considered a net benefit.

Indeed, there is substantial evidence that such logic holds when the challenges of place are not only economic but climatic as well. Even in Russia's Far North, where conditions are often quite bleak, research has shown that outmigration slowed dramatically after the 1990s not only owing to changing economic conditions, but also because of the social capital invested in place, the lack of clear alternatives, and the "psychic costs" of migration that often outweighed what others might view as simple cost/benefit calculations.[132]

In a study titled "How the North Became Home: Attachment to Place among Industrial Migrants in the Murmansk Region of Russia," Bolotova and Stammler find a strong attachment to place even among people living in industrial towns above the Arctic Circle. They describe a "process whereby an environment that is seen as 'harsh,' or 'hostile' by outsiders, and cities that are often considered neither beautiful nor worth living in, have become home."[133] Ironically, it appears that the very harshness of such locations can over time create a strong sense of community and of mutual reliance and bonding with fellow residents.

One can find such attachment to place even in Norilsk, known as "the northernmost city in the world" and home to Norilsk Nickel, which is said to be "the world's largest mining and metallurgy complex." But Norilsk is also known as one of "the world's most polluted places" and has such brutal environmental and living conditions that life expectancy is ten years shorter than elsewhere in Russia.[134] Not surprisingly, there was massive outmigration in the post-Soviet years, including efforts at "managed decline."[135] Yet many who remain in the city of 177,000, even those not employed in the plant, claim to love living there.[136] This is due in part, as Marlene Laruelle and Sophie Hohmann found, to the residents' "pioneering spirit and the image of the *Severyane*, the 'people from the North,' who succeed by hard labor and a strong work ethic."[137]

Such rootedness and attachment to place are undervalued by the World Bank and the Russian government in their relocation efforts, since, as Bolotova and Stammler argue, "social, cultural, and other non-material variables" can "overrule even material incentives for relocation."[138] Indeed, as the notion of cultural embeddedness suggests, the very preferences of individuals can be profoundly shaped over time by their cultural milieu. As a result, relocation programs, initiated by the World Bank and carried out by the Russian government, have proven largely ineffective. Such programs have targeted "surplus populations"—that is, pensioners and other nonworking residents—with the ultimate goal of leaving behind only those engaged in profitable economic activity. However, whereas retirees in northern regions of the US often seek to move to Florida, in the Russian case pensioners in Arctic industrial towns have done just the opposite: a significant number would take the government's housing incentive and purchase a dwelling in the south of Russia but transfer it to one of their offspring, while themselves remaining in the Far North.[139]

Such attachment to place and resistance to relocate extends not only to industrial towns in Russia's Arctic region but also to the region's many villages. As Paul Goble has written, the Russian government lacks the funds to continue to subsidize people living in isolated villages in the Far North, "but it also lacks the money that would be needed to shut down these settlements and move their residents to cities."[140] At the time of the 2010 census, Russia had around 153,000 villages, and 60,000 of them had fewer than one hundred residents. Most still exist, and many are becoming increasingly isolated because of crumbling transportation infrastructure. According to a report from the Russian Academy for Economics and State Service, it would cost a minimum of 150 million rubles ($2.5 million) to close down a single village and another 1.2 million rubles ($20,000) to move each worker.[141]

Still, in economic terms at least, in the long run it would be less costly to close the villages than to maintain them. But as Goble argues, even if the government had the funds for relocation, it would still have to handle "the opposition it would face from the villagers if it were to try," since "a significant share of the population of these villages has little or no interest in moving away from where they call home."[142] According to Vladimir Klimanov of the Moscow Institute for Social Sciences, "There are not so many successful cases of forced liquidation of settlements." The consequence is that the government has instead employed a strategy of "optimization" whereby hospitals, schools, and kindergartens in isolated villages are closed, and the roads or rail lines connecting them to the outside world are not maintained or repaired.[143] Yet such a strategy would hardly appear optimum for a political leadership that depends in part on the support of rural voters. Moreover, while such "controlled shrinkage" might prove effective for small villages over time as the elderly population dies out, a similar scenario in an urban industrial center would almost certainly prove more problematic.

Beyond the Far North, residents retain their attachment even in environmentally challenging and indeed toxic towns such as Asbest—whose very name proclaims its main product. Female pensioners in Asbest are not only proud of having worked in the city's main plant for forty years, but declare that "we built this city with our hands." Working-age men might complain about "this hick town" where "life sucks [zhivut khrenovo]," but they still find it habitable enough to remain. Even young mothers pushing strollers (who might most be concerned about the city's conditions) explain that "we've lived in St. Petersburg, Yekaterinburg, but our city still pulls us in."[144] Yet Asbest is hardly without conflict: the mostly female workers at the Asbest brick factory (a subsidiary enterprise in the town) have protested loudly over their unpaid wages.[145]

The monotowns form only part of a larger problem of managing Russia's deindustrialization. Here it is worth considering Russia's metallurgical industry, which includes several large plants centered in monotowns, as well as others that are located in urban centers alongside other industries. In many ways, the metal industry has been a bright spot in Russia's Putin-era economy, as many steel factories benefited significantly from the boom in global commodity prices in the decade prior to the 2008 crisis. They did so largely by taking advantage of Russia's relatively low costs in raw materials, electricity, and labor, inputs that are central to the profitability of the industry.[146] Low costs for electricity were partly a legacy of the Soviet period and partly the result of cross-industry subsidies negotiated between regional leaders and oligarchs.[147] As for labor costs, Russian wages in the metallurgical industry are lower than those of most of its competitors, especially those in advanced capitalist countries.[148]

Yet while the metals industry benefited greatly from the boom years, like a number of other Russian sectors it remained vulnerable to commodity price volatility.[149] Metallurgical plants and related industries in such regions as Vologda, Chelyabinsk, Lipetsk, Sverdlovsk, and Kemerovo were hit sharply by the 2008 crisis, with production dropping by one-third or more. Though the populations suffered through the loss of income, open unemployment was kept largely hidden by various interventions. Shortly after the crisis, Zubarevich argued that "the metallurgical regions . . . are 'standing in line' as candidates for depression [*depressivnost'*] in the foreseeable future."[150]

As Chris Miller argues in his study of "Putinomics," steel firms "had to place social and political stability before profit. Magnitogorsk's ability to improve productivity was limited by implicit prohibitions on firing excess workers. Russian steel firms remained far from optimal productivity, employing too many administrative workers, for example. As of late 2007, Russian steel firms had three times as many employees per ton of steel produced than did American companies. Reaching optimal efficiency levels that year, according to one estimate, would have required firing 140,000 workers."[151]

There is some evidence that, since then, several large metallurgical enterprises began to cut the number of workers substantially. In 2013, six major steelmakers were said to cut their payrolls by 33,500, reducing employment by over 9 percent from 2012.[152] According to one observer, "five years ago during the collapse in steel trade . . . such a job cull would have been impossible because the Kremlin warned the mill proprietors against mass layoffs."[153] It remains unclear, however, whether the giant metallurgical combines have simply shed workers in such large numbers without costly make-work schemes. One of the most dramatic cases is the Novolipetsk Metallurgical Combine. The plant was said to reduce its labor force from roughly fifty thousand in 2001 to twenty-nine thousand by

2011, a 40 percent reduction. While two-thirds of the cuts were said to come from individual separations, at least one-third came by spinning off workers into new firms created by the company.[154] Other metallurgical monotowns—such as Magnitogorsk, Nizhnii Tagil, and Novokuznetsk—despite the stated substantial reduction in the workforces of their steel plants, were placed in "category 3" of the government's monotown list, meaning they were cities determined to have a "stable social and economic situation," with registered unemployment no higher than the Russian average.[155]

In 1999, Severstal employed fifty thousand people in Cherepovets; by 2017 it was just half that number, with six thousand workers let go in 2013 alone. Yet somehow the official unemployment level remained unchanged at 1.24 percent.[156] A major explanation would appear to be that forty-five hundred of the laid-off workers were reemployed by enterprises funded by the company, and another ten thousand were given jobs at new companies supported by the steelmaker's "business incubator." Explained Alexey Mordashov, the steel titan who owns Severstal, "I believe there is a sort of social contract in many companies. I don't pretend everyone is happy, not at all. But in general [Severstal] has a certain, I hope, social contract."[157]

Whatever the extent of the actual restructuring, the boom-and-bust nature of the industry continued to be felt. While a number of export-oriented metallurgical plants in Russia benefited from the devaluation of the ruble toward the end of 2014, since their costs were kept low relative to sales in foreign currency, by 2015 world steel prices hit their lowest point in eleven years, which compounded the slack demand from Russia's own economic downturn.[158] Yet while the devalued ruble continued to help Russia's industry, workers were not necessarily enjoying the benefits. Given the gap between production costs in rubles and sales prices in dollars, firms could continue to pay their workers a low ruble wage while capturing the bulk of the profits from the exchange rates.[159] Nevertheless, firms in the steel sector continue to struggle.[160]

The fortunes of Russia's metallurgical giants underscored the problem with the monotown label: these cities and towns, and their city-forming enterprises, were hardly monochromatic. Cherepovets in particular is held up by government officials as a success story and touted as the first monotown slated to leave the government's monotown list. But critics have questioned whether it ever belonged there. Cherepovets, dominated by the conglomerate Severstal, whose owner, Mordashov, is one of Russia's wealthiest oligarchs, had received 800 million rubles ($13 million) in federal funds because of its monotown designation. In line with the Audit Chamber's allegations, others argued that the monotown list was subject to "manipulation" and that it "mostly resembles the strength of regional lobbyists."[161] As a result, the current plans are to cut the official monotown list roughly in half, to about 150 cities and towns. This has led to complaints from some of the more vulnerable monotowns. A local official in Irkutsk Oblast protested that "if we are suddenly removed from the monotown list and deprived of state support and benefits, this will be the collapse of all the hopes of local residents. There's nothing and no one else we can turn to."[162] During a visit to the vast KAMAZ truck factory in Naberezhnye Chelny, when pressed by workers about the end of monotown support, Putin promised the support would continue.[163] As one journalist put it, "the president of Russia has repeatedly addressed the topic of monotowns. He stressed that the situation should be saved, because people should not suffer from the death of city-forming enterprises."[164] Yet the promised sums to be distributed through the Monotown Fund remained paltry: 5.5 billion rubles annually for the next three years.[165]

It is important to recognize that, in themselves, the monotowns merely represent an extreme form of a broader problem. Sergei Besdelov, an economist and official with the Russian Chamber of Commerce and Industry, had a curt solution to the monotown problem: "If it's cheaper to destroy a monotown [than revive it], then the question answers itself." Yet he was quick to add, "I believe that we should not talk only about monotowns. Everywhere there are places where people live poorly, where the level of infrastructure, health care, and the state of the economy leaves much to be desired. In this sense, a monotown is no different from another small locality." Yet, he added, the government has failed to reveal the full extent of this challenge.[166]

Russia's monotowns—one-industry towns left over from the Soviet era—create a significant challenge for Russia's political leadership. They form one part of Russia's industrial inheritance from Soviet planners, which includes large enterprises centered in many small-to-medium-size cities, dispersed across Russia's vast territory, often located in harsh climates. Many are unprofitable, and even those that are better positioned are vulnerable to economic shocks and volatility in global commodity prices. Entire towns are dependent on the continued operation of these enterprises. Moreover, the monotowns form only part of a larger problem of managing Russia's deindustrialization.

The problem of Russia's monotowns came to the fore with the 2008–9 global economic crisis, when fear of a new "Novocherkassk" workers' rebellion seemed to come to life in the town of Pikalyovo, where Putin personally intervened to resolve the crisis. Further crises were avoided, but only through administrative measures and costly subsidies to prevent mass layoffs and plant closures.

While the worst fears of monotowns being a Russian "time bomb" now appear to have been exaggerated, the problems are chronic, and government officials speak of the "red hundred" of the most troubled monotowns. Official plans for supporting the monotowns, which entail both massive job creation and inducements for private investment, have been called utopian by critics. Yet the proposals of liberal economists and others, for reducing subsidies, encouraging outmigration, and allowing for the "controlled shrinkage" of these company towns, appear perhaps at least as unrealistic, for the simple reason that many people do not want to leave.

Indeed, the reasons for the low level of migration in Russia, even from depressed areas, are not only economic, but social and political as well. Simply put, many people have become attached to place, even to places that few others would consider habitable, an attachment that can take the form of "aggressive immobility."[167] Even when migration does happen from monotowns or depressed urban centers, a substantial population almost always remains. Such a consideration is largely missed by the World Bank and other liberal reformers, who claim low mobility must be due to the country's industrial and labor policies.

Still, the economic logic is hard to deny. In the long run it may be true, as Leonid Bershidsky argues, that "the Grim Reaper is coming for the once-bustling little towns where people had moved from the villages. In a country with too much space and too few people, much of the territory is doomed to be a huge fly-over zone."[168] Yet unless that process happens very gradually—a pace that would undercut the goal of economic growth—attempts to uproot people from places they call home will almost inevitably lead to protest.

The dilemma extends beyond geography and economics. The 2008 economic crisis not only brought Russia's monotowns to the fore but also marked a shift by the country's leadership toward greater state control over the economy, more emphasis on the "social responsibility" of the country's oligarchs, and, as we shall see in chapter 7, an increased populist turn toward nationalist and socially conservative rhetoric.[169]

So the challenge of the monotowns remains. As Stefan Hedlund, a longtime observer of Russia's economy, reflects, "the non-decision on what to do with the monotowns provides perhaps the most important reflection on how the Russian government is searching—fruitlessly—for a new economic growth model and development strategy." He argues that "they should be simply phased out and resources freed up for more productive ventures," while at the same time observing that "voters in the Russian rustbelt form the bedrock of political support for the regime, which fears the anger that would follow from aggressive enterprise closure."[170]

Does the Russian government—as powerful and in control as it would appear to be—really fear the anger from rust belt workers in its monotowns? With Russia's dominant trade union federation allied with the Kremlin, with considerable restrictions on strikes and protests firmly in place, and with Russia's working class said to form the bedrock of the regime's political support, does such fear have any solid basis? We turn to such questions in the next chapter.

LABOR PROTEST IN RUSSIA'S HYBRID REGIME

So far, this book-length study about the politics of labor in Russia has had relatively little to say about labor relations and trade unions. While a central argument of this study is the regime's perceived vulnerability to socioeconomic protest, we have focused only tangentially on the causes and extent of protest by Russian workers. This chapter will fill that gap and concentrate attention on unions, labor relations, and worker protest. It will argue that regarding labor, Russia's political leadership, as it has with its attempts to control civil society generally, has created a paradox: by seeming to protect itself from any semblance of an independently organized labor movement, it has left itself open to spontaneous protest that has the potential to become quickly politicized.

Despite considerable research over the years, some key questions about Russian workers remain unanswered: to what extent are workers able to assert their interests, and to what extent do they remain patient, resigned, or quiescent? When they do protest, are their demands "defensive" or "offensive"? Are those demands directed at managers and owners, or at government officials? Do protests tend to be led by unions (whether "legacy" or alternative), or are they more often wildcat actions? How much are workers' actions shaped mainly by their mentality, such as habitual patterns or ideological legacies, and how much are they shaped by structural constraints, such as economic conditions? Not least, to what extent have Russian industrial relations been transformed over the last two to three decades, and how much do workers and workplaces remain weighed down by the Soviet legacy?

In order to understand the significance of labor protest today and the potential threat it poses, we need to examine some formative episodes in Russian labor relations, such as the strike wave of the late 1990s and the adoption of the new Labor Code shortly after Putin came to power. This chapter will then probe the choice workers make between pursuing individual strategies—whether redress through the courts or exit to the informal economy—or acting collectively to address their grievances, and explore the types of conflicts that generate overt protest, how the authorities tend to respond, and the struggle of workers and others to make sure their demands are heard.

Russian Unions, Legacy and Alternative

As with Russia's industrial landscape, Russia's labor unions were substantially shaped by the Soviet past. In contrast to unions in advanced capitalist societies, workers, managers, and union officials alike viewed Soviet enterprise-level unions as arms of management, and unions and managers often provided a common front in bargaining with central planners. Unions rarely saw themselves as independent advocates of workers in adversarial bargaining with managers. They had very little say over such fundamental issues as wages, which were centrally determined, and collective agreements contained little beyond what was stated in Soviet labor law. As a result, workers were more likely to approach their supervisor rather than their union representative with a workplace grievance. The complaints that workers addressed to unions typically concerned the goods and services that the unions distributed, arguably their main role in the Soviet system.[1]

Erik Olin Wright's three sources of workers' bargaining power can help make sense of the power of workers within the Soviet political economy and the subsequent transformation of that power in the post-Soviet context.[2] The first source is "associational power," from collective workers' organizations such as unions and political parties. There are also two types of "structural power," stemming from workers' place in the economic system: "marketplace bargaining power," such as from tight labor markets, and "workplace bargaining power," from the strategic location of certain groups of workers. Despite all the rhetoric, workers clearly lacked associational power in the Soviet system, but given the labor shortage, they did have marketplace power. Even with the de facto prohibition on strikes, they also had workplace power, since the shortage of labor and other necessary materials meant that labor's cooperation was often necessary in key areas of production. Such bargaining that did take place occurred informally, on the shop floor between workers and line managers, based on workers' individual power to exit their jobs given the shortage of labor.[3]

Much of this changed dramatically with the end of the Soviet Union. With the transition from communism to capitalism, the labor shortage was replaced with the threat of unemployment, and Russian workers lost much of their structural power. With the promise of a more democratic system, workers might have hoped to increase their associational power. Yet Russia's trade unions remain dominated by the Federation of Independent Trade Unions of Russia (FNPR), the successor to the communist-led union federation of the Soviet period.

Russian unionization rates have declined dramatically from the Soviet days of compulsory trade union membership. According to the union federation in 2018, "trade unions affiliated with the FNPR account for over twenty million members, which is about 95 percent of all organized workers in Russia."[4] About one-fifth of those members, however, were nonworking students or pensioners. Still, roughly one-quarter of those employed in Russia are union members, and about half of all those working in large and medium enterprises belong to unions.[5] Mikhail Shmakov (the union's president since 1993) could claim that the FNPR remains "the biggest non-governmental association in the Russian Federation."[6] Alternative unions exist, and together claim a (very likely inflated) membership of close to five million, an estimate unchanged since 2000.[7]

Despite its still-sizable membership, large structure, and a near monopoly on worker representation in Russia, the FNPR is a clear example of a "legacy union": a union whose resources are the result of its privileged yet subordinate position in the previous (in this case communist) regime.[8] As Russia's business newspaper *Vedomosti* put it, "luckily for many businessmen, workers' associations in Russia are survivals of the Soviet era and are not unions in the real sense of the word." Or as close observers of Russia's civil society stated, "FNPR unions are para-statal organizations intended to manage workers rather than represent them."[9]

Much of the FNPR membership remains a rather passive holdover from the Soviet era of compulsory membership, with workers often not knowing whether they were union members or not.[10] Nor do unions garner much trust from workers or the general public. A survey from 2008 conducted by the state-owned polling agency VTsIOM found that of those respondents with a trade union at the workplace, 64 percent "do not believe it helps the living standards of their staff," and only 11 percent held the opposite view.[11] Such views have not faded with time: a Levada Center poll from September 2017 found that unions remained near the bottom of public institutions in terms of trust, with only 22 percent of the population expressing trust of unions, placing unions ahead only of political parties (19 percent) and big business (18 percent).[12]

While the FNPR took a confrontational stance against Yeltsin's economic reforms in the early 1990s, siding with Yeltsin's opponents who were defending the Russian "White House" during the dramatic confrontation of October

1993, the dénouement of the "October events" (which included the shelling of Russia's parliament) was a pivotal turning point for the FNPR. In the aftermath, the Yeltsin administration threatened to take away the significant properties and other assets the federation had inherited from the Soviet period. Shmakov was appointed head of the federation, and the FNPR began its shift to an accommodationist policy toward the Yeltsin government, an approach that increased significantly under Putin's leadership.

The Strike Wave of the Late 1990s

As we saw in chapter 2, while Russia avoided mass unemployment in the 1990s, by the end of the decade the resulting low wages erupted in a crisis in wage arrears. While mass layoffs were avoided, the result was a very significant if peculiar strike wave from 1996 through 1999. Defying the stereotype of quiescence, the strike wave demonstrated that Russian workers were able to mobilize on a massive scale. Not only industrial workers, but also teachers, doctors, and nuclear scientists went on strike and blocked traffic in a number of Russian regions.[13] Yet as Greene and Robertson point out, "from an international perspective, the strikes of the Yeltsin era were quite unusual," in part because most were prompted not by traditional worker grievances; instead, "more than 95 percent of strikes were about unpaid wages, legally owed by employers."[14] Graeme Robertson convincingly argues that wage arrears "had become the dominant economic problem in Russia in the second half of the 1990s."[15]

A large proportion of these strikes, however, were actually coordinated by regional political elites (with the blessing of managers, as well as the FNPR) trying to gain leverage in bargaining or political struggles with Moscow.[16] For example, Primorsky Krai governor Yevgeny Nazdratenko bused strikers in to blockade the Trans-Siberian railway in order to pry greater support from Moscow.[17] Such a phenomenon provides further evidence, at least for the 1996–99 strike wave, that the dominant trade unions remained allied with managers as well as regional elites.[18]

Nevertheless, a significant number of the protest actions occurred spontaneously, reflecting a tremendous amount of anger and frustration.[19] Coal miners did not need Governor Nazdratenko to show them how to block major railways: already in 1994, in a desperate attempt to obtain their promised wages, Kuzbass miners blocked the Trans-Siberian Railway and invited Vladimir Zhirinovsky to intervene on their behalf, while in another case, miners refused to resurface from their mine until their demands were addressed.[20] By 1998 such actions by miners culminated in the "rail wars," when in May and June of that year miners from

Sakhalin, Primorsky Krai, Kemerovo, and Komi, seeking back wages, repeatedly blockaded the Trans-Siberian and other major railways. The blockade effectively divided the country in half and shut down the country's main source of transportation, causing millions of rubles in economic losses.[21] Surveys showed that despite the hardships the rail blockades imposed, between 50 and 60 percent of the Russian population supported the miners' actions.[22] Beginning in August, miners encamped on Gorbatyi Most in front of the Russian White House, banging their helmets on the cobblestones every half hour to remind government officials of their presence. By that month approximately $12.5 billion in back pay was owed to Russian workers.[23] The nonpayment of wages extended to Russian soldiers, contributing to morale problems in the military.[24]

It was in this context that the Russian government failed to reach an agreement with the IMF on austerity measures, delaying the next $670 million disbursement of the IMF's three-year, $9 billion loan.[25] All along, the Russian government had been desperately trying to defend the ruble's value and maintain payments on Russia's debt to international creditors. Yet by August the government devalued the ruble and declared a moratorium on the repayment of its foreign debt. These steps were justified by the need to pay off back wages to coal miners and others to "ease the alarmingly high social tensions in the country."[26] Indeed, to a significant extent the government had faced a crucial dilemma: to pay international lenders and defend the ruble, or pay protesting miners and others back wages. Soon after the August 1998 devaluation of the ruble, one of Russia's oligarchs, Vladimir Potanin, "flustered financial markets when he warned that Russia would sooner default on its [foreign] debt than risk disrupting 'social peace.'"[27] It was then that President Yeltsin warned the internal affairs minister, Sergei Stepashin, that "the situation in the country could explode."[28]

While protests by coal miners and others helped push the Russian government toward default and devaluation, and the miners achieved some concessions from their rail blockades, the collapse of the ruble severely impacted the wages of Russian workers, and the strike wave reached its height after the ruble's collapse.[29] Overall, the strike wave provided "considerable support for a direct connection between economic hardship and strikes" in Russia.[30]

Given the steep drop in economic activity and the loss of workplace bargaining power, it is perhaps not surprising that, following the logic of Joshua Clover's argument, the protests were less often strikes halting production and more often actions blocking transport (or "circulation") or other dramatic acts to draw attention to the workers' plight.[31] Indeed, a significant portion of worker protests during this period involved extreme measures: the hostage-taking of managers; the seizure of factories by work collectives contesting privatization; the hunger strikes and even the self-immolation of those not getting paid. Between 1997 and

2000 Interior Ministry reports recorded at least thirty cases of self-immolation or suicide by protesting workers, more than 840 separate hunger strikes, 94 cases of rail blockades, and 356 cases of highways being blocked, as well as 40 cases of building or factory occupations. Various forms of direct action accounted for over 25 percent of all protests during this period, with hunger strikes alone accounting for 14.5 percent of all protest events.[32]

Putin Comes to Power

With this strike wave as backdrop, "upon assuming power, Putin quickly undertook measures to curb regional leaders, unions, and others who might challenge his rule."[33] The different union camps provided distinct challenges. FNPR unions, alongside managers and regional leaders, were seen as complicit in generating protests, while alternative unions often pushed for dramatic collective action. According to Robertson, "this had not gone unnoted in the Kremlin, and one of the first institutional reforms on the agenda of the new Putin administration was a major overhaul of labor legislation that would change the position of the largest labor unions and effectively incorporate them into the Kremlin system."[34]

Thus, the strike wave directly prompted Putin's push for a new labor code soon after becoming president in 2000, both as a first step in controlling regional elites through his new "vertical of power" and to prevent spontaneous protests and direct actions from getting out of government control. There had been previous attempts to enact a new labor code, since the existing one (although modified) dated from the Brezhnev era; the government and employers, along with the World Bank, the IMF, and multinational corporations, had long derided provisions they viewed as incompatible with a market economy, such as the trade unions' right to veto layoffs (a provision that had little meaning in the Soviet era, given the labor shortage).[35] The initial plan proposed by the new government was part of a liberal reform program known as "Strategy 2010," drawn up by a team chaired by economist German Gref.[36] The plan was based closely on a version prepared by the IMF and aimed at significantly restricting the rights of Russia's unions.

The previous attempts at reforming the labor code had been thwarted by opposition from the Communist Party's considerable presence in parliament; but with the Duma elections of 1999 that obstacle was removed as the party's presence decreased. The new parliament, however, included a number of trade unionists. A "group of eight" union leaders in the Duma mobilized a campaign against the proposal, succeeding in framing Gref as a "cutthroat liberal" and his plan "as utterly capitalist," thereby dooming it.[37] Following its defeat, Ashwin and

Kozina concluded that "the struggle over the Labor Code reveals that Putin's concern for social order trumps economic liberalism. It also shows that, despite the unions' limited capacity for mobilization, the government is wary of outright confrontation."[38]

Yet rather than conceding defeat, the Putin government built a new coalition, splitting the unionist parliamentarians by granting the FNPR something close to monopoly status.[39] While all unions were opposed to the government's initial draft, the FNPR and independent unions were soon bitterly divided over the compromise version reached by the government and the FNPR, the version that was eventually passed by the Duma. Independent unions raised a number of objections, most particularly over removing the union "veto" over a worker's firing (though unions could state an opinion on the matter).[40] Yet their main concern was that under the new labor code, management must negotiate only with a union that commands a majority of the workforce. Specifically, when an enterprise has more than one union, the unions should form a single organ representing the trade unions in proportion to their membership, but if they could not agree to do so within five days, the union containing a majority of members would represent all workers.[41] The provision was clearly a threat to the smaller, alternative trade unions, since, as one Russian expert noted, "the old and new unions have been openly at war with one another," and "it is almost impossible to find cases in which they have acted jointly to defend the interests of workers."[42] A decade after the law was passed, a leading Russian labor researcher found that "the most important problem of the alternative unions continues to be their institutional exclusion, which is largely a consequence of the existing labor code."[43]

The marginalizing of alternative unions had significant consequences, since, while they remain small, their institutional exclusion contributes to their militancy. As for the FNPR, the increasingly popular Putin soon endorsed Shmakov in his reelection as head of the union federation.[44] As Robertson concludes, "with the introduction of the new Labor Code, the government fully integrated the official unions into a system of hierarchically managed interest intermediation at the expense of more democratic and representative alternatives."[45] Grigoriev and Dekalchuk go further, arguing that in order to get the labor reform through a still-chaotic Duma, "the government ventured to reorganize the party landscape through uniting the pro-Putin forces into a single, more manageable entity," pushing the OVR and Unity parties to merge as United Russia, the party that would dominate the Duma well into the future. Thus, they conclude, a byproduct of the drive to push the new labor code through parliament "was that it contributed to the nascent corporatism in state-society relations."[46]

Over time, the FNPR itself formed a partnership with United Russia, and the two groups have since coordinated "protest" actions that appear more like political campaigns.[47] In 2011, the same year the "Russia without Putin" protest wave began, the FNPR joined the Russian People's Front, a coalition set up by Putin between United Russia and various officially recognized and supported civil society organizations. The FNPR's Shmakov was seen meeting regularly with Putin; one of Shmakov's strengths was that he could claim regular access to the corridors of power in the Kremlin. Given such a reliance on the state, however, any attempt by the FNPR to challenge state policy would require a radical transformation, a step it has shown no inclination to take. In a sign that the government also takes this relationship quite seriously, it supported a bid, later aborted, to replace Shmakov with Andrei Isayev, one of the top leaders of United Russia (as well as of the FNPR).[48]

Nominally at least, the Russian government and the FNPR sought to create a western European–style system of "social partnership" for industrial relations, with tripartite commissions on various levels including representatives from unions, employers, and the state. Rather than an avenue for bargaining and compromise, however, with the FNPR's acquiescence such institutions have largely aimed at defusing conflict. Even in the wake of the 2008–9 economic crisis, when union members were experiencing the greatest hardship they had faced in years, the federation prided itself on ensuring social stability above all. The FNPR commissioned an "independent study" of its activities during the crisis that reached "an important conclusion: in times of crisis the value of trade unions to ensure social stability has increased significantly."[49]

One might argue that the Russian labor market—with its flexible wages alongside relatively low unemployment—reflects the success of social partnership, since traditionally, strong corporatist arrangements often resulted in a compromise of unions accepting wage restraint in exchange for full employment.[50] Yet, as we have seen, "wage restraint" begins to sound like a cruel euphemism when there is little to no wage floor (with the minimum wage and unemployment benefits for many years well below subsistence level) and where economic downturns are met with delays in paying any wage at all. Outside of a few sectors discussed below, Russia's unions have had little to no impact on wage levels; that is, the union "wage premium"—the greater wage that union workers receive compared to their nonunion counterparts, which in the US remains about 20 percent—in Russia is virtually nonexistent.[51] Simply put, the inability of unions to influence wages has directly shaped Russia's extreme wage flexibility, its low wages and low labor productivity, and the failure of unions to reverse Russia's huge growth in inequality.

One of the main reasons for the inability of Russia's unions to influence wage rates is that, in the workplace as well as at the national level, most FNPR unions adhere more closely to Soviet practice than act as advocates for workers in an often-antagonistic bargaining relationship with management. One study of

Russian workplaces finds that FNPR unions tend to continue to operate under a "distributive model," whereby they are "viewed by employers as a subdivision of the human resources department, the job of which is to motivate and support worker morale, or to help in distributing social benefits. As a result, most unions are involved in distributing resources, as in Soviet times."[52]

Not only do Russia's unions, on the whole, fail to push for higher wages for their members; given weak membership ties, they have a very limited ability to mobilize their members. According to union officials themselves, union membership plays little to no role in whether a worker decides to engage in a workplace protest or not.[53] For most FNPR unions, in the workplace as well as at the national level, the main goal is to preempt conflict, to engage in a "hierarchical dialogue" with employers, and to "try to avoid open protest actions by all possible means." Should a conflict break out, these unions may intervene, but mainly to act as a "buffer" between workers and employers.[54]

Given the FNPR's large and diverse structure, there are important exceptions to such generalities.[55] Yet the major exceptions come from Russia's alternative unions, which tend by their very nature to be more combative. In contrast to the "distributive model" more typical of FNPR workplace unions, alternative unions are closer to a social movement or "protest model" of unionism. Though their membership is small, alternative unions are directly connected with much of the recent strike and protest activity described below.[56] Alternative unions generally attract younger and more able-bodied workers, including those found in multinational corporations; and unlike FNPR unions, they don't include managers in their membership.[57] Union staff are often unpaid activists, and, as distinct from most FNPR unions, some alternative unions avoid any formal contact with the enterprise hierarchy, to prevent potential vulnerability to managerial pressure. Alternative unions view the threat of protest as the main source of their bargaining power with employers, and regard leading protest actions as one of their basic functions, though they can take such actions only with the active support of their members. Not surprisingly then, as Vladislav Inozemtsev has argued, "there is abundant evidence that the Russian authorities are wary of any sign that an independent trade union movement might be in the offing and they are hostile to any form of professional solidarity."[58]

Labor Law and Individual Strategies

The obstacles to labor protest in Russia extend beyond Russia's dominant unions and their ties to past practices. Russian labor law also places severe restrictions on the right of workers to use their ultimate source of power: to refuse to work, or to strike. Since strikes were simply not supposed to occur in the Soviet Union, there was never a Soviet strike law. The law on strikes (or more specifically, the Law on Collective Labor Disputes) was first written in 1991, extensively revised in 1995, and following the strike wave of the late 1990s the legal avenues for engaging in strikes were further restricted with the new Labor Code.[59] The law itself is arcane and lays out extremely detailed procedures that must be followed before a strike can be considered legal.[60] Rather absurdly, the law states that unions must not only announce beforehand the start date for the strike, but also the date when the strike will end. Even FNPR president Shmakov has expressed concern, stating "in world practice, Russia has the longest list of activities where strikes are banned. It is practically impossible to stage a legal strike."[61]

The upshot is that spontaneous strikes are almost always illegal, as are solidarity strikes, political strikes, or strikes about any issue that does not appear in the labor contract. This is a significant problem, since most overt conflicts have been spontaneous, "wildcat" actions, often deemed illegal, and participating workers can simply be dismissed for absenteeism. Since FNPR unions are often opposed to such strike activity, those accused of illegal strikes can find it difficult to obtain legal representation.[62] The law on strikes has been so restrictive that at various times government officials have considered expanding the scope of legal strikes, while at the same time increasing penalties for engaging in strikes with "noneconomic or political demands." Such discussion clearly suggests the government's concerns that workers have few legal and effective channels through which to express grievances, but also their understanding that, in the absence of such channels, workers' spontaneous actions can quickly become politicized. As will become clear, such concerns are not unfounded.

While it is not surprising that organizations such the ILO might criticize Russia's restrictive labor relations, less predictable has been the criticism from the OECD, an organization hardly known for its pro-labor views, though it states its recommendations for Russia's labor laws quite clearly: "In particular, ease conditions for more than one trade union to participate in the collective bargaining process at the firm-level. Better enforce the provisions guaranteeing workers' representation. Relax the very strict provisions on the right to strike."[63]

Since the struggle over the Labor Code shifted from creating greater labor flexibility to building a form of state corporatism and controlling strikes, Russian business leaders and the business press have continued to complain about the need to make Russia's labor laws more flexible, "enabling entrepreneurs to get rid of excess personnel in a more timely fashion."[64] Some experts also contend that Russia's labor laws remain rigid, place significant obstacles before employers in terms of firings and temporary contracts, and maintain inefficient forms and levels of employment.[65] International comparisons would suggest this is true:

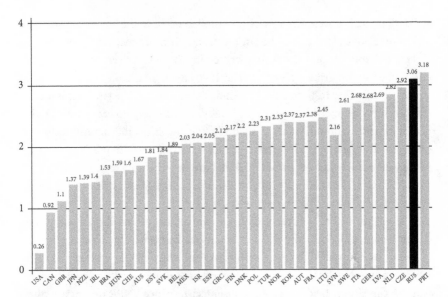

FIGURE 5.1. Strictness of employment protection (individual dismissals)

Source: OECD.

Note: Russian and Brazilian data from 2012; British and Slovenian data from 2014; Lithuanian data from 2015; all else from 2013.

according to the OECD, Russia is second only to Portugal in terms of its strictness of employment protection laws regarding individual dismissals (see figure 5.1).

Yet one must also consider how effectively such laws (or laws in general) are enforced in Russia. While Russia's adherence to the rule of law was highly questionable in the 1990s, when the threats of violence rather than legal norms shaped the behavior of many economic actors, even by 2017 the World Bank claimed that Russia ranked below Brazil, Mexico, and Ukraine in terms of rule of law, and just above Belarus (see figure 5.2).[66] If the rigidity of employment protection legislation is a major factor in preventing employers from firing workers, one would have to assume that those particular laws were somehow enforced differently from other laws (including, for example, laws prohibiting wage arrears). Yet according to one study, a major problem facing Russian industrial relations is "the legal nihilism of employers, who often ignore the provisions of the Labor Code and collective agreements."[67] As *Vedomosti* points out, "managers have learned to force unnecessary or unwanted employees to leave 'of their own volition' or 'by agreement between the parties,'" essentially violating employment protection laws at will, a point on which the World Bank also agrees.[68] According to a survey of those directly involved in enforcing employment protection legislation, only 8 percent of employers' representatives, 3 percent of judges and regional trade

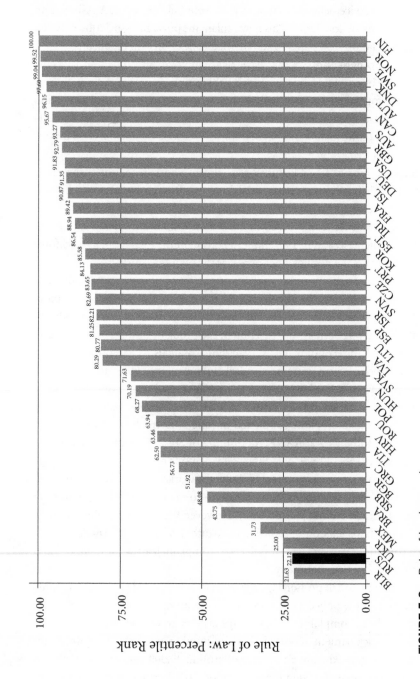

FIGURE 5.2. Rule of law by country

Source: Worldwide Governance Indicators.

union officials, and none of the surveyed labor inspectors or officials of the Public Employment Service believed that such laws were fully enforced. As Gimpelson and Kapeliushnikov conclude, "This may explain the puzzling association between stringent regulations (on paper) and remarkable flexibility (in practice)."[69]

Indeed, in other countries that have rigid employment protection laws, the result is quite often "dual labor markets": stable employment for those with contracts in the formal sector (especially if they are unionized), and a large portion of workers existing outside those protections in the informal sector. Yet interestingly, in Russia informality and "legal nihilism" pervade the formal (and unionized) sector as well.

Since violations of labor law in Russia appear widespread, not surprisingly workers and their advocates have sought redress through the courts. This was especially the case in the late 1990s. The number of wage complaints handled by public courts rose from 19,000 in 1993 to 1.3 million in 1998—an almost seventy-fold increase, and in 1997 alone, 6 percent of the total Russian workforce sought redress for the nonpayment of wages through the courts.[70]

While Putin sought more liberal laws on the firing of workers with the new Labor Code, his leadership also increased the criminal penalties for employers failing to pay wages to include imprisonment, no doubt a popular move in the wake of the wage arrears crisis. Though the problem of wage arrears largely evaporated with the economic recovery in the early 2000s, as economic growth in Russia declined in recent years (particularly following the 2008 crisis), incidents of the violation of labor laws appear to have increased, and workers are once again turning to the courts. According to a survey of sixteen hundred workers in thirty-five Russian regions conducted in June 2017 by the Center for Social and Political Monitoring at RANEPA's Institute of Social Sciences, nearly half of all surveyed workers (42 percent) reported violations of labor rights, with wage arrears the most common complaint. Tellingly, workers were over seven times more likely to complain about labor violations to managers (36.7 percent) than they were to trade unions (5.1 percent). However, while a worsening economy led to more labor violations, according to coauthor of the study Andrei Pokida, in such conditions workers were less likely to complain, fearing for their jobs and for the survival of their company.[71]

Yet despite the small proportion of workers who appealed to the courts (only 4.1 percent of those polled), given worsening economic conditions the absolute number of those complaining about wage arrears grew. The Supreme Court's adjudication department reported that the number of legal complaints over wage arrears increased from an average of around 29,000 per month in 2007 to a monthly average of 40,600 in the first half of 2017. Further, over 95 percent of those cases were decided in favor of plaintiffs.[72]

Following the logic of Russia's political leaders, it is undoubtedly preferable for workers to complain through an individualized, slow, and deliberative legal process than through collective action. Such individual paths fit with other preferred avenues for registering grievances, such as writing letters to authorities about specific problems or complaining during President Putin's yearly "direct line" television show.[73] Such isolated and localized forms of complaint provide critical feedback about major social problems without threatening those in power with collective action that might spin out of control.[74]

As Gimpelson and Kapeliushnikov argue, "The prevalence of individual exit strategies over collective action serves as a kind of shock absorber, partly easing social tensions and turning them into a hidden form."[75] Such exit strategies include informal work arrangements that provide a crucial buffer for many workers and an individualized alternative to oppressive employers. As we have noted, Jeremy Morris has well documented working-class resilience in Russia where workers don't merely survive, but through various strategies make their postcommunist and increasingly postindustrial working-class milieu "habitable."[76] While not purely isolated individuals, in the sense that Morris's informants form close bonds with a small circle of friends, these mostly remain tight circles of mutual adaptation, with little direct impact on broader society. Hence despite the many grievances that Russia's workers might have, from low wages and wage arrears, to violations of labor rights and ineffectual trade unions, to dismal prospects in dying monotowns, the incentives for workers lie mostly in relatively low-cost (if low reward) individual avenues for defending their social standing, rather than attempting to undertake the challenge of high-risk collective action. Workers, not least those in monotowns, remain for the most part dispersed, scattered, secluded, so that even the protests that do break out can be dampened like isolated fires.[77] Thus, in the views of some observers, provided there is no great shock to prod them to action, workers are likely to react to Russia's gradual deindustrialization like the proverbial frog that sits in a pot of lukewarm water as the flame is slowly turned up to the boiling point, when it becomes too late to leap out. At least unless those workers come to believe that, besides protest, there is no other way out.

Russian Labor Protests and Economic Conditions

Thus, the question of a boiling point, or a threshold of pain that prompts labor protest, is a crucial one. Social or economic grievances, perhaps connected to cutbacks in social benefits or worsening economic conditions, could prompt a significant amount of protest as they have in the past. To have a broader impact, such protest would need to extend beyond local levels and combine into larger cross-regional actions and reach the scale at which state-controlled media and government officials are compelled to publicly address it. The questions therefore become what might prompt such protests, and what might prod them to spread?

Given the dire conditions in Russia during the 1990s, it hardly seemed surprising that workers would protest. Yet as counterintuitive as it may seem, considerable empirical evidence suggest that labor protests around the world are more likely when economic conditions are good—that is, during taught labor markets when workers aren't afraid of losing their jobs and feel confident that they can demand better pay and work conditions. According to Roberto Franzosi, "the association between strike frequency and the business cycle is one of the clearest findings of econometric research."[78] But Russia's labor protests in the 1990s were countercyclical, rising when the economy went down, as compared to the typical practice elsewhere of protests being "pro-cyclical," rising alongside a growing economy.[79] Thus not only was Russia's labor market out of sync with global norms; its pattern of labor protest looked rather peculiar as well.

With the end of the economic crisis in 2000, wage arrears were replaced with substantial wage increases, and following the Russian pattern, strikes also declined dramatically after their peak in 1999. Consistent growth, however, appeared to embolden Russia's workers, with a number of sources reporting a sharp increase in labor protests beginning around 2006.[80] Significantly, these new protests appeared to signal a qualitative change in Russian labor relations. Some argued that this new strike activity in Russia reflected a waning of the Soviet legacy and marked a "normalization" or convergence toward the practice of other countries.[81] Greene and Robertson argued that in contrast to past countercyclical strikes in Russia—defensive responses to economic decline—the new wave was pro-cyclical, more typical, they argue, of both OECD and developing countries, and that "the majority of new strikes involve demands for improvements in wages and work conditions."[82] The newspaper *Trud* (once the official union paper in the Soviet period, now largely reflecting the government view on social issues), in reviewing "20 years of strike in Russia," argued that in contrast to the often desperate and illegal strikes in the past, by 2007 "acts of protest in Russia began to acquire a civilized character."[83] From a different perspective, Irina Kozina found that the new strike wave, differing from past "defensive" strikes often aimed at government officials, had an "offensive" character, reflecting "class consciousness" and a "labor-capital" struggle over the distribution of profits within the enterprise.[84]

Some described this as a period of "classical" industrial relations for Russia, with workers asserting their interests in growing economic sectors, such as the oil and gas and auto manufacturing industries.[85] Indeed, workers were particularly militant in some of the foreign firms that had entered the Russian market during the boom, leading to the formation of new, alternative unions, such as the Inter-regional Trade Union of Autoworkers (MPRA in the Russian acronym).[86] The union was formed initially by workers at Russia's Ford plant, and spread from there to others in the auto industry. In a fascinating comparison of labor relations in Volkswagen plants in Russia and Slovakia, Hinz and Morris found that Russian workers were able to leverage their structural power, which came from tight labor markets, and also from the fact that the Russian VW plant (in contrast to the Slovakian one) was producing exclusively for the Russian market, effectively eliminating the threat that VW might relocate the plant to another country with cheaper labor.[87] In auto and other expanding sectors workers gained concessions by threatening to disrupt profitable production through strikes, rather than resorting to the desperate measures of the past. They were also likely to direct their demands toward enterprise management, rather than asking government officials to intervene on their behalf. Taken together, these protest actions suggested that Russian workers and workplaces were indeed shedding the Soviet legacy and converging toward world industrial relations practice.[88]

The picture changed dramatically, however, with the 2008–9 recession. Given the sudden and substantial drop in economic output, there was renewed talk of potential social unrest.[89] As we have seen, considerable attention was placed on monotowns, especially after the protest in Pikalyovo.[90] Yet following the Russian labor market model, while unemployment increased in 2008–9, mass dismissals did not take place, and enterprise managers reverted to their earlier practices of reducing pay by putting workers on shorter work hours, on unpaid leave, or simply not paying wages (putting them in arrears).[91] Protests grew as a result, with defensive demands once again predominant.

Russia's economic decline during this recession was deep but relatively brief. The economy rebounded fairly quickly, as did key sectors such as the automobile industry.[92] Writing in the wake of that recession, Vinogradova, Kozina, and Cook argued that in Russia "labor activism is at a crossroads." While one path might lead to a reinforcement of old patterns of dependence and immobility punctuated by periods of defensive protest actions, another direction was possible, since "new trends, which changed the patterns of quiescence and dissociation, have emerged: more solidarity, more union leadership, more workers' self-identification as a party bargaining with management and owners, and demands for decent wages and working conditions."[93]

The economic downturn of 2014–16, however, did little to nurture this alternative path of a more offensive-minded Russian workforce. But neither were workers quiescent. Instead, Russian labor protest remained countercyclical, with strikes increasing alongside economic hardship, with mainly defensive protest demands. This conclusion becomes clear thanks to the compilation of labor protest data by a number of Russian researchers. Official strike statistics are nearly useless, in part since Russia's highly restrictive strike law makes legal strikes nearly impossible to carry out, and strikes deemed outside the law simply go unrecorded. For instance, during the depth of Russia's economic crisis in 2009, the statistical agency claimed that only one strike took place during the entire year.[94]

A number of Russia researchers have begun to systematically study Russian labor conflict. The most impressive database has been compiled at the Center for Social and Labor Rights (CSLR) by Petr Bizyukov, who has gathered data on labor protests since 2008,[95] based on a compilation of news accounts and internet reports.[96] Unlike Rosstat, the CSLR database measures "labor protest," which can include simply the "advancing of demands." Given the legal restrictions on strikes, however, Russian workers often protest through other means. The CSLR data include "stop actions," a category that contains various forms of refusals to work (including slowdowns, or in Russian parlance "Italian strikes"). The CSLR database suggests a picture of labor protest very different from that of the Rosstat strike data: while Rosstat recorded five strikes in Russia in 2015 and three in 2016, the CSLR database recorded a yearly average of 414 protests for 2015–16, with an average of 163 "stop actions" each year.

Although relying on other definitions and slightly different methodologies, other research centers have begun compiling labor protest data as well. A research center on "Social-Labor Conflicts" (SLC), based at a unit of the St. Petersburg Trade Union University (affiliated with the FNPR), has been systematically following labor protests since 2013. Russia's Center for Economic and Political Reforms (CEPR) has also begun to monitor labor protests, though only since the beginning of 2016.[97]

To be sure, there are limits to the understanding of labor protest in Russia based on the data collected by these organizations.[98] Nevertheless, the existing data allow for certain deductions and conclusions. The databases make clear that labor protests continue to increase during downturns. Following the economic decline in 2014, the CSLR database recorded a 40 percent jump in protests in 2015 from the previous year, and a further jump in 2016, when protests were 76 percent higher than the average recorded from 2008 through 2013, a period that included Russia's last economic crisis. During those six years, only five months recorded thirty or more labor protests; but thirty protests or more took place in twenty-one of the thirty months from October 2014 through March 2017. That is, the likelihood that any month would experience more than thirty labor protests went from 7 percent in the earlier period to 70 percent during the recent recession, a tenfold increase. The absolute number of "stop actions" recorded by CSLR over this period also increased substantially, though their portion of overall protests remains roughly the same. Thus, one question concerns why labor protests were greater following 2014 than they were in 2008–9, when the drop in economic output was greater.[99]

Though using different definitions of protest, the SLC database found that the number of "social-labor conflicts" grew from 140 in 2014 to 161 in 2015 and to 186 in 2016.[100] Though the third monitoring project, conducted by the CEPR, lacks comparable data from earlier years, it also monitors what it calls "high profile [rezonansnye] cases" of labor tension or "conflict situations," such as incidents of wage arrears, mass layoffs, and reductions in working hours that might lead to overt protests. In 2016 it recorded 1,141 such "conflict situations," though only a small fraction of these (207) led to an overt protest, while seventy-eight (or over 90 percent) of Russia's regions were impacted by these cases with the potential for more overt protest.[101]

By 2017 the number of protests recorded by at least two of the databases began to decline. The CSLR database reported 334 labor protest for the year, down from 2016 (419) and 2015 (409) but still significantly higher than the average yearly protests (241) from 2008 to 2014. The SLC database recorded 176 "social-labor conflicts" in 2017, 166 in 2018, and 171 in 2019 (down from the 186 in 2016 but still higher than those in 2015 and 2014).[102] The CEPR monitoring found that through the first three quarters of 2017 (the latest data available from that source) the number of overt labor protests declined from the previous year, but the number of "conflict situations" remained quite high and increased through the third quarter. Yet by 2019 the CSLR reported an uptick in labor protest from the previous year, and for the first half of 2020 the SLC noted a rise in social-labor conflicts (the latest data available for both sources).[103]

While there are limitations to the evidence, when measured against GDP growth or changes in real wages, the data are consistent with Russia's familiar countercyclical pattern of labor protest, where protests increase during periods of economic hardship. In figure 5.3 the number of monthly protests as recorded by the CSLR is mapped against changes in real wages (using change in GDP would present a similar picture). The available evidence makes clear that there is an inverse relationship with Russian labor protests and economic conditions. That is, labor protests in Russia are hardly becoming pro-cyclical; rather, as in the past, they increase during an economic downturn.[104]

Not surprisingly, since the protests were connected to economic contraction, the various databases find that workers advanced more defensive demands during the economic downturn of 2008–9 and after 2014. What is noteworthy, however, is how quickly those protest demands reverted to those seen during the protest wave of the 1990s, almost as if the intervening boom years had never

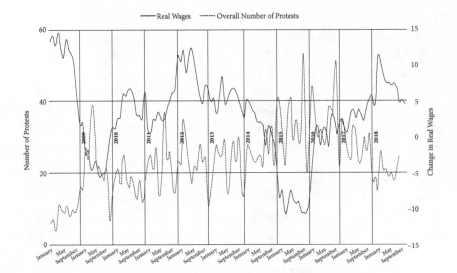

FIGURE 5.3.   Changes in real wages versus labor protests (January 2008–
November 2018)

Sources: Labor protest: Bizyukov and trudprava.ru. Real wages: Gimpelson et al. 2017 and Rosstat.

happened. Once again, Russian employers were much more likely to respond
to the economic contraction by reducing wages or withholding them altogether
than through mass layoffs. While layoffs did indeed take place, and while wage
arrears are not nearly as high as they were during the 1990s, wage arrears have
once again become the main impetus for protest, with all three databases reporting that wage arrears were the leading cause of protest, often by a considerable
margin. The SPU found that over 60 percent of all labor conflicts from 2016 to
2018 were over wage arrears; according to the CEPR, while 12.4 percent of labor
protests in 2016 were about mass layoffs, 87.7 percent centered on lower wages,
many around wage arrears.[105]

Another similarity with protests in the late 1990s, again testifying to the lack
of fundamental change in Russian labor relations, is that some workers began
resorting to extreme forms of protest. While nowhere near the same magnitude as
in the past, protests involving threats to health and life, including hunger strikes,
self-mutilation (such as the opening of veins), and threatening suicides (such as
by jumping off a crane or through self-immolation), were reported by various
regional and local news sites.[106] According to CSLR data, before the 2014 recession the number of extreme protests had declined, which appeared to strengthen
the argument that Russian labor strikes and protests were converging toward
the norm elsewhere. The reappearance of extreme forms of protest, however, is

a result not only of renewed economic difficulties, but also attests to the lack of effective institutional mechanisms for resolving economic and social problems, an absence that reveals itself during a crisis. While such examples are anecdotal, they are clearly evidence of individuals who believe they have exhausted all other options, or, in a phrase, have no other way out.

Perhaps consistent with their defensive nature, the geographic locus of labor protests has been shifting as well. The share of protests is declining in major cities but growing in smaller provincial cities, where in the past people preferred to seek work in the informal economy as an alternative survival strategy. Protests have taken place not only in isolated and clearly troubled enterprises. With the economic constraints impacting federal budgets as well as private firms, workers in state-financed projects, some of them with a relatively high profile, have also been protesting. For instance, as seen in chapter 3, the problem of wage arrears and layoffs and threats of closures has hit several industrial firms connected to the defense sector. The construction sector has been especially hard hit, with workers building the Vostochnyi Cosmodrome protesting over unpaid wages, as well as those who built stadiums for the 2018 World Cup in Moscow, St. Petersburg, Nizhnii Novgorod, Kaliningrad, and Rostov-on-Don.[107]

Prospects for the Spread of Labor Protest

Still, while Russian authorities were clearly alarmed by the prospect of labor protest in 2008–9, they were able to take measures (such as providing subsidies and preventing mass layoffs) that dampened those protests, and they took similar actions after 2014. Moreover, as the economy began to recover, however haltingly, in 2010 and again in 2017, labor protests began to decline. As long as the Russian economy can achieve modest growth, it would appear that the potential for labor protest to threaten social and political stability is limited. Future recessions, however, will be difficult to avoid, particularly if the country's economy remains closely tied to the volatile global commodity markets. Further, a prolonged period of slow economic growth, even if not outright stagnation, could allow grievances to accumulate. The challenge for Russia's leadership then would be to keep protests isolated, preventing them from reaching a scale sufficient to signal a significant level of dissatisfaction from an important segment of Russian society.

What potential is there then that labor protest might increase and spread? Here we return to Charles Tilly's two factors—which he termed "netness" and "catness"—that are central to successful mobilization.[108] Again, netness refers to networks connecting groups to one another, in this case primarily labor unions.

Catness refers to the perception of belonging to a common category with others, such as disparate workers impacted by a change in work rules or labor law.

Regarding netness, Russia's workers remain hampered, since, as we have seen, the dominant union federation, the FNPR, is generally conflict-averse. Indeed, sizable numbers of labor protests take place without any union participation at all. The CSLR database found that 53 percent of protests in 2016 were spontaneous and involved "only workers," with workplace unions involved in only 29 percent of protests.[109] The SLC database reported that 77 percent of worker protests were "unorganized" in 2018.[110] Reflecting on this earlier, E. Makarov, director of the SLC data center, noted that this "indicat[es] the growth of spontaneous worker actions and their unregulated character."[111] This is a significant admission, given that the SLC data are gathered by an FNPR-affiliated organization, and Makarov himself is a deputy chairman of the union federation.

Without assertive unions, many labor protests, when they do erupt, remain localized, without a network that might help them spread. Indeed, the FNPR's Makarov finds "the overwhelming majority of social-labor conflicts take place outside the sphere of existing legal frameworks," a point that Bizyukov of the CSLR has emphasized repeatedly as well.[112] Moreover, the very fact that these protests rise up spontaneously, without existing organizations or clear institutional channels to guide them, can make their appearance and subsequent path unpredictable. In such an environment, it is hardly surprising that at least in some cases workers reach for extreme forms of protest, including threats—or the actual carrying out—of personal bodily harm in order to attract attention to their plight.

On one level, the tendency to revert to past patterns—with employers avoiding mass layoffs but workers quietly suffering from labor-rights violations including wage arrears, until such suffering becomes intolerable and they spontaneously protest, as in the *bunt* of the Russian peasant past—suggests the persistence of age-old paternalism and worker quiescence. Yet, in addition to the adroit individual strategies that workers deploy to make their environments habitable, Russia's alternative unions directly challenge the contention that Russian workers remain hopelessly mired in mentalities from the past. Though small in number and often harassed by officials at various levels, alternative unions have had an impact beyond their numbers, and their assertiveness increased during the more pro-cyclical strikes before the 2008 economic crisis. We will see a concrete example of this in chapter 6, where we will examine the MPRA, a particularly assertive union that arose in the auto industry. This suggests that a significant segment of Russia's working population responds rather rationally to opportunities stemming from changing economic conditions. Following Erik Wright's notion of workers' power, they are able to act as if fully aware of their structural power, not only protesting out of desperation when times are hard but also becoming more militant when the economy grows and labor markets are tight. Yet that also means that the scope of action for Russia's alternative unions is constrained not only by considerable political restrictions, but also by Russia's economy, particularly its dependence on the global commodities market. Thus, unless and until economic conditions in Russia change, the prospects would appear limited for the rise of the assertive, offensive-minded alternative unions witnessed during the economic boom of the 2000s.

Workers can also be mobilized by what Tilly called catness—that is, becoming united through belonging to the same category. For example, for public-sector workers, the same authorities are typically responsible for setting their wages and working conditions across different localities, but not so private-sector workers. This creates a dilemma for authorities, since in times of slower economic growth and limited income from oil revenues, there is an increasing need to raise revenue or cut expenditures (or both), including for social programs. Yet raising taxes or cutting benefits has the potential to spur more protests, since such government actions impact disparate workers and others as a single category.

Thus, just as the Russian state is constrained from, say, closing down inefficient large enterprises in a monotown out of fear of spurring protest, it is also constrained more broadly by what Russians refer to as the "social sphere." This became clear even as the oil boom was still well under way, when in 2005 the attempt by Russian authorities to replace the universal social benefits given to the elderly with cash payments led to spontaneous protests in a large number of Russian cities. As many as three hundred thousand protesters appeared on the streets, in eighty out of Russia's eighty-nine regions, in what was characterized as the largest case of social unrest in the country since the Soviet coal miners' strikes in 1989.[113]

Though the protests became known in Russia as the *sitsevaia* revolution, from the cheap print dresses worn by elderly Russian women, the protest actions themselves often became intense, as when demonstrators blocked roads in Bashkortostan or broke through armed guards to storm the mayor's office in Tolyatti. As Robertson concludes, "In each case, it appears the protests were local, organized in isolation from one another."[114] Indeed, the sudden, spontaneous spread of the protests over such a vast space was not simply the result of imitation or diffusion (especially given state control over major media); rather, an abrupt change in government policy gave common cause to an otherwise isolated category of individuals across the country, a process we will see repeated with the mobilization of Russia's truckers in chapter 8.

Moreover, as Petrov, Lipman, and Hale note, the spontaneous nature of the protests meant that they were "evidently quite unexpected and terrifying for the authorities, who had also not anticipated the [previous year's] Orange Revolution in Ukraine, and who thus feared that they might have badly miscalculated revolutionary potential much closer to home."[115] Despite President Putin having been overwhelmingly reelected the previous year, polls found that 81 percent of Russians believed that the government had botched the rollout of the reform.[116] This was no doubt all the more distressing since at the time pensioners were commonly viewed as a core pro-Putin constituency. The government quickly backed down, with the concessions costing more than the reforms would have saved.

Pensioners are of course former workers (even though many in Russia continue to work while drawing a pension), so this was hardly a labor protest. Yet as we shall see with the example of the truck drivers, workers can also become united through policy changes that impact them as a single category. Moreover, the bungled attempt to monetize in-kind benefits points to dilemmas at the core of Russia's welfare state, which is often described by critics as bloated and inefficient, but which remains an area of great importance to the Russian public. Needless to say, the pensioners' protest significantly dampened the government's enthusiasm for undertaking reforms to social benefits.

Russia's welfare state directly impacts a significant segment of the workforce. Liberal economists inside and outside Russia complain about overemployment in what Russians call the "budget sector"—workers employed by the state, especially in health care and education. Gimpelson and Kapeliushnikov argue that "the over bloated budgetary sector waits for its restructuring."[117] The World Bank contends that almost 30 percent of Russia's workers are employed in "nonmarket services," a percentage that is ten points higher than in comparator market economies. The bank argues further that "the additional employment consists mostly of low-wage labor hired in poor regions, such as janitors, street cleaners, and workers helping in hospitals and schools. These jobs aim to alleviate the hardship of unemployment, but they reflect the inadequate mobility of the Russian labor market, which they then compound by tying people to locations where they are not productive."[118]

Bryn Rosenfeld finds evidence of the political effectiveness of this support, however economically inefficient it may be, when middle-class professionals employed in the budget sector were much less likely than private-sector workers to support the 2011–12 antigovernment protests.[119] Putin has clearly tried to maintain this support, for instance by promising to increase the pay of workers in education and health care in his May Decrees in 2012 and again in 2018. Yet such promises have fallen short, in part because the federal government has placed the burden of funding these salary increases onto often-indebted regional budgets. This meant that the decrees "could not but result in massive dismissals in the public welfare sector."[120]

In short, the dilemmas facing Russia's social sphere parallel and often overlap with those of the industrial sector. Critics charge that Russia's social spending is excessive (relative to revenue) and that the budget sector is inefficient and over-manned. Yet the sector, and such social benefits that exist, remain an important element in social stability and the regime's political support.

Not surprisingly then, attempts to "optimize" (the euphemism preferred by Russian authorities) the budget sector can lead to protest. This was true in 2004–5, when teachers and medical workers undertook short work stoppages throughout the country, demonstrating their ability to mobilize through their union "network" power, and the FNPR-affiliated unions then demonstrated a willingness to engage in at least symbolic actions. Since then, and especially fol-lowing the 2012 welfare restructuring, such workers have increased their network power by forming interregional independent unions—"Teacher" and "University Solidarity" in the education sector, "Action" in the health sector—all belonging to the Confederation of Labor (KTR), the major alternative union umbrella. While small in number, as with other alternative unions they have shown their militancy through strike action.[121] For example, when "optimization" in health involved plans to close some twenty-eight hospitals and clinics in Moscow and lay off thousands of medical workers in November and December 2014, thousands of those workers began marching in the streets.[122] Putin quickly and publicly backed away from the reforms, stating they required further study and deliberation. Yet years later health care workers were continuing to organize protest actions.[123]

Moreover, budget cuts can impact otherwise isolated public sector work-ers within and across regions. While coordinated cross-regional labor protests remain rare in Russia, they have increased since 2014, led less often by indus-trial workers and more by public-sector employees such as teachers and medical workers.[124]

Given strains on federal and regional budgets, it is not surprising that the pro-test databases note an increase in budget-sector protests. Without a significant increase in revenue—which, as we shall see with Russia's truckers, can also lead to protest—or a dramatic shift in spending priorities, further budget cuts, and resulting protests, would appear difficult to avoid. Yet, as with Russia's pension-ers, budget-sector workers are considered to be a core constituency of the Putin leadership, and protests by such workers can take on an additional symbolic sig-nificance, signaling a weakening of Russia's social stability.

Thus, limited economic growth, when combined with budget pressures and calls for austerity, has the potential to create what we might call "catness soli-darity," when groups with similar complaints find common cause.[125] This has certainly been the case with budget-sector workers, but joint protests can also occur over issues such as wage arrears. As protests grow in number, they can clump together when protests in one enterprise in a region combine with others. Further, protests with traditional labor demands can join with protests over other social and economic concerns. For instance, in Ivanovo in December 2015, workers protesting wage arrears were joined by pensioners protesting potential cuts to retirement benefits.[126] Russia's truckers protested in solidarity with farmers from Kuban objecting to what they claimed were illegal land seizures, as well as with miners from Rostov threatening a hunger strike over unpaid wages. All of this suggests that for many Russian workers, the challenge is less about breaking out of a state of quiescence and resignation and more about seeking that their demands actually get heard. Yet as we have noted, for that to happen the protests will likely need to reach a certain threshold level, making labor protests a difficult topic for those in power to ignore.

The Authorities' Response

The question of whether or not protest reaches that threshold is clearly connected to the response of Russian authorities. In his study of protest in Russia's hybrid regime, Robertson argues that Russian officials react to protest with some combination of coercion, channeling, and concessions, with channeling referring to attempts to divert or co-opt protesters through state-sponsored organizations. However, FNPR unions, the groups ostensibly positioned to divert or channel worker protests, have generally proven ineffective in doing so.

The CEPR, headed by Nikolai Mironov, has compiled its own study of what it terms the authorities' "most typical tactics" in response to social and labor protests in recent years. The study's overall assessment is blunt: "The authorities demonstrate an inability to effectively resolve conflict. Their intervention often exacerbates the conflict, and speaks to the lack of a system in Russia able to deal with social protests and problems that cause them."[127] More specifically, the report notes that, as a rule, even protesters with exclusively "private" demands (such as wage arrears or the closure of private enterprises) appeal to public authorities; the SPU also finds protesters overwhelmingly appealing to government officials as opposed to managers and owners of private workplaces.

As we saw at the beginning of this chapter, when Putin came to power he successfully established a "vertical of power" in part to stop regional officials from harnessing labor and other protest as a means of extracting concessions and financial support from federal authorities. Yet doing so created a different set of incentives with its own problems. Local and regional leaders, rather than using conflict to their advantage, are now held accountable for suppressing it. Thus, officials often respond to protest (in what the CEPR refers to as "tactic no. 1") by combining repression aimed at activists with attempts to ignore their actions altogether, in order to "silence the media to prevent publicizing the protest, and, more importantly, to prevent the protest's federalization"—in other words the reverse of what many regional leaders sought in the late 1990s. The CEPR report, however, argues that this tactic is usually ineffective, as it often leads to the worsening of the conflict by driving it underground so that a new conflict reappears later, perhaps in the form of hunger strikes or road blockages. One reason suppressing media coverage of such protests worsens them is that doing so leads to a lack of information not only on the part of the authorities, but also for those affected, who are often left to rely on rumors. The attempt to ignore protests can radicalize participants precisely because, from the workers' point of view, the whole point of engaging in public protest is to draw the attention of the authorities.

Thus, the second (or fallback) tactic for local and regional leaders is to become involved only when the situation worsens and the conflict escalates. While the intervention that follows is often effective in resolving the problem, the tactic "creates significant risks for the government and its reputation," since by this late stage the protests may have succeeded in gaining the attention of the central media, "leading to the federalization of the conflict, which regional authorities want to avoid."[128] Yet the CEPR report notes that conflicts in large enterprises in particular can often only be resolved though federal intervention.

In short, local authorities try to quickly repress and otherwise ignore social and labor conflicts, since reacting openly would draw attention to their existence, which would be seen by those above as a shortcoming. But quelling attention to the conflict can lead to its deepening, as both authorities and protesters lack information, and protesters may take more radical actions to ensure that their demands are heard, perhaps by those higher up the political power structure.

Whether viewed from the perspective of labor or management and the state, Russia's system of labor relations appears largely dysfunctional. The Russian state, in order to promote stability, has discouraged "labor shedding" and relied on the tradition of workplace dependence, but at the cost of wage arrears and festering monotowns. The restrictions on strikes and the subordination of the FNPR have limited legal strikes but have led to simmering discontent, providing few if any institutional channels to contain protest when it breaks out. Thus, Russia's labor relations leave workers with very limited means to protest or resolve conflict, but as a result the Russian state is left with deep concerns about social stability. The dilemma extends beyond the industrial sector to include the social sphere, since budget-sector workers are both a basis of political support and a potential source of labor protest, and much the same can be said of social spending and benefits generally. While widespread labor and social unrest might appear unlikely, a significant change in economic conditions, whether a steep drop in the price of oil or a prolonged period of stagnating wages, could alter that calculation significantly.

Still, one might argue that the fear of a Russian "social explosion" was and is misplaced. In the next chapter, we will examine how such a feared social explosion was avoided in Tolyatti, Russia's largest monotown, despite massive downsizing in the "city-forming enterprise." Yet rather than illustrating a model for the authorities to follow elsewhere, the case demonstrates the unintended consequences of trying to avoid large-scale labor conflict. There, the costly measures aimed at avoiding some conflicts ended up creating others.

DOWNSIZING IN "RUSSIA'S DETROIT"

How did Russia's largest monotown—sometimes referred to as "Russia's Detroit," given the dominance of its auto industry—survive layoffs on a massive scale? What were the consequences of those layoffs? In answering these questions, I take a closer look at several of the themes discussed previously. First, I investigate another example of Russia's industrial policy, this time through the automobile sector. I also detail the rise of Russia's leading alternative union through that sector, and how its strengths and limitations mirrored those of the auto industry. Much of this chapter focuses on AvtoVAZ, Russia's leading auto factory, located in Russia's largest monotown, Tolyatti. Just like the US city of Detroit, Tolyatti, along with AvtoVAZ, has experienced hard times. Indeed, the case of AvtoVAZ seems to provide a counter-example to one of the central claims of this book: massive layoffs took place here without large-scale social unrest, let alone a social explosion. Yet on closer inspection we find that the downsizing of AvtoVAZ was accompanied with huge subsidies and considerable state intervention, some of which, rather than easing social tensions, made the situation even more combustible.

The Soviet Auto Giant

In the late 1960s, in an effort to improve their production technology and meet the growing consumer demands of its population, Soviet leaders concluded a cooperation agreement with the Italian firm FIAT, and created an entire city around a new automobile factory on the Volga. The plant was called AvtoVAZ (for Volga Automobile Factory), and the town was named Tolyatti, after the Italian Communist Party leader Palmiro Togliatti. As this historian Lewis Siegelbaum recounted, "The entire workforce and members of their families, estimated to be 130,000 people, would be housed in what for all intents and purposes was a new city."[1] Unlike company towns in advanced capitalist societies that typically waned with the arrival of the automobile age, or the Soviet monotowns such as Magnitogorsk that were built in the 1930s during Stalinist industrialization, Tolyatti was created decades later (just as the process of deindustrialization was about to begin elsewhere). The plant produced the Lada and Zhiguli models, based on a modified version of the Fiat 124, and it soon became the Soviet Union's leading car producer, with shares as high as 70–80 percent of the Soviet market. As one source put it, "Soviet automobile production was afflicted only by supply bottlenecks—lack of quality or price were no obstacle to sales."[2]

The city was laid out in such a way that its housing, streets, and public transport could get its initial workforce of thirty-five thousand workers to the factory gates in thirty minutes or less. In Siegelbaum's estimation, "the overwhelmingly youthful population that swelled the city had the opportunity to work and live in as close to ideal conditions as the USSR was capable of mustering for its industrial working class."[3] Thus it might not only have been nostalgia filtered through the subsequent conditions of AvtoVAZ that led a husband and wife to recount to a documentary film crew their happy memories of living and working in Tolyatti in the late Soviet period:

> [HUSBAND:] I came here in 1975, I was twenty-four years old.
>
> [WIFE:] I moved here later, in 1988. I was also twenty-four years old.
>
> [HUSBAND] Back then people weren't driven by fear, they were motivated by being given responsibility. They didn't work just for money.
>
> [WIFE] They were proud to work here.
>
> [HUSBAND] There were trade unions.
>
> [WIFE] People used to feel grateful to have a job at the plant. They would receive a flat, the kindergartens were for free . . . the factory owned many recreation resorts and sanatoriums. Going on vacation used to cost kopecks. Everyone could afford it. We all used to go pretty often. We could go to the seaside. . . .
>
> [HUSBAND]—with the whole family.
>
> [WIFE] There were vacation resorts here. We could take twenty-one days off. Imagine going on a three-week vacation for the whole family

nowadays and paying like 1,000 rubles? And the food was great, it could be by the Volga river.

[HUSBAND] These were the most beautiful times I've ever had.

[WIFE] We quite miss it. The life was merrier, more interesting, people were nicer.[4]

Tolyatti grew to become the Soviet Union's largest monotown—a city of seven hundred thousand, where as recently as 2009 one out of seven residents—not just working-age adults—worked at the auto plant, with many others employed in production and services tied to the factory.

In 1992, less than a year after the collapse of the Soviet Union, AvtoVAZ was privatized. In typical post-Soviet fashion, managers and former party officials acquired the company's assets, while the plant's main trade union stood idly by. Managers created private trading companies that then sold AvtoVAZ cars, returning payment to the factory with enough delay that, given steep inflation, the funds were greatly devalued.[5] In other cases, cars were brazenly stolen from the factory and delivered to private dealers by criminal gangs. Boris Berezovsky, who later boasted of being an "oligarch," made his first millions through AvtoVAZ, becoming its largest private dealer, in what by a number of credible accounts was largely a criminal operation.[6] Indeed, by 1997, according to one source, "AvtoVAZ perhaps had become the most gangster-ridden leading industrial company in Russia." The so-called "car wars" turned Tolyatti into the crime capital of the country: two hundred murders took place in Tolyatti in 1997 alone, and sixty-five of the victims were company managers, dealers, and business rivals, including two board members.[7]

While AvtoVAZ was making millions for the well-connected, the factory itself was hemorrhaging money. The Soviet-era Lada was of such poor quality that once Russia was open to global competition, it lost a significant portion of its market share to the import of used vehicles. By 1996, the company was Russia's largest tax debtor, owing $2.6 billion to various government budgets.[8] Workers went unpaid, and there were reports of management relying on criminal gangs to break strikes and enforce labor discipline.[9] That same year, President Boris Yeltsin agreed to a $3.3 billion subsidy to AvtoVAZ in what was effectively a debt-equity swap. While the collapse of the ruble in 1998 made the Lada more competitive relative to foreign models, and production rose that year to over seven hundred thousand vehicles, the next year the government provided $700 million in aid, and another $800 million in 2002.[10] By 2005 the company was de facto renationalized, as the state corporation Rostec became the majority shareholder.

Yet state ownership resulted in little change in management personnel or practice, or in updating the vehicles produced. The lack of modernizing production was a problem—while the Lada was inexpensive, many viewed the car as cheap in both senses of the word. Besides being uncomfortable and prone to breakdowns, it was also viewed by experts as unsafe: the Russian magazine *Avtorevu* reported that in a crash test collision at forty miles per hour with a stationary barrier, the driver of a rear-wheel-drive Lada would be crushed to death by the steering wheel.[11] The reason for the lack of the plant's modernization, as one source put it, was that "employment policy and the prevention of social protests in the event of possible job cuts were the government's main concern." Even while investment to modernize was not forthcoming, "subsidies continued to flow to maintain jobs."[12] This was due not only to the importance of the factory for the city—AvtoVAZ was the reason the city existed after all— but its significance to the region as well. In the Soviet period the Samara region depended to a considerable degree on its defense industry, especially in aviation.[13] When the military industry collapsed in the 1990s, the region became even more dependent on AvtoVAZ, which was by far the dominant employer in all of Samara. As Thomas Remington noted, it is "hard to imagine how the region could have absorbed the loss of employment and social services that would have been triggered by the complete collapse of its major defense, aviation, and automotive industries."[14]

As we have seen, one of the ways that Russia's industrial regions survived the 1990s and beyond was by balancing the interests of business elites to extract profits with the goals of regional leaders to maintain social stability (and thereby maintain their positions). In Samara, Konstantin Titov remained governor from 1991 to 2007 by doing just that. While he publicly declared his pro-market ideology, he remained very concerned with avoiding unemployment and social instability. Titov not only sought support for AvtoVAZ; he also persuaded the auto giant to assist with his strategy for the region's industrial development. This was crucial, since not only did the firm itself have a massive impact on the region, but twenty-seven other enterprises made components for Lada vehicles, and AvtoVAZ had a controlling share in most of them.[15] Therefore the firm's backing of Titov's plan for regional development "was vital, because to a large degree the plan rested on AvtoVAZ's willingness to contract with local suppliers for its inputs."[16]

In his balancing of economic and social goals Titov was, in Remington's words, "one of the most successful governors in Russia."[17] Yet Titov was also politically independent, refusing to join United Russia and demonstrating his political ambition beyond the region by running for president against Putin in 2000 (and losing badly). He held on as governor of Samara until 2007, when he was replaced by Vladimir Artiakov, a member of United Russia, and who—underscoring the significance of the plant to the region and the federal government—had been the head of AvtoVAZ since 2005.[18]

Import Substitution in the Auto Sector

As with the military industry, Russia's leadership has viewed the automobile sector as strategically important, though in this case based less on national security grounds and more explicitly as a source of well-paying jobs. Much like the bailout of the US auto industry in 2008, Russia's auto sector has received substantial state support over the years. But rather than simply propping up the manufacturers of the old Soviet-era Ladas and Volgas, during the oil boom of the 2000s the Russian government looked to the auto industry as one avenue for diversifying the Russian economy beyond its reliance on oil and gas.[19] The well-known challenges of the "oil curse," however, weakened that strategy, as real wages increased and the ruble appreciated, undermining the cost advantages of domestic producers. In an analysis of the Russian automobile industry, Rudolf Traub-Merz found that "by 2005 automobile imports claimed a market share of 30 per cent with a clear tendency to eclipse domestic models. Largely stuck at the technological level of 1990, which in turn scarcely surpassed the level of 1975, Russian models were no longer competitive and the domestic automobile industry faced oblivion amidst the oil price boom."[20]

Given the threat of the industry's oblivion (which, needless to say, would have led to huge job losses), the Russian government sought to confront the sector's technological lag and the state's continued subsidization of employment, and implemented an explicit import substitution policy for the auto sector. Specifically, beginning with decrees in 2005 and 2006, with additional steps added later, the policies privileged domestically produced automobiles over imports. The steps included tariffs on imports, as well as reduced taxes, custom duties, and other incentives for foreign carmakers to open auto assembly plants in Russia rather than importing finished vehicles.

Such incentives proved attractive to foreign automakers, since Russia's population at over 140 million remained a large market by European standards, especially when consumer demand was boosted by high prices for the country's oil and gas exports. This led to a surge in the Russian auto sector, which "became one of the world's most thriving markets."[21] Foreign automakers sited production within Russia to meet this demand and get inside the country's protectionist bubble. While automakers like Volkswagen invested in plants in countries like Slovakia exclusively for export, they built plants in Russia to take advantage of the domestic market.[22] In terms of car production inside Russia, the import substitution policy appeared largely successful: while imports were as high as 59 percent of auto sales in 2009, by 2013 they had declined to 25.4 percent.[23]

Militant Auto Unions

The policy also appeared successful for workers in the automobile sector, where one of the strongest alternative union organizations, the MPRA (Interregional Labor Union of Automobile Workers) was formed by workers from two automobile plants (Ford in Vsevolozhsk and AvtoVAZ) in 2006, just as the import substitution policy had begun. The MPRA led some of the most successful labor actions in Russia, such as the 2007 strike at the Ford plant, where workers halted production and barred entry to the plant, and by doing so won wage gains of 11 percent and a contract guaranteeing wage indexation of 1 percent above inflation.[24] The Ford contracts became an inspiration for other workers in the industry, and the MPRA spread to other auto plants such as Volkswagen in Kaluga. Workers in these plants played a key part in the "pro-cyclical" and more assertive labor protests that began around this time. Workers at AvtoVAZ also went on strike in 2007, at one point demanding wage increases to 25,000 rubles per month, defiantly echoing a campaign promise of the ruling United Russia party.[25] The case of the MPRA points to the potential strengths but also to the limitations of Russia's unions and their ability to advance the interests of their members.

Hinz and Morris argue convincingly that the success of Russia's autoworkers can be explained by Erik Olin Wright's "working-class power" approach, as the economic boom of the 2000s boosted the structural power of the sector's workers.[26] They were able to capitalize on their marketplace power because of tightened labor markets, especially for skilled workers. Their workplace power was enhanced by a surge in the Russian auto industry, which benefited from the rise in demand alongside economic growth, as well as from the import substitution policy.

Russia's auto industry was hard hit by the 2008–9 recession. In part because of swift government intervention, however, the industry soon rebounded, making the Russian auto market the second largest in Europe, slightly behind that of Germany.[27] As the outlook improved, autoworkers again went on the offensive. For example, in March 2012, while the protests against electoral fraud were still taking place in Moscow and St. Petersburg, not far from Moscow workers at Benteler

Automotive, an auto parts supplier for the Volkswagen plant, undertook a three-day strike that nearly shut down the VW plant, in order to gain recognition of their MPRA-affiliated union. According to Ilya Matveev, "after the intervention of the regional authorities, the striking workers won recognition for their union and then, after three months of bitter collective bargaining, signed one of the best collective agreements in the industry."[28]

Russia's autoworkers and the MPRA provide a sharp counterexample to claims that workers (and by extension, the Russian masses) are constrained by a paternalist mentality and tend to accede to authority, provided their basic needs are met. True, as we have seen, Russian labor protests are more likely when conditions for workers are adverse or even intolerable, as in the case of wage arrears. Yet Russian autoworkers, especially those working at foreign-owned plants, were able to recognize and press their advantage when the opportunity presented itself. Unfortunately for the autoworkers, their structural power—as with Russia's economy overall—was fueled by high prices for oil and gas, and by foreign capital attracted by that oil-fed demand. This became clear with the collapse of the oil boom in 2014, which once again pushed Russia's auto industry into a deep crisis. With that the structural power of Russia's autoworkers, and the assertive demands that that power allowed them to advance, receded along with the withdrawal of foreign capital. Instead of seeking a greater share of profits, the MPRA was forced to fight to prevent layoffs.

Interestingly, however, the MPRA didn't simply fold under pressure. The organizing tools and experience that workers gained during their brief window of structural power allowed them to retain a measure of "associational power" even when that structural power had largely dissipated. Rather than shrinking, the MPRA gradually grew with the addition of union groups that arose from labor conflicts and protests in various industries and regions of Russia and which then turned to the MPRA for assistance. As a result, the trade union transformed itself into an interregional and cross-industrial network accommodating alternative trade unions, regardless of their industrial or professional affiliation. With changes in its organizational structure, the MPRA began to look more like a "hub organization" coordinating territorial branches in a number of Russian regions rather than a traditional trade union built on primary workplace units within a given industry. It even changed its name, with its Russian abbreviation (MPRA) no longer referring exclusively to autoworkers but instead signifying the Interregional Trade Union Workers Association.[29] The MPRA remained a significant vehicle for labor organizing, so much so that the Russian authorities undertook a court action to have the union declared illegal in the run-up to Putin's 2018 reelection campaign, though that action was later annulled by the Supreme Court.[30]

Protectionist Boomerang

The waxing and waning of the structural power of Russia's autoworkers also points to two serious defects in Russia's industrial policy for the sector. First, while the policy aimed in large part at boosting or at least maintaining employment in car factories, ironically the surge of investment from foreign car manufacturers in Russia put domestic producers such as AvtoVAZ under significant pressure. Thus, while in 2005 Russian manufacturers accounted for 60 percent of cars sold in the country, by 2014 that share had plunged to 18.5 percent (while the share from foreign car manufactures with plants in Russia rose from 12 percent in 2004 to 71.2 percent by 2014).[31] Once again, rather than following the East Asian model of strategically supporting domestic industries with the goal of building a comparative advantage in exports, the Russian policy was directed toward the domestic market. In contrast to countries such as China, foreign carmakers seeking access to Russia's market were not required to enter into joint ventures with Russian firms, nor were they given mandates or incentives for the transfer of technology. As a result, while employment was boosted in the plants of foreign firms sited in Russia, domestic producers such as AvtoVAZ suffered.

The second shortcoming was that much of that foreign investment was attracted by oil-fueled demand and thus was subject to the boom-and-bust cycles of global commodity markets. This can be seen in the extent to which Russian car sales mirrored the global price of oil. While Russia's auto industry was hard hit by the 2008–9 recession, it soon rebounded. The collapse of the oil boom in

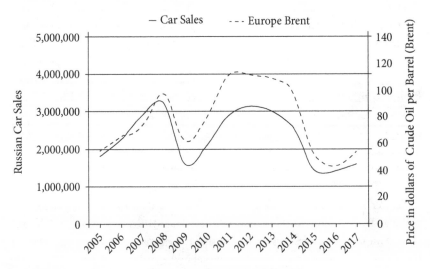

FIGURE 6.1.   Car sales and oil prices, Russia (2005–17)

Sources: Traub-Merz, "Automotive Industry in Russia"; Oica.net statista.com.

2014, however, "wrenched the sector into a profound crisis." By 2015, Traub-Merz argued, the Russian automobile industry was "fighting for its life with uncertain prospects."[32] Distressed by huge losses, foreign firms were "all cutting costs by reducing production and staff. This include[d] reductions in the number of shifts, temporary closures, monetary packages for voluntary termination of employment, short-time working and forced dismissals."[33] Meanwhile, though Russia had negotiated a sunset clause allowing for import tariffs on cars when it entered the WTO in 2012, that provision was set to expire in 2018.

Testifying to the continued volatility of the sector, Russia's auto industry recovered somewhat by 2017. With labor costs now lower than those in China, foreign companies that are able to produce cars in Russia up to international standards can export "made in Russia" cars to countries in the post-Soviet space. Yet given the weakness of those markets, the exports number only in the tens of thousands.[34] Moreover, the recovery of the domestic market was helped in part by state intervention: the government has subsidized interest rates for car loans, and in July 2017 it promised an additional 7.5 billion rubles ($97 million) for loans for a first car or a family car.[35] While Soviet-era leaders all rode in Soviet-made cars, most high-ranking Russian officials, including Putin, preferred the luxury of a German Mercedes.[36] That changed with the rollout of the Kortezh (Russian for "motorcade") limousine, built with an engine from Porsche.[37] Yet beyond the Russian government, which purchases the car for its top officials, it is unclear who else might buy such a vehicle. As one source put it, "The first edition will not exceed 250–300 units and will be a symbolic gesture rather than a real industrial development."[38]

Thus, as with its approach to industry generally, Russia in its various policies toward its auto sector has been curiously ineffective. The laissez-faire approach of the 1990s proved disastrous for the hugely inefficient and noncompetitive Soviet car industry. Though the subsequent, more statist leadership of Putin explicitly sought to build a coherent industrial policy, the result was an ineffective mix of liberal and mercantilist precepts, an intervention that was more thumbs than fingers. Further, the attempts to protect industry, in large part to ensure that layoffs did not lead to social unrest, resulted in unintended consequences that rebounded politically. This was clearly the case for AvtoVAZ and the city of Tolyatti.

AvtoVAZ in Crisis

The policy measures taken by the government beginning in 2005 and 2006 to support the auto industry incentivized foreign firms to produce inside Russia, undercutting domestic Russian manufacturers rather than protecting them.

As Traub-Merz notes, "The government only exacerbated AvtoVAZ's sales crisis with its import substitution intervention."[39] With the Russian market growing during the oil boom of the mid-2000s, the government also sought foreign investors for AvtoVAZ. Given the pent-up demand, foreign multinationals wanted access, with GM, Fiat, and Renault seeking to invest directly in the company. Renault won the competition, and in 2008 it invested $1 billion in capital and acquired a 25 percent stake in AvtoVAZ, with Rostec (the state-owned holding company that specializes in strategically important firms and industries) and Troika Dialog (now known as Sberbank CIB, a subsidiary of state-owned Sberbank) controlling another 25 percent each.[40] With business booming, in 2008 AvtoVAZ produced eight hundred thousand cars, a record for the plant. Boris Aleshin, the company's CEO, boasted that he hoped to sell one million cars that year.[41] That was just before the global economic crisis hit.

With the crisis, Russia's auto industry, and AvtoVAZ in particular, quickly went from boom to bust.[42] By the end of 2008, "AvtoVaz was on the verge of collapse." Lada sales had dropped by 50 percent to only 350,000 vehicles, and over 150,000 remained unsold on the factory's lots.[43] Production was halted from December to January, and although the factory restarted in February, it stopped two weeks later when the plant's suppliers, who had not been paid for past deliveries, refused to deliver more parts until payments were made. The company was selling little more than half the cars it needed to in order to break even, despite offering the Lada at a 20 percent discount.[44] The plant's workers, which still numbered over one hundred thousand, with many more involved in auto parts production and subsidiary services, were hit with a sharp reduction in wages.

During this time, the firm still accounted for at least 60 percent of the city's revenues.[45] As a "city-forming enterprise," in the Soviet period AvtoVAZ had provided vital social services for Tolyatti, such as day care centers, hospitals, and housing. Yet rather astonishingly, in 2009 AvtoVAZ was still spending about 170 billion rubles (roughly $60 million) a year on such social programs for the city.[46] Indeed, while a major goal of post-Soviet privatization had been for industrial firms to dispense with the provision of "social services," in many ways the connection between Tolyatti and AvtoVAZ got stronger in the post-Soviet period. As Siegelbaum noted, "one is hard-pressed to think of another city its size that is so completely dominated by one company."[47] While in the Soviet period AvtoVAZ was one component—if an extremely large one—of the Ministry of Automobile Production, in the post-Soviet era Tolyatti became truly a "company town."

Underscoring the dependence of the entire region on the plant, while Russia's GDP shrank by 9.5 percent year on year in the first quarter of 2009, Samara's GDP declined by 38 percent.[48] According to an editorial in the business newspaper *Vedomosti*, while almost no one in the government believed it made economic sense to continue to prop up the tottering auto giant, it was politically impossible to bankrupt a factory on which a town and an entire region were so dependent. "The fear that all of [the workers] will go on strike keeps the country's leaders from the obvious step, which just prolongs the plant's expensive agony."[49]

The government's initial response was to double down on its import substitution policy. Since used imports continued to be a major competitor for the inexpensively priced (but unreliable) Lada, Russia aggressively hiked the import duty on used cars, which then doubled in terms of their ruble price, making them noncompetitive.[50] Yet this quick action to stave off a crisis for AvtoVAZ, Tolyatti, and Samara unexpectedly led to another crisis: protests by Russia's used-car importers.

Ironically, while the import tariffs were intended to protect jobs in one region and industry, they threatened jobs in another. In Vladivostok, a port city five hundred miles from Japan, importers, dealers, parts wholesalers, and mechanics had built a thriving industry from secondhand imports, which many viewed as a better purchase than newer domestic vehicles.[51] The industry had risen in part as a response to deindustrialization. As one auto dealer put it, "Here, there are no enterprises; all the factories have fallen apart. To feed ourselves—because here there are no other factories or enterprises and so forth—we had to go into the auto business."[52]

Some years earlier, protests by drivers and others prevented a planned halt to the use of right-hand-drive cars from Japan.[53] As a result of the import tariffs, by December 2008 protests by dealers and consumers of used cars broke out in a large number of cities in Russia, in what until then were some of the biggest street demonstrations since Putin had come to power. The largest protests were centered in Russia's Far East, especially Vladivostok, where thousands demonstrated in various protests in December and January.

In the first demonstration in Vladivostok in early December, an estimated two thousand protesters carried signs demanding "No to Taxes" and "Enough Coddling Oligarchs at the Expense of the People!"[54] During a protest in mid-December, drivers in Vladivostok blocked traffic in several locations, which led the regional parliament to vote to appeal to federal authorities for a reversal of the tariff.[55]

The protests clearly startled Russian leaders. A subsequent protest in Vladivostok in late December was broken up by riot police, who were flown in all the way from Moscow. Protesters (and journalists) were reportedly beaten, and over one hundred arrested, with organizers receiving intimidating phone calls warning them to avoid criticizing the government.[56]

Yet the repression had the opposite of the intended effect, as the protests quickly became politicized. As Mischa Gabowitsch described the situation, "the regional chairman of United Russia stepped down, the liberal and communist opposition parties declared their support for the protesters, and the protest wave led to the emergence of a new political movement, TIGR, that no longer focused on car-related topics but demanded the resignation of Russia's president and government."[57] Vladimir Bespalov, a Communist Party member who help organize the protest, described how repression contributed to politicization by uniting the opposition: "They threatened us. They pressured us. But our victory resulted from the fact that not just the Communist Party came out and participated, but rather a coalition of left-wing and right-wing opposition forces. They are frightened. For the first time in years, the central square is ours. This is the first victory of this coalition."[58]

As the protests continued into January, with banners that read "Kremlin, we are against you," the organizers' demands included the removal of Vladivostok governor Sergei Darkin, a return to the direct election of regional leaders, and the resignation of the federal government, with chants in the crowd calling for the resignation of Putin himself.[59] The protests in the Far East coincided with related protests in the western enclave of Kaliningrad. As Gabowitsch notes, "the scope of the protests and their rapid evolution from specific causes to general demands for political change came as surprises for the presidential administration and United Russia."[60]

For his part, Governor Darkin, a Putin appointee, argued that while he sympathized with those suffering as a result of the tariff, he also recognized that about two million workers were employed by Russia's automakers. "So of course, you have to protect the Russian auto industry."[61] Alexander Pikulenko, an auto industry analyst with the radio station Echo Moskvy, argued that the government was right to focus its support on the automakers rather than protests that were taking place far from Moscow: "As we know, revolutions never happen in the suburbs. They always happen in the capital."[62] While that may be true, the mere talk of revolution, stemming from the unintended result of actions taken to prevent social unrest elsewhere, must certainly have unnerved Russian leaders, particularly as the economic crisis continued.

The used-car import tariffs were not enough to save AvtoVAZ. In October 2008, Igor Sechin, then deputy prime minister and Putin's close associate, organized an industrywide brainstorming session on how to rescue AvtoVAZ, and he soon announced a $1 billion loan for the company from the state bank VEB.[63] Yet with about fifteen thousand workers sent on unpaid leave, more drastic action was needed. Putin, then prime minister, visited the plant in March 2009, soon after the import-tax protests. As Remington notes, while meeting with Samara's governor (and former head of AvtoVAZ), "Putin hardly needed to impress on Artiakov the point that maintaining employment at the firm and preserving social stability in the region were the governor's responsibility. (This was because, as Putin helpfully reminded him, 'there are about one million people living there who are tied to that enterprise')."[64] Putin told the plant's workers that he was buying a Lada-Kalina 4x4 (which, in the summer of 2010, he would drive with great fanfare from Khabarovsk to Chita). He made considerable promises of financial support for the factory. Among other assurances, he said in response to a question about the plant's kindergartens that the government would pay 621 million rubles for social programs that had long been paid for by AvtoVAZ. Putin added, "This is another gift to AvtoVAZ from the Russian government."[65]

Yet such promises by themselves hardly improved the situation. With the company teetering on bankruptcy, in 2009 the plant shut down for the month of August and reopened in September with only one of two shifts, with workers on half pay. The resulting pay cuts pushed lower-waged workers below the poverty line. When AvtoVAZ, with Renault now as a minority shareholder, announced that thirty thousand workers—over one-quarter of the workforce—would be let go, the government immediately intervened, initially banning the layoffs.[66] When the layoffs finally moved forward, twenty-seven thousand were said to be let go, close to half of whom were pensioners, another fifty-five hundred workers nearing retirement, and five thousand white-collar workers. Over nine thousand of those laid off were "given new jobs in subsidiary organizations under AvtoVAZ's auspices."[67] Thus, the Russian government eventually allowed the large layoffs to proceed but only after significant intervention and providing a massive bailout. Still, there were signs that workers' sentiments were simmering just below the boiling point. One assembly line worker described how many of his fellow disgruntled workers were banging on screw-in parts with hammers, effectively saying "I won't do the nut properly to spite my boss."[68] Rumors were circulating that while the pay of workers had been slashed, top bosses were still being paid lavish salaries.

With the plant's social situation and the outlay of such large subsidies unsustainable, the Russian state, AvtoVAZ managers, the Samara government, and the Renault corporation wrestled over a radical restructuring plan for the firm. The eventual agreement was reached in November, only "after heated arguments."[69] In the end, the Russian federal government would contribute an outlay of roughly 1.67 billion euros, while the Samara regional government would pay the wage costs of 14,600 former AvtoVAZ employees who now worked for two subsidiaries of AvtoVAZ.[70] Another scheme involved the relocation of AvtoVAZ workers and their families to a new industrial plant in Tikhvin, in Leningrad Oblast. The ICT financial industrial group, with state support, was set to employ thirty-five hundred laid-off workers from AvtoVAZ, with the company building housing for the new workers. While acknowledging the need for the state to assist relocating workers from depressed cities, Natalia Zubarevich noted the absurdity of creating a new company town: "They're exchanging one problem for another, and with state money. Tikhvin is a second Pikalyovo."[71]

The costly social services that the factory had long been responsible for were finally transferred to the local and regional governments. For its part, Renault promised to transfer its technology and production platform, valued at 240 million euros, for its Romanian-made Dacia automobile. Yet, in Traub-Merz's estimation, "Renault emerged the winner from this dispute." The rescue package, secured in the depth of the economic crisis, amounted to a paradigm shift. AvtoVAZ would now be "managed on commercial principles," with the plant's employment policy under the sole control of foreign management.[72]

Partly owing to state support, Russia's auto industry (and economy overall) soon rebounded from the 2008–9 recession. The government continued its support for the auto industry in 2010, using a "scrappage premium" for older cars in an attempt to boost sales of new vehicles. Likely with an eye toward renewed demand from Russian consumers, by 2012 Renault sought to leverage its position further. Investing an additional $742 million, Renault increased its ownership share (Nissan also invested some $376 million for a minority stake). With this, the Renault-Nissan alliance gained majority control, occupying eight of the fifteen seats on the supervisory board, and the right to name top management. In effect, the former Soviet auto giant became "a regional affiliate of an international company."[73]

While AvtoVAZ production rebounded from the plant's low levels of 2009, significant problems remained. Because of competition from Russian-based foreign car manufacturers, in 2013 the factory sold almost 20 percent fewer cars than the year before, and profits turned again to losses. AvtoVAZ was said to have reduced its payroll to sixty-six thousand workers by the end of 2013, though it remained unclear how many former workers were employed by the firm's subsidiaries or paid in some form by the federal or regional governments.[74] Nevertheless the firm was talking about further "massive sackings" involving an additional thirteen thousand workers.[75]

The Renault-Nissan alliance was headed at the time by Carlos Ghosn, subsequently notorious for fleeing Japan to avoid being arrested for withholding the full amount of his compensation from authorities. Ghosn had first risen to prominence in France in the 1990s when he engaged in radical restructuring of Renault through means that earned him the moniker of "Le cost killer." When subsequently asked about the nickname, he said, "It's sexy, there's blood in it, there's meanness."[76] When Renault acquired a stake in Nissan, Ghosn was sent to Japan to head the company. Despite mass layoffs then being a rarity in Japan, within months he closed five factories and cut about twenty-one thousand jobs, or about 14 percent of the workforce.[77]

In January 2014, with Putin's blessing, the management of Renault-Nissan brought in a new CEO for AvtoVAZ: Bo Inge Andersson, a Swedish national and former top manager at GM who was initially brought to Russia by the oligarch Oleg Deripaska to head the GAZ automobile factory in Nizhny Novgorod. There he gained a reputation for a willingness to slash costs and cut jobs. His plans were ambitious. In Andersson's words, "productivity [at AvtoVAZ] was 20 cars per employee per year in 2013. We should double it to 40 by year-end and 60 is our next target."[78]

Yet when oil prices dropped toward the end of 2014, just months after he took the helm, the Russian automobile industry again went into a deep tailspin. The economic contraction provided Andersson, as a foreign CEO focused on the bottom line, with even greater incentive to cut costs. Within two years, Andersson reduced employment in the plant still further, cutting the number of workers to forty-four thousand.[79] But a major focus of his cost-cutting measures was on the firm's suppliers. Shortly after the earlier crisis in 2009, Renault-Nissan management acknowledged in a report to the government that its cars were "of extremely low quality," though it blamed the firm's Russian suppliers, some of whom, stemming from Soviet practice, were monopolists.[80] By 2016, materials and components still made up about 75 percent of the cost of AvtoVAZ's cars.[81] From the view of a foreign CEO whose singular goal was to return the plant to profitability, the answer was straightforward: if the Russian suppliers couldn't deliver quality parts at affordable prices, then foreign producers would. Following this logic, Andersson linked AvtoVAZ to Renault-Nissan's purchasing organization and signed contracts with foreign auto-parts manufacturers, sharply reducing the level of local content in the Russian Lada.

The shift to an exclusively economic logic for the auto giant had profound consequences. As noted, Titov, the previous governor, while considered a pro-market reformer, had sought AvtoVAZ's help in developing the region's industry, but doing so depended on the use of local auto-parts suppliers. Sergei Tselikov, director of an agency that analyzed the Russian automobile sector, defended the previous government bailouts of AvtoVAZ based on the impact the firm had on parts suppliers. He warned, "The localization level of foreign models assembled in Russia does not exceed 10 percent, whereas the Lada is almost entirely made of Russian-made parts. If it collapses, a wave of bankruptcies may follow."[82] This raised a fundamental question: Was AvtoVAZ primarily a money-making firm within a multinational corporation that happened to be based in Russia, or was it primarily a large Russian employer in a company town that also sought to make a profit (or at least break even)? Under Andersson's leadership, the firm took a decisive turn toward the former position.

Layoffs and Their Consequences

The course charted by Andersson could hardly avoid a clash of cultures. For one, Andersson and his team had substantial complaints about AvtoVAZ's Russian workforce. According to the firm's vice president of corporate development, a Czech national brought in by Andersson, management did not need to "befriend" the workers:

> Our task is to show the path to the eager ones and bid farewell to the ones who don't want to follow it. There were about one thousand people working in these workshops a month ago. Maintenance teams for who knows what, people who had no idea what their job actually was. When we checked on them one day at 8:30 a.m. they were sleeping, playing chess, or just having tea. When we came again an hour later the only thing that changed was that they had locked the door. We kicked them all out.[83]

As Andersson himself complained to a team of Czech documentary filmmakers,

> Most people here think that everything was fine. So when I arrived, the problems started. And they actually think that. I mean, everyone was stealing enough to have a decent life, everyone expected that the government would bail them out, everyone understood that they could never be laid off. Now we have fired fifteen thousand people, and they know I will not stop.[84]

Not surprisingly, workers at the plant had a rather different perspective about the factory's work regime. As Andrey Kuranov, a twenty-seven-year-old working in the plant's chassis shop, recalled, "Andersson came in 2013, and started introducing all sorts of nonsense that our people couldn't understand—to get your bonus, you had to go to work constantly, you couldn't take a sick day, no days off for blood donation." He continued, "Everyone complained. Workers used to come to work with tears in their eyes."[85]

That same year, Anna Perova, a sixty-two-year-old transport worker who would later go on to chair the Edinstvo union at the plant, lost her fingers above her knuckles in a stamping press. A judge ruled that this was a "light injury" and awarded her 50,000 rubles ($1,500) in compensation. Since she could no longer work the press, her pay was cut by more than half. Six months later, in the same workshop, another worker lost three fingers in the press, and still another lost her whole hand.[86] Perova alleges that the injuries stem from workers being asked to work twelve-hour shifts. While the plant operates twenty-four hours a day, with three eight-hour shifts, workers are often asked to work an additional four hours of overtime. In November 2017, a fifty-eight-year-old worker leaving from his twelve-hour shift collapsed and died before the ambulance arrived. Three months later, AvtoVAZ workers reported through the Russian social media site VKontakte that a cutter at the factory had died while working an overnight shift. Production continued, and the body was simply covered up in the shop until the shift ended in the morning.[87]

What is remarkable is how, on the surface at least, the massive layoffs and other pressures at AvtoVAZ appeared to take place with limited backlash. The plant's main trade union, affiliated with the FNPR, lived up to its label as a "legacy union." While its membership was nominally large—said to be twenty-five thousand as late as 2017—and it retained from the Soviet past vast resources for providing social benefits, with representation on the local tripartite commission, it played an astonishingly minimal role in defending workers' interests during this tumultuous period. It had never organized a strike in its half-century of existence, preferring, its leaders said, to peacefully negotiate with management. Several of its leaders were said to occupy top posts at the plants.[88] The union reportedly stood by Andersson during the massive layoffs, conceding that this was the only way to get wage increases for the workers who would remain.[89]

Within AvtoVAZ there was a second, alternative union, known as Edinstvo (Unity), which had risen during a strike in 1989, still in the perestroika era, when the official union refused to back the strikers. Edinstvo thus became the first independent union in Russia's automobile industry, and it clearly exemplified Russia's more assertive alternative unions: 20 percent of its dues went toward a strike fund, and it led a number of labor actions through the 1990s.[90] By 2000 it claimed 3,425 members.[91] During the oil boom years, when the auto sector thrived, Edinstvo became more offensive-minded and helped found the MPRA. Yet AvtoVAZ's management sought to ignore Edinstvo, and it was excluded from the local tripartite commission. Thus, the unions at AvtoVAZ closely conform to the overall picture of Russia's union structure: the legacy union was large but largely compliant with management, whereas the alternative union was small but forceful and prone to protest. As Anna Perova, the transport worker who headed Edinstvo, explained, "since I joined Edinstvo, I tell everyone: 'Guys, until you start striking, you'll be treated like lambs to the slaughter.'"[92]

Yet over time successful strikes became more difficult to carry out, partly because of the firm's darkening economic prospects, but also because management increasingly used the legal restrictions on strikes to punish strikers. As Aleksei, an AvtoVAZ worker, explained, striking without legal backing left workers exposed: "The [union] chairman can come out with a flag, the people are with him, and then the people will get it in the neck." He continued: "Unions have had all their forms of protest removed. Today, the union is no one."[93] Workers who were not laid off were reportedly threatened with firing if they did protest.[94] As Viktor, another plant worker, complained, "There is a very bad mood in the factory now. To tell the truth, the workers are afraid. Daily we have to sign papers saying that we won't attend any gatherings. Any meetings. That we won't tell anyone anything."[95] Such pressures appeared successful: by 2010, a year after the global economic crisis and the first round of mass layoffs, Edinstvo's membership was reportedly down to three hundred, and by 2018, only around one hundred remained.

While repression is certainly part of the explanation for the lack of major unrest following the AvtoVAZ sackings, another significant factor appears to be the efforts aimed at softening the impact of the layoffs. While Tolyatti was a monotown with a population of over 700,000, where as late as 2009 the dominant factory employed close to 100,000 (with many more residents employed in subsidiary production and services), astonishingly, in 2016, when AvtoVAZ claimed to have slashed employment by more than half to 43,500 workers, the city's official unemployment rate was reportedly 2.3 percent.[96] As we have seen, Russia's official unemployment rate is grossly understated, and the director of the town's employment center said ten thousand residents were looking for work.[97] Even so, the fate of the other forty-five thousand or so former autoworkers remains a puzzle. As we have seen, earlier layoffs were aimed at those nearing pension age, with the plant promising to pay a supplement for a number of years to those agreeing to take an early pension. A substantial portion of workers were simply transferred to auxiliary enterprises within the AvtoVAZ orbit. By November 2015 Tolyatti was officially recognized as a category 1 (or "red") monotown, enabling it to apply for financial development aid from the Federal Monotown Development Fund and allowing it to create a special economic zone (TOSER) on its territory in the hope of attracting further investments.[98] By June 2016, the zone employed roughly twenty-five hundred people, and another zone in the area employed an additional thousand.[99] A significant number of workers may have migrated out of the town and region, with one report stating that Tolyatti had experienced a net emigration of five thousand residents in the first eight months of 2015 alone.[100] Yet such a level of outmigration is difficult to square with the available data: Rosstat's estimate of the city's population in 2017 was only nine thousand less than the results of the 2010 census. As Kuranov, the twenty-seven-year-old chassis shop worker, explained, "People say you need to leave Tolyatti. But where? Moscow? Petersburg? Who needs you there? There's no hills of gold there."[101]

Indeed, the main answer to the puzzle appeared to lie elsewhere: the director of Tolyatti's employment center conceded that as of March 2016, almost forty-five thousand of the town's residents were "employed in enterprises with temporary employment" (*na predpriiatiiakh s ogranichennoi zaniatost'iu*).[102] Whether such temporary employment was being funded by regional or federal budgets, or by AvtoVAZ, was left unexplained. By 2017, however, the firm—"in order to lower tensions on the labor market"—was pleading with the government to pay the costs for laid-off workers who had been transferred to the industrial park with "the preservation of their pay and social benefits" paid for by AvtoVAZ.[103]

Conflict

Not surprisingly, even with various measures such as temporary work and severance payments to soften the blow, the layoffs did lead to protests. Though their study is an aggregate one and doesn't examine the exact location and cause of each protest, Lankina and Voznaya found that from 2007 to 2012, after Moscow city and St. Petersburg, Samara recorded the most protests of Russia's many regions.[104] Not surprisingly, most of the AvtoVAZ protests were led by MPRA/Edinstvo.

The protests themselves did little to dampen Andersson's resolve. He grumbled to his managers about the protests, "Here people complain and cry like babies, and we give them something else. And people are smart because if they cry they get something. But I mean if you do nothing you should not have a good salary. Because you don't earn anything."[105]

Yet the most dramatic protests were led not by workers of AvtoVAZ but by those employed at the plant's parts suppliers, who were now being shut out through Andersson's economizing measures. Employees at the Volzhskii Machine-Building Factory, whose output was dependent on sales to AvtoVAZ, struck in February 2014 over wage arrears, but by the next year the plant, which had employed three thousand workers, was due to close altogether.[106] In 2016 workers at a whole range of enterprises in Tolyatti and nearby Zhigulevsk protested, mostly over wage arrears.[107] Workers at AvtoVAZagregat (AVA), AvtoVAZ's largest parts supplier, together with its three subsidiaries (AvtoVAZagregatTrans, PoshivAvtoVAZagregat, and AvtoVAZagregatPlast), led the most widely publicized protests. AVA and its subsidiaries halted production in June 2015 when its contract with AvtoVAZ was canceled. The company's twenty-three hundred workers were left abruptly without pay, though Russian law stated that laid-off workers were entitled to two-thirds of their former pay.[108]

The AVA workers began to protest and set up a "Workers' Initiative Group" led by longtime employee Antonina Larina. She pressed the workers' case at a meeting at the local prosecutor's office, which began a legal investigation.[109] While the representatives of a number of government agencies attended the meeting, AVA's management chose to ignore it. In further confirmation of the inability of the legacy unions to defend workers' interests, even during such an existential crisis, there is no mention of the plant's FNPR-affiliated union attending the meeting, even in the union's own newspaper. As the demands for the missing severance payments increased, the union told its workers that it was unable to get in contact with the factory management and suggested that the workers find another job.[110]

While the union was ineffectual, Larina continued to press the workers' case, and she soon found support from the local Communist Party (CPRF). Bolstered by the backing of an outside force, Larina began to suggest more direct action, such as blocking the highway connecting Tolyatti to Samara city. Her position was strengthened further when it became clear that AvtoVAZ was planning to lay off an additional ten to twenty thousand workers, raising the potential that worker protest could spread.[111]

Edinstvo/MPRA announced a new protest on September 20 with the demand that AvtoVAZ be renationalized. Their chosen date for the protest happened to coincide with the day that Alexei Navalny had set for his latest antigovernment protest. Not surprisingly, Tolyatti's authorities refused to sanction a protest on that date, yet a protest took place a week later, let by Edinstvo and CPRF. It attracted between seven hundred and fifteen hundred participants, a not insignificant number for a Putin-era protest in a provincial city. Protesters waved banners in support of AVA workers, but the demands went further, denouncing the "asocial policies" of AvtoVAZ management who continued to lay off workers.

Amid chants for "Strike!" "Nationalization!" "Out with the bourgeoisie!" Edinstvo chair Perova, wearing an MPRA jacket, took the microphone and addressed the crowd about how workers at the plant were being treated:

> It's like "you're the most honest, the most wonderful worker" if you come in according to the schedule. It doesn't matter if you're drunk, incapable, or lazy. What matters is you came. But now you have to work like me. Don't sleep! Go to the plant and work. And what do we get for that? Just kopeks. Peanuts! We don't need any kids who might fall ill, relatives or parents that can die. Someone will take them to the cemetery without your help. That is all disgusting! What's left to us? We are not allowed to get sick, we can just croak at the workplace and off to the cemetery with us.[112]

While protesters criticized the government, most of their ire was aimed at two individuals: Viktor Kozlov, the director of AVA, and Bo Andersson, the CEO of AvtoVAZ. Larina demanded that Kozlov give back the money he had stolen from workers and that he should "give the factory back to the workers." As for AvtoVAZ, the protesters began to argue that its problems stemmed from its being run by a foreign capitalist who "had no social obligations toward the workers." In their view, Andersson, whom many AvtoVAZ workers referred to as "that American," wanted to turn the factory into a "screwdriver department" for Renault-Nissan, where Russian workers would simply assemble cars from imported parts. The workers at the protest spoke fondly of an earlier time when AvtoVAZ was owned by the state, "before the plant was handed to the foreigners."[113] Needless to say, in the wake of Russia's seizure of Crimea and resulting sanctions and counter-sanctions, such criticisms arose alongside heightened tension between Russia and the West, as the Putin leadership sought to base its legitimacy less on economic performance and more on assertive nationalism.

When the FNPR union did finally respond, with a gathering of its own about a week or so after the Edinstvo/CPFR protest, it was a weak affair. Instead of red flags, those attending the union rally held Russian flags and banners with the AvtoVAZ logo. The event captured little attention, and according to local media, the speeches were simply read from printed texts and contained tepid demands. Those gathered looked puzzled as to why they were there, often glancing down at their watches. The local tripartite committee, which met on September 29, just two days after the larger protest, failed to even address the demands of AVA's workers.[114] Again, the legacy union in this case proved unwilling or incapable of acting as representatives of workers' interests before management, even to become a "shock absorber" during a period of intense conflict.

At a meeting of delegates to a conference of plant employees, Andersson adopted a critical tone. He began by saying that when he first arrived, he looked at the toilets, which were dirty, leaking, and without toilet paper. "I was told that this was AvtoVAZ's tradition. And for many years you accepted it." He then went on to cite the many changes he had brought to the plant. His speech was followed by that of a plant employee, who addressed the conference while Andersson, looking on uncomfortably, sat directly to his left. The speech was interrupted several times by applause:

> Greetings, dear delegates. You heard from the President of AvtoVAZ that the workers must be cherished, that he would dismiss a minimum number of people, and that Russian specialists deserve respect and they deserve good wages. It all ended up quite different. You may say that there were only one thousand people [recently] laid-off. But we all know that thousands of workers left because they'd been afraid that they'd be

made redundant. Yes, we've heard many times that compared to other factories, we have too many employees and too low productivity. But no one takes into account that AvtoVAZ is the last remaining Russian manufacturer capable of completing the entire car production cycle. All of this brings us to an unsettling conclusion: we will become just an assembly line for licensed foreign cars. Please think about that and save AvtoVAZ as a Russian manufacturer.[115]

While the protests had lost some steam by November 2015, at this point they reached the attention of Russia's leaders, who began to express concern about rising social tensions in Tolyatti. The ire of Sergei Chemezov, the head of Rostec, was raised by "pickets in Tolyatti." While at this point a minority shareholder in AvtoVAZ, Rostec was a powerful government entity, and Chemezov himself was a close personal friend of Putin. Chemezov became openly critical of Andersson's "throwing people on the streets." He added that while mass layoffs "may be a European practice, we consider this unacceptable; it's necessary to behave more responsively [*nado vesti sebia gibche*]."[116]

By January of 2016 CPRF leaders at the federal level began denouncing AvtoVAZ's leadership on nationalist grounds. In February Leonid Kalashnikov, a state Duma representative from Samara Oblast and CPRF member, who was the first deputy secretary of the Duma's committee on international affairs, published an "open letter" to Prime Minister Medvedev in which he accused the "foreign citizen" Andersson of "destroying the company" through a policy of ending contracts with Russian suppliers in favor of foreign ones. He complained that the official Renault-Nissan/Rostec alliance was registered as a legal entity in the Netherlands, a NATO member. Kalashnikov accused Rostec and Medvedev (who had visited Tolyatti earlier that month) of ignoring the plight of AvtoVAZ and AVA workers. In a fit of fury, he claimed Andersson was guilty of espionage and sabotage.[117]

By the next month, March 2016, Chemezov announced that Andersson would step down as AvtoVAZ CEO, just two years after he assumed the post. Part of the explanation for Andersson's being pushed out had to do with the continued financial losses at the plant. Despite the mass layoffs, AvtoVAZ reported losses of over 25 billion rubles ($686 million) in 2014, with the losses rising to 74 billion rubles ($1 billion) in 2015.[118] Losses were felt across Russia's auto industry as a whole, however, as demand dropped by 50 percent in the Russian car market from 2014 to 2015 along with the drop in oil revenues.[119]

But there were other compelling reasons why Andersson was removed from his post. A major concern was that his policy of integrating with foreign supply chains threatened the viability of Russian suppliers. Whereas Chemezov wanted technology from the Renault-Nissan alliance to upgrade the productivity of

Russia's parts manufacturers, Andersson simply viewed those firms as noncompetitive. This in turn threatened the interests of Rostec (and thus Chemezov), since among its holdings was United Automotive Technologies, the largest auto parts supplier in Russia, with about 40 percent of its sales going to AvtoVAZ.[120] Still, according to Traub-Merz, opposition to Andersson's management "stemmed largely from [his] radical personnel policy," with his Russian critics "prioritizing social concerns about jobs and localization interests over prices and quality considerations."[121] In particular, it was noted that since AvtoVAZ refused to purchase car seats from AVA, it "left the plant on the verge of bankruptcy."[122] Moreover, Andersson had sliced the number of employees from seventy thousand to forty-four thousand in just two years. Yet it was not simply the number of workers who had been let go that was being questioned; it was the manner in which that was done. According the Chemezov, even more workers had been laid off following the 2008–9 crisis, but Andersson let workers go with little concern for their retraining or reemployment. As the business newspaper *RBK* recounted Chemezov's words, during the 2008–9 round of layoffs, "there was no uproar [*shum*], it was a carefully structured process, we worked together with the regional authorities and the Ministry of Labor. We found new jobs, transferred people, provided them with training, they got a new profession."[123] What Chemezov left unspoken was the substantial cost to the government (as well as to AvtoVAZ) of preventing any uproar from the earlier layoffs.

Interestingly, Andersson's approach of steep job cuts combined with dropping ties to inefficient Russian parts suppliers appeared to do little to improve productivity at the plant. While the cuts in the number of workers were substantial, so was the drop in the plant's auto sales, so that the productivity increases—the number of cars produced per worker—were minimal. While in 2005 the plant produced 6.10 cars per employee, the number was only slightly better by 2016 (see figure 6.2).

The new AvtoVAZ director, Nicolas Maure, was also a foreigner, who had headed Renault's Dacia car factory in Romania. According to Lenta.ru, he might have caught the eye of AvtoVAZ's board because he had successfully reached a compromise during a major strike at Dacia, where over 80 percent of the workers were unionized.[124] As the new CEO, he changed the plant's social policy, initiating a program to provide funds to help dismissed employees start their own businesses, and another program to more efficiently redistribute workers within the firm, from overstaffed to understaffed departments. Once Maure was in place, AvtoVAZ planned to increase the share of local suppliers and to send twelve hundred workers to a new call center run by (state-owned) Sberbank, created in a building the plant no longer needed.[125] For employees willing to take early retirement, AvtoVAZ promised to subsidize their monthly pensions for a five-year period.[126]

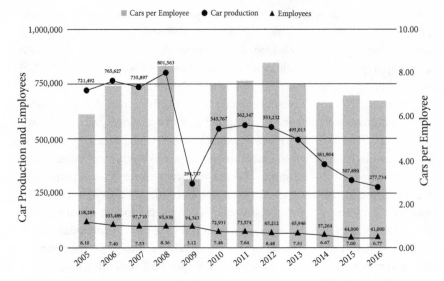

FIGURE 6.2.   AvtoVAZ car production per employee

Sources: Traub-Merz, "Automotive Industry in Russia"; Oica.net; Spark-Interfax system.

The replacement of Andersson with a new CEO more sensitive to work-ers' concerns appeared to dampen protest in Tolyatti for a time. Nonetheless, Maure was still the CEO of a firm majority-owned by the multinational alliance Renault-Nissan, and he was determined to cut labor costs further, though he explained the methods of doing so should be "softer."[127] As a result, the plant shifted to a reduced, four-day workweek for most of 2016. Moreover, Maure—who had earlier admitted that the Romanian strike was one of the most severe crises he ever faced—had plans to automate more production at the plant. As he put it, "robots don't strike."[128]

Still, AvtoVAZ's losses continued through 2016 (at 45 billion rubles) and the first quarter of 2017 (at a lower rate of 2.8 billion rubles). Wrestling also contin-ued over the amount of state subsidies to the firm. As noted, AvtoVAZ pleaded with the state to pay for the large number of workers who had been transferred to the industrial park and whose salaries and social benefits were still being paid by AvtoVAZ until sufficient investors were found to create new jobs there.[129] While Russia's labor and economic ministries wanted to maintain subsidies to the firm, the Ministry of Finance wanted to cut them to as little as 600 million rubles ($10 million) a year.

By mid 2017 the plant's position had improved somewhat, as had Russia's auto industry overall. For the first half of the year, AvtoVAZ recorded a tiny profit, the first since 2012. Still, some industry analysts cautioned that given Russia's dependence on the global oil market, there was no telling how long the trend would continue.[130] The recovery had been helped in part by government subsidies to reduce interest rates for auto loans, a program the government renewed in July 2017.[131]

Yet the change in AvtoVAZ management and the upswing in the auto industry came too late to help the workers of AVA, who were still seeking payment of the wages owed to them. They faced a challenge in that majority ownership of the firm was held by KopperBerg Ltd., an offshore company registered in the British Virgin Islands, and it appeared likely that any funds to pay the workers might have quietly slipped out of the country.[132] Media attention on AVA spurred by the protests continued, prompting Samara's governor, Nikolai Merkushkin, to take action.

Merkushkin had replaced Governor Artiakov in 2012. He was appointed by Putin from his position as governor of the Republic of Mordovia, where he had developed a reputation for strong-handed and paternalistic rule. In Samara that approach would eventually lead to scandal. Initially Merkushkin's actions brought satisfaction to some of AVA's workers. Viktor Kozlov, the CEO of AVA, was arrested at a Moscow airport, after which Merkushkin demanded that Kozlov's brother, Alexei—who happened to be the majority shareholder of KopperBerg—come to Samara to sign a document promising to pay the unpaid wages to AVA workers. When Alexei did so, his brother was released. Another legal case was opened against Viktor Kozlov. The AVA workers were paid in March 2016, and Merkushkin, through the Samara government, gave them each an additional "social benefit" payment of 10,000 rubles ($172).[133]

The problems were not fully resolved, however. Like Russian nesting dolls, just as AVA had been totally dependent on the much larger AvtoVAZ for its survival, the seven hundred workers of AVA's three smaller subsidiaries—AvtoVAZagregatPlast, PoshivAvtoVAZagregat, and AvtoVAZagregatTrans—had still not been paid, despite the governor's promises. In August 2016, in a scene that was captured on video, shared online, and then shown on national media, a worker from PoshivAvtoVAZagregat asked governor Merkushkin at a public forum in Tolyatti about the promised wage payments:

> [WORKER] Nikolai Ivanovich, I am a former worker with the long-suffering enterprise. I would like to know, when will our wages be paid? It's already been two years, and there have been so many promises. . . .
>
> [MERKUSHKIN] Well here's what I want to say. If you're going to talk in such a tone, [the answer is] never! Never! Go ask the people who are inciting you.

[WORKER] Excuse me please, but I believe I am speaking normally. Because this is already the second year without our wages.

[MERKUSHKIN] I know. You listen! You listen to me now. It's when the American ambassador came here to incite these people, and then within a month they revealed themselves to the whole world. The whole world![134]

Besides the rather incoherent nature of Merkushkin's outburst, his bullying attack on a female worker who was asking about wages that had been legally owed to her for over two years became scandalous.[135] Moreover, this occurred at a time when a number of Russian leaders were increasingly employing nationalist rhetoric in a transparent attempt to distract the population from economic concerns. Yet in claiming that complaints about wage arrears in a small firm in Tolyatti stemmed from a conspiracy hatched in Washington, Merkushkin raised such attempts to a patently absurd level.[136]

Needless to say, Merkushkin's outburst did little to satisfy AVA's unpaid workers. Two days after he denounced the worker complaining of wage arrears, eighty workers blockaded the highway between Tolyatti and Samara, though the protest ended quickly.[137] The following day, August 30, 2016, AVA was formally declared bankrupt, and it remains unclear if the workers from AVA's three subsidiaries ever received their pay. By September 2017 Merkushkin was removed from office, with the Russian press speculating he was removed at the behest of Rostec chairman Chemezov.[138]

What can we conclude from the case of AvtoVAZ and Tolyatti? Despite the massive layoffs at AvtoVAZ—which had downsized from close to one hundred thousand employees in 2006 to forty-one thousand ten years later—the feared social explosion did not happen. One might reasonably conclude that such fears were widely misplaced. A closer look, however, suggests a more complex interpretation. The government's first attempt to reduce social tensions at AvtoVAZ and other Russian automakers during the 2008–9 crisis was to raise taxes on the imports of used cars, yet this led to a protest movement in the Far East that was put down with repression and quickly became radicalized, however briefly. While the layoffs that did occur during the crisis were made without an "uproar," as Chemezov later boasted in explaining why Andersson was fired, doing so required massive subsidies, paid by both the Russian government and AvtoVAZ. A further large round of layoffs followed, especially once another crisis hit the auto industry in 2014, but only at the behest of a foreign CEO, who soon became the target of workers' ire. That same CEO, operating on market principles as the representative of a multinational corporation, caused further distress by effectively bankrupting

Russian parts suppliers that had been de facto subsidiaries of AvtoVAZ. That AvtoVAZ was repeatedly bailed out, while AVA was left to bankruptcy, illustrates how large firms in Russia are kept afloat through state intervention, but smaller and medium-size firms come and go largely on their own. In this case, however, workers from the smaller firms protested. While this hardly led to a social explosion, it gained national media attention. This is the very outcome, as we have seen, that regional and national elites seek to avoid, as it leads to unwelcome scrutiny and, as in this case, can cause governors to lose their jobs.[139]

That protests reached such a threshold stemmed in large part from the fact that, despite the paternalistic efforts of management and government to deal with the various predicaments, workers themselves were largely shut out of the process. Even in a case of existential crises for these workplaces—massive layoffs in the case of AvtoVAZ, bankruptcy and unpaid wages for the workers of AVA—Russia's legacy unions, by far the largest official representative of their interests, failed to provide them with any visible defense. Some twenty-five years after the end of the Soviet system, these unions continued to view themselves as something of a "transmission belt" between management and workers, rather than as advocates of workers in an adversarial relationship with managers, particularly during times of cutbacks and layoffs. Alternative unions, in this case MPRA/Edinstvo, with fewer members and resources, were effectively shut out of the tripartite process. Short of protest, this left no institutional channel for workers to express their grievances during what was for most of them perhaps the most dramatic period of their working lives.[140]

Since workers in a firm headed for bankruptcy have little recourse to the strike weapon—production is already halted after all—the goal of protest becomes seeking media attention for their plight. This AVA workers did by joining with members of the "systemic opposition" (the local CPRF) and suggesting a possible alliance with the "nonsystemic opposition" (calling for a demonstration on the same day as Alexei Navalny's planned nationwide protests). While the number of AVA workers was small, when their protest demands coincided with those of workers at AvtoVAZ—where another round of layoffs was announced, signaling the potential for larger protests to follow—their cause got national media attention, and their protests appeared to spur Rostec head Chemezov's criticisms of Andersson, soon leading to his departure.

While Andersson was for a time a convenient scapegoat for the Russian government, AvtoVAZ's problems have hardly been solved. Tens of thousands of workers have been let go, and the extent of government intervention and the cost of subsidies (both past and present) have been substantial. While the AvtoVAZ workers' criticism of Andersson ("that American") may have appeared xenophobic, it was also a pretty accurate assessment of the dilemma the plant faced.

The problems caused by Andersson's approach to management—which Che-mezov criticized as alien to Russia—pointed to a fundamental impasse: Was the former Soviet auto giant AvtoVAZ simply another profit center for a foreign mul-tinational, or was it to remain a source of employment and pride for the people of Tolyatti? More broadly, the case demonstrated a significant challenge for Russia's political economy: How does it satisfy the demands of foreign capital in order to attract sufficient investment and technology to move beyond a dependence on raw commodities exports, while meeting the social expectations of workers and society at large, and the regime's own need for stability and political survival?

The mass layoffs at AvtoVAZ were not (at least to date) politically destabiliz-ing. One might argue that if the Putin team could survive such layoffs at Russia's largest monotown, it has little to fear about unrest elsewhere. Yet there are rea-sons to question that assessment. The Russian state has devoted enormous subsi-dies over the years to AvtoVAZ and continues to employ various schemes to prop up Tolyatti. Put another way, by paying close attention, the Russian government was able to buttress its largest and most visible monotown. But there are literally hundreds of others, and one wonders how many will get similar attention.

Still, the protests that did take place in Tolyatti have been limited. So far, the potential for labor protests to grow from local social and economic demands to more radical demands that could become politically destabilizing would appear to be largely theoretical. Yet in the next chapters we will explore the reasons why Russia's leadership fears such a scenario and see, through the example of the rapid politicization of Russia's truck drivers, that such a scenario is not merely theoretical.

THE SPECTER OF A COLOR
REVOLUTION

Even with everything discussed so far—the problems of extremely flexible and often exceedingly low wages, the chronic problems of monotowns, the lack of institutional outlets for worker grievances leading to spontaneous and at times extreme outbursts, the significant state interventions and subsidies that were needed to prevent the crisis at AvtoVAZ and Tolyatti from exploding—one might argue that it remains far from clear that workers present a real threat to Russia's ruling elite. Tolyatti is the biggest of Russia's monotowns, and while the interventions there might have been costly, most other monotowns are considerably smaller, and many are isolated, almost by definition. When crises do flare up, leading to significant protest, as in Pikalyovo, Russia's president can swoop in with a timely intervention, appearing in the role of the savior. Unions, for reasons we have seen, are hardly well positioned to lead a strong protest movement. The so-called color revolutions that have removed leaders in postcommunist states from power have typically centered on allegations of electoral fraud, and—at least until the Belarus protests (explored in chapter 9)—rarely have workers played a central role. Moreover, and one hardly needs to add, in Russia as in other states with authoritarian tendencies, repression can be quite effective. In short, outside of a major economic catastrophe such as Russia experienced in the 1990s, widespread labor protest leading to political destabilization would appear to be a low-probability event.

All these factors notwithstanding, however, while political destabilization from any source might not be a likely outcome for Russia's leaders, they can hardly rule it out. I have discussed in theoretical terms the challenges to authoritarian and hybrid regimes stemming from economic-based protests in particular. Here I spell out in greater detail the Russian leadership's fear of labor and related social-economic protest, the challenges such protests pose, and the specific steps taken to prevent such protest. In short, I seek to answer the following: How can a state be so strong, yet so afraid?

Defending Stability in Tough Times

Putin came to power in 1999 as the prime minister serving a deeply unpopular President Yeltsin. While Yeltsin survived the wave of protests in the late 1990s, the entire Yeltsin government and entourage were, in the public's mind, deeply implicated in the cataclysm of the 1990s, especially the huge increase in poverty and the rapid privatization that was widely viewed as enriching a handful of oligarchs. When Putin assumed the presidency in early 2000, many observers believed he was given the post in order to protect the Yeltsin "family"—those most closely associated with Yeltsin, including powerful oligarchs—from prosecution and possible loss of their assets.

As president, Putin soon made the promise of "stability," in contrast to the chaos of the 1990s, a cornerstone of his claim to legitimacy.[1] The perceived threats to that stability began early on. Already in 1999, the NATO bombing of Russia's longtime ally Serbia outraged even pro-Western liberals in Russia.[2] That action directly contributed to the overthrow of Slobodan Milošević the following year, in the first of the color revolutions. For Russia's new leadership, this suggested a twofold threat to stability: an external threat, from Western governments seeking "regime change," and an internal threat, in that foreign influences sought to provoke domestic populations into rising up against their own governments. The "Bulldozer Revolution" in Serbia was soon followed by the "Rose Revolution" in Georgia in 2003, the "Orange Revolution" in Ukraine in 2004, and the "Tulip Revolution" in Kyrgyzstan in 2005.

For the leaders of Russia and other post-Soviet states, witnessing governments in neighboring countries fall through mass protest was hardly a welcome experience. Thus, what has been described as the "creeping authoritarianism" of Putin's presidency did not take place in a vacuum. Russian (and other post-Soviet) leaders began to engage in "preemptive authoritarianism," seeking to eliminate threats before they arose.[3] Putin's government enacted restrictive electoral reforms in 2005 and a law to curtail NGOs in 2006. The Russian leadership created its own youth movement, Nashi, to counter the youth movements that were seen as driving the color revolutions in other countries. With such concerns in mind, Kremlin leaders began overtly to question the legitimacy of liberal democracy, alleging that it was a foreign influence alien to Russian culture.[4]

Given such anxieties over foreign intervention and youth-led protests, any threat from workers would appear to be a lower-level concern. As we have seen, however, the challenge posed by workers began before Putin came to power and predated any concern with color revolutions. By the mid-1990s, it was clear that the nonpayment of wages and the resulting protests reflected the failure of trade unions or other institutions to effectively channel the grievances of workers and others in a time of wrenching social change. As Simon Clarke noted at that time, this "underlies the dual fear that the bulk of the population will, in its passive moment, vote for the authoritarian leader who can make the most radical promises and, in its active moment, take to the streets in outbursts of mass civil unrest."[5] The crisis of wage arrears reached its apex in 1999, just as Putin became prime minister. As we saw in chapter 5, coal miners and others protesting unpaid wages led the "rail wars" that helped push the Russian government to devalue the ruble, and that action led to a steep decline in living standards and a still greater spike in wage arrears, leading to still more strikes and protests. Thus, Putin first came to power just as a major wave of labor protest was cresting.

The economic growth that opportunely coincided with Putin's assumption of office helped stave off immediate fears of mass protest. Yet the new government hardly remained passive. As we have seen, Putin soon made the nonpayment of wages a serious crime, but he also significantly revamped Russia's labor code, severely restricting the right to strike, hindering the more militant alternative unions, with the result that the FNPR became increasingly loyal to Putin's leadership. By 2002, Irene Stephenson, the Russian-based representative of the AFL-CIO, which had sought to improve labor rights in the country by assisting alternative unions (while deliberately avoiding the FNPR), was denied entry at a Moscow airport "based on information provided by the FSB."[6]

To be sure, labor protest was hardly the only concern in the minds of Russia's leadership as Putin consolidated his power. Over time Putin successfully subdued the Duma, rebellious regional elites, independent oligarchs, and the media. Labor protest receded as the economy improved, which not only vanquished wage arrears but led to significant wage increases. These wage increases, and economic growth generally, unquestionably contributed to the popularity of Putin's leadership.[7] In an echo of the Brezhnev era, as Richard Sakwa argued, Putin had built a new "type of 'social contract' whereby the government promised rising standards of living in exchange for restrictions on independent popular political participation."[8] Petrov, Lipman, and Hale specified this further as a "non-intrusion pact" between state and society: a promise of "steady economic growth, Russia's perceived return to global leadership, a sense of stability, nonintrusive government, and a feeling that the country is being guided by a strong and capable leader" in exchange for society's staying out of politics.[9]

Still, economic growth did not remove the threat of labor protest entirely. Rather, as with the automobile sector, by the mid-2000s workers in profitable industries became more militant, and through more "pro-cyclical" strike activity began to advance demands for improved working conditions and a greater share of profits.

Yet with the global economic crisis of 2008, labor protest reappeared as a major threat, as the crisis revealed that little effort had been made during the boom years to resolve Russia's various labor dilemmas, all the more so since the Putin regime had sought to legitimate its power by emphasizing "stability."

With the crisis, the status quo became untenable, and the measures taken to prevent its worsening impact were profound. According to Konstantin Gaaze, "in July 2008, as the financial crisis took hold in the United States, Russia's oligarchs—oil executives, steelmakers, retailers, and industrialists—had started asking the government for support." By October of that year, "the crisis suddenly took on a social dimension: the country's large corporations started threatening the government with mass layoffs."[10] As we have seen, measures were implemented to prop up the auto industry, including the tax on the imports of used cars, which itself led to significant—and quickly politicized—protests in Russia's Far East. The crisis also spurred the huge bailout of AvtoVAZ, followed by the Renault corporation taking greater control over Russia's largest auto producer. Much focus was placed on Russia's other monotowns, particularly after Putin's intervention in Pikalyovo. As described by Daniel Treisman, "After the disorienting first months [of the crisis], the Kremlin settled on a political strategy. The focus was on using the media to show that Putin was personally in command and—as prime minister—was energetically fighting the fires as they arose, in a style that became known as 'manual control.'"[11]

Yet beyond the specific steps taken to avert particular emergencies, a new "Putin coalition" formed in response to the overall crisis. According to Gaaze, the process "resembled a collection of economic and social prosthetics," leading to "an unimaginable alliance of workers, state employees, and capitalists whose economic interests did not always coincide." As signaled by the "bending of the oligarch" Deripaska in Pikalyovo (chapter 4), the rules of the game changed for business elites, who were told to avoid mass layoffs despite the steep drop in demand, and as a result they "moderated their appetites regarding commercial viability of production." Yet "in exchange, they received cheap loans from government banks worth billions of rubles."[12] Under the language of the "social responsibility of business," economic incentives shifted away from market signals and more toward political connections, where "public-private partnerships" in practice meant competing with rivals for greater government support. Labor protest was thus kept in check, and support for Putin grew from "workers of the enterprises that Putin's administration had favored, saved, and supported." According to Gaaze, by 2017 "the much-touted figure of 86 percent approval ratings for Putin was born not only thanks to the annexation of Crimea, but also because of the money that Putin's administration spent in the late 2000s to fight the financial crisis."[13]

Moreover, for Gaaze the increasing state control (*ogosudarstvleniia*) of the economy in response to the 2008 crisis led to the "accidental formation of Russia's war coalition" that made war and confrontation with the West possible in 2014. Undoubtedly, the perceived poor performance of Russia's military during its brief 2008 war with Georgia led to calls for increased military spending. Such demands were strengthened during the crisis by struggling enterprises producing military goods and employing large numbers of people (chapter 3). Over time, greater state support for various firms and industries led to demands for greater protectionism and less reliance on Western capital markets and therefore less concern about subsequent sanctions and counter-sanctions.

The government's response to the 2008–9 crisis appeared to be quite effective in the short run, and the Russian economy recovered fairly quickly. Yet the state support for industry, while beneficial to certain groups, was not perceived as such by all. Despite the rebound in economic growth, popular support for Prime Minister Putin and President Medvedev continued to sag, leading to lower approval ratings from 2008 to 2011.[14] Some argued that the connection between economic growth and political legitimacy, which the Putin leadership had enjoyed from 2000 to 2008, had become decoupled, helping to contribute to the protest wave of 2011–12.[15]

Thus while the foundation of Putin's subsequent return to sky-high approval ratings may have been laid by state support for industry and its workers during the 2008 crisis, the protest movement that burst forth in Moscow and St. Petersburg in December 2011 was most often credited to the political awakening of Russia's urban middle class.[16] As the political commentator Yevgenia Albats told the *New York Times*, "Today we have proved that civil society does exist in Russia, that the middle class does exist and that this country is not lost."[17] The phrase most often heard in Russia to describe this group was the "creative class," meant to denote educated, internet-savvy urbanites, the kind said to reside in vibrant "global cities." Liberal reformers inside and outside Russia placed much hope that this new middle class—concerned more with political freedoms than base economic issues—would galvanize opposition to the Putin regime. The labeling of these protests as "middle class" has been challenged on various grounds, however. Bryn Rosenfeld for one found that "state-sector professionals" were significantly less likely to join the protests, suggesting that they might form another part of the "Putin coalition."[18]

Nevertheless, without question the protests were a grave shock to Russia's leadership. They significantly added to existing fears of a color revolution. The Arab Spring revolutions, beginning in 2011, just months before the Russian protests, only increased this fear, as seemingly unshakable authoritarian regimes proved susceptible to mass protests that arose unpredictably, seemingly out of nowhere.

Yet Russia's 2011–12 protest wave, while certainly dramatic in the Russian context, crested fairly quickly, without anything approaching a color revolution. It did so in large part because the abstract political demands of the protesters—for fair elections and a "Russia without Putin!"—did not match up with the more concrete socioeconomic concerns of much of Russia's population, especially those residing outside of Moscow and St. Petersburg. Indeed, there was much speculation that Putin's core support came from the working class in Russia's provinces, based on certain shared values. Krastev and Holmes argued that Putin won the March 2012 presidential election "by mobilizing antimodern Russia against modern Russia, and by mobilizing the countryside against Moscow."[19]

There is evidence to suggest however that such a narrative was overly simplistic and that Putin was already having trouble maintaining support in Russia's hinterlands. Focus group studies in sixteen Russian regions, carried out by the Center for Strategic Research in Moscow, found that while provincial Russians were fiercely nonideological and much less concerned with the abstract slogans of protesters in the capital, they were "most concerned with the state's dwindling ability to provide essential services, such as health care, education, housing, personal security, and effective courts" and expressed deep skepticism that national politicians could provide such services effectively.[20] Likewise, assessing surveys from the Levada Center, Treisman finds that when Putin's approval ratings began to decline in 2010, "support for the Kremlin fell quite uniformly, declining in all social, economic, and geographic categories" and thus not just from the "creative class" in Moscow and St. Petersburg. In fact, by late 2011, the lowest approval ratings for Putin and Medvedev were found not in the two largest cities, but in large provincial cities. "Expressed readiness to protest was also higher in the provincial cities."[21] While none of this speaks directly to working-class support, it does suggest that the level of material conditions in, and federal support for, Russia's regions matters greatly to regime legitimacy. Moreover, a study of "the calculus of non-protest in Russia" found that while there were many protests in the country from 2000 to 2013, most were local protests over socioeconomic issues. While about 20 percent of the population was ready to engage in "political" protests, the remaining 80 percent or so was either against democratic reforms or indifferent to them. The authors of the study found that the reason for this hesitancy from the bulk of the population was connected to their "concerns over the highly uncertain redistributive consequences of political reforms"—in other words, their fears that political liberals would bring back the economic liberalism of the 1990s, with adverse effects on their standard of living.[22] In this view, the protest behavior in Russia's regions stemmed less from provincial prejudice than from a rational calculation of the material well-being to be gained by backing the current regime rather than the political opposition. Yet with the end of the boom years of the 2000s, a change in that calculus posed a potential challenge to Russia's leaders.

Doubtlessly recognizing this, Putin sought to respond to the 2011–12 protests by playing on tropes he had long employed, seeking to widen the cultural divide between liberal intellectuals and more traditional Russians in the country's provinces. Clearly Putin has long appealed to significant segments of Russian society by projecting an image of a strong male figure, riding shirtless on a horse through the taiga, among many other publicized feats of machismo.[23] The projection of Putin as a real Russian *muzhik* resonated in particular with a male working class that suffered a loss in social status as well as material well-being in the 1990s and which continued to struggle with the changes in work and life brought about by Russia's further insertion into the global capitalist economy.[24] In speaking with male workers in Russia, one often hears Putin praised as decisive, as someone who gets things done, as in "the guy said what he was going to do, and then he did it" (*muzhik skazal, i muzhik sdelal*).

This ability to connect as a strong and culturally recognizable figure to working-class men (and often women) became even more useful as a contrast to the allegedly more effete cosmopolitan intelligentsia that led the 2011–12 protests. The very public prosecution of Pussy Riot soon followed, alongside the promotion of the Russian Orthodox Church as the defender of traditional conservative values. United Russia's law against homosexual "propaganda" in opposition to the libertine morality of Western societies soon followed.[25]

While the 2011–12 protests were still under way, Putin also sought to more directly exploit class (and regional) resentments to discredit the protesters. This approach became clear in the heavily publicized remarks of Igor Kholmanskikh, a foreman from the Urals tractor and tank factory Uralvagonzavod.[26] As described at the beginning of this book, Kholmanskikh appeared on national television in December 2011 during one of Putin's "direct line" call-in shows while the first protests were under way. Standing on the factory floor surrounded by his fellow workers and referring directly to the protests,

Kholmanskikh stated that "if the militia . . . can't handle it, then me and the guys [*muzhiki*] are ready to come out and defend stability."

The Kremlin played up this event considerably. As part of Putin's reelection campaign, the plant's roughly thirty thousand workers were mobilized: "Activities included pro-Putin webpages, participation in pro-Putin rallies, and 'corporate voting.'"[27] After his reelection to the presidency in 2012, Putin reconnected with Kholmanskikh and Uralvagonzavod workers on a "tele-bridge" broadcast where he accepted Kholmanskikh's congratulations and thanked him and his workers for their "common victory." While the workers were pictured on and around a tank, Putin added that Kholmanskikh and the plant's workers had shown by their actions that they were "two levels of intellect higher" than the protesters. Their actions, he continued, showed that "the real Russian people, the Russian working man, the man of labor [*chelovek truda*] . . . are a head taller than any do-nothings, than any chatterbox."[28] In a widely publicized step, Putin later appointed Kholmanskikh—despite his lack of relevant credentials—as the presidential representative for the Urals Federal Region.[29] For his part, Kholmanskikh, whom one pro-Kremlin pundit called "the samurai of Tagil" (Uralvagonzavod is located in Nizhnii Tagil), took to organizing events such as a roundtable discussion about "the man of labor," where he defended his "workers' counterrevolution."[30]

Putin apparently continued to view industrial workers as a central part of his political base as he prepared for his 2018 reelection campaign. He chose to announce his intention to run for reelection at the GAZ automobile factory in Nizhnii Novgorod, at a celebration of the plant's eighty-fifth anniversary. In response to a question from one of the plant's workers about his plans for the election, Putin responded, "There is probably no better place or better occasion to make such an announcement." "Everyone in this audience, without exception, supports you," replied a worker.[31]

Employing language from the Soviet period, one might say there were "objective" reasons for Russia's industrial and state-sector workers to support Putin's leadership, beyond their ideological leanings or their limited worldviews (as liberal oppositionists sometimes alleged). Speaking in the broadest possible terms, as long as economic growth was sufficient, both the government and workers in "second Russia" shared an interest in maintaining the status quo. Russia's elite could continue extracting rents, and workers could count on jobs and at least some modest increase in income. Particularly given the lack of a mechanism whereby workers and other segments of society could negotiate with the government over policy outcomes, a destabilizing political crisis was something to avoid.

Indeed, while Kholmanskikh became a human embodiment of Putin's working-class support, there were reasons to view this support as more conditional and

transactional than one based on shared traditional values. In his original statement during the 2011 call-in show, Kholmanskikh preceded his talk of support
for Putin with this remark: "Mr. Putin, you visited our plant in hard times and
helped us. . . . Today, thousands of people at our plant have work, get paid for
their work and have a good outlook for the future. This stability is important to
us. We don't want to return to the past."[32]

After the election, Putin not only elevated Kholmanskikh but rewarded Uralvagonzavod in concrete terms. He went to the plant in one of his very first post-
election trips and announced that the government would purchase twenty-three
hundred "new generation" tanks from the factory, for which it would pay the
factory in advance in full. The announcement contradicted earlier Ministry of
Defense statements about tank purchases, and the promised 100 percent prepay-
ment ran counter to standard practice for defense orders, which typically require
firms to take out loans.[33]

By 2015, however, economic conditions at the factory had changed, and Uralvagonzavod was faced with bankruptcy.[34] The plant has struggled for survival
since, partly because its business model relies on the sale of railcars as well as state-
ordered tanks, and in February 2016, railcar (but not tank) workers had their pay
cut by one-third, and in June, three thousand workers were furloughed.[35] That
same year the plant was brought under the control of Rostec.

Putin continued to visit the plant, most recently after his 2018 presidential
election victory. But given the more challenging economic conditions, the positive impact of such attention from the top was clearly wearing off, as residents
began to complain bitterly about their hardships. As Morozov, a welder at the
plant, put it, "We've needed a change at the top for a long time now."[36] More
troubling still were reports that by February 2019 five of the plant's workers
had committed suicide. That month, in the latest of those acts, a twenty-seven-
year-old cutter had hanged himself at the plant after a meeting with managers.[37]
In such circumstances, it was hard to imagine how many Uralvagonzavod workers were now willing to "defend stability."

Indeed, while the Russian economy had recovered fairly quickly from the deep
recession in 2008–9, economic growth failed to return to the levels that Russians
had grown accustomed to from 1999 to 2008. By the end of 2012, growth began
to stagnate, and by 2014 the country headed into another recession. The Russian
leadership was faced with the challenge of seeking an alternative source of legitimacy in place of the dynamic economic growth that, outside of the 2008–9 crisis,
Russians had enjoyed since Putin first came to power.

Yet in 2014 another event directly challenged the stability that the Putin leadership sought to project. Ukraine's Maidan uprising led to another color revolution, as the pro-Russian president of Ukraine, Viktor Yanukovych, was forced to

flee the country. To this, Russia's leadership reacted with the seizure of Crimea, the fomenting and supporting of armed separatists in Ukraine's Donbass region, and the ramping up of nationalist rhetoric and propaganda inside Russia. This was soon followed by Western sanctions that were imposed in response to Russia's actions in Ukraine, and then by the drop in global oil prices in mid-2014, which only deepened Russia's economic woes.

Thus, it would appear that Russia had moved to a militarized basis for legitimacy. Putin's approval ratings famously shot up from roughly 60 percent to over 80 percent following its takeover of Crimea. In the words of Gleb Pavlovsky, the Ukrainian revolution led Russia's leaders to implement a "Russian counter-revolution," seeking to inoculate Russian society from a revolution of its own.[38] According to Vladimir Ryzhkov, Putin's "first social contract in the early and mid-2000s was based on the principle that most Russians would accept the government's restrictions on personal freedoms and democracy as long as they received higher standards of living." But the seizure of Crimea shifted the focus of most Russians onto another value: "returning Russia to its great-power status," which gave Putin's legitimacy a "second wind."[39]

During his fieldwork in Russian working-class communities, Jeremy Morris reports that his informants almost uniformly supported Russia's seizure of Crimea. Even in Tolyatti, despite the massive downsizing at AvtoVAZ, the economic hardship did not appear to dent the strong support residents gave to Putin. Indeed, the Kremlin's nationalist rhetoric helped shift the blame for AvtoVAZ's mass layoffs to the company's foreign managers. Even the leader of Edinstvo, the alternative union at AvtoVAZ (and part of MPRA), argued in 2016 that "the nationalistic, patriotic, imperial sentiments hold sway. If you're talking about Putin, people support him," adding that in assessing Putin, "they don't pay attention to their own impoverished existence."[40]

This shift to a legitimacy based on restoring Russia to great-power status built upon the socially conservative and patriarchal ideology Putin had already increasingly relied on. Such was the cultural context as Putin repositioned himself yet again as a figure standing up to the West following the seizure of Crimea.

Over time, however, it became increasingly clear that nationalism and pride in Russia's resurgence on the global stage, as well as the emphasis on traditional paternalistic values, could not long overcome the experience of many Russians of a stagnating standard of living. In the Russian metaphor, the television—the ideology of state propaganda—began losing out to the refrigerator—the material struggles of everyday life. Moreover, that propaganda could appear patently absurd, as when Samara's governor Merkushkin accused a woman asking about wage arrears of being tied to a foreign plot connected to the US ambassador. By the fall of 2017, Yevgenii Gontmakher argued that the slogan "Crimea is ours!"

had lost its "festival-like character" and had become no more evocative than say-ing "Kaliningrad is ours!"[41] As Smyth and Soboleva note, "Polling data suggest that the pool of reliable voters secured by symbolic politics—while cohesive—is considerably smaller than the support yielded by sustained economic growth."[42]

The All-Important "Social Sphere"

Thus, while the shift from political legitimacy based on economic performance to one buttressed by social conservatism and assertiveness in foreign affairs pro-duced a sharp spike in popular support, such a "rally round the flag" effect was always going to be temporary. The problem for Kremlin leaders was that while nationalist values resonated with many Russians, the core concerns of the bulk of the population lay elsewhere. Those concerns have long centered on socioeco-nomic issues. Denis Volkov, a sociologist and expert at the Levada Center, Russia's leading independent polling agency, states this quite clearly: "During a quarter of a century of sociological surveying, the majority of Russians have been con-cerned primarily by economic issues: inflation, low wages, insufficient social pay-ments (up to 70 percent of people), poverty, destitution, declines in the standard of living (up to 50 percent), and the risk of unemployment (up to 40 percent)."[43]

This fundamental point has repeatedly been missed by Russia's liberal opposi-tion, whose 2011–12 protest slogans focused overwhelmingly on abstract politi-cal issues and thus failed to mobilize the rest of a seemingly complacent society. But as Volkov notes, "half of the population wants changes, although they are not the changes that the democratic community is talking about." He added, "The majority of supporters of reform want changes in the social sphere rather than in politics." As Sil and Chen put it, "Although public opinion surveys generally indicate a preference for some form of 'democracy' in the abstract, much more significant are the substantive expectations that a state, democratic or not, ought to be able to do a better job in providing such valued public goods as social order, economic stability, guaranteed welfare and a greater measure of distribu-tive justice."[44]

If the Kremlin leadership actively promotes a politics that is culturally to the right on the political spectrum, much of Russia's opposition promotes a future that is not only more politically liberal but economically liberal as well. Yet polling data demonstrate that a clear plurality of Russians continue to prefer a "mixed" economy of planning and market, with more of the remainder prefer-ring a planned to a market economy. Indeed, surveys have consistently shown a social democratic if not socialist orientation as the dominant one in Russian society.[45] According to the Levada Center's Aleksei Levinson, "If we take the left to mean socialist ideas in the strictest sense . . . then these represent the most widespread views in the bulk of the population. . . . I believe that the dominant views here are without a doubt [those of] the left."[46]

There has been a surprising lack of successful political parties on the left of the spectrum in Russia, with the revealing exception of the Communist Party of the Russian Federation (CPRF). While the CPRF may have been Russia's largest opposition party since the early 1990s, it is considered to be part of the "systemic" (and hence nonthreatening) opposition and for years suffered from the perennial and uninspiring leadership of Gennadi Zyuganov, who, rather than run unsuccessfully for the presidency for the fifth time, finally yielded his place in the March 2018 presidential elections to a younger but still uninspiring candidate. More tellingly, beginning in the mid-1990s, the CPRF began to speak of the "nation" as much or even more than "class," so that despite being the one nominally left party of any prominence in Russia, it became vulnerable to the even more patriotic discourse of Putin, whose policies the CPFR has largely supported.[47] Interestingly, when CPRF deputy Kalashnikov sharply denounced the government's handling of AvtoVAZ, he did so largely along nationalistic grounds.

Thus, while the promotion of conservative and nationalist values has helped provide legitimacy to Putin, it would only be a slight exaggeration to say that for Russia's leadership, social policy represents a minefield. The notion of a welfare state ("*sotsial'noe gosudarstvo*") is enshrined in Russia's constitution, and the polling data make clear that while most Russians are not very concerned about politics, they are centrally concerned with socioeconomic issues, with clear expectations that the state is responsible for a providing a certain (if minimal) level of social welfare. As Holm-Hansen and colleagues put it, "delivering social welfare in amounts and ways in line with the population's expectations is one of the pillars upon which the current Russian regime bases its legitimacy."[48] Moreover, there is evidence that the Russian population's concerns for state-supplied social welfare, rather than waning as some Soviet-era vestige, increased after the 2008 crisis.[49]

These concerns are directly connected to the potential for protest, as seen for example by the pensioners' revolt over the monetization of benefits in 2005. While Russia's leadership seeks to economize on social spending, particularly given its emphasis on fiscal conservatism, it also amends and mitigates its welfare reforms in both the planning and implementation stages to avoid the risk of destabilizing protests or steep losses in legitimacy.[50] With some exceptions, the Kremlin has proven fairly adept at finding that balance and avoiding undue social disruption. Yet such concerns undoubtedly increased in 2014 when global oil prices dropped from the high level seen in the 2000s, reflecting the continued vulnerability of the Russian economy to unpredictable shifts in global commodity markets. Lower oil prices not only put a crimp in Russia's economy; they arguably change the relations between state and society. When oil prices were high, with oil and gas revenues accounting for a substantial part of the federal budget, the Russian government could afford to use oil industry rents to help maintain regime legitimacy through the "non-intrusion pact," where society is provided for and otherwise left alone, as long as it stays out of politics.[51] When prices are low, however, the state needs society both to give up more of its dwindling income as revenue and to quietly accept a lower level of benefits. When prices remain low, the pressure to raise taxes and cut expenditures continues to build.

Putin has repeatedly displayed his understanding of the political importance of social spending and benefits. In particular, he has viewed "budget sector" workers as a core part of his political base. During the protest wave of 2011–12, Putin issued his "May Decrees" of 2012. In one of the most prominent, he vowed to boost the salaries of health and education workers and other public employees. The pledges included such steps as raising the pay of teachers at a minimum to the average pay of their region, and doctors to double the average regional pay. Experts warned at the time that such increases could only be achieved through deficit spending, which is precisely what happened, though the debts appeared on the ledgers of regional budgets rather than the federal one. Within the first year after the May decrees, the average regional budget deficit doubled from 4 percent in 2012 to 8 percent in 2013.[52] As pressure to fulfill the decrees mounted, deficit spending continued, and in some regions it reached unsustainable amounts. Kudrin and Gurvich claimed that the "sharp wage increases in certain branches of the public sector" were spreading to the entire economy, with wage increases significantly above productivity.[53] Yet five years after the 2012 decrees, as Putin prepared another presidential campaign, those decrees were far from being fulfilled. Despite the growing deficits, it was becoming clear that statistics were being manipulated to make it seem as if teachers were being paid more. Survey evidence suggested that a majority of teachers reported that their pay had not grown (after taking inflation into account) and believed that they were being massively underpaid.[54] Doctors were similarly disillusioned.[55]

As noted in discussing public-sector protest in chapter 5, the Russian authorities were well aware that the connection between economizing on social spending and the risk of public protest was not merely hypothetical. The Kremlin had to concern itself not only with labor protests, or protests over the welfare state and inadequate social spending, but also with a host of concrete socioeconomic issues. These grew to include protests over housing renovations in Moscow, the demands of deceived investors and shareholders, protests over increases in utility rates and by those in unsustainable debt, protests over deaths from preventable building fires, against raising the pension age, and protests over toxic garbage dumps placed next to population centers. According to Russia's Center for Social and Labor Rights, in the first quarter of 2019, while there were 39 labor protests and 11 "trade union actions," there were 73 protests over environmental and local (*gradozashchitnyi*) issues and 157 over social and daily life (*sotsial'no-bytovoi*) concerns.[56] As with all such protests, the challenge for those in power is to keep them small in scale and isolated, rather than allowing them to spread and combine in a way that threatens political legitimacy or, in the worst case, leads to an uprising of protest reminiscent of a color revolution.

Social Problems and "National Security"

Further evidence of the Kremlin's concern over socioeconomic protest and its potential to lead to political destabilization comes from Russia's reaction to the 2014 Maidan revolution, where a popular uprising led to bloodshed and the melting away of Ukraine's security services, with President Yanukovych fleeing for a safe haven in Russia. The reaction in the Kremlin led not only to a sharp increase in nationalist rhetoric but also to attempts to inoculate the Russian population against any similar attempt at revolution, particularly through a state media campaign that emphasized the chaos in Ukraine following the country's "fascist" and illegal "coup." This counterrevolutionary campaign certainly had some impact. For example, when protest leaders at the AvtoVAZ automobile plant in Tolyatti began to raise political demands at one demonstration, including shouts of "Down with Putin!" and "We need a Maidan!" (*nado maidan sobirat'*), they were met with a response from other workers that "We don't need any Maidan" (*ne nado nam maidana*).[57]

Perhaps most frightening for Kremlin leaders was the inability or unwillingness of Ukraine's security forces to stand their ground in the face of massive protests. As Russian military analyst Aleksandr Golts has argued, referring to the failed coup at the end of the Soviet period, "The experience of 1991 hangs over Putin, when Soviet paratroopers having held conversations with the KGB special forces replied that 'no, we will not shoot'" at the population. That fear explains why the Kremlin leader created the National Guard (Rosgvardiya), which he believes will "fulfill any order."[58] The four hundred thousand–strong National Guard was explicitly created to prevent a color revolution, including one stemming from protests aimed at stopping corruption. By December 2014, a year after the start of the Maidan revolution, the new Military Doctrine of the Russian Federation argued that modern military conflicts involved the "integrated use of military force and nonmilitary political, economic, informational and other measures, implemented with extensive use of the populace's protest potential."[59] An adviser to the National Guard expressed these concerns even more explicitly:

> The scenario for how events unfold is known from the color revolutions. The organizers get millions of people shouting "Down with the government!" to take to the streets. The authorities start to lose control. Next come sanctions and an integrated attack on the country's economy. The armed forces don't know what to do. All of this leads the country to collapse. This is how a modern war could unfold. The emergence of the National Guard is a response to the challenge to our society, to the threat posed by the use of so-called nonviolent resistance, which it would be more accurate to call a "color revolution."[60]

The increased fear of a color revolution clearly stemmed from the events next door in Ukraine, which the Russian leadership believed was fomented from outside. Kremlin advisers increasingly began to see the hidden hand of the West (and especially the US) promoting "regime change" through color revolutions in the post-Soviet states. In May 2014, the Russian Ministry of Defense's third "Moscow Conference on International Security" was focused almost exclusively on the threat posed by color revolutions, with top national security officials from Russia and Belarus characterizing such revolutions as a form of hybrid warfare hatched in the West.[61] As the Russian National Security Strategy, published in December 2015, stated, "The practice of overthrowing legitimate political regimes and provoking intrastate instability and conflicts is becoming increasingly widespread." An analysis by the US Defense Intelligence Agency (DIA) noted that the 2015 document significantly expanded the sections on internal stability, economy, and culture from previous versions. The DIA noted further that the Russian strategy "identified new threats to state and public security posed by foreign nongovernmental organizations (NGOs), 'color revolutions,' and the use of social media to foment unrest and undermine political and social stability, reflecting Russian officials' allegations that Western powers seek to provoke regime change in Russia."[62]

Even in the minds of Russian officials seemingly obsessed with Western interference, however, the threat of color revolution could not be simply attributed to foreign scheming. Russia's increasing alarm about popular uprisings was also driven by concerns about the economy, specifically regarding the sudden drop in oil prices, which also occurred in 2014, the same year as the Maidan revolution. Thus, the 2015 National Security Strategy explicitly connected national defense and internal stability with the state of the economy. Of the strategy's eight "national security priorities," one was titled "Improving the Quality of Life of Russian Citizens"—which included the importance of reducing inequality—with another section titled "Economic Growth." The strategy included ten "Main Indicators of the State of National Security," four of which were economic measures: GDP per capita, inflation, unemployment, and Gini inequality.[63] In essence, Russia's national security documents lay bare the central dilemma facing the country's political economy. On the one hand, the National Security Strategy's section on economic growth makes clear what would be needed: "The main strategic threats to national security in the sphere of the economy are its low competitiveness, the persistence of the export/raw-materials model of development and a high level of dependence on external economic circumstances." To this list it added such factors as a labor shortage, the extent of the shadow economy, and regional inequality.[64]

Yet tackling these problems in earnest would almost certainly lead to social hardship and thereby increase the potential for socioeconomic protest; consequently Russia's military doctrine also speaks of the threat of "the populace's protest potential." While Russia's new security force, the National Guard, was ostensibly created to defend against the threat of terrorism, terrorist acts tend to come from sole actors or small groups, hardly justifying a four hundred thousand–strong paramilitary force. Yet repression and acts of violence against nonviolent protesters can backfire, as was seen in Ukraine's Maidan revolution, when the security forces' firing on protesters led to greater protests. This may be one reason why the ruling United Russia party has tasked its "Youth Guard" to be ready to mobilize on the streets as counter-protesters against any popular demonstrations.

Still, a more detached and sober analysis would likely find the potential for a Russian color revolution to be fairly low. As we have noted, many of the color revolutions elsewhere have arisen over charges of widespread fraud in elections, whereas support for President Putin, and even United Russia, has been sufficiently high so that—at least so far—blatant fraud to change election outcomes (as opposed to turnout levels or victory margins) hasn't been needed. As we have also seen, when political protests did break out over charges of electoral fraud in 2011–12, Putin succeeded in heightening social divisions between "real Russians" in the industrial and rural hinterlands and the cosmopolitan professionals in the major cities. Indeed, most color revolutions have not been directly ignited by the types of socioeconomic concerns we have examined in this book, though that began to change in 2020 in Belarus. Still, at least since the 2005 protests over the attempted monetization of benefits, Russia's leadership has "sought to delineate a legitimate sphere of protest over economic demands from an illegitimate sphere of attempts to politicize the situation."[65] This has led to a sharp discursive divide in Russia between socioeconomic protests on the one hand and political protests on the other.[66] Yet for those in power, the real danger is that this divide might be breached, with the socioeconomic demands that drive (often localized) protests in Russia's regions leading to demands for political change. In the next chapter we examine a case of just such a breach, with Russia's truck drivers, seemingly at the core of Putin's political base, moving rapidly from a simple economic grievance to demands to bring down Russia's political leadership.

4

RUSSIA'S TRUCKERS AND THE ROAD TO RADICALIZATION

To what extent might protests over socioeconomic issues become politicized in the Russian context? To be sure, Yeltsin remained president through economic conditions much worse than what Russia has experienced since, and faced a much greater level of labor and related protest, with a much lower level of approval. Moreover, the political contexts between the strike wave in the 1990s and the labor protests in the Putin era, in the first decades of the twenty-first century, are dramatically different. Then, labor protests were closely connected to, and at times driven by, political parties and regional leaders fighting for political influence and representation in the Duma. In contrast, the participants in current labor protests often explicitly reject political interference, fearing an attempt to harness their protest for the political ambitions of others. This thinking pervades the work of Russia's unions as well. Unions typically seek to distance their protests from overt political demands and underline their exclusively economic character. Even alternative unions, whose protests are regularly infused with the language of class struggle, nevertheless often intentionally emphasize that their demands are purely economic.

This is a clear contrast with labor protests in the 1990s, which would often include the demand "Yeltsin, resign!" In keeping with the age-old Russian notion of the "good tsar," today's protesters are more likely to demand—as did many of the truckers in their initial protest in 2015—"President, help us!" (in the earlier period, a slogan of "Yeltsin, help us!" would have sounded absurd).[1] The majority of Putin-era conflicts have remained focused on the local level, with protesters appealing for help and trying to attract attention to a particular problem rather than demanding more general political changes.

On closer inspection, however, the analytical distinction between political and economic concerns appears artificial, regardless of whether that distinction is imposed by outside observers or the protesters themselves. For one, too often discussion of protest in post-Soviet authoritarian societies has centered on whether protests might lead to the downfall of a political regime, as if society faces a binary choice between stability and revolution. Authoritarian leaders must concern themselves with events that might signal to other elites or centers of opposition that those in power are not infallible. In political systems that tolerate little overt opposition, protests are certainly the types of events that can signal potential vulnerability, even if those protests are limited and in themselves pose no direct threat.

In Russia as elsewhere, states that rely heavily on commodity exports often exert greater control over their economies. State control over the economy can become a source of authoritarian power, but it can also become a potential vulnerability. Justifiably or not, liberal capitalist economies claim a separation between the realms of public and private, political and economic; while political leaders in those societies are often blamed (or praised) for overall economic conditions, they are much less likely to be called on to solve specific economic grievances. In more authoritarian settings with greater state control over the economy, particularly those with a more personalistic leadership (as with Putin), that leader might successfully swoop in to play the role of savior during a local economic crisis. Yet a leader who fails to play that role, or does so unsuccessfully, can quickly be viewed as the source of the problem rather than its salvation. In Goodwin's comprehensive account, social revolutions occur when significant sections of society come to believe that their situation is untenable and that a personalistic leader has gained such control over their daily lives that the only "way out" is to remove that leader from power.[2]

As noted in the first chapter, for these reasons the Kremlin has long "sought to delineate a legitimate sphere of protest over economic demands from an illegitimate sphere of attempts to politicize the situation."[3] This has contributed to a sharp "discursive divide" in Russia between socioeconomic protests on the one hand and political protests on the other.[4] Yet that divide becomes blurred when considering an issue such as corruption. The Levada Center's Denis Volkov argues that polling data make clear that most Russians want socioeconomic changes, not political ones. Yet, he adds, "corruption is worthy of special mention. About 30 percent of those polled regard it as an acute social problem, making it a notable subject among secondary issues. High-profile corruption scandals, however, attract the attention of a far greater proportion of the population."[5]

The opposition leader Alexei Navalny has well understood that outrage over corruption can form a potent bridge connecting economic concerns to political demands. For example, the fifty-minute video produced by Navalny and his associates titled *Don't Call Him "Dimon,"* which provided extensive documentation of the vast wealth accumulated by Prime Minister Medvedev, was a brilliant strategy, and the video inspired dramatic protests in a large number of cities and towns in March and June 2017.[6]

From the view of the political leadership, exposing the illicit wealth of government officials is deeply troubling. It raises the question about how firmly even top leaders control their personal assets in a political system where corruption is systemic and political power is the ultimate determinant of one's right to property. After the Maidan revolution, not only was Ukrainian president Yanukovych chased from office, but he lost control of his wealth as well. Hence the Kremlin's deep fear of a color revolution: as Yanukovych's fate makes clear, whatever vast holdings Russian leaders and their moneyed associates currently enjoy, a fall from the political heights can mean losing wealth as well as power.

Moreover, charges of ill-gotten wealth take on greater weight in the popular imagination when people are struggling to meet their basic needs. While the Putin leadership survived the 2011–12 protest wave, Russia's economy was then still enjoying significant economic growth. Since then, following lower oil prices and economic sanctions, economic growth has slowed considerably, and real wages have remained stagnant or worse. Moreover, while the 2011–12 protests focused on often abstract political demands, Navalny, though overtly political, cleverly plays on sentiments of social injustice during challenging economic times. For instance, while Putin finally fulfilled his long-standing promise of raising the minimum wage to subsistence levels, Navalny called for a rise in the minimum wage to 25,000 rubles per month, more than twice the current level. As a journalist described one of Navalny's speeches, he "spoke about the contrast between government elites' luxurious lifestyles and the region's sagging wages; about rising utility fees, despite falling energy prices; about the pitiful state of the roads."[7]

Navalny's actions have demonstrated the potential for political demands to take on an economic dimension, to widen their attraction and add to their potency. This would certainly be one plausible reason why Navalny was targeted with poisoning by means of the nerve agent Novichok. Yet a rather different example—that of Russia's truck drivers—illustrates how very limited economic grievances can become rapidly politicized, and its participants radicalized in the process. While Navalny has long and openly positioned himself as part of Russia's political opposition, prior to their protest Russia's mostly male and working-class truckers would have been considered (quite likely even by themselves) as part of a pro-Putin "silent majority." Such a dramatic turnaround would likely make their example truly alarming for those in power.[8] Thus, their path to radicalization is worth exploring in detail.

In an illustration of just how rapidly the truckers' demands changed, one in-depth study sought to explain the "failed politicization" of the Russian truckers' movement, arguing that the "rigid divide between economic and political pro-test" in Russia prevented the truckers from "real politicization and radicaliza-tion."[9] Yet when viewed over a slightly longer period, the case of Russia's truckers proves precisely the opposite.

The conflict began over a simple tax issue. On November 2015 the Russian government announced a new road tax on load-bearing tractor-trailers, in order, it was argued, to help pay for the wear and tear heavy loads placed on Russia's highways. Through a system called "Platon" (from the Russian *oplata za tonnu*, or pay per ton), trucks weighing over twelve tons would be charged four rubles per kilometer, with the charges incurred through a satellite-based tracking device.[10]

The fee charged might seem small, but many truckers argued that they were barely breaking even and were already paying both a transport tax and a fuel tax. Moreover, many of Russia's truck drivers are independent owner-operators: Rus-sia's approximately 1.9 million trucks are owned by 1.14 million individuals and companies.[11] In that sense, most Russian truckers are small businessmen, albeit ones surviving on very small margins.

Shortly after the tax was announced, Alexander Kotov, the head of the Interre-gional Trade Union of Professional Drivers (MPVP), called (in a YouTube video) for truckers to drive to Moscow to demand negotiations with the government. Seeking to broaden the appeal of the truckers' demands, he argued that since the costs would be passed on to consumers, "Platon doesn't only rob truck drivers, it robs the whole population of the Russian Federation."[12] Soon, truckers in forty-three of Russia's eighty-five regions and more than seventy cities took to the streets in various forms of protest. In some cases they drove in "snail" convoys at less than ten miles per hour, while in others they blockaded highways altogether. The protests persisted through December 2015, with truckers in some regions refusing to drive in January.

As with the spontaneous protests that followed the government's attempt to monetize benefits in 2005, "the intensity of protests caught the political system completely off guard."[13] By late December, 78 percent of the Russian population stated they were aware of the protests, and in another poll 63 percent said they supported it (with 70 percent of Muscovites in support).[14]

Moreover, in contrast to the "middle-class" protesters of 2011–12, Russia's truck drivers could hardly be "framed as isolated from 'the people' and their everyday concerns."[15] This led some more excitable commentators, including those from Russia's liberal opposition, to argue that the truckers' protest might be the beginning of the end for the Putin regime. The former oligarch and Putin opponent Mikhail Khodorkovskii claimed that the truck drivers' protests signaled "an inevitable revolution" in Russia.[16] Paul Gregory, a long-term observer of the Russian economy, asked whether Putin had "met his match" in the country's truckers, speculating that "apolitical Russian long-distance truck drivers can set off a Russian Spring, just as a small Tunisian merchant set off the Arab Spring, in response to public revulsion over corruption and mismanagement."[17]

Yet not long afterward, one Russian following the protests noted that on social networks many leftists and liberals "were disappointed the truckers were not organizing a revolution."[18] With hindsight, it appears far-fetched indeed to expect that truck drivers concerned about a road tax would suddenly become revolutionaries. This was hardly the first time that Russia's liberal opposition had projected its hopes for a political revolution onto the latest socioeconomic protest. However, the conclusion that within a few months various interventions by outsiders and decisions by the truckers themselves had "prevented radicalization and rendered the protests largely toothless" also proved unfounded.[19]

To be certain, the authorities were quick to try to quell the protest. Drivers in front of the "snail columns" were arrested. According to one driver, truckers were pulled over and compelled to sign "a statement saying 'I refuse to take part in the protest action and the law has been explained to me.'"[20] The Duma quickly passed a law restricting driving in convoys (avtoprobegi). Jardar Østbø reported that "law enforcement had warned that if there were any political slogans, the protesters would be detained."[21] Yet, as is their standard practice, the authorities held out carrots as well as wielded sticks: the fines for failing to pay the tax were lowered substantially, a transport tax deduction was offered, and the tax itself was lowered by more than 50 percent, at least temporarily.

The truckers were hardly mollified. When they called for a nationwide strike in March 2016, months after their initial protest, they issued a set of demands: an end to the Platon toll system and punishment for those responsible for implementing it; an end to fees for major repairs for apartment buildings and a two-year halt to increases on utility rates; and a reinstatement of discounted public transport for pensioners and the disabled. Whereas earlier the truckers were trying to broaden their appeal by arguing that a tax on truckers would increase prices for all consumers, now the truckers were clearly trying to draw support from other disaffected groups. As Viktoriia Lomasko recounted their rationale, "These are basic demands, because they affect everyone. Everyone gets old, and everyone has parents."[22] Still, these demands clearly remained socioeconomic rather than political in nature.

Much of the subsequent discussion of the truckers centered on this very question. Some observers noted that one of the most prominent demands from the

December 2015 protests was "President, Help Us!" Others argued that the road tax was seen by truckers as a violation of Putin's implicit "non-intrusion pact." As one protest placard stated, "Let people work in peace!"[23] Anotoly, a truck driver from St. Petersburg, put it this way: "I have two loans, the apartment is mortgaged, and three kids. I am not interested in politics: let me work!!!"[24]

Yet the line dividing economic from political demands was far from clearly drawn. For one, the truckers were well aware of credible charges of corruption surrounding the Platon tax system. The company operating the system, which received 20 percent of all the funds collected, was half-owned by Igor' Rotenberg, the son of Arkady Rotenberg, a former judo partner and now billionaire friend of Vladimir Putin.[25] Within a month of their protest, drivers were placing signs on the back of their trucks announcing "Remember, Rotenberg: the tire iron is under the seat," with other placards proclaiming "we want to feed our wives and children, not the oligarchs." Believing that the central media was ignoring their protests—an important spur to their subsequent radicalization—the truckers also deployed signs depicting Russia's three main TV networks as the see-no-evil, hear-no-evil, speak-no-evil monkeys.[26]

In the first months after the initial protest, representatives of various parties in the systemic and nonsystemic opposition (including CPRF, Kommunisty Rossii, Yabloko, and Alexei Navalny), along with other political actors, worked hard to unite with the protests, offering assistance and organizational support. The truckers, however, deliberately maintained a nonpolitical stance. According to Lomasko, who spent considerable time with the truckers in their encampment in Khimki on the outskirts of Moscow, the truckers would tell everyone who visited that they were not involved in politics. As one put it at the time, "You have to have the knack of politics to make political demands."[27]

But sharp divisions soon appeared among the truckers regarding political demands and alliances. By late March 2016, observers were reporting a "schism" between the leaders of the protests, with some urging to keep political parties at arm's length, while others made their political demands explicit. According to Østbø, the "orthodox" wing of the movement was led by Andrei Bazhutin, who in seeking to build an independent union without the influence of political parties was seen as pursuing an "apolitical" strategy, "keeping the organization on the 'correct' side of the economic/political discursive divide."[28] Meanwhile, the "politicizers" among the truckers included Yurii Bubnov, who stated, "My main demand is the resignation of the government. And then . . . to initiate a procedure towards impeachment of the president for failing to prevent violations of the Constitution."[29] Even earlier, at a meeting with the Presidential Council for Human Rights and Civil Society in December, trucker Igor Pasynkov fumed that "a vertical, feudal decision-making process in the context of capitalist production will, at best, result in a peaceful and almost bloodless storming of the Bastille, or, at worst, to a prolonged Hundred Years' War."[30]

Such differences continued by early April 2016, when a rally in Moscow against the Platon system featured the political parties PARNAS, Democratic Choice, Yabloko, and the Communist Party. The truckers in the Khimki encampment and their allies in various regions had met via Skype and voted against taking part in the rally. They argued that the organizers of the rally were not themselves truckers and therefore couldn't fully understand their problems. They were also wary of "march[ing] under any flags." As Lomasko reports the truckers' thinking, making a distinction between "the people" and political parties, "it was crucial ordinary people trusted them, but ordinary people no longer trusted any of the parties."[31] Yet about a dozen truckers from Vologda decided to drive into Moscow for the rally, where the slogans quickly turned political. As Yevgeny, a Vologda driver, put it, "They are right to say, 'Down with Putin!' It was he and his cronies who dreamed up Platon." He added, "You have to take advantage of every conflict. We're not ashamed of ourselves. We didn't lie home in bed." While the truckers in the Khimki camp were not happy with the drivers from Vologda for attending, one of the latter argued, "Politics and life are dirty. What, do you want to be squeaky clean? What difference does it make whom we unite with? What matters is they're also opposed to Platon."[32]

One reason the Khimki drivers sought to avoid political entanglements was that they wanted to create their own organization first. A truckers' trade union existed already. Kotov, the head of the MPVP, had spearheaded the initial protest through his YouTube appeal. But before long Kotov appeared to be trying to dampen the protests. He had earlier led his union's column at an "anti-Maidan" and pro-Kremlin demonstration.[33] At the very beginning of the Khimki encampment, as Mikhail Kurbatov, a driver from Nizhny Novgorod, recalled, "When Kotov noticed how few of us had showed up, he said: 'Let's call it a day and just go home.' The response was: 'No, we won't back out. We are here, we'll stay here and we'll carry on.' That was the moment when Andrei Bazhutin said: 'You're destroying the protest, look how many people support you!' The leader we all had been counting on just wimped out."[34]

Unhappy with the existing union, the drivers sought to organize their own but faced the technical hurdle that many of them were both workers and employers at the same time; therefore, rather than calling it a "union," they chose to form an "association of carriers." Yet organizing proved difficult. "In the early days, we pushed everyone away and were suspicious of each other. We didn't know each other then," Sergei Vladimirov, a trucker at the Khimki camp, would remember.[35] Kurbatov explained, "We were perfect strangers [yet] everybody was outraged and ready to stand their ground." He added, "We realized we needed an organization. But we were total rookies, nobody had any hands-on experience in public activism."[36]

On April 30, 2016, about four months after the start of their protests, the truckers held the founding congress of the Association of Russian Carriers (Ob'edinenie perevozchikov Rossii, or OPR) at the Lenin State Farm in the Moscow region. By their count, about three hundred drivers from thirty-one regions attended the congress. A majority elected Bazhutin chair of the OPR.[37] According to Bazhutin, "in the early days, chaos reigned, but the guys are like soldiers now." Stressing their desire to gain media attention for their cause, he added, "We have figured out what 'newsworthy' means and how to give interviews."[38]

While the decision to create an organization to press their demands may have appeared to some as orthodox and apolitical, the truckers were already heading down the road of radicalization. As we have seen, one reason the truckers avoided political alliances was their distrust of political parties (one shared, they argued, with much of the public). But another was the class divide between Russia's intelligentsia and its working class.

The journalist and commentator Arkady Babchenko noted, on the blog of opposition leader Garry Kasparov, that with every socioeconomic protest in Russia, whether it comes from truckers or miners on hunger strike over unpaid wages, liberal intellectuals tend to ask whether it will lead to a revolution.[39] The problem, Babchenko complained, was that Russian liberals "do not comprehend their own people." This was certainly a fair point, as there has long been a clear cultural as well as class divide between Russian intellectuals and "their own people," not least the working class. Yet Babchenko goes further, asking, "When will you finally understand, my dear caring idealistic liberal friends?" adding that that there will be no revolution, because "the people" care only about small localized problems like trucker taxes and garbage dumps, and otherwise support Putin wholeheartedly. Instead of revolution, Babchenko argues, "here there will be only uprisings [*bunt*]." To make his point clear, he adds, "The uprisings of naked asses [*golikh zh***]."[40]

While such language might seem patronizing in the extreme, when Tamara Eidelman, herself a prominent member of the liberal intelligentsia, decided to go to the Khimki camp and offer some lectures on civil disobedience, she recounted that "my acquaintances tried to scare me by saying the truckers were zombies."[41] Her friends told her, "They won't understand a thing." "They support Putin and won't give you the time of day." They advised her that she had better expand her vocabulary, since the truckers' language was full of curse words.[42] She herself was persuaded. "I pictured burly men who yawned as they listened to my arguments and might even, for all I knew, shout, 'Why are we listening to this? We are not interested.'"[43] But, as it turned out, "I looked around and could see they really

were interested. I saw I was surrounded not by ferocious wild men, but by atten-
tive listeners with intelligent faces." Together they discussed the protest tactics
of Gandhi. Reacting to a lesson on the bus boycotts organized by Martin Luther
King Jr., they responded, "That's great! They hit them in their wallets!" As Eidelman recounted, "The questions rained down one after the other. Of course they
mainly boiled down to the famous 'What is to be done?'"[44] Thus, while many
truckers initially sought to maintain a divide between economic and explicitly
political demands, they remained open to escalation regarding tactics.

In fact, the truckers soon escalated their demands as well as their tactics, and
with time those demands became political indeed. The truckers' radicalization
was prompted in part by meeting with other individuals and groups protesting
various issues. By late March 2016, some of the truckers joined the march com-
memorating the assassination of opposition leader Boris Nemtsov. According to
one, "When they said we were a 'fifth column,' we realized how easy it was to throw
mud at anyone." Added another, "Killing a man in Red Square is a brazen thing to
do." Earlier the truckers had supported Muscovites who were seeking to protect
the Torfyanka park from the development of a new church, and came to the aid of
protesters there who were being physically attacked by religious activists.[45]

The sense that their demands were being ignored by the authorities contributed further to the escalation of those demands. Repression by the authorities
was effective in dispersing many of the truckers (as was the indebtedness they
incurred while not working, and the strain on their families while the truckers were away from home). Yet repression also emboldened a number of those
who remained. This was clearly the case for Bazhutin, who was not only first
arrested in 2015 during the initial protests, but was also threatened with having
his children taken away by state authorities.[46] He claimed he had been arrested a
dozen times, had been fined 60,000 rubles, threatened with the loss of his apartment, and at various times deprived of his driver's license (and thus his means
of income).[47] As he put it, "Over the last two years I have lived through things
I couldn't have imagined before."[48]

By March 2017, when the government did not meet their demands, and the
road tariff increased, the truckers escalated their protest with an "all-Russian
strike." According to the OPR at least, more than half a million truck drivers
joined in, with major protests taking place in Dagestan, where almost 100 percent of the truckers refused to drive. They also claimed their protest lasted from
March 27 to mid-June 2017.[49] Whatever the scale, given the presence of the OPR,
the March 2017 protest was much better organized than the initial largely spontaneous protest of November–December 2015.

Moreover, the truckers' demands had become explicitly political within a short
period of time. During their initial protest in December 2015, the most political

demand was for the resignation of the minister of transportation. Yet by March 2017, just over a year later, in addition to their economic demands, the truckers called for "the resignation of the government and no-confidence in the president." Further still, the truckers adopted language from Navalny's anticorruption protests that had coincidentally begun at the same time, targeting (as did the Navalny protests) Prime Minister Medvedev by name. By the time of demonstrations on May 1 in Moscow and St. Petersburg, political demands dominated the truckers' placards and slogans, second only to the total cancellation of Platon.[50] Thirty truckers were among the 825 individuals arrested in Moscow during the Navalny-inspired anticorruption protests on June 12, 2017, and truckers participated in protests in at least eight other cities on that day.[51] As one OPR leader in Chelyabinsk put it, in an echo of Navalny's claims about the corruption of Medvedev and other leaders, it wasn't trucks but yachts that were destroying Russia's roads.[52] As the protests continued to be met by repression as well as silence from government officials and state media, the politicization deepened. Whereas the March 26 strike announcement sandwiched the demand for the resignation of the government and no-confidence in the president between economic demands (it was number four out of six demands), by July that demand was moved to number one, and on the OPR website was printed in boldface type.[53]

In another dramatic step away from the truckers' plea for help from Putin, on June 23, 2017, Bazhutin, leader of the OPR, announced his intention to run for president in 2018.[54] While his candidacy was quixotic and was clearly intended to draw attention to the truckers' cause, this was a fundamental transformation for a leader who had recently been described as "apolitical" and as seeking to keep the truckers "on the 'correct' side of the economic/political discursive divide."[55] In explaining why he decided to run, Bazhutin claimed that "all the other prospective candidates are professional politicians." He added, "They're divorced from real life. While I come right from the working environment, for me it's quite easy to find common language in any labor collective."[56] He claimed his support came not only from truckers but from other disaffected groups, such as small entrepreneurs, the Housing Justice movement protesting apartment demolitions, from foreign-currency debtors, taxi drivers, deceived shareholders, "and other associations of people who [have] suffered injustice at the hands of the government."[57]

In the end, Bazhutin did not succeed becoming an official candidate. As his campaign unfolded, OPR, the truckers' association he headed and counted on to support his candidacy, was declared a "foreign agent."[58] The charge resulted not only in a stigma but also a fine, and it restricted the group from providing the necessary support for his candidacy. Later that month Bazhutin was arrested and detained for fifteen days, for driving the family car without a license, which he had been deprived of for participating in protests the past March. He claimed the authorities were waiting for a pretext, as bailiffs had visited his home that morning, and interior ministry police had been stationed outside. Upon his release he was detained again, this time on charges stemming from a protest the previous April. Unable to gather the necessary signatures, he decided to abandon his candidacy.[59]

While Bazhutin's candidacy might appear self-serving, and his radicalization exceptional, other truckers described a similar transformation. Aleksei Borisov, a leader of the OPR branch in Ryazn, explained,

> When the tax was announced, many of us went to Moscow in search of the truth. We didn't think about politics, we simply wanted to explain to Putin that we would not be able to work, that we would go bankrupt. We sincerely believed that he didn't know about it, and somehow we would tell him and somehow he would understand and. . . . It seems funny now, but that's what I believed. Journalists and volunteers, friends and family, sympathizers and people who had yet to make up their minds came to visit us. But no one from the government would talk with us. The majority of the information from the mass media was either non-existent or unreliable. We spent four and half months in that camp. . . . Much became clear. I turned off the television and saw the light.[60]

Explaining Radicalization

By itself, the truckers' protest hardly represented a direct threat to the Russian leadership. True, the truckers' organization OPR claims to have ten thousand members and chapters in sixty-six cities, as far away as Chita and Yakutia, each with an official "coordinator" whose name, picture, and contact information is listed on the OPR website.[61] The truckers' protest actions continued, such as a December 2017 strike timed to coincide with Arkady Rotenberg's birthday.[62]

Still, while such protests by the truckers have been reported widely in the regional and opposition press, they continued to be ignored by Russia's central media.[63] Although repression has emboldened some truckers, many others, already struggling to provide for themselves and their families, were deterred. A number rebelled silently as individuals, by seeking to thwart the Platon tracking system, rather than risk the consequences of collective action.

While in the end the truckers' movement portended no direct threat, let alone a revolution, their example illustrates a number of significant challenges for Russia's political leaders. For one, their protest illustrates the limits of what Petrov, Lipman, and Hale have called the "non-intrusion pact," in which society is provided for and otherwise left alone, as long as it stays out of politics.[64] The truckers' protest was not a typical labor conflict, where workers in a single work-place or company protest over the conditions of their work. Indeed, as owner-operators, the independent truckers look less like workers than small business-men, though ones struggling at the margins. As analyst Dmitrii Oreshkin has argued, the truckers' protest can best be seen as a taxpayers' revolt.[65] Should oil prices remain down from their historic highs of the 2000s, however, and the Putin leadership remain committed to macroeconomic stability, similar tax increases may prove impossible to avoid.

Second and relatedly, the truckers' case provides a perfect illustration of Tilly's concept of "catness": the potential for individuals to become mobilized collec-tively because they belong to a single category.[66] Before the imposition of the tax, the truckers were isolated and spread throughout Russia's far-flung regions—"perfect strangers," as one of them put it—with little ability or inclination to act collectively. That quickly changed, however, when the government imposed a new tax on them as a group.

The ability of the truckers to sustain collective action was stymied initially by Tilly's other element for successful mobilization, that of "netness," or networks and organization. The existing trade union for truck drivers (MPVP), rather than assisting in mobilization, instead proved to be a "mediating spoiler," in keep-ing with Russia's dominant (and often co-opted) trade union movement.[67] Yet within a few months of their initial mobilization, the truckers formed their own organization, despite considerable obstacles.

The truckers' example reveals the limitations of imposing sharp analytical divides between social and economic demands on the one hand and political demands on the other. What had appeared to be the "failed politicization" of the truckers' movement soon turned out to be anything but. To be sure, while there is often a divide in Russia between socioeconomic and political protest demands, the reasons behind that division are more complex than is commonly assumed. One reason, which the truckers themselves acknowledge, is reflexive support for Putin, especially among the working class, as exemplified in the slogan "Pres-ident, help us!"—only a slight variation of the much older Russian phrase, "If only the tsar knew!"

Yet another explanation for the divide in demands is that the authorities have made clear, to the truckers and others, that social and economic protests are in some sense legitimate, while political protests are not, and that the latter would be dealt with harshly. Thus, when protesters themselves insist their demands are not political, it may reflect less the intensity of their concerns and more the desire to appear more legitimate, to obtain redress from the authorities, and to avoid repression. Consequently the truckers initially sought to gain support for their demands not by making them political but by claiming the road tax would lead to price hikes, and then by adding demands against utility rate hikes and in support of pensioners. Nevertheless, even when the truckers explicitly rejected political demands, the economic-political distinction became blurred, as when one of their early protest placards threatened oligarch (and Putin ally) Rotenberg with a crowbar.

In an illiberal regime where the state looms large over the economic as well as the political sphere, socioeconomic protests are often politicized by their very nature. This is certainly the case in Russia, since, at a minimum, social or economic demands almost always entail an appeal to authorities for redress. Moreover, Russia's political leadership—embodied in Putin himself—often claims to be the ultimate protector and savior of the population. Yet further politicization becomes a distinct possibility when workers come to believe that government officials are unable or unwilling to address their demands.[68] Thus the flip side of the belief in the "good tsar" is discovering (as Russian workers over a century ago did in the wake of the Bloody Sunday protest of 1905) that the top leader does indeed know of their distress and is choosing to respond with silence or worse.

Much theoretical and comparative work on social movements suggests that such realizations become more likely once workers and others have mobilized and begin to act collectively.[69] Having broken out of their isolation, they are now able to discuss Russia's "accursed questions": Who is to blame, and what is to be done?

Yet even as the truckers began to ask those questions and became radicalized in the process, they continued for some time to disavow politics. But they did so not out of lack of interest, or because they revered Putin and viewed Russia's political system as legitimate. On the contrary, a major reason for disavowing an explicitly political strategy was that they distrusted the political process. When asked toward the end of 2017 if the OPR was "ready to go political as an organization," driver Kurbatov replied that the organization's "underlying principle excludes support for any political party. We distance ourselves from any joint actions." He explained:

> All these political organizations are horses of the same color. You bet on a chestnut horse, I bet on a black one—it doesn't matter, because it [is] still the horse owner who gets the profit. Political parties in Russia are not meant to articulate somebody's problems, they are a means to blow off steam. If you find yourself in trouble, you go and seek comfort with your Mom, because you know you'll get a pat on the back, while your Dad will just say: "You had that coming." You get your pat, you feel good, but that's it. The problem is still there. Political parties offer the same

"pats on the back" intended to make you feel okay so you can get it out of your system. But they never solve problems.[70]

While political parties were to be avoided because they were ineffective, the same thinking did not extend to like-minded social movements. According to Kurbatov, "Yes, we do collaborate with grassroots movements." He mentioned the Khimki truckers coming to the aid of the defenders of the Torfyanka and Dubki city parks in Moscow, and the Housing Justice movement (Narodnym dvizheniem za zhil'e).

> We helped the Kuban farmers who had planned a march on Moscow. They contacted us and asked for help, we dispatched some truckers to Rostov-on-Don to work out a joint strategy. But everyone got busted by the police not far from Rostov. I went there and we spent two weeks in Rostov trying to get everybody out of jail. We tried reaching out to the Gukovo coalminers near Rostov [who were protesting long-standing wage arrears] but they seem to avoid us like the plague. They are so full with "Putin, help us!" crap, still believe that the President is kept in the dark and will come to their aid as soon as he learns the truth. They turned out to be not ready for direct action.[71]

Although working with social movements that have economic grievances, while avoiding political entanglements, may in some literal sense maintain a distinction between economic and political protests, as Kurbatov explained, the line was clearly blurred. "We're open to anybody who supports freedom, equality and justice—we're going in their direction. Our motto is 'The enemy of my enemy is my friend.'"[72]

The truckers did not pose a direct threat to the Putin regime. This is true for a variety of reasons, not least the continued repressive power of the Russian state. Nevertheless, the case of Russia's truckers is undoubtedly troubling for those in power: the imposition of a simple tax spurred a movement of "perfect strangers" from Chita to Dagestan, who within two years went from pleading "President, help us" to calling for no-confidence in Putin and advancing a candidate from their ranks to unseat him. The issue of a tax increase illustrates how fiscal pressures can create painful tradeoffs in social policy. This point is crucial, because a drop in oil prices not only puts a crimp in Russia's economy; it arguably changes the very relations between state and society. When oil prices were high, with oil and gas revenues accounting for a substantial part of the federal budget, the Russian government could afford to use oil industry "rents" to help maintain regime legitimacy without overly extracting taxes from the general population. When oil prices drop, however, the state needs society either to give up more of its dwindling income as revenue or to quietly accept a lower level of benefits, or both. Should oil prices remain low and the government's reserve funds become drained, the need to raise taxes and cut expenditures will grow, a process that has been proven to generate significant social protest. As we have just seen, such protests can become quickly politicized. While the truckers were never going to lead a color revolution by themselves, their example serves as a flashing warning light to any further attempts to impose austerity, increase revenue, or cut subsidies and benefits.

HOW DIFFERENT IS RUSSIA?
THE COMPARATIVE CONTEXT

In placing Russia in comparative context, this chapter will first take a brief look at company towns and deindustrialization elsewhere, finding considerable differences between Russia and the countries of advanced capitalism, yet noting a similar political backlash between global cities and lagging regions. I examine the challenges other middle-income countries have faced between balancing the need for economic growth and integration into the global economy with preventing destabilizing social and political unrest. I then turn to the postcommunist cases of east central Europe, exploring how the communist legacy has hindered labor and the political left and facilitated the rise of right-wing nationalism, even as migration within the EU provides a partial outlet. Finally, I explore illustrative post-Soviet cases, especially Ukraine and Belarus, as well as China. There are deep parallels between the labor regimes in Russia, Ukraine, and Belarus. In Ukraine, deindustrialization coincided with even greater economic decline, resulting in protest and revolution. In Belarus, deindustrialization and mass privatization were largely avoided, but economic grievances, combined with a dictator clinging to office, led workers to deploy their symbolic power in an attempt to bring down that dictator. In contrast, massive deindustrialization in China led to widespread protest with little sign of political instability, occurring as it did alongside almost unprecedented levels of economic growth and the creation of entirely new cities. For Russia's leaders, the Chinese case appears as an unrealizable dream, while the Ukrainian and Belarusian scenarios represent their nightmare.

Deindustrialization has been a daunting process throughout the advanced capitalist economies in recent decades, and the difficulties of "rust belt" cities are well known. The process started in 1970s in advanced capitalism, if not before.[1] In contrast, Russia passed through a different phase of industrial development and deindustrialization, industrializing much later and "catching up" in the Soviet period, guided by the much heavier hand of the state.[2]

The differences become clear when comparing company towns in advanced capitalist societies and Russia. There were large numbers of company towns in the United States, for instance, though most arose in the earlier phase of industrialization in the late nineteenth and early twentieth century.[3] Company towns existed in the pre-Soviet period as well, such as Iuzovka (later named Stalino and then Donetsk in post-Soviet Ukraine).[4] Yet as we have seen, the vast majority of Russian monotowns were created with Soviet industrialization starting in the 1930s, and one of the newest monotowns—Tolyatti—was first established as late as the 1960s. Moreover, while almost all the company towns in the US (as in other in advanced countries) underwent a long period of decline and were abandoned or absorbed into other agglomerations some time ago, Russia's monotowns, while far from homogeneous, have survived into the twenty-first century.[5] Likewise, in Russia deindustrialization was largely held at bay until the 1990s, when the process began with a jolt. In short, Russia's experience with industrial transformation has been out of sync in world-historical time, making the integration into the global capitalist economy—starting at the last decade of the twentieth century—all the more difficult.

The differences with Russia include space as well as time. For example, the World Bank suggests that Pittsburgh and Glasgow provide positive lessons for Russia's urban reinvention, and Germany's Ruhr region is held by some to be the most successful case of postindustrial transformation.[6] Yet Pittsburgh, Glasgow, and the Ruhr are large urban agglomerations that do not suffer from the geographic isolation and inhospitable climates of many of Russia's industrial towns, nor were they to the same degree dependent on a single industry—or in some cases a single enterprise—as are many of Russia's monotowns. The largest company towns, in both the US and Russia, were steel towns: Gary, Indiana, and Magnitogorsk respectively. Gary, however, was built on the outskirts of Chicago, then America's second-largest city, whereas Magnitogorsk was sparsely inhabited. While as of this writing Magnitogorsk is faring well, given current steel prices and a devalued ruble, other Russian monotowns and industrial centers struggle with unprofitability and geographic isolation.

Further still, as we have noted throughout, deindustrialization in Russia has been carried out in a dramatically different fashion from deindustrialization in the advanced capitalist world: much less through plant closures (especially of large enterprises) and unemployment, but rather through low and very flexible wages and attrition.[7] Industrial employment has declined significantly, but not as much as in some other comparable cases (see figure 2.2). Thus, so far Russia has relied on workforce atrophy and individual worker exit, which, while reducing employment levels, have kept inefficient enterprises open without providing meaningful alternatives.

And yet, industrial transformation is hardly an isolated economic phenomenon: even with the significant different deindustrialization experiences between Russia and the West, the class and regional divisions—and the politics they generate—are strikingly similar. The votes for Brexit and Donald Trump, as well as the rise of right-wing populist figures and parties in western Europe, forced the mainstream political elites in those countries to confront, in the most literal sense, the very different worlds the professional classes and the working classes inhabit, as urban centers connected to the global economy thrived, while seething resentments grew in many rural and rust belt communities.[8]

German sociologist Wolfgang Streeck, reflecting on the causes behind what he terms "Trumpism," argued that "among the structural cracks in contemporary societies in which Trumpism flourishes is a rapidly growing cleavage between cities and their deindustrialized, more or less rural, hinterland. Cities are the growth pole of postindustrial societies. They are international, cosmopolitan, and politically pro-immigration, in part because their success in global competition depends on their ability to attract talent from all over the world."[9]

Much has been made about the phenomenon of postcommunist nostalgia, as at least certain segments of those societies look back wistfully on the sureties of the communist past.[10] Yet it is worth speculating whether this nostalgia is truly "postcommunist" as opposed to "postindustrial." Scholars of deindustrialization elsewhere note significant nostalgia in working-class communities that struggle with, among other things, trying to maintain relationships that are torn apart by economic decline. Though levels of interregional migration tend to be much higher in the US and western Europe than in Russia, one finds attachment to place in areas of industrial decline—places of "devastation" that are still "home"—there as well.[11] While politicians might seek to play to these sentiments, by promising, for example, to make their country great again, in these communities, as in the postcommunist cases, the nostalgia is typically more ambivalent than rose-colored.[12]

Yet given Russia's significant differences with the advanced capitalist world, perhaps the more apt comparisons lie elsewhere. As noted in chapter 1, Russia is an anomaly among its BRIC counterparts, in that while it has been an "emerging market," its challenge is not industrializing but deindustrializing.[13] Still, Russia in many ways is a normal country, in the sense that it shares middle-income status with many other countries in the world, along with many of the same challenges: low productivity and low wages, and high levels of informality and inequality.[14] Middle-income status and high levels of inequality are often closely correlated with clientelism, populism, and "hybrid" political regimes. As we have noted, liberal economists and others have argued for a path out of the middle-income trap: investing in human capital and core urban centers as a means to increase productivity. Yet the challenge is not simply technocratic, but one that entails forming a political "growth coalition" that can disrupt existing political arrangements and modes of legitimation. Hybrid regimes are particularly vulnerable to protests stemming from unpopular social policies as well as economic crises and declining standards of living. Thus, as in Russia, governments in many middle-income countries face the challenge of balancing the need for economic growth and strategic integration into the global economy with preventing destabilizing social and political unrest.

Still, one might argue that in eastern Europe at least—those countries that share the postcommunist legacy with Russia—the destabilizing backlash that was expected to arise with the end of communism and the rapid adoption of capitalism did not take place, at least not initially.[15] Especially in the early postcommunist period, with the communist experience largely framed as one imposed by Soviet occupation, ideologies from the left of the political spectrum were tainted by the legacy of Communist Party rule, and labor unions were viewed as complicit.[16] The one major union exception was Poland's Solidarity, and yet Poland's first postcommunist government, nominally headed by Solidarity, implemented what became known as "shock therapy."[17]

With labor and other segments of society in disarray, yet with an overall popular yearning to become "normal" countries and join the West, the pace and scope of economic transformation in eastern Europe appeared unprecedented. As Appel and Orenstein conclude, "No world region has embraced neoliberalism as enthusiastically and persistently as post-Communist Europe. The adoption of neoliberal policies in the former Communist countries since 1989 has been unparalleled in speed and scope, far exceeding the expectations of analysts and practitioners."[18]

The enlargement of the European Union, rather than leading to a transfer of the traditional European "social model" to the east, led instead to greater divergence between new and old member states, as the new members experienced higher levels of inequality and considerably weaker unions and forms and levels of collective bargaining.[19] Ten years after enlargement, there was a "hollowing and backsliding of industrial democracy" in the east, with fewer strikes from workers, though public-sector workers began to press demands, albeit less as "workers" and more as "citizens."[20] In macroeconomic terms, Poland's transformation, for

one, has been stunningly successful.[21] Yet in the process a significant number
of Poles were pushed into impoverishment. Much like Russians making their
monotowns "habitable," they transformed their initial degradation and helpless-
ness into a resourcefulness that extended to scrap collecting and even basic hunt-
ing and gathering.[22]

Indeed, overall discontent in the region was expressed less in collective fashion
and more in the form of individual exit, such as by workers diverting into the
informal economy. In striking contrast to their counterparts in Russia, workers
in the new EU member states took advantage of the provision for free movement
of labor to leave for work in higher-wage countries. The inflow of workers from
these countries to the UK was roughly ten times greater than the British government had predicted, and the overall flow of migrants from the new member
states to the old was at least twice that projected by the European Commission.[23]
While the migration was often seen as a "brain drain," as the young and relatively
skilled often emigrated, the result was a tightened labor market beneficial to the
workers that remained.

Low labor costs and flexible work arrangements, combined with neoliberal
policies, were successful in attracting foreign investment to the east. Before long,
Slovakia became the world's largest per capita producer of automobiles. Yet the
overall result was that these countries were transformed into "dependent market
economies," with crucial economic sectors, such as banking, controlled by foreign capital.[24] A major consequence was instability: in surrendering significant
state regulation of the economy and relying on the fickle nature of foreign investment, these countries were left vulnerable to crisis.[25]

It should hardly be surprising then that "the global financial crisis of 2008
shook the [postcommunist countries] to the core."[26] As Adam Tooze notes, since
these countries were so highly leveraged, "all the most severe casualties of the
2008–2009 crisis are to be found among the transition economies of the former
Eastern bloc."[27] Suddenly, the economic policies long pursued by these countries
were viewed in a much harsher light. As Appel and Orenstein conclude, "The
global financial crisis of 2008 finally created the populist reaction to neoliberalism that had long been feared."[28] This, too, should not have been surprising.
While the predicted backlash from workers and other "losers" from postcommunism had failed to materialize in a substantial way for two decades, for some
critics it was clear that such a backlash was looming.[29] Indeed, the "patience"
that labor and other social groups long exhibited appeared to end with the 2008
crisis.[30]

Given the growing disparities between global cities and lagging regions, it
is fairly predictable that the illiberal leaders in Poland, Hungary, and elsewhere
in eastern Europe were "predominantly provincial in origin" and attracted

considerable support "especially outside the globally networked metropolitan centers."[31] Yet the populist reaction in the region took a particular form. While leaders in Poland and Hungary in particular, in line with much of the far-right politics that rose up elsewhere in the 2010s, expressed strong nationalist and xenophobic views, they also took steps—not only symbolic but material as well—that acknowledged what some have referred to as the "leftist bias" in postcommunist societies. Based on their analysis of data from the World Values Survey, Pop-Eleches and Tucker find that, compared with counterparts elsewhere, citizens in postcommunist societies on average are significantly less supportive of markets and more supportive of state-provided social welfare. The authors find that this "leftist bias"—a political orientation they term "left-authoritarian"—is greater in postcommunist citizens who express less support for democracy.[32] Thus, in Hungary, Victor Orbán came to power in 2010 promising an end to austerity, imposing restrictions on foreign banks and denouncing the IMF, while members of Poland's Law and Justice Party called for an end to "dependent development" while providing support to vulnerable groups and directing aid to smaller towns and struggling regions.

It may be true that such material support was fairly limited, perhaps amounting to "authoritarian neoliberalism," with cultural conservatism and xenophobia meant to act as a tonic soothing the pain of more stringent economic policies.[33] And without the safety valve of mass labor emigration, one wonders what the politics in the region might look like. Nevertheless, we can conclude that at the very least, in the wake of the 2008 crisis, a different legitimation strategy was needed for many countries in the region. The postcommunist countries of eastern Europe have many differences from Russia, not least their membership in the EU. Yet these countries and Russia share a paradox: a "leftist bias" in the population's overall views of markets and welfare, accompanied by a stunning lack of those entities traditionally associated with left politics, especially effective trade unions and parties with a left orientation.

Farther east (the Baltic states aside), the communist legacy was even more deeply ingrained in the former Soviet states. For example, in the most industrialized of the former Soviet republics—Kazakhstan, Ukraine, and Belarus, as well as Russia—the former communist "legacy" union dominated the field of labor representation. Further, all these countries wrestle with monotowns.[34]

In Kazakhstan, something close to authoritarianism prevailed. This did not, however, prevent potentially destabilizing labor protests from occasionally breaking through the countries' calm exteriors. As in Russia, in Kazakhstan labor protest is limited, with severe restrictions on the right to strike, repression of independent unions, and state support for the FTUK, the country's "legacy union."[35] Yet in another close parallel with Russia, since the dominant union is more concerned with preserving labor peace than in defending the interests of aggrieved workers, protests, when they do break out, are often wildcat in nature, with demands that can quickly escalate. One such protest in the Kazakh oil town of Zhanaozen, in December 2011, escalated to the point that police opened fire on workers, with at least sixteen killed and another one hundred injured.[36]

A number of other post-Soviet countries, where authoritarianism is less entrenched, have achieved, in Lucan Way's characterization, "pluralism by default."[37] Moldova, Armenia, and Georgia, as three examples, must wrestle with "the specter of revolution."[38] This has certainly been true of Ukraine, which besides Russia is the most populous post-Soviet state.

Despite Ukraine's clear differences with Russia—the language and cultural divide; greater dependence on foreign capital, given the lack of oil and gas reserves; and a politics of "pluralism by default" rather than a "vertical of power"—the Soviet legacy has left Ukraine with fundamental similarities with Russia, not least in the area of labor relations. Not only does the legacy union—the Federation of Trade Unions of Ukraine (FPU)—dominate in Ukraine, as the FNPR does in Russia, but the FPU follows the FNPR's emphasis on the distribution of social benefits, an approach that "leave[s] no space for militancy."[39] As in Russia, "on the shop floor, the legitimate voice of the workers is the foreman rather than the formal union representative." At the factory level, "the union is just an auxiliary wing of the management."[40] As one critic put it, despite their numerical strength in formal membership, "it's as if our unions have disappeared from our political and economic life."[41]

The formation of Ukraine's post-Soviet industrial relations began, as in Russia, during the economic collapse of the 1990s, when following a general strike by coal miners in the Donbass in 1993—involving 230 of the region's 250 mines and 400 other enterprises—a coalition was formed between the "red directors" and industrial workers in order to "avoid a 'social explosion.'"[42] From then on, "the FPU consistently discouraged strike action in the name of social stability and maintained its privileged position in the scheme of distribution of social insurance funds," as well as holding on to union properties inherited from the Soviet era.[43]

The parallels with Russia continue: While workers left industrial jobs, they typically did so as a result of low pay rather than massive layoffs.[44] The minimum wage has consistently been less than the government-estimated living wage.[45] As in Russia, lax enforcement of labor regulations helps produce an environment where management vastly overpowers workers, with employees forced to work overtime without pay or go on forced vacations.[46] Oligarchic groups—which one observer referred to as "job givers"—took advantage of the post-Soviet model of worker dependence on factories and the oligarch's provision of favors to shape election outcomes.[47] Workers make their situations habitable through informal personal networks, taking out loans, and relying on subsistence agriculture.[48] Legal restrictions make lawful strikes difficult to hold, and partly as a result, state agencies consistently underreport strike activity (for instance, reporting "zero" strikes in years when there are dozens). The leading demand behind strikes and labor protests has typically been wage arrears, accounting for between 35 to 47 percent of such protests in recent years.[49] Taken together, these commonalities underscore that Russia's approach to labor relations and deindustrialization is not something unique to the Putin-era political economy but stems from the Soviet legacy, the methods of postcommunist privatization, and the striving of oligarchs and political power holders to maintain stability and thus their wealth and power.[50]

While Ukraine has lagged considerably behind Russia in terms of economic growth and standard of living, it too enjoyed the boom in commodity prices in the 2000s. This allowed for "reinforcing and maintaining the post-Soviet hegemonic expectations from the factory, union, and state. This social contract implied several unspoken mutual commitments, under which workers were to maintain social peace and loyalty to the enterprise, while the owner of the enterprise guaranteed preserving jobs, a lax attitude, and certain levels of monetary and nonmonetary income."[51]

Yet, as with the boom itself, this "hegemonic configuration" was not sustainable, especially after the 2008 economic crisis. As Tooze notes, the route to the 2014 Maidan revolution was twisted, "but the path it would travel down was mapped out already" by the earlier crisis.[52] Like its postcommunist counterparts farther to the west, Ukraine had become increasingly dependent on foreign borrowing, particularly since the Orange Revolution of 2004. With the 2008 crisis, Ukraine's steel sector—which accounted for 42 percent of the country's foreign currency earnings—was deeply impacted, since "no sector was worse hit by the crash in global investment spending than steel."[53] Though layoffs were limited, millions of Ukrainian workers were left without pay. After Latvia, Ukraine suffered the worst contraction of any economy in the world.

This added a heap of pain on top of long-standing misery for Ukraine. As Tooze notes, the pre-crisis "social contract" meant that "while a tiny minority grew fabulously rich, the standard of living for the least well-off was kept at a tolerable level only by a system of pensions and energy subsidies that consumed 17 percent of GDP." With the 2008 crisis, Ukraine had little choice but to turn to the IMF for emergency loans, but those came "with demands for changes in taxes and benefits that made it impossible for a government to sustain legitimacy."[54] Before long, President Yushchenko's approval ratings were in the low single digits, and Viktor Yanukovych, whose rigged election victory in 2004 was overturned by the 2004 Orange Revolution, was elected president, this time fairly, two years later.

Yet by 2013, average incomes were barely higher than they had been in 1989, during the height of Soviet perestroika.[55] While it would certainly be mistaken to claim that these concerns alone led to the 2014 Maidan revolution, in Ukraine there was a clear connection between social and economic hardship and destabilizing political protest. Labor-related protests had grown for the three years prior to the Maidan uprising.[56] When the Yanukovych government wavered over turning to the EU rather than Russia, it had to consider that the conditionality of EU and IMF assistance entailed such measures as lengthening the workweek and increasing the prices for basic necessities like electricity.[57] In the estimate of some, the terms were "onerous," and accepting them "would have been a political disaster."[58] But for Yanukovych the disaster came anyway.

The violence that broke out in eastern Ukraine following the Maidan revolution was the product of many factors, Russian intervention chief among them. But the Donbass was not only the most industrialized region in Ukraine; it was also the region where labor was most volatile, especially in the mining sector, where independent unions had first risen up during the massive strikes in the late Soviet era.[59] There were half a million coal miners employed in Ukraine in 2014, most of them concentrated in the Donbass. Already struggling with mine closures—137 had been closed since 1996—the region's miners were dependent on subsidies from Kiev, which had been increased under President Yanukovych, a Donbass native.[60] His sudden removal from office, combined with a promise by the new government to turn to Europe, clearly threatened to reduce those subsidies considerably.[61] Strikes and labor protests soon followed in the wake of the Maidan revolution. In the end, most coal miners were caught in the middle when the violence escalated, with the separatists engaged in theft and extortion. The region's fraught labor politics certainly contributed to the volatile mix.

Again, there are important differences between Ukraine and Russia; among other things, Ukraine is riven by divisions between regions and oligarchic clans in a way that Russia is not. Yet for the Russian leadership, one lesson from Ukraine must certainly be that worsening economic conditions and a declining standard of living—but also the austerity measures that some claim are needed to boost growth and improve those conditions—can lead to protest, destabilization, and even a color revolution. In the Ukrainian case, it led to the ultimate nightmare for post-Soviet leaders: President Yanukovych not only lost political power and was forced from office, but was compelled to flee the country and leave his personal wealth and property behind.[62]

With Alexander Lukashenko—often referred to as "Europe's last dictator"— firmly ensconced as president, Belarus would seem to be an unlikely place for a color revolution. For some years the Lukashenko regime maintained social and political stability through severe restrictions on civil society, including steps aimed at "preempting" protests that might lead to political destabilization.[63] In what some called "socialism with Russian subsidies," Belarus has been supported for years by Russia, with subsides that by some estimates amounted to around $10 billion a year.[64] This allowed for popular steps to boost legitimacy, such as hikes in public-sector wages.

Yet, according to the International Trade Union Confederation, Belarus has "no guarantee of [labor] rights," its fixed-term (one-year) contracts are a "a form of forced labor," and the restrictions on legal strikes are even greater than those in Russia (and Ukraine).[65] According to Volodymyr Artiukh and Denys Gorbach, the "Belarusian factory regime combines the worst from the Soviet past and the Western capitalist present."[66] Moreover, as the subsidies from Russia began to decline, social and economic conditions worsened. By the spring of 2017, falling living standards and the third recession since 2009 prompted Belarus to implement a "parasite tax"—taxing those neither officially employed nor registered as unemployed (thus clearly aimed at those in the underground economy). The tax prompted spontaneous street protests, and in the end hundreds were detained and at least five hundred sentenced to jail, with many more fined.

Following those protests, Arkady Moshes concluded that "the protests demonstrated [that] the old social contract in Belarus, within which a post-socialist distributive economic model used to provide enough benefits for the population and guarantee their non-participation in politics, is eroding." In a clear parallel to what we have argued for Russia, Moshes added, "The regime's ability to address this latent problem by starting macroeconomic reforms is limited." This is due largely to "the realization that embarking on economic reform may worsen standards [of living], which will in turn threaten the regime's political position. However, the longer reforms are postponed, the more painful and costly for the population they will eventually be." Moreover, Moshes continued—presciently given later events—"If the system now fails to provide for the population's minimum needs or if the authorities introduce measures that are provocative, such as the 'parasites tax,' protest sentiment will grow and Belarusian 'stability' will be in jeopardy."[67]

The provocative step that did jeopardize Belarusian stability came in August 2020 through clearly falsified election results, which proclaimed Lukashenko's reelection as president yet again. This prompted a now-familiar scenario of a color revolution: within days after the election, crowds of people, particularly the young and well educated, took to the streets, demanding free and fair elections. Yet there was a major difference in the Belarus case: given worsening economic conditions, the protests were soon joined by workers in a number of major industrial enterprises, amid calls for a general strike. By one count, over eighty industrial, trade, and service organizations joined the protests, as did workers in medical, educational, and other organizations. These included some of Belarus's largest and most prominent industrial workplaces: the thirty largest enterprises whose workers were involved in the protests accounted for close to one-third of the country's GDP.[68] Workers formed strike committees in a number of prominent factories, including the Belaruskali Potash Company, the Minsk Tractor Plant, and the Minsk Automobile Plant. The Hrodna City Strike Committee was said to unite workers in twenty-one different companies. The opposition Coordination Council called for a general strike for October 25, though by this time considerable state (and workplace) repression, as well as Russia's declarative backing of Lukashenko, dampened protest activity. Still, Artiukh and Gorbach conclude, "labor unrest represented a culmination of the protest wave."[69]

The worker protests in Belarus were exceptional in their spread and scale, as well as their participation in a color revolution (where elsewhere such labor participation has typically been limited). Yet while the language of strikes was used, the methods employed were more often protest meetings, marches, and petitions, with few actual workplace stoppages. Independent unions announced an "Italian strike" (a "work to rule" tactic), though this may have entailed primarily symbolic actions on the shop floor.[70] The worker protests were exceptional in another way as well: in contrast to the worker protests I have discussed—and certainly that of Russia's truckers, who began with a very limited economic grievance—the demands by Belarus's workers were immediately and largely political, denouncing falsified elections and police brutality.[71]

The reasons behind that politicization are not hard to find. Lukashenko had been in power, in progressively dictatorial fashion, since 1994. Further, the economy, characterized by some as "state capitalism," remained largely un-privatized (in contrast to Ukraine and Russia), with the majority of protesting workplaces either state-owned or dependent on government funding. Seen in this light, it is perhaps unsurprising that workers did not express economic grievances; they did not perceive themselves as economically exploited so much as placed in a political stranglehold, increasingly by Lukashenko himself. As Artiukh and Gorbach put it, they protested less as workers and more as citizens.[72] Given this, workers were able to overcome the class divisions that have appeared in Russia and elsewhere and unite with liberal protesters, without overly focusing on the potential economic consequences that a liberal post-Lukashenko regime might bring about.

The Belarus labor protests clearly demonstrated one point: workers in the post-Soviet space retain considerable symbolic power, even if lacking in organizational power. This is especially pertinent given a leader like Lukashenko, who championed himself as a fellow *muzhik* and a protector of working-class jobs and interests. Indeed, as Natalya Chernyshova argues, workers were seen as Lukashenko's "traditional constituency," and others referred to them as "the leader's base."[73] Lukashenko himself certainly saw workers that way, since he went directly to the protesting factories, telling the workers that they were betraying his trust and that their protests were to him like a knife in the back (*udar v spinu*).[74] Yet rather than backing down, the workers responded by chanting "Go away!" and "It's time for you to go!" One worker stood toe to toe with Lukashenko and, looking him in the eye, said, "The people are tired!" and it was clear of whom they were tired. As Chernyshova put it, Lukashenko "had never been publicly challenged, and this was visibly an unpleasant shock."[75] According to Ben Aris, strikes at state-owned factories were "a body blow for Lukashenko. The blue-collar workers at the big Soviet-era enterprises have always been his core supporters."[76]

Other groups protesting Lukashenko clearly grasped the symbolic power of workers: as Artiukh and Gorbach noted, "Workers were received as heroes on the streets, greeted with banners and chants, invited to talks on opposition media, offered solidarity at the factory gates and material compensation for unemployment."[77] Protests by students and middle-class professionals might be challenging, but strikes and protests by workers could become crippling for a leader like Lukashenko. The embattled president blamed the protests on the work of foreign governments and complained the actions were being led by "criminals and the unemployed." Yet such rhetoric was hardly effective when the protesters were marching in work uniforms out of factory gates.

As of this writing, Lukashenko has survived the protests, largely through repression and mass arrests, including of labor leaders and workers detained at the workplace. Russia's backing, however, has quite likely played a decisive role, and arguably the regime would not endure without it.

Massive deindustrialization and economic hardship, while leading to widespread protest, do not always lead to destabilization, let alone revolution. As Xi Chen put it, "One of the biggest puzzles of China's reform era is how the government was able to implement a stunning enterprise restructuring program amid widespread worker protests."[78] Indeed, in Russia, widespread labor protest appears less as a reality and more as a specter—a looming threat of what might take place if the state pursued mass layoffs, the closure of large enterprises, or substantial austerity measures. To project what the leadership might face with such closures, Russia could look east to China, which did not simply revise the Maoist-era social contract, but carried out what some referred to as "smashing the iron rice bowl."[79] Between 1993 and 2006, over sixty million workers—more than the entire population of France—lost their jobs at state-owned and urban collective sector enterprises. This amounted to more than 40 percent of jobs being lost in the formal urban sector in under fifteen years.[80]

Lee describes the impact on one rust belt province in China's northeast: "Once the heartland of the socialist planned economy and home to some of China's most prominent state-owned industrial enterprises, Liaoning has decayed into a wasteland of bankruptcy." Predictably, Liaoning Province was also transformed into a "hotbed of working-class protest by its many unemployed workers and pensioners."[81] Across China, the layoffs led to "widespread contention by workers," with "at least hundreds, probably thousands, of episodes of laid-off workers' contention in China every year between about 1998 and 2008."[82] Such protests typically involved workers blocking street traffic, lying across railroads, or staging sit-ins in front of government buildings. Across the country, government statistics recorded eighty-seven thousand cases of "riots and demonstrations" in 2004 alone.[83] As Lee concludes, in the eyes of the Chinese leaders these protests "presented a palpable threat to social stability."[84] William Hurst concurs, adding that they "produced deep-seated worries among China's elite about the stability and security of society and the political system."[85]

To be sure, these protests did not ultimately destabilize Chinese society and threaten the political leadership. As Russia's leaders are no doubt aware, however, there are substantial differences between Russia and China. Most obviously, in contrast to Russia's continued reliance on commodity exports, China became known as the workshop of the world, exporting manufactured goods while essentially importing jobs that had been outsourced from the advanced industrial world.[86] Thus, substantial plant closures in some regions took place alongside massive job creation in others. Second and relatedly, in contrast to Russia's relatively low levels of interregional mobility, in recent decades hundreds of millions of Chinese have migrated to jobs in the booming cities. Massive deindustrialization was therefore buffered by almost unprecedented levels of economic growth and the creation of entirely new cities, made possible by a mobile population.

This destruction alongside enormous expansion allowed the Chinese leadership to exploit divisions within its workforce. In explaining how China avoided labor protests from leading to political instability, Chen concludes that "the government's mastery in undermining the trust and solidarity among workers played an essential role."[87] Natural divisions exist between a more stable industrial workforce on the one hand and migrant labor brought in from the countryside with many fewer rights on the other.[88] There are also divisions in the government's treatment of older and younger workers.[89] Migrant workers can also become divided by sector.[90] But much of the division stems from substantial variations in the regional political economy in China. Even looking exclusively at workers laid off from state-owned enterprises, Hurst finds substantial variation in regional labor-market conditions and state capacity, leading to very different forms of protests and types of grievances with substantially different political implications.[91] Manfred Elfstrom also finds "broad, regional differences in Chinese labor politics—between the northeast and southeast, between the coast and the interior, between the old industrial bases of the planned economy and new centers of foreign investment," and even between otherwise similar "booming export hubs with large numbers of migrant workers."[92]

Not surprisingly then, worker protests in China have largely remained "cellular" in the sense that they are typically aimed at managers of individual workplaces and local political leaders. Ching Kwan Lee argues that the localized nature of these protests reflects the Chinese leadership's success in creating a "decentralized legal authoritarianism," where local rather than national leaders are perceived as responsible for both the economic conditions in their regions and for enforcing the legal rights of workers.[93]

Certainly, there are substantial variations between Russia's many regions, especially in terms of living standards but also regarding approaches to governance.[94] It is highly questionable, however, whether most Russians view government authority to be as decentralized as it is in China. True, while economic conditions in Russia were objectively worse in the 1990s, at that time Yeltsin had succeeded in creating the perception of a "liberal" economy, one in which the state was perceived—with reason—to be not fully in control, and it remained unclear who exactly was to blame.[95] Yet in contrast, while Putin's popularity stemmed in large part from the economic boom in his first years in power, he also demonstrably established a "vertical of power," making it clear that his hand was firmly on the tiller. While his crisis interventions might involve dressing down or firing subordinates, in so doing he makes himself appear to be ultimately responsible for the social and economic state of affairs.

A further and somewhat ironic contrast with China is worth mentioning. In a study of labor relations in auto plants in Russia and China, Martin Krzywdzinski finds that legacies from the past remain stronger in the former than the latter, despite China's continued rule by the Communist Party. There are multiple reasons, but in Russia's case the auto plants, like AvtoVAZ, are based directly on their Soviet foundations and have a much older workforce, with an institutional memory of the enterprise paternalism of the Soviet past. In contrast, as China became the world's largest producer of automobiles, it did so not by retrofitting communist-era factories but by building new "greenfield" plants and enlisting a massive wave of young workers to fill them.[96]

In sum, Russia's industrialization and deindustrialization, compared with that in advanced capitalist societies, took place in different forms and under very different circumstances, both in space and time, in the sense that its industrial centers were much more dispersed across its considerable landmass, and both its industrial phase and subsequent deindustrialization were out of sync with the world's leading economies. Even so, there are striking similarities in contemporary politics between Russia and the West, in the backlash stemming from declining industrial regions and the political coalitions that have sprung up in response. If Russia differs from advanced capitalist societies, it is also distinct from its fellow BRIC countries as well, in that the latter are largely still in the process of industrializing. Nevertheless, Russia shares with those countries the formidable challenge of trying to escape from the middle-income trap. As we have seen, doing so entails not simply pursuing the right mix of policies, but creating a political coalition in support of growth, in which labor must either be included or successfully shunted aside. The postcommunist countries of eastern Europe provide a closer parallel to the Russian case, and partly owing to the communist legacy they were able to implement neoliberal policies with only minimal pushback from labor. The backlash came, however, following the economic crisis of 2008, though it took the form of nationalist and right-wing populism rather than a more traditionally left-based wave of labor protest. Instead of erupting with collective voice, workers in these countries took advantage of their EU membership to depart on a massive scale to the more prosperous countries to the west.

Not surprisingly, the former Soviet republics most closely resemble the Russian case. Soviet-era industrialization left them with monotowns, as well as with labor representation dominated by a legacy union from the communist period. Ukraine and Belarus in particular demonstrate a number of remarkable parallels with Russia. Both countries clearly show that worsening socioeconomic conditions can incite political instability, with crucial consequences for political leaders. China, on the other hand, demonstrates that massive layoffs and large plant closures, even when leading to waves of protest, do not necessarily create political instability. In China, however, the protests have been absorbed by economic and political conditions about which Russian leaders can only dream.

OVERCOMING RUSSIA'S LABOR DILEMMA

We have seen how Russian society survived the traumatic economic collapse of the 1990s, and—defying predictions—did so without producing mass unemployment. While avoiding the feared "social explosion," Russia was left with a peculiar labor market: one where employment levels were kept fairly steady, but at the expense of extremely flexible, and usually very low, wages. Most large enterprises remained open, skewing Russian industrial employment at the expense of small to medium-size firms. These practices survived not only through the 1990s but through boom-and-bust cycles ever since.

We found that one consequence has been Russia's very low labor productivity, a key driver—maybe *the* key driver—of economic growth. Productivity matters for Russia particularly since the country faces a demographic challenge in the decline of its working-age population. Upgrading the use of technology could boost productivity, but Russian employers have little incentive to do so, since wages remain so low. Thus Russia finds itself in what we have termed a low-productivity trap. Yet government policies to date have focused more on industrial policies aimed, in no small part, at maintaining employment in key sectors.

Top officials, from Putin on down, have declared that boosting labor productivity has become a paramount goal, in order to kick-start economic growth. One avenue for doing so is to focus, in Kudrin's phrase, on "cities instead of oil"—that is, to direct government attention and resources toward building a handful of "global cities" beyond Moscow and St. Petersburg. Such an approach makes a lot of sense, as large, dynamic cities have become the growth centers of economic globalization. However, such an approach—now official government policy—runs directly counter to the facts on the ground in Russia. Almost uniquely, rather than a handful of major cities, Russia has hundreds of small and medium-size cities, dispersed across its massive land area. These include over three hundred officially designated monotowns, many of them built around struggling industrial enterprises from the Soviet era. Many residents defy economic logic by remaining attached to place, engaging in what has been termed "aggressive immobility."[1] These places become potential flashpoints of protest during economic crises, and the government has used subsidies and a number of investment schemes to keep them afloat. Needless to say, a major policy plan to shift investment elsewhere runs no small risk of greater protest down the road.

On the surface, it might seem that any potential danger to the political authorities stemming from such labor protest would be minimal. Vladimir Putin came to power just as a major wave of labor protest crested; amid economic growth that replaced wage arrears with substantial wage increases, he pushed through a new Labor Code that, among other things, cemented the FNPR as a loyal "legacy" union and marginalized the more militant alternative unions. He also succeeded in placing significant legal restrictions on strikes, which according to official statistics often number only in the single digits per year. Yet, whether viewed from the perspective of labor or management and the state, Russia's system of labor relations appears largely dysfunctional. The avoidance of mass layoffs has come at the cost of renewed wage arrears and festering monotowns. The restrictions on strikes and the subordination of the FNPR have limited legal strikes but also led to simmering discontent, providing few if any institutional channels to contain protest, which, when it breaks out, is typically spontaneous and uncontrolled. Thus, Russia's labor relations leave workers with very limited means to resolve conflict, but consequently the state is left with deep concerns about social stability. The dilemma extends beyond the industrial sector to include the social sphere, since so-called budget-sector workers are both a basis of political support and a potential source of protest. While widespread labor unrest might appear unlikely, a significant change in economic conditions, whether a steep drop in the price of oil or a prolonged period of stagnating wages, could alter that calculation significantly.

Still, the example of Tolyatti—Russia's largest monotown—would seem to suggest such obstacles can be overcome. There, in "Russia's Detroit," the workforce in Russia's largest auto plant was cut by more than half, without any social explosion. Yet, closer inspection reveals a much more complex picture: the workforce reduction was accomplished only with massive government interventions and subsidies. One of those interventions, to stem protests from autoworkers, led to protests from car importers that became so quickly politicized that they were put down only with the help of riot police. The transformation at Tolyatti also entailed turning Russia's largest automobile firm into the subsidiary of a multinational corporation, with a foreign CEO brought in to radically downsize the labor force. That scenario coincided rather uncomfortably with the Russian government's turn toward a more belligerent nationalism; while the foreign CEO was forced out by the Russian government, by that time the labor conflict had spread to the firm's abandoned Russian parts suppliers, leading to a scandal whereby the region's governor (since deposed), Nikolai Merkushkin, publicly blamed a worker's complaints about wage arrears on an international conspiracy hatched by the CIA.

While absurd, the sentiment behind Merkushkin's outburst reflected the fears that other government officials have expressed about the danger of a Russian color revolution. Before the Belarus case at least, those uprisings that have deposed leaders in neighboring countries have rarely been led by workers; however, the Putin leadership, by basing its legitimacy for many years on providing economic growth and stability, and then by attempting to ally itself with Russia's industrial heartland against the ostensibly middle-class and more cosmopolitan protesters in Russia's two major cities, has left itself vulnerable to protests from workers and other more plebeian Russians. Nationalist rhetoric and actions could serve as a distraction for a time, but without significant economic growth, basic grievances continue to build. This is especially true when the bulk of the population is most concerned with the government providing a minimally acceptable level of social support and benefits.

One way for the government to prevent such grievances from approaching anything like a color revolution is to create a strict divide between economic and political protests. Yet, for a number of reasons, such a division is fairly porous in practice. Russia's truckers provide a particularly vivid example: a simple road tax instantly united otherwise isolated drivers from Chita to Dagestan. At first, the truckers' most prominent slogan was "President, help us!" But with the authorities both repressing their protests and ignoring their demands, they formed an independent union and in little over a year began demanding the resignation of the government, with a leader of the movement campaigning against Putin for the presidency. While the government survived the truckers' protests, the episode provided yet another signal that, at a time of lower revenues from oil and gas exports, Russia's leaders had to proceed very cautiously when considering tax increases or benefit cuts.

One long-standing question has been whether Russian workers (and by extension, Russians generally) are quiescent, owing to, as some have argued, a paternalistic mentality. To characterize Russian workers as patient or long-suffering, however, is difficult to square with the experience of the coal miners who helped bring about the end of the Soviet Union (not to mention the workers in the Russian Revolution of 1917), or with the more recent outbursts that have led to rail or road blockades and other dramatic actions. Such spontaneous worker actions might suggest some form of cultural continuity, with long periods of suffering and patience interspersed with revolutionary uprisings.

Yet a related question has been whether Russian labor protests are primarily defensive and countercyclical, increasing when times are bad, or pro-cyclical, with workers protesting to demand a greater share of profits when times are good. The experience of Russia's autoworkers and others during the oil boom years of the 2000s strongly indicates that Russian workers, far from being mired in mentalities from the past, are capable of exploiting structural advantages when those opportunities arise. Yet labor protests in Russia are overwhelmingly defensive in nature, often centered on concerns such as unpaid wages. When examined alongside the autoworkers' actions, this suggests that the defensive protests of Russia's workers reflect less any cultural inclination and more their limited structural power in a deindustrializing economy, in particular one that faces the boom-and-bust cycles of global commodities markets. In, say, a monotown where the city-forming enterprise is struggling to remain open, refusing to work in order to extract a greater share of profits makes little sense.

Paralleling the tendency to see Russian workers as either long-suffering or prone to spontaneous uprisings is the inclination by others to view protest actions as potentially leading to revolution and regime change, and if not, then as relatively minor events in an otherwise stable polity and society. Yet—and this is a key point—the protests themselves, the issues they raise, and the manner in which they are being conducted point to substantial chronic problems that will be difficult to resolve, especially if economic growth remains slow or stagnant. But as Chris Miller has pointed out, for the Kremlin, economic efficiency and growth have been lower priorities than social, and ultimately political, stability.[2]

For a number of reasons, above all the leadership's goal of maintaining social stability, the Russian government has continued to prop up monotowns and other struggling large enterprises. Such support will become much more difficult during a period of slow economic growth or stagnation. In such conditions, managing struggling monotowns will be but one of the trials that test Kremlin leaders, and subsidies or other support for industry will be but one of the pressing demands on state funds. Herein lies a central dilemma: by preventing mass layoffs, the government can maintain social stability, but only at the cost of economic growth, the absence of which is itself a potential threat to social stability. Continuing to pay such costs would seem to be misguided, since with weak trade unions and extremely low official strike rates, the threat of widespread worker unrest in Russia would appear to be low. With few effective channels through which workers can express their grievances, however, a real potential exists for labor protest to become radicalized, creating a serious threat to regime legitimacy.

To be sure, claims that monotowns are a "time bomb" for the Russian state are almost certainly overstated.[3] When crises do flare up, even when they create significant attention as they did in Pikalyovo, Russia's president can swoop in with a timely intervention, appearing in the role of the savior. Rather than leading to a greater conflagration, protests in monotowns or other industrial communities might be put out like isolated wildfires, all the more so since unions, for reasons we have seen, are often not involved, and even when they are (as in Pikalyovo), they often lack sufficient network power—the "netness"—to create broader and stronger protests. Indeed, monotown protests can be less about labor per se than about "place"—that is, conflicts about conditions in the towns themselves rather than the status of the city-forming enterprise. The last straw for Pikalyovo residents was the shutting down of their hot-water system; likewise the protests over placing landfills for urban garbage in communities far from Moscow underscores the resentment that dwellers in small towns have for the political elite and the relative privilege of big-city inhabitants. But the chance of a broader protest movement arising in unison over such local issues remains slim.

The socioeconomic protests that have spread are less often those joined through netness, and more often the result of "catness"—protests that unite otherwise isolated individuals and groups when state actions impact them as a single category. This can happen through a change in social benefits, as with the 2005 attempt to monetize benefits, or through an increase in taxes, as happened more recently with Russia's truckers. That such protest movements arose over policy changes to taxes and benefits suggests that the threat of social unrest to Kremlin leaders extends well beyond industrial workers. As with any modern state, the Russian government must be able to extract resources from its population (such as through taxes) while maintaining enough legitimacy to avoid rebellion. When oil prices drop below a certain level, it becomes more difficult for Russian leaders to maintain what some have called the non-intrusion pact, whereby society is largely left alone, provided it refrains from political demands. Yet the problem for Russia lies deeper, in that while many Russians appear to be willing to leave politics to others, there is overwhelming support for what the Russian constitution terms a "social state." While the specific provisions might appear meager, there is clear evidence that the main concerns for a majority of Russians lie in the realm of social welfare, in areas such as health, education, and pensions.

Moreover, the concept of "worker" itself, in Russia as in most any contemporary society, extends beyond the industrial laborer to include the full range of subordinate employees.[4] As we have seen, labor protesters in Russia include not only factory workers and truckers, but teachers and health care workers, among others. On the one hand, employees in state-owned enterprises and budget-sector workers have become a core source of support—at least at times—for the Putin regime. On the other hand, maintaining that support entails a direct cost to the budget, a cost that rises under conditions of slower economic growth. Yet when fiscal pressures increase, experience strongly suggests that cutting benefits can lead to protest—but so can raising taxes.[5]

Still, to what extent might protest with social and economic demands—as opposed to explicitly political protest—be destabilizing? Some have found a "discursive divide" in Russia between economic and political protest, a divide that the government has encouraged by claiming the former is legitimate while the latter not. Yet that divide turns out to be porous, as we have seen with the rapidly politicized protests over car import tariffs in 2008–9, as well as the example of Russia's truckers.[6]

Putin has expertly worked to maintain that divide, in part by deflecting economic and class anger onto other targets. As we first saw in the Igor Kholmanskikh episode, Putin has sought to divide the "two Russias," playing off working-class resentments in the industrial heartland against the more educated professionals in the metropolitan centers. He has added cultural politics to such class resentments, pitting the urban and cosmopolitan "do nothings" tainted by Western libertine values against those with the faith, tradition, and values of "real Russia."

While that strategy proved effective in Russia in the wake of the 2011–12 "Russia without Putin" protests, the massive demonstrations next door in Belarus in the late summer and fall of 2020 attest to the limits of such an approach, even in a highly coercive political system. The Belarus uprising also proved that workers could indeed join a "color revolution," even one with overwhelmingly political demands. As Arkady Moshes predicted in the wake of the "parasite tax" protests three years earlier, the anger of Belarusian workers sprang from a foundation of worsening social and economic conditions.[7] In that context, rather than acting as the "leader's base," workers turned sharply against Lukashenko.[8] This clearly shocked the Belarusian president, who went directly to protesting factories, telling workers that their actions to him were like a "knife in the back." The workers responded with boos and jeers.

One explanation for the almost exclusively political demands from Belarusian workers would be the country's political economy, where many workplaces remain state-owned. Rather than experiencing their hardship as stemming from exploitative oligarchs or private owners, workers readily blamed the state, embodied in the personalistic rule of Lukashenko.[9] This might appear to be a significant contrast with Russia, where much of the economy has been privatized. Yet given Russia's own version of (increasing) state capitalism, similar hardships there might also well be attributed to a political system—sometimes referred to as one of "manual control"—at the top of which sits Putin. The post-Soviet color revolutions, as with the Arab Spring uprisings, and indeed many of the social revolutions of the twentieth century, most often occur when a personalistic ruler is viewed as individually responsible for intolerable conditions, and the only clear way out is to get rid of "him" (it's almost always a him).[10]

When workers join these protests, they present an acute challenge to such rulers. When protests become political in Russia and in Belarus, the rulers have sought to portray the demonstrators as feckless youth backed by foreign agents. In language paralleling that which Putin used during the 2011–12 Russian protests, Lukashenko complained that the 2020 Belarusian protests were being led by "criminals and the unemployed." Such rhetoric will almost certainly fall flat when the protesters are marching in work uniforms out of factory gates. While authoritarian rulers might rely on social divisions to encourage riot police to beat college-educated youth, overt repression against workers—the same class from which many police are drawn—could much more easily result in security force refusals and defections.

Sharp class divisions, of course, are not unique to Russia, or Belarus. If global economic forces are driving greater inequalities between metropolitan centers and struggling industrial regions, a politics of resentment will almost inevitably follow.[11] Interestingly, given this populist backlash, even some of the economically liberal international institutions are fundamentally revising their recommendations. For example, in a recent report, the OECD argues that given "large and persistent inequalities in regional economic performance" in many parts of the world, there is a growing "need for place-based policies to address them." The report makes the case that those place-based policies—the very policies that the World Bank has argued strenuously against for Russia—"are especially important in light of growing public discontent with the economic, social and political status quo," since "geographical patterns of public discontent are closely related to the degree of regional inequalities."[12]

The extent of this discontent, and its potential political consequences, are often missed by economic liberals, in and out of Russia, who argue for greater market liberalization. Within Russian elite circles the debate is usually framed as one between liberals and "statists," with the latter seen as defending the status quo, or pushing for even greater state control over the economy. There is little doubt that they have self-interested reasons for doing so. But there are important reasons beyond "rent-seeking" officials that prevent Russia from moving to greater market efficiency. For example, government plans for supporting monotowns, which entail both large-scale job creation and inducements for private investment, have been called utopian by critics. Yet the proposals of the World Bank and Russian economists for reducing subsidies, encouraging outmigration, and allowing for the "controlled shrinkage" of these company towns appear at least as unrealistic. While outsiders have spelled out the economic costs of the Russian government's implicit policy of "keeping the lights on" in struggling factories and industries, they fail to explore fully the social and political consequences of turning the lights off.[13] In the long run it may be true, as Leonid Bershidsky argues, that "the Grim Reaper is coming for the once-bustling little towns where people had moved from the villages. In a country with too much space and too few people, much of the territory is doomed to be a huge flyover zone."[14] Yet unless that process happens very gradually—a pace that would undercut the goal of economic growth— such policies will almost inevitably lead to protest.

While economic liberals tend to ignore the political costs of their plans, political liberals—particularly those pushing for broader democratic change—too often fail to view the social and economic concerns of many Russians with much sympathy. As much work in classic political sociology makes clear, revolutions almost always involve class coalitions, and are rarely if ever led by a single social entity such as the "middle class" or the "working class" alone.[15] Russian protest movements have exposed a deep class divide in Russia, one that those in power have exploited to great effect. As we have seen in chapter 8 on the truckers' protest, liberal oppositionists in Russia can yearn for workers to become democratic revolutionists one moment, and in the next disparage them in the most patronizing manner.

There is a countervailing sentiment on the part of workers in Russia, who are often wary of having their protests co-opted by the agendas of liberal protest leaders. Coal miners of the perestroika era, like workers today, complained of being treated "like cattle," or, in a different metaphor, of climbing on a bus being driven by liberals to a destination beyond their control.[16] For many miners, that destination became the Yeltsin-led 1990s. To many Russians, the memory of that decade, when reformers of various stripes pushed neoliberal transformation until society nearly boiled over, remains vivid.[17] It may not be a matter of ignorance for workers to stay clear of political opposition movements and parties. Russian workers as a whole are not uniting behind the preferences of liberal economists that they should become socially and geographically mobile, and neither are they acting as desired by liberal oppositionists, providing the muscle behind politically motivated protest. Yet most workers are also not the dutiful patriots that Putin and his circle would wish them to be. Not surprisingly, they have their own interests.

There is a contradiction in the politics of many of Russia's liberals: they call for free and fair elections, yet while many would not call the bulk of the country's population (as Babchenko did) "naked asses," they too often look down on the attitudes of average Russians, the very ones whose voices would count in a true democracy. Indeed, if Russia were ever to experience a true democracy—that is, a government that clearly reflects popular interests and sentiment—it would not necessarily make Russia more "Western." Such a democracy (admittedly idealized) would make the state more accountable to, and shaped in the preferences of, average Russians, who are clearly not economically liberal; nor are politically liberal ideals necessarily their top priority. Instead, the evidence strongly suggests their preferences lie in some version of socialism, social democracy, or in support of a "social state." To phrase the issue more pointedly, if a Russian government were to pursue a more a dramatically free-market or neoliberal transformation, that might require even more authoritarianism, rather than more democracy.[18]

To argue, as this book has, that the country's leadership has refrained from embarking on certain socially painful economic reforms—that is, that the fear of social unrest places limits on Russia's increasingly authoritarian state—is not to say that Putin's Russia is somehow opposed to economic liberalism. While liberal technocrats and statists often wrestle each other to gain influence over Kremlin policy, and though the Russian state has gained demonstrably greater control over the economy, the state's role in that economy is arguably at once both statist and neoliberal.[19] Rather than being a contradiction, as others have argued, the neoliberal state under globalized capitalism is rarely small or laissez-faire but rather geared toward to the demands of capital accumulation.[20] The Putin-era economy is built on the foundations of the liberal transformation of the Yeltsin era; it soon implemented a flat tax, and more recently has retained a tight grip on macroeconomic and fiscal stability. Inequality has grown; while some of the names have shifted, oligarchs and billionaires have flourished under Putin.[21]

But if the Russian economy is neither fully liberal or statist, the country's political system is not entirely authoritarian. Elections, however restricted, can still serve as focal points for protest; Putin's approval ratings clearly remain a Kremlin obsession. In such a political hybrid, social protest stemming from painful economic reforms can pose a threat of a kind that would not appear in a more overtly authoritarian system that can rely more explicitly on coercion. Military dictators in Chile and Argentina, for example, had unionists and other leftists who opposed painful neoliberal reforms thrown from helicopters. To the dilemmas of a hybrid regime, one must add the historical and ideological legacy of the Soviet state, where figures of workers were placed on pedestals. While those monuments have largely disappeared, the memory of that past has not. Pinochet would hardly have laid flowers at a Chilean Novocherkassk, nor would he have helicoptered in to deliver a nationally televised dressing-down to a Chilean oligarch over a workers' protest.[22]

Almost unavoidably in discussing contemporary Russia, we have invoked Putin's name to a considerable degree and pondered the possibilities for and likelihood of a Russian color revolution; however, it should be clear by now that the shape of Russia's political economy is not simply the result of the Kremlin's rent-seeking "kleptocrats."[23] Rather, as Alena Ledeneva has argued, the Russian political economy appears to be much more systemic, and likely to survive into any post-Putin leadership.[24] The limits to transforming that system extend beyond the patron-client relations of Russia's political elite, to managing the expectations, demands, and potential breaking point of Russia's workers and broader society.

Even with all that we have discussed so far—the problems of extremely flexible and often exceedingly low wages, the chronic problems of monotowns, the lack of institutional outlets for worker grievances leading to spontaneous and at times extreme outbursts, the significant state interventions and subsidies that were needed to prevent the crisis at AvtoVAZ and Tolyatti from exploding, the rapid politicization of Russia's truckers in response to a simple road tax—it remains unclear that workers present a direct threat to Russia's ruling elite. Yet the probability is hardly zero, and the stakes are high. The fear of social instability—and ultimately political instability—remains. In the absence of high oil and gas revenues, the Russian economy must either find new sources of economic growth or face stagnation. Either scenario—market reforms or economic stagnation—raises the possibility, even probability, of social unrest. That is the dilemma at the core of this book.

The goal here is not to suggest policy options for the Russian government. There are no ready avenues for escaping this dilemma. The only alternative to further neoliberal reforms imposed on society in the hopes of jump-starting economic growth, or economic stagnation alongside an evermore severe paternalism, would be to permit society to organize, allow real trade unions to assert the interests of their members, to push up wages and benefits for the unemployed and the poor. This would hardly be a utopia—Russia would almost certainly remain a middle-income country (or an upper-middle one). Whatever possibilities there might have been to make its industry competitive have arguably passed, and Russia will quite likely remain primarily a producer of commodities for the global market and—while hardly poor by comparative standards—thus stuck on the semi-periphery of the global capitalist system.[25]

This self-organized civil society would at least allow Russia's citizens to take an active part in shaping their own destiny, even if it involves negotiating the pace and the form of the country's further deindustrialization. But such a self-organized society would pose a direct threat to Russia's power holders, not only to their grip on political power but to the vast wealth they have accumulated. It might pose a challenge to the vision of many in Russia's political opposition as well, since a true Russian democracy would not likely lead to a neoliberal cosmopolitanism, as most Russians, workers and others, express a desire for something closer to socialism or social democracy, and not austerity and a handful of thriving metropolitan centers alongside postindustrial ghost towns.

Notes

1. THE POLITICAL CONSEQUENCES OF RUSSIAN DEINDUSTRIALIZATION

1. ITAR-TASS, "President Appoints Railway Car Building Plant's Workshop Manager Presidential Envoy in Urals."

2. Krastev and Holmes, "Autopsy of Managed Democracy"; Aron, "Russia's 'Monotowns' Time Bomb."

3. Zubarevich, "Chetyre Rossii"; Zubarevich, "Four Russias."

4. Miller, *Putinomics*, 97.

5. Gaddy and Ickes, *Bear Traps on Russia's Road to Modernization*; Kudrin and Gurvich, "Novaia model' rosta dlia Rossiiskoi ekonomiki"; Ledeneva, *Can Russia Modernise?*; Dawisha, *Putin's Kleptocracy*.

6. Robertson, *Politics of Protest in Hybrid Regimes*, 62.

7. An important exception was Serbia's "Bulldozer Revolution," where a strike by coal miners at the Kolubara mine, which produced roughly half the country's electricity, played a crucial role in Milošević's downfall. Erlanger, "Serbian Strikers, Joined by 20,000, Face Down Police."

8. Indeed, many have argued that authoritarians in contemporary societies are most likely to be threatened by protests in major cities. Wallace, "Cities, Redistribution, and Authoritarian Regime Survival."

9. Clarke, *Conflict and Change in the Russian Industrial Enterprise*, 13, 40.

10. Kolesnikov, "Dilemma diktatorov: Pochemu Lukashenko ne ukhodit."

11. Chernyshova, "Very Belarusian Affair"; Edwards, "Belarusian Workers Support Protesters with Growing Strikes."

12. Scott, *Seeing Like a State*.

13. Offe, *Contradictions of the Welfare State*.

14. According to Credit Suisse in its 2016 *Global Wealth Report*, "the top decile of wealth-holders owns 89% of all household wealth in Russia. This is significantly higher than any other major economic power": Shorrocks et al., "Global Wealth Report 2016," 53. See also Novokmet, Piketty, and Zucman, "From Soviets to Oligarchs." Countries such as Brazil and South Africa can certainly rival Russia in terms of wealth inequality. Measures of income (as opposed to wealth) inequality would find somewhat lower levels for Russia comparatively.

15. Haggard and Kaufman, *Dictators and Democrats*; Lichbach, "Will Rational People Rebel against Inequality?"; White, McAllister, and Munro, "Economic Inequality and Political Stability in Russia and China."

16. Ledeneva, *Can Russia Modernise?*

17. Haggard and Kaufman, "Introduction: Institutions and Economic Adjustment," 32.

18. Evans, *Embedded Autonomy*; Deyo, *Beneath the Miracle*.

19. Haggard and Kaufman, "Introduction: Institutions and Economic Adjustment," 32.

20. Svolik, *Politics of Authoritarian Rule*. See also Gandhi and Przeworski, "Cooperation, Cooptation, and Rebellion under Dictatorships."

21. Hale, *Patronal Politics*.

22. Acemoglu and Robinson, *Economic Origins of Dictatorship and Democracy*; Gandhi and Przeworski, "Cooperation, Cooptation, and Rebellion under Dictatorships"; Knutsen and Rasmussen, "Autocratic Welfare State."

23. Compare Collier, *Paths toward Democracy*, and Rueschemeyer, Huber, and Stephens, *Capitalist Development and Democracy*, with Acemoglu and Robinson, *Economic Origins of Dictatorship and Democracy*.

24. For a challenge to that view of the middle class see Rosenfeld, "Reevaluating the Middle-Class Protest Paradigm."

25. Doner and Schneider, "Middle-Income Trap," 4.

26. Brancati, *Democracy Protests*; Haggard and Kaufman, *Dictators and Democrats*; Acemoglu and Robinson, *Economic Origins of Dictatorship and Democracy*; Mesquita and Smith, "Leader Survival, Revolutions, and the Nature of Government Finance"; Treisman, "Income, Democracy, and Leader Turnover"; Guriev and Treisman, "Popularity of Authoritarian Leaders."

27. Brancati, *Democracy Protests*.

28. Shih, *Economic Shocks and Authoritarian Stability*.

29. Rosenfeld, "Popularity Costs of Economic Crisis under Electoral Authoritarianism."

30. Wines, "World; O.K., the Ruble's Junk."

31. Mandel, "'Why Is There No Revolt?'"; Ashwin, *Russian Workers*; Kubicek, *Organized Labor in Postcommunist States*. For a revisionist view see Sil, "Fluidity of Labor Politics in Postcommunist Transitions."

32. Kolesnikov, "By Bread Alone."

33. Zubarevich, "Strana gotova szhimat'sya i vyzhivat'."

34. Wynn, *Workers, Strikes, and Pogroms*; Kuromiya, *Freedom and Terror in the Donbas*.

35. Gorbachev, *Zhizn' i reformy*, 460.

36. Crowley, *Hot Coal, Cold Steel*.

37. Przeworski, *Democracy and the Market*; Haggard and Kaufman, *Political Economy of Democratic Transitions*.

38. Crowley, "Explaining Labor Weakness in Post-Communist Europe"; Kubicek, *Organized Labor in Postcommunist States*.

39. Greskovits, *Political Economy of Protest and Patience*; Appel and Orenstein, *From Triumph to Crisis*.

40. Silver, *Forces of Labor*.

41. Wengle, *Post-Soviet Power*, 47, emphasis in original.

42. Mitchell, *Carbon Democracy*.

43. Voskoboynikov, "Structural Change, Expanding Informality and Labor Productivity Growth in Russia," 407.

44. Clover, *Riot. Strike. Riot.*

45. Romanov, "Regional Elite in the Epoch of Bankruptcy," 224.

46. Taubman, *Governing Soviet Cities*, 54.

47. S. Collier, *Post-Soviet Social*. For a fascinating and comprehensive exploration of Russia's monotowns from an urban design perspective (including Soviet-inspired monotowns in China and India), see Strange, *Monotown*.

48. World Bank, "Russia: Reshaping Economic Geography," 40; Collier, *Post-Soviet Social*.

49. Morris, *Everyday Post-Socialism*.

50. The literature is extensive, but see Florida, *Rise of the Creative Class*; Mellander et al., *Creative Class Goes Global*. For a more critical take see Rossi, *Cities in Global Capitalism*; Sassen, *Global City*; Harvey, *Cosmopolitanism and the Geographies of Freedom*; Harvey, *Limits to Capital*.

51. Aris, "Russia Is Stuck."

52. Greene, "Running to Stand Still"; Morris, *Everyday Post-Socialism*.

53. Gabowitsch, *Protest in Putin's Russia*.

54. Collier, *Paths toward Democracy*, 15; Murillo, "From Populism to Neoliberalism."

55. Crowley, "Russia's Labor Legacy"; Caraway, "Pathways of Dominance and Displacement."

56. Tilly, *From Mobilization to Revolution*.

57. Evans and Sil, "Dynamics of Labor Militancy in the Extractive Sector"; Anner and Liu, "Harmonious Unions and Rebellious Workers"; Pye, "Plantation Precariat."

58. Robertson, *Politics of Protest in Hybrid Regimes*, 168–69.

59. Goodwin, *No Other Way Out*.

60. Petrov, Lipman, and Hale, "Three Dilemmas of Hybrid Regime Governance."

61. In some ways, this places much of the post-Soviet leadership, despite the transition to capitalism, in a position similar to that of the Soviet *nomenklatura* of the post-Stalinist years, where maintaining power became paramount, since losing one's political position meant losing access to the considerable privileges that went with it, as Khrushchev found once he was deposed. Hence the importance of the "stability of cadres" to the Brezhnev-era elite.

62. Robertson, *Politics of Protest in Hybrid Regimes*, 179.

63. Østbø, "Between Opportunist Revolutionaries and Mediating Spoilers."

64. Robertson, *Politics of Protest in Hybrid Regimes*, 11.

65. Silitski, "Preempting Democracy"; Silitski, "Year after the Color Revolutions."

66. Inozemtsev, "Sources of Putin's Regime."

67. Tooze, *Crashed*.

68. Tilly, *From Mobilization to Revolution*.

69. Moore, *Social Origins of Dictatorship and Democracy*.

70. Robertson, *Politics of Protest in Hybrid Regimes*.

71. Wengle, *Post-Soviet Power*.

72. Remington, *Politics of Inequality in Russia*.

73. Greene, *Moscow in Movement*; Greene and Robertson, *Putin v. the People*. However, see Greene and Robertson, "Politics, Justice and the New Russian Strike."

74. Gabowitsch, *Protest in Putin's Russia*. For an exception to the general tendency to ignore workers see Wood, *Russia without Putin*, especially 68–75.

2. RUSSIA'S PECULIAR LABOR MARKET AND THE FEAR OF SOCIAL EXPLOSION

1. Kotkin, *Magnetic Mountain*.

2. Connor, *Accidental Proletariat*; Crowley, *Hot Coal, Cold Steel*. The USSR was the world's largest producer of crude steel, with production peaking in 1988 at 163 million metric tons (though some estimates claimed that half of Soviet steel output was wasted because of poor quality). Miller, *Putinomics*, 94.

3. Miller, *Putinomics*.

4. Kornai, *Economics of Shortage*.

5. Regarding food items, in one large but by no means extreme example, in the late Soviet period the steel factory Zapsib in Novokuznetsk, with over thirty thousand workers, controlled several vacation centers and eight pioneer camps, some as far away as Central Asia and Crimea. The plant had its own state farm, to which various shops sent gas and other materials, as well as workers at harvest time, and also had its own meat-producing rabbit farm and an aquaculture program. The entire operation was supervised by the steel plant's "deputy director for agriculture." Food production was further expanded when the plant contracted with a Moscow engineering cooperative to build

a shop for producing sausage and other meat products at the plant. In addition to the plant cafeterias, which provided workers with their main meal of the day at subsidized prices, the plant had twelve stores selling foodstuffs inside the production shops and two more selling consumer goods. In addition to food, the plant also provided workers with other items in short supply such as housing, televisions, and automobiles. Crowley, *Hot Coal, Cold Steel.*

6. Ashwin, *Russian Workers.*

7. Crowley, *Hot Coal, Cold Steel*; Ashwin, *Russian Workers*; Kubicek, *Organized Labor in Postcommunist States.*

8. Ashwin and Clarke, *Russian Trade Unions and Industrial Relations in Transition*, 30.

9. Crowley, *Hot Coal, Cold Steel.*

10. Hirschman, *Exit, Voice, and Loyalty.*

11. Hauslohner, "Gorbachev's Social Contract."

12. Baron, *Bloody Saturday in the Soviet Union*; Turovsky, "Novocherkassk Massacre."

13. Regardless of the empirical validity of the claim that price rises in the Soviet Union would lead to protest, this perception was widespread, inside and outside the Soviet Union.

14. Crowley, *Hot Coal, Cold Steel.* The strike began in March 1991, ending only with Gorbachev's signing of the "9+1 agreement," which promised to dramatically reshape the Soviet Union. The pending implementation of that agreement prompted the failed coup, the final nail in the Soviet coffin.

15. Gorbachev, *Zhizn' i reformy*, 460.

16. Crawford, "Post-Communist Political Economy," 27–28.

17. Barnes, *Owning Russia*, 75–76, cited in Wood, *Russia without Putin*, 36.

18. Inozemtsev, "Russia's Economic Modernization," 9.

19. Barnes, *Owning Russia.*

20. Inozemtsev, "Russia's Economic Modernization," 10.

21. Given the resulting hardship, much has been written about the plight of Russia's workers in the 1990s. We will recount only the broad outlines here, focusing on how the directions taken then continue to impact current conditions. See Clarke, *Conflict and Change in the Russian Industrial Enterprise*; Clarke, *Structural Adjustment without Mass Unemployment?*; Cook, "Trade Unions, Management, and the State in Contemporary Russia"; Crowley, "Social Explosion That Wasn't"; Kubicek, *Organized Labor in Postcommunist States.*

22. Gimpelson and Kapeliushnikov, "Labor Market Adjustment," 720n1.

23. International Monetary Fund and Organisation for Economic Co-operation and Development, *Study of the Soviet Economy*, vol. 2.

24. Clarke, *Structural Adjustment without Mass Unemployment?*, 18.

25. Milanovic, *Income, Inequality, and Poverty*, 29; Clarke, *Structural Adjustment without Mass Unemployment?*; Gimpelson and Kapeliushnikov, "Labor Market Adjustment."

26. Although official figures may fail to capture informal economic activity, other measures put the decline at only slightly lower levels. On this see Milanovic, *Income, Inequality, and Poverty.*

27. By contrast, in the postcommunist countries of Poland, Bulgaria, and Slovakia, unemployment levels approached 20 percent for much of the 2000s. Gimpelson, Kapeliushnikov, and Roshchin, *Rossiiskii rynok truda*, 13.

28. Ashwin, *Russian Workers*, 9.

29. Ashwin, *Russian Workers.*

30. One expert at a forum on corporate raiding counseled that an "armed detachment" (*silovoe podrazdelenie*) will want to avoid fighting with a crowd of workers in front of cameras. He added, however, that "you have to establish a relationship with your

employees in advance. You cannot just get . . . them to go out there for you on 'ready, set, go': workers usually hate their managers." Markus, "Secure Property as a Bottom-Up Process," 253. In one example, workers at the Krasnoyarsk Aluminum Plant were said to support the existing director in a privatization struggle, because the plant "retained its Soviet-era wealth of social benefits, ranging from medical services to kindergartens." This despite the fact that the director was being held on money laundering and murder charges. *Moscow Times*, April 28, 2000.

31. Kabalina, "Privatisation and Restructuring of Enterprises," 288.

32. Gimpelson and Kapeliushnikov, "Labor Market Adjustment."

33. Standing, "Reviving Dead Souls."

34. Remington, *Politics of Inequality in Russia*.

35. Within constraints, managers attempted to do just that. Facing the exodus of their best workers, managers abandoned "the attempt to 'preserve the labor collective' as a whole in favor of a strategy of 'preserving the skeleton of the labor collective'" by providing relatively higher wages to key workers and letting less desired workers leave because of poor wages and work conditions. Clarke, "Labor Relations and Class Formation."

36. Schwartz, "Employment Restructuring in Russian Industrial Enterprises," 65–66.

37. Gimpelson, Kapeliushnikov, and Roshchin, *Rossiiskii rynok truda*, 15.

38. Gimpelson and Kapeliushnikov, "Labor Market Adjustment," 8.

39. Remington, *Politics of Inequality in Russia*, 214.

40. Remington, 51.

41. See Guy Standing, "Reviving Dead Souls."

42. Remington, *Politics of Inequality in Russia*, 52; Woodruff, *Money Unmade*.

43. Woodruff, *Money Unmade*, 132–33; Collier, *Post-Soviet Social*.

44. One source claims that during the height of privatization from 1992 to 1995, 20 percent of military plants in Russia were declared bankrupt and closed, though the size of those plants was not specified. "Analiz protsessov privatizatsii," cited in Ushakin, *Patriotism of Despair*, 8.

45. Romanov, "Regional Elite in the Epoch of Bankruptcy," 224, citing *Samarskie Izvestiya*, September 27, 1994.

46. Schumpeter, *Capitalism, Socialism and Democracy*.

47. Nelson, "Politics of Economic Transformation."

48. Woodruff, *Money Unmade*, 115; Wengle, *Post-Soviet Power*.

49. Woodruff, *Money Unmade*, 115n9.

50. Wengle, *Post-Soviet Power*, 4.

51. Wengle, 5, 14; Woodruff, *Money Unmade*.

52. Wengle, *Post-Soviet Power*, 193–94.

53. Remington, *Politics of Inequality in Russia*, 76.

54. Remington, 107, 108, 211.

55. Romanov, "Regional Elite in the Epoch of Bankruptcy," 224.

56. Guy Standing points to the "considerable financial incentives to induce firms to put workers on lay-off rather than make them formally unemployed," such as avoiding severance payments. "Reviving Dead Souls," 153.

57. Gaddy and Ickes, *Russia's Virtual Economy*; Woodruff, *Money Unmade*.

58. Crowley, "Social Explosion That Wasn't"; Kubicek, *Organized Labor in Postcommunist States*; Javeline, *Protest and the Politics of Blame*; Cook, "Trade Unions, Management, and the State in Contemporary Russia."

59. For example, according a Meeting Report of the Kennan Institute, Anders Åslund argued "it is important to note that there has been little to no labor unrest in Russia, which may be proof that the situation is not so dire." "Achievement and Failures

in Russian Reform," Meeting Report, Kennan Institute for Advanced Russian Studies, vol. 14, no. 13, 1997.

60. Robertson, *Politics of Protest in Hybrid Regimes*.

61. Gimpelson, Kapeliushnikov, and Roshchin, *Rossiiskii rynok truda*, 24.

62. Alasheev and Kiblitskaya, "How to Survive on a Russian's Wage."

63. Shorrocks and Kolenikov, "Poverty Trends in Russia during the Transition."

64. Gerber and Hout, "Tightening Up," 695.

65. Alasheev and Kiblitskaya, "How to Survive on a Russian's Wage." While teachers in Voronezh Oblast were offered fences and tombs from a local cemetery instead of cash wages, in Tula Oblast, authorities in the town of Kimovsk, having received manure from collective farms to pay off the farms' debts, redistributed the manure to teachers in the place of back pay. The teachers received some 1,000 tons of manure, but 125,000 tons were required to pay off all their back wages. *Izvestiya*, November 26, 1999, as reported in ICEM, "Russia Campaign: Strikes and Protests."

66. Earle and Peter, "Equilibrium Wage Arrears"; Desai and Idson, *Work without Wages*; Javeline, *Protest and the Politics of Blame*.

67. RF Human Rights Commissioner, "1999 Report of RF Human Rights Commissioner."

68. Working, "Russia's Patchwork Economy." With such low wages, workers looked elsewhere for income. Young men stripped copper wire from utility poles to sell as scrap. Unfortunately, in a number of cases the wires were live and led to gruesome injuries. This however did not deter others, and sometimes the very same individuals, from taking such action. "Power Line Thieves Loot Russia, Often Risking Death or Maiming," *New York Times*, April 18, 2000.

69. It noted further that despite the steep drop in output, "the working conditions of more than 43 percent of the laboring public are inconsistent with public health standards," and "the rate of industrial accidents has risen sharply." RF Human Rights Commissioner, "1999 Report of RF Human Rights Commissioner."

70. Javeline, "Labor Challenges and the Problem of Quiescence."

71. Between 1990 and 1995, the number of working-age people who died from alcohol-related causes more than tripled, while in the same period the number of registered disabled rose by 1.4 times, the number of murders more than doubled, and the number of suicides rose by 1.6 times. Standing, "Reviving Dead Souls," 154.

72. Clarke, *Conflict and Change in the Russian Industrial Enterprise*, 3, 13, 40.

73. *Nezavisimaya Gazeta*, May 19, 1998; Fred Weir, as posted in Johnson's Russia List, no. 2143, April 9, 1998. Here Chernovets manages to combine in a few sentences the tropes of the Russian people as patient with their history of leading revolutions.

74. *Financial Times*, August 19, 1998.

75. *Izvestia*, September 23, 1998.

76. Gimpelson, Kapeliushnikov, and Roshchin, *Rossiiskii rynok truda*, 53.

77. Gimpelson and Kapeliushnikov, "Anticipation and Management of Restructuring in Russia," 10, 38.

78. Clarke, *Structural Adjustment without Mass Unemployment?*, 10–11.

79. Gimpelson and Kapeliushnikov, "Labor Market Adjustment."

80. Gimpelson, Kapeliushnikov, and Roshchin, *Rossiiskii rynok truda*, 13.

81. Rossiiskaya Federatsiya, "Federal'naya Sluzhba Gosudarstvennoi Statistiki."

82. Gimpelson and Kapeliushnikov, "Labor Market Adjustment," 3.

83. Remington, *Politics of Inequality in Russia*, 71.

84. Gimpelson and Kapeliushnikov, "Labor Market Adjustment," 10, 12.

85. Gimpelson, Kapeliushnikov, and Roshchin, *Rossiiskii rynok truda*, 29.

86. Inozemtsev, "Sources of Putin's Regime," 3.
87. World Bank, "Russia: Reshaping Economic Geography," 67.
88. Remington, *Politics of Inequality in Russia*, 204.
89. World Bank, "Russia: Reshaping Economic Geography," 67.
90. Inozemtsev, "Chto tyanet nas obratno v SSSR?"
91. Gaddy and Ickes, *Bear Traps on Russia's Road to Modernization*.
92. Gimpelson and Kapeliushnikov, "Anticipation and Management of Restructuring in Russia," 12.
93. Rosstat, "Finansy Rossii," 102.
94. AP Archive, *Putin Comments on Iraq, Economy and Other Issues*.
95. Inozemtsev, "Russia's Economic Modernization."
96. Inozemtsev, "Russia Shouldn't Work but It Does."
97. Gaddy and Ickes, "Russian Economy through 2020," 166. Though he is more sympathetic to the desire to avoid social upheaval, see also Remington, *Politics of Inequality in Russia*; Wengle, *Post-Soviet Power*.
98. Remington, *Politics of Inequality in Russia*, 75.
99. Wengle, *Post-Soviet Power*, 270.
100. Wengle, 92–93.
101. Heleniak, "International Comparisons of Population Mobility in Russia."
102. Wengle, *Post-Soviet Power*, 93.
103. Gimpelson and Kapeliushnikov, "Anticipation and Management of Restructuring in Russia," 3.
104. Baev, "Russia Is Steered Back toward Petro-Stagnation."
105. Zubarevich, "Gubernatoropad." As Lamberova and Treisman note, "governors and mayors are responsible for maintaining social order and ensuring electoral victories in their jurisdictions, and are managed in this regard by the political operatives of the Presidential Administration in the Kremlin." Lamberova and Treisman, "Economic Shocks and Authoritarian Responses."
106. Inozemtsev, "Sources of Putin's Regime," 4.

3. RUSSIA'S LABOR PRODUCTIVITY TRAP

1. Krugman, *Age of Diminished Expectations*.
2. Kudrin and Gurvich, "New Growth Model for the Russian Economy," 17.
3. Gaddy and Ickes, *Bear Traps on Russia's Road to Modernization*, 97.
4. President of Russia, "Vladimir Putin's Annual News Conference."
5. Inozemtsev, "Russia's Economic Modernization"; Kotz and Weir, *Russia's Path from Gorbachev to Putin*; Stiglitz, *Globalization and Its Discontents*.
6. World Bank, "Russia: Reshaping Economic Geography," 108.
7. Gimpelson, Kapeliushnikov, and Roshchin, *Rossiiskii rynok truda*, 13.
8. Kudrin and Gurvich, "New Growth Model for the Russian Economy," 17.
9. Kudrin and Gurvich, 6.
10. Kudrin and Gurvich, 20–21. Needless to say, labor is a central factor of production. Thus the authors explicitly call on the government to "eliminate excess employment where it exists" (27).
11. Rossiiskaya Federatsiya, "Federal'naya Sluzhba Gosudarstvennoi Statistiki."
12. Gimpelson, Kapeliushnikov, and Roshchin, *Rossiiskii rynok truda*, 94.
13. Gimpelson, Kapeliushnikov, and Roshchin, 97, 105.
14. Gimpelson, Kapeliushnikov, and Roshchin, *Rossiiskii rynok truda*.
15. Rosbalt, "Analitik."

16. Thus Kudrin and Gurvich argue, "A shrinking labor force . . . puts additional upward pressure on wages." Kudrin and Gurvich, "New Growth Model for the Russian Economy," 27.

17. Schenk, *Why Control Immigration?*

18. Economy Times, "Ol'ga Golodets."

19. W.M. Mercer Consulting, "Worldwide Benefit and Employment Guidelines 2001/2002."

20. Kuvshinova, "Rabota bez zarabotka."

21. Rambler, "Golodets o roste bednosti"; Olimpieva, "Tragedy of the Working Poor and the Populism of Russia's Presidential Campaign."

22. RBC, "Putin poruchil uravniat' MROT i prozhitochnyi minimum k nachalu 2019 goda"; TASS, "Putin Signs Law on Minimum Wage Hike to $195 Starting 2020."

23. "I believe that the Constitution should include a provision that the minimum wage in Russia must not be below the subsistence minimum of the economically active people. We have a law on this, but we should formalize this requirement in the Constitution." President of Russia, "Presidential Address to the Federal Assembly."

24. Meyer (Olimpieva), "Tragedy of the Working Poor and the Populism of Russia's Presidential Campaign"; Lyashok, "Povyshenie MROT."

25. Meyer (Olimpieva), "Tragedy of the Working Poor and the Populism of Russia's Presidential Campaign"; Gimpelson, Kapeliushnikov, and Roshchin, *Rossiiskii rynok truda*, 73.

26. World Bank, "Russia's Recovery," 14.

27. World Bank, 13.

28. Meyer (Olimpieva), "Tragedy of the Working Poor and the Populism of Russia's Presidential Campaign."

29. Meduza, "At 39 Percent of GDP, Russia's Shadow Economy Is the Fourth Largest in the World." Ironically, one obstacle to the further growth of Russia's informal economy comes from workers' already low wages: in order to survive with limited income, an increasing number of Russians have gone into debt. But in order to take on debt, many need to provide proof of income, which can only come from a formal-sector job. I am grateful to Liliya Karimova for this point.

30. Morris, *Everyday Post-Socialism.*

31. Mukhametshina, "Piataia chast' Rossiiskikh uchitelei dumaiut ob ukhode iz shkoly."

32. OECD, *Russia*, 94–95.

33. Voskoboynikov, "Structural Change, Expanding Informality and Labor Productivity Growth in Russia."

34. In Russia the tradeoff is not merely theoretical: the size of the informal economy is almost directly (if inversely) correlated with the level of unemployment. When one goes up, the other goes down. Gimpelson, Kapeliushnikov, and Roshchin, *Rossiiskii rynok truda*, 79.

35. Gimpelson and Kapeliushnikov, "Anticipation and Management of Restructuring in the Russia," 20.

36. OECD, *Russia*, 38.

37. OECD, 31.

38. Linz and Semykina, "How Do Workers Fare during Transition?"; Gimpelson and Oshchepkov, "Does More Unemployment Cause More Fear of Unemployment?"; Gimpelson and Monusova, "Strakh bezrabotitsi."

39. Gimpelson and Oshchepkov, "Does More Unemployment Cause More Fear of Unemployment?" By contrast, in the US and the UK, the number of workers who feared losing their jobs in the 1990s was under 10 percent. However, the number of

workers fearing job loss was high in many other postcommunist countries besides Russia. Gimpelson and Kapeliushnikov, "Labor Market Adjustment."

40. Gimpelson and Kapeliushnikov, "Labor Market Adjustment," 22.

41. CEPR, "ZdravoZakhoronenie."

42. Bear Market Brief, "Analytical Center Counts 12 Million among Working Poor." See also Zvezdina, "Eksperty rasskazali o stavke nizhe 25 tys. rub. u poloviny vrachei."

43. Podtserob, "Pochemu v Rossii vygodno byt' 'rabotaiushchim bednym.'"

44. Hille and Foy, "Russia's Next Revolution."

45. Kudrin and Gurvich, "New Growth Model for the Russian Economy."

46. Hille and Foy, "Russia's Next Revolution."

47. Gimpelson and Kapeliushnikov, "Labor Market Adjustment."

48. OECD, *Russia*; Morris, *Everyday Post-Socialism*.

49. Gimpelson, Kapeliushnikov, and Roshchin, *Rossiiskii rynok truda*. Though see the attempts to address this problem at the regional level: Remington, "Business-Government Cooperation in VET."

50. Gaddy and Ickes, "Russia after the Global Financial Crisis," 293.

51. Morris, *Everyday Post-Socialism*.

52. Inozemtsev, "Nas malo, no eto ne vazhno."

53. Deyo, *Beneath the Miracle*; Wade, *Governing the Market*; Chang, *Bad Samaritans*.

54. Sharma, "Next Economic Powerhouse?"; Sharma, *Rise and Fall of Nations*.

55. Sharma, "Next Economic Powerhouse?"

56. Inozemtsev, "Russia's Economic Modernization," 10–11.

57. Chang, *Bad Samaritans*.

58. Inozemtsev, "Russia's Economic Modernization," 10–11.

59. Szakonyi, "Monopolies Rising."

60. Miles, "Russia Was Most Protectionist Nation in 2013."

61. World Bank, "Russia: Reshaping Economic Geography," 42.

62. World Bank, 116.

63. Gaddy and Ickes, *Bear Traps on Russia's Road to Modernization*.

64. Gaddy and Ickes, *Bear Traps on Russia's Road to Modernization*. See also Commander, Nikoloski, and Plekhanov, "Employment Concentration and Resource Allocation."

65. I am grateful to Vladimir Gimpelson for this point.

66. Tkachev, "Issledovanie RBK."

67. Mereminskaia, "Konkurentsii ne stalo bol'she"; Szakonyi, "Monopolies Rising."

68. Sil, "Privatization, Labor Politics, and the Firm in Post-Soviet Russia," 209.

69. Kudrin and Gurvich, "New Growth Model for the Russian Economy"; Kornai, *Economics of Shortage*.

70. Kudrin and Gurvich, "New Growth Model for the Russian Economy," 20. As for the ability of such firms to borrow funds on favorable terms, by 2016 state-owned banks in Russia were distributing more than 71 percent of corporate loans. Szakonyi, "Monopolies Rising."

71. Leutert, "China's State Enterprise Reform."

72. FAS Russia, "Report on Competition Policy in Russian Federation in 2016 to OECD."

73. Szakonyi, "Monopolies Rising."

74. Szakonyi.

75. Golikova, Gonchar, and Kuznetsov, "Rossiiskaia promyshlennost' na pereput'e."

76. Kudrin and Gurvich, "New Growth Model for the Russian Economy," 23–24.

77. Tkachev and Feinberg, "Zerkalo zastoia."

78. Szakonyi, "Monopolies Rising."

79. Remington, *Presidential Decrees in Russia*; *Vedomosti*, "Vladimir Gimpel'son: Gde vziat' 25 mln."

80. Gaddy, *Price of the Past*; Mikhailova, "Where Russians Should Live," 3.

81. Cooper, "Military Dimension of a More Militant Russia," 130.

82. Hakvåg, "Russian Defense Spending after 2010."

83. Gaaze, "Accidental Formation of Russia's War Coalition."

84. As recorded in Hakvåg, "Russian Defense Spending after 2010."

85. "Russian National Security Strategy, December 2015—Full-Text Translation."

86. Hakvåg, "Russian Defense Spending after 2010," 505.

87. Yakovlev, "What Is Russia Trying to Defend?," 152.

88. As quoted in Hakvåg, "Russian Defense Spending after 2010."

89. Litovkin, "S 'bulavoi' napereves."

90. Golts, "Militarizm i konkurentosposobnost' Rossii," 6.

91. Hakvåg, "Russian Defense Spending after 2010," 505.

92. Hakvåg, 505; Zubarevich, "Tri tipa regionov."

93. TsEPR, "Monitoring sotsial'no-ekonomicheskoi napriazhennosti v trudovoi sfere v 2016 godu," 8–9.

94. Golts, "Militarizm i konkurentosposobnost' Rossii."

95. World Bank, "Russia: Reshaping Economic Geography," 101.

96. Though in typical top-down fashion, the Russian government is trying to change that, with plans to launch a new medium-range passenger airliner, the MC-21, to replace the outdated Soviet-era Tupolev Tu-154s. Rahimov, "Eurasian Union."

97. Gaddy and Ickes, *Bear Traps on Russia's Road to Modernization*.

98. Gaddy and Ickes argue further than "loser regions" are generally anti-growth, given their interests in self-preservation. They quote Viktor Tolokonskiy, governor of Novosibirsk, from August 2000: "Under conditions of total openness of the economy . . . we here in Siberia should not expect any serious investment activity at all. Our costs of production are too high, residential housing and office manufacturing facilities are too expensive, and our transport costs and wages are higher than in southeastern Asia." Gaddy and Ickes, *Bear Traps on Russia's Road to Modernization*, 75.

99. Kudrin and Gurvich, "New Growth Model for the Russian Economy," 23.

100. Balzer, "What Have We Learned," 3.

101. Frye, Reuter, and Szakonyi, "Political Machines at Work."

102. Frye, Reuter, and Szakonyi, "Hitting Them with Carrots."

103. Though the surveys did not reveal the political content of the workplace campaigning, by most accounts business leaders are often closely allied with United Russia, and those that aren't are often threatened with a loss of state support.

104. Frye, Reuter, and Szakonyi, "Political Machines at Work," 217.

105. Frye, Reuter, and Szakonyi, "Hitting Them with Carrots."

106. Rochlitz, "Political Loyalty vs Economic Performance," 1; Rochlitz et al., "Performance Incentives and Economic Growth." Frye and colleagues find that regions more supportive of United Russia during elections received greater social transfers and more targeted investment funds than other regions. During the financial crisis, politically loyal regions were even more richly rewarded. Frye et al., "Through Thick and through Thin."

107. Miller and Ivanov, "Regiony vstupili v bor'bu za iavku."

108. Jarmas, "Yes, the Kremlin Is Worried—"; Nagornykh, "Na vyborakh zadeistvuiut korporativnyi resurs."

109. Golubkova, "Exclusive."

110. Burmistrova, "Rosatom otsenit protestnye nastroeniia"; Bell, "Kto zaplatit za obraz budushchego dlia."

111. Kozlov, "Kreml' nachal monitoring ekonomicheskikh sobytii, vliiaiushchikh na regional'nye nastroeniia."

112. Rosenfeld, "Reevaluating the Middle-Class Protest Paradigm." This suggests the need to expand the traditional conception of "worker" beyond the industrial workplace. As we shall see when discussing labor protest in chapter 5, protest from public sector workers, including those in health and education, can have a particular impact.

113. Gimpelson and Oshchepkov, "Does More Unemployment Cause More Fear of Unemployment?," 4. Moreover, as we shall see in chapter 9, outside of the Baltic states, the "Russia model" of labor market adjustment has been replicated in much of the former Soviet Union, strongly suggesting the need for explanations that extend beyond Russia's current leadership.

4. MONOTOWNS AND RUSSIA'S POST-SOVIET URBAN GEOGRAPHY

1. Florida, *Rise of the Creative Class*; Mellander et al., *Creative Class Goes Global*.

2. Rossi, *Cities in Global Capitalism*, 5.

3. Sassen, *Global City*; Sassen, *Globalization and Its Discontents*.

4. Harvey, *Cosmopolitanism and the Geographies of Freedom*; Harvey, *Limits to Capital*.

5. Coletta et al., *Creating Smart Cities*; Song et al., *Smart Cities*. For a critical take on the concept of the "smart city" see Townsend, *Smart Cities*.

6. Leonard, "Spatial Development and Innovation in Russia."

7. Kudrin, "Goroda vmesto nefti"; Tsentr strategicheskikh razrabotok, "Tekhnologii umnogo goroda v rossiiskikh gorodakh."

8. Kudrin, "Goroda vmesto nefti."

9. Gazeta.ru, "Kudrin: Moskva i Sankt-Peterburg."

10. Tsentr strategicheskikh razrabotok, "Tekhnologii umnogo goroda v rossiiskikh gorodakh."

11. Kudrin, "Goroda vmesto nefti."

12. "Razvitie gorodov dolzhno stat' dvizhushchei siloi dlia strany, zaiavil Putin." Within days, however, his campaign website altered the statement so that it referred to "the whole country," promising to make sure that small cities and villages had access to all necessary goods and services: "Razvitie gorodov dolzhno stat' dvizhushchei siloi dlia vsei strany."

13. Pravitel'svo Rossiiskoi Federatsii, "Stratagiia prostranstvennogo razvitiia."

14. Pravitel'svo Rossiiskoi Federatsii, "Kompleksnogo plana modernizatsii"; Bershidsky, "Putin Turns Swathes of Russia."

15. Zubarevich, "Chetyre Rossii"; Zubarevich, "Four Russias."

16. Collier, *Post-Soviet Social*, chap. 8.

17. Morris, *Everyday Post-Socialism*.

18. Greene, "Running to Stand Still."

19. Gabowitsch, *Protest in Putin's Russia*.

20. World Bank, "Russia: Reshaping Economic Geography," 58; Rosstat, "Federal'naia sluzhba gosudarstvennoi statistiki. Chislennost' naseleniia Rossiiskoi Federatsii po munitsipal'nym obrazovaniiam na 1 ianvaria 2020 goda."

21. United Nations, "World Urbanization Prospects"; City Population, "City Population"; US Census Bureau, "American FactFinder—Results"; Collier, *Post-Soviet Social*, 111–12.

22. "Zipf's Law for Cities."

23. Further, as the World Bank notes, Russia's second-tier cities are also not large enough. Cities ranked between third and tenth by population account for only 6.6 percent

of Russia's population. This share is well below that found in Brazil, Japan, and Poland, where cities in the same ranks account for between 8 and 11 percent of the respective populations. World Bank Group, "Rolling Back Russia's Spatial Disparities," 9.

24. World Bank Group, 9.

25. World Bank, "Russia: Reshaping Economic Geography"; Statistics Canada, "Statistics Canada"; Australian Bureau of Statistics.

26. Mikhailova, "Gulag, WWII and the Long-Run Patterns of Soviet City Growth"; Barenberg, *Gulag Town, Company Town.*

27. Gaddy and Ickes, *Bear Traps on Russia's Road to Modernization*, 51.

28. Mikhailova, "Where Russians Should Live."

29. World Bank, "Russia: Reshaping Economic Geography," 33.

30. Hill and Gaddy, *Siberian Curse*; Gaddy and Ickes, *Bear Traps on Russia's Road to Modernization.*

31. World Bank, "Russia: Reshaping Economic Geography," 66.

32. World Bank, "Challenge of Russia's Monotowns." In one indication that regions themselves did not profit from the sale of their products on global markets, despite the hard currency the oil extracted from Perm Oblast earned in the 1970s and '80s, neither the residents of the region nor its regional elites directly profited. Rogers, *Depths of Russia.*

33. World Bank, "Russia: Reshaping Economic Geography," 28, 77.

34. Wengle, *Post-Soviet Power.*

35. Gaddy and Ickes, "Russian Economy through 2020," 165.

36. On the struggles and protests in Russian monotowns in the 1990s see Evans, "Protest Patterns in Provincial Russia"; Evans, "Local Democracy in a Hybrid State."

37. World Bank, "Russia: Reshaping Economic Geography," 41.

38. World Bank, 42.

39. Gontmakher, "Stenarii': Novocherkassk-2009."

40. Oreshkin, "2nd-Largest Potemkin Village in History."

41. Elder, "Vladimir Putin Takes Oleg Deripaska to Task."

42. Ledeneva, *Can Russia Modernise?*

43. Sperling, *Sex, Politics, and Putin.*

44. Fortescue, "Russian Economy and Business." For a detailed account see Maksimov, "Yavlenie Rossii v Pikalyovo."

45. Tooze, *Crashed*, 224, 226; Lamberova and Treisman, "Economic Shocks and Authoritarian Responses."

46. Ledeneva, *Can Russia Modernise?*, 107.

47. Wengle, *Post-Soviet Power*, 97. According to Dmitry Zemlyanksy of Moscow State University, "The effect of that show lingers until today," adding that "after what happened in Pikalyovo, in all Deripaska towns, they keep on a certain number of employees even in companies that should be shut down, just because of the fear of Putin." As quoted in Hille and Foy, "Russia's Next Revolution."

48. Krichevskii, "PostPikalevskaia Rossiia."

49. Crowley, "Monotowns and the Political Economy of Industrial Restructuring in Russia."

50. Sobesednik, "'Sindrom' Pikalevo." See also Yakutin and Matern, "'Sindrom Pikalievo' v ekonomike Rossii."

51. Aron, "Russia's 'Monotowns' Time Bomb"; Aron, "Darkness on the Edge of Monotown."

52. Zubarevich, *Regiony Rossii*, 92.

53. Zubarevich, 83, 87.

54. Zubarevich, 86.

55. The main criteria for inclusion on the list is that the leading enterprise provides at least 20 percent of overall employment in the town and that it engages in resource extraction (excluding oil and gas), industrial production, or the reworking of industrial products. One reason for the decline in the government's count of monotowns is that the criteria now exclude those from the oil and gas industry. Pravitel'stvo Rossii, "Ob utverzhdenii perechnya monogorodov."

56. See, for example, the many sources cited by Zamyatina and Pilyasov, *Innovatsionnyi poisk v monoprofil'nykh gorodakh.*

57. Zamyatina and Pilyasov, 7; Zubarevich, *Regiony Rossii.*

58. Il'ina, "Strategiya modernizatsii monogorodov Rossii."

59. Zamyatina and Pilyasov, *Innovatsionnyi poisk v monoprofil'nykh gorodakh.*

60. For an-depth look at how such variation can impact the likelihood of protest see A. Evans, "Protest Patterns in Provincial Russia."

61. Zubarevich, *Regiony Rossii,* 86.

62. World Bank, "Challenge of Russia's Monotowns," 24.

63. Commander, Nikoloski, and Plekhanov, "Employment Concentration and Resource Allocation," 10.

64. Pravitel'stvo Rossii, "Ob utverzhdenii perechnya monogorodov"; Pravitel'stvo Rossii, "O kriteriyakh otneseniya."

65. Pravitel'stvo Rossii, "O kriteriyakh otneseniya."

66. Pravitel'stvo Rossii, "O kriteriyakh otneseniya." On the FSO see Pertsev and Solopov, "What Putin Reads"; Sinelschikova, "'Putin's People.'"

67. They use two definitions of one-company towns: the first where 5 percent of the town's total population is employed at a single enterprise, and the second where 10 percent is. The first definition makes up 13–17 percent of manufacturing employment nationwide, including over one-third in the Urals Federal District, Russia's industrial core. Commander, Nikoloski, and Plekhanov, "Employment Concentration and Resource Allocation."

68. Nemtsova, "On the Edge of Siberia's Dark Blue Heart."

69. RFE/RL, "Dual Rallies over Baikal Paper Mill."

70. *Siberian Times,* "'There Is No Way Back.'"

71. Zamyatina and Pilyasov, "Single-Industry Towns of Russia," 59.

72. World Bank, "Challenge of Russia's Monotowns."

73. Prezident Rossii, "Soveshchanie po voprosam stabil'nogo razvitiia monogorodov."

74. Solov'eva, "Zhitelei monogorodov prevratiat v predprinimatelei."

75. Solov'eva, "FSO i profsoiuzy pomogaiut sledit' za sotsial'nym dinamitom." See also Hedlund, "Russia's Monotowns—Evidence of an Increasingly Obsolete Economy."

76. Miliukova, "FSO zafiksirovala ukhudshenie situatsii v monogorodakh."

77. Malysheva, "Krizis okhvatil monogoroda."

78. Tepliakov, "Sergei Mukhortov."

79. Fond razvitiia monogorodov, "Strategiia razvitiia nekommercheskoi organizatsii' do 2020 g."; Solov'eva, "FSO i profsoiuzy pomogaiut sledit' za sotsial'nym dinamitom."

80. World Bank, "Russia: Reshaping Economic Geography," 18.

81. World Bank, 12.

82. Harvey, "From Managerialism to Entrepreneurialism."

83. Zamyatina and Pilyasov, "Single-Industry Towns of Russia," 60.

84. Zubarevich, *Regiony Rossii.*

85. World Bank, "Russia: Reshaping Economic Geography," 106; Zubarevich, "Geopolitical Priorities in Russia's Regional Policies," 51.

86. Zubarevich, "Geopolitical Priorities in Russia's Regional Policies," 51.

87. Inozemtsev, "Russia's Economic Modernization."

88. "Monogoroda.rf."

89. Zamyatina and Pilyasov, "Single-Industry Towns of Russia"; Zamyatina and Pilyasov, *Innovatsionnyi poisk v monoprofil'nykh gorodakh.*

90. Solov'eva, "Zhitelei monogorodov prevratiat v predprinimatelei."

91. Fond razvitiia monogorodov, "Strategiia razvitiia nekommercheskoi organizatsii' do 2020 g., 2.

92. Fond razvitiia monogorodov, 3.

93. Fond razvitiia monogorodov, 3.

94. Tepliakov, "Sergei Mukhortov." That would explain the government's decision to "freeze" the number of designated monotowns. TASS, "Spisok monogorodov v rossii 'zamorozhen' do kontsa 2018 goda."

95. Vesti.ru, "Dying Soviet 'Monotowns' to Be Repurposed!" The ratio of temporary to permanent jobs was left unstated. Nevertheless, at least one government promise had been fulfilled: in 2011 Prime Minister Putin proclaimed that two hundred thousand new jobs would be created in monotowns by 2015. *Izvestiya*, "Putin ozhidaet znachitel'nogo snizheniya urovnya bezrabotitsy k godu 2015."

96. TASS, "Schetnaia Palata." For previous criticism from the Audit Chamber see Solov'eva, "Zhitelei monogorodov prevratiat v predprinimatelei"; Malysheva, "Krizis okhvatil monogoroda."

97. Fond razvitiia monogorodov, "Strategiia razvitiia nekommercheskoi organizatsii."

98. Solov'eva, "Zhitelei monogorodov prevratiat v predprinimatelei"; Malysheva, "Krizis okhvatil monogoroda."

99. Cited in Malysheva, "Krizis okhvatil monogoroda."

100. *Izvestiya*, "Putin ozhidaet znachitel'nogo snizheniya urovnya bezrabotitsy k godu 2015."

101. World Bank, "Russia: Reshaping Economic Geography," 12, 34.

102. World Bank, 18, 34.

103. World Bank, 17.

104. Bershidsky, "Putin Turns Swathes of Russia."

105. World Bank, "Russia: Reshaping Economic Geography," 112.

106. Zubarevich, *Regiony Rossii.* Such estimates vary considerably, though they all point to substantial differences between the US and Russia. The World Bank claims that the average American moves twelve times in his or her lifetime, whereas the average Russian moves only twice. According to Gaddy and Ickes, Russia's internal migration rate is about 1.2 percent, compared with over 5 percent in the US and Canada. World Bank, "Russia : Reshaping Economic Geography"; Gaddy and Ickes, *Bear Traps on Russia's Road to Modernization*, 56.

107. Mikhailova, "Where Russians Should Live," 39; Heleniak, "Out-Migration and Depopulation of the Russian North during the 1990s."

108. Gaddy and Ickes, *Bear Traps on Russia's Road to Modernization*, 55–56.

109. World Bank, "Russia: Reshaping Economic Geography," 25; Andrienko and Guriev, "Determinants of Interregional Mobility in Russia."

110. Federal'naia sluzhba gosudarstvennoi statistiki, "Chislennost' naseleniia Rossiiskoi Federatsii po munitsipal'nym obrazovaniiam"; Federal'naia sluzhba gosudarstvennoi statistiki, "Itogi Vserossiiskoi perepisi naseleniia 2010 goda."

111. Morris, *Everyday Post-Socialism.*

112. Plusnin et al., *Wandering Workers.*

113. I am grateful to Lewis Siegelbaum for this point.

114. Stoliarova, "'Oni prakticheski pustye.'"

115. Shiklomanov et al., "Dealing with the Bust in Vorkuta, Russia."

116. Remington, *Politics of Inequality in Russia.*

117. Meardi, *Social Failures of EU Enlargement*.

118. Ashwin, *Russian Workers*. According to a local housing official, explaining why people remained despite the dramatic loss of jobs in AvtoVAZ, the town's city-forming enterprise, "Over the years, people in Tolyatti have acquired comfortable apartments": Tovkailo, Tyomkin, and Nazarova, "AvtoVAZ Workers Offered Chance to Move." Tolyatti and AvtoVAZ are discussed in greater detail in chapter 6.

119. World Bank, "Russia: Reshaping Economic Geography," 36.

120. Commander, Nikoloski, and Plekhanov, "Employment Concentration and Resource Allocation."

121. Andrienko and Guriev, "Determinants of Interregional Mobility in Russia."

122. Zamyatina and Pilyasov, "Single-Industry Towns of Russia," 59. The authors argue, however, that "it is precisely the local community, and not abstract indicators, that determines the destiny of single-industry territories, including making radical decisions" for their future.

123. World Bank, "Russia: Reshaping Economic Geography," 118. The Russian economist Denis Raksha says all such residents should be moved, since otherwise state expenditures on maintaining infrastructure amount to "money going down the drain." Stoliarova, "'Oni prakticheski pustye.'"

124. World Bank, "Russia: Reshaping Economic Geography," 26, 114, emphasis added.

125. Zamyatina and Pilyasov, "Single-Industry Towns of Russia."

126. Granovetter, "Economic Action and Social Structure."

127. Zamyatina and Pilyasov, "Single-Industry Towns of Russia," 56, emphasis in original.

128. Zamyatina and Pilyasov, 57–58.

129. Zamyatina and Pilyasov, "Single-Industry Towns of Russia," 57–58.

130. Nedoseka and Karbainov, "Sotsial'noe Samochuvstvie Zhitelei Postsovetskogo Monogoroda."

131. Morris, *Everyday Post-Socialism*; Shiklomanov et al., "Dealing with the Bust in Vorkuta, Russia."

132. Dixon and Graybill, "Uncertainty in the Urban Form," 24.

133. Bolotova and Stammler, "How the North Became Home." See also Bolotova, Karaseva, and Vasilyeva, "Mobility and Sense of Place among Youth in the Russian Arctic."

134. Walsh, "Urban Wastelands."

135. Laruelle and Hohmann, "Biography of a Polar City."

136. Buder, "Toxic City of Norilsk, Russia."

137. Laruelle and Hohmann, "Biography of a Polar City."

138. Bolotova and Stammler, "How the North Became Home," 194.

139. Bolotova and Stammler.

140. Goble, "Moscow Can't Afford to Support Russia's Villages."

141. Goble.

142. Goble.

143. Varsegov, Blaginina, and Adamovich, "V glubinku dorogu prolozhim, sozhzhem milliardy rublei," as cited in Goble, "Window on Eurasia—New Series."

144. Nevidimye goroda, "Asbest the Best." The quotations are taken from the website "Invisible Cities," which contains oddly beautiful pictures of a number of Russian monotowns, as well as some insightful commentary from the residents themselves. Interestingly, the very same language is used by Bolotova and Stammler's informants in describing their attachment to towns in the Far North: "We built this city," and the North "pulls us in" (*sever tyanet*). Bolotova and Stammler, "How the North Became Home."

145. Narodnoe televidenie Asbesta, *Obrashchenie rabotnikov Kirpichnogo zavoda k Iazevu*; Narodnoe televidenie Asbesta, *Rabotnikam Kirpichnogo zavoda*; Narodnoe

televidenie Asbesta, "'Iazev, gde zarplata za 3 mesiatsa?'" Women can often be employed in less-profitable subsidiary firms rather than in a monotown's "city-forming enterprise."

146. Miller, *Putinomics*, 95; Fortescue, "Russian Steel Industry, 1990–2009."

147. Wengle, *Post-Soviet Power.*

148. Miller, *Putinomics*, 95; Fortescue, "Russian Steel Industry, 1990–2009."

149. World Bank, "Challenge of Russia's Monotowns," 24.

150. Zubarevich, *Regiony Rossii*, 61.

151. Miller, *Putinomics*, 96–97. In 2009 labor productivity in the Russian steel industry, while better than that of a number of other sectors, was only one-third the productivity of the industry in the US. Klintsov, Shvakman, and Solzhenitsyn, "How Russia Could Be More Productive."

152. Petlevoy, "Metallurgicheskie kompanii uvolili."

153. Helmer, "Kremlin Loses Fear of Regional Demonstrations."

154. Gimpelson and Kapeliushnikov, "Anticipation and Management of Restructuring in the Russia," 22.

155. Other criteria for inclusion in category 3 included the finding that the "city-forming enterprise" had no plans to lay off more than 3 percent of the workforce and that the population judges the social-economic situation in the city to be good/satisfactory (*blagopoluchnoe*) according to sociological surveys carried out by FSO. Pravitel'stvo Rossii, "O kriteriyakh otneseniya."

156. Petlevoy, "Metallurgicheskie kompanii uvolili v proshlom godu 33,500 chelovek"; Helmer, "Kremlin Loses Fear of Regional Demonstrations." To be precise, as with the other metallurgical companies, the layoffs at Severstal were from all of its operations, but the Cherepovets plant is by far the company's largest employer.

157. Hille and Foy, "Russia's Next Revolution."

158. Stubbs, "Prospects Brighten for Russian Steelmakers as Economy Improves."

159. Fedorinova and Lemeshko, "Russia Steel Mills Become World Beaters after Ruble's Slide."

160. Ebel, "In World Cup's Shadow, Layoffs and Anger at Russian Factory." Nor does the relative success of a metallurgical factory necessarily guard against other grievances from monotown residents, as in the gas explosion that killed thirty-one apartment dwellers in Magnitogorsk in December 2018: Zheleznova, "Bezalabernost' protiv terrorizma."

161. Yankov, "Monogoroda s problemami i bez."

162. Polinkevich, "Zachem predlagaiut sokratit' monogoroda?"

163. Latukhina, "Putin obeshchal prodolzhit' podderzhku monogorodov."

164. Dyakina, "Esli monogorod deshevle razrushit', to vyvod naprashivaetsia sam soboi."

165. RIAPO, "Na podderzhku monogorodov budet ezhegodno vydeliat'sia 5,5 mlrd rublei."

166. Dyakina, "Esli monogorod deshevle razrushit', to vyvod naprashivaetsia sam soboi."

167. Morris, *Everyday Post-Socialism*; Greene, "Running to Stand Still."

168. Bershidsky, "Putin Turns Swathes of Russia."

169. Gaaze, "Accidental Formation of Russia's War Coalition."

170. Hedlund, "Russia's Monotowns—Evidence of an Increasingly Obsolete Economy."

5. LABOR PROTEST IN RUSSIA'S HYBRID REGIME

1. See, for example, the contentious union meeting at a Ukrainian coal mine captured in the documentary by Icarus Films, *Perestroika from Below.*

2. Wright, "Working-Class Power, Capitalist-Class Interests, and Class Compromise." See also Silver, *Forces of Labor*; Grdešić, "Exceptionalism and Its Limits."

3. Burawoy and Krotov, "Soviet Transition from Socialism to Capitalism"; Crowley, *Hot Coal, Cold Steel*; Sil, "Privatization, Labor Politics, and the Firm in Post-Soviet Russia."

4. FNPR, "Federatsiia Nezavisimykh Profsoiuzov Rossii—ofitsial'nyi sait."

5. Gimpelson, Kapeliushnikov, and Roshchin, *Rossiiskii rynok truda*, 22.

6. Shmakov, "Press Conference with Independent Trade Unions Federation Chairman Mikhail Shmakov"; Gordon and Klopov, *Poteri i obreteniia v Rossii devianostykh*, 218.

7. Olimpieva, "'Free' and 'Official' Labor Unions in Russia," 2; Ashwin and Clarke, *Russian Trade Unions and Industrial Relations in Transition*.

8. Caraway, "Pathways of Dominance and Displacement"; Caraway, Cook, and Crowley, *Working through the Past*.

9. Greene and Robertson, "Politics, Justice and the New Russian Strike," 75–76.

10. Karelina, "Tendentsii izmeneniya chislennosti professional'nykh soyuzov," 48.

11. *Moscow News*, "Weak Trade Unions Suit Business, but Might Hit Back in a Crisis."

12. Mukhametshina, Bocharova, and Churakova, "Protesty profsoiuzov."

13. Robertson, *Politics of Protest in Hybrid Regimes*; Petkov and Shklyar, "Russian Regions after the Crisis."

14. Greene and Robertson, "Politics, Justice and the New Russian Strike," 78. See also Desai and Idson, *Work without Wages*.

15. Robertson, *Politics of Protest in Hybrid Regimes*, 135.

16. Robertson, *Politics of Protest in Hybrid Regimes*; Cook, "Trade Unions, Management, and the State in Contemporary Russia."

17. Remington, *Politics of Inequality in Russia*, 92–93.

18. That these strikes were also a form of political bargaining with Moscow helps explain why a high proportion of strikes took place in the "budget" sector, since the low wages and wage arrears of these workers were largely a function of the central state budget. From 1992 to 1999, more than half of all strikes in Russia (whether measured by days not worked or workers involved) took place in the education sector, and even when paid promptly, Russia's teachers received astonishingly low compensation. International Labour Office, *Year-Book of Labour Statistics*; Cook, *Postcommunist Welfare States*, 137, 187.

19. Katsva, "Kollektivnye deistviya v konste 90-kh godov"; Kozina, "Profsoyuzy v kollektivnykh trudovykh konfliktakh." Much depended on local conditions. See Evans, "Protest Patterns in Provincial Russia."

20. Borisov, Bizyukova, and Burnyshev, "Conflict in a Coal-Mining Enterprise"; Bizyukov, "Underground Miners' Strikes."

21. Cooper, "Russian Financial Crisis." During the spring and summer of 1998, the tactic of blocking major rail connections across Russia, and in particular the Trans-Siberian Railway, had become so common that by May regional Interior Ministry offices began listing rail blockades in a separate section of their reports to Moscow. Greene and Robertson, "Politics, Justice and the New Russian Strike."

22. Solovenko and Kust, "Social Attitudes to Miners' Protests during the Transition to Market Relations (1992–1999)," 663; Gordon and Klopov, *Poteri i obreteniia v Rossii devianostykh*, 325.

23. Department of State, Office of Website Management, *Russia*, 11.

24. Cooper, "Russian Financial Crisis."

25. Petkov and Shklyar, "Russian Regions after the Crisis."

26. *Financial Times*, August 19, 1998.

27. *New York Times*, September 27, 1998, section 3, p. 1.

28. *Izvestia*, September 23, 1998.

29. Rutland, "Russia: Entrenched Elites Ride Out the Crisis."

30. Robertson, "Strikes and Labor Organization in Hybrid Regimes," 795.

31. Clover, *Riot. Strike. Riot.*

32. Robertson, *Politics of Protest in Hybrid Regimes*, 53–54. As Roberston notes (p. 55), "in Russia there is a strong tradition of hunger-striking prisoners that stretches at least from the Decembrists of the 1820s through Stalin's Gulag to Brezhnev era dissidents. What is interesting is the adoption of the tactics of the incarcerated by workers across Russia."

33. Robertson, 132.

34. Robertson, 150.

35. Sil, "Fluidity of Labor Politics in Postcommunist Transitions"; Cook, "Russian Labour," 324; Gimpelson and Lippoldt, *Russian Labour Market*.

36. Grigoriev and Dekalchuk, "Collective Learning and Regime Dynamics under Uncertainty"; Grigoriev, "Labor Reform in Putin's Russia."

37. Grigoriev and Dekalchuk, "Collective Learning and Regime Dynamics under Uncertainty," 489.

38. Ashwin and Kozina, "Russia," 289. See also Chen and Sil, "Communist Legacies, Postcommunist Transformations, and the Fate of Organized Labor in Russia and China"; Ashwin and Clarke, *Russian Trade Unions and Industrial Relations in Transition*, 65–66.

39. Grigoriev and Dekalchuk, "Collective Learning and Regime Dynamics under Uncertainty," 490.

40. Olimpieva, "Labor Unions in Contemporary Russia." As Minister of Labor Pochinok characterized the labor code, perhaps boastfully, "the new code will really remove unions from the economic sphere, they really will lose very serious possibilities, which they had before," since they "will no longer have economic levers." Moskovskii Tsentr Karnegi, "Stenogramma osnovnykh vystuplenii na seminare 'Reforma trugodovo zakonodatel'stva.'"

41. *Rossiiskaya Gazeta*, "Trudovoi kodeks Rossiiskoi Federatsii ot 30 Dekabrya 2001 g. n 197-F3."

42. Bizyukov, "Al'ternativnie profsoyuzi na puti osvoyeniya sotsial'nogo prostranstva," 30. See also Greene and Robertson, "Politics, Justice and the New Russian Strike."

43. Olimpieva, "'Free' and 'Official' Labor Unions in Russia," 4.

44. Grigoriev and Dekalchuk, "Collective Learning and Regime Dynamics under Uncertainty," 490.

45. Robertson, *Politics of Protest in Hybrid Regimes*, 151.

46. Grigoriev and Dekalchuk, "Collective Learning and Regime Dynamics under Uncertainty," 492, 490.

47. Greene and Robertson, "Politics, Justice and the New Russian Strike."

48. Sadovskaya, "Pod Shmakovym zashatalos' kreslo."

49. *Tribuna*, "FNPR proshla nezavisimuiu e'kspertizu."

50. Panitch, "Development of Corporatism in Liberal Democracies."

51. Gabriel and Schmitz, "Longitudinal Analysis of the Union Wage Premium for US Workers"; Standing, "Reviving Dead Souls."

52. Olimpieva, "'Free' and 'Official' Labor Unions in Russia," 5; Kagarlitsky, "Labor Code in Bad Need of Revision"; Ashwin, "Social Partnership or a 'Complete Sellout'?" To be sure, this distributive model has shifted since the Soviet period, since "there have been changes in the sources, size, and content of the goods that are distributed and the unions are constantly seeking new types of services and support for their members (for example, credit unions, special insurance systems, etc.). As a result, there is great diversity in the

distributive models, ranging from 'mutual help' to 'business services.'" Olimpieva, "'Free' and 'Official' Labor Unions in Russia," 5.

53. Olimpieva, "Labor Unions in Contemporary Russia"; Olimpieva, *Rossiiskie prof-soyuzy v sisteme regulirovaniya sotsial'no-trudovykh otnoshenii*. In a definitive study of FNPR-led protests at the end of the Yeltsin era, a survey concluded that trade union membership had no effect on whether or not individuals joined the protest. Javeline, *Protest and the Politics of Blame.*

54. Olimpieva, "Labor Unions in Contemporary Russia," 210.

55. For example, the FNPR-affiliated union head in Pikalyovo helped lead the protests there, though that brought criticism from FNPR officials at a higher level. Olimpieva, "Labor Unions in Contemporary Russia," 281.

56. Olimpieva, *Rossiiskie profsoyuzy v sisteme regulirovaniya sotsial'no-trudovykh otnoshenii*; Olimpieva, "'Free' and 'Official' Labor Unions in Russia."

57. Kozina, "Zabastovki v sovremennoi Rossii."

58. Inozemtsev, "Russia's Economic Modernization." On the efforts of enterprise managers and local officials to suppress alternative unions see Evans, "Protest Patterns in Provincial Russia."

59. According to Irina Olimpieva, "The most radical change [of the new Labor Code] affected the possibility for labor protests." Olimpieva, "Labor Unions in Contemporary Russia," 274.

60. Experts calculate that it would take no fewer than forty-two days to carry out all the required preliminary pre-strike procedures. Crowley, "Liberal Transformation," 163–64; Ashwin and Clarke, *Russian Trade Unions and Industrial Relations in Transition*; Kozina, "Zabastovki v sovremennoi Rossii," 15.

61. *Itar-Tass Daily*, January 29, 2008.

62. Kozina, "Zabastovki v sovremennoi Rossii."

63. OECD, *Russia.*

64. *Vedomosti*, "Freedom from Labor."

65. Gimpelson, Kapeliushnikov, and Roshchin, *Rossiiskii rynok truda*, 17.

66. Volkov, *Violent Entrepreneurs*; Markus, "Secure Property as a Bottom-Up Process."

67. Kalashnikov and Shrov, "Trudovye otnosheniia v Rossii," 73.

68. *Vedomosti*, "Freedom from Labor"; World Bank, *Reducing Poverty through Growth and Social Policy Reform in Russia*, 96–97.

69. Gimpelson and Kapeliushnikov, "Labor Market Adjustment," 714.

70. RF Human Rights Commissioner, "1999 Report of RF Human Rights Commissioner"; Christensen, "Labor under Putin."

71. Aptekar', "Stoit li sudit'sia za zarplatu," translated by the Russian Reader.

72. Despite business complaints about Russia's strict EPL, but fitting with Russia's labor market model, the Supreme Court reported remarkably fewer complaints about unlawful dismissals: there were 17,934 such suits in 2007 and only 4,316 in the first six months of 2017. Thus, as late as 2017, complaints about unlawful dismissals were a small fraction of the complaints over wage arrears, and they declined over time despite a worsening economic climate. Moreover, lawsuits over dismissals were less likely to be decided favorably for workers: only 40.5 percent in the first half of 2017. Aptekar', "Stoit li sudit'sia za zarplatu."

73. Lussier, "Contacting and Complaining."

74. Lussier; Henry, "Complaint-Making as Political Participation in Contemporary Russia."

75. Gimpelson, Kapeliushnikov, and Roshchin, *Rossiiskii rynok truda*, 25.

76. Morris, *Everyday Post-Socialism.*

77. Clément calls these protests "everyday activism," centered on everyday life experience. Clément, "Social Mobilizations and the Question of Social Justice in Contemporary Russia."

78. Franzosi, "One Hundred Years of Strike Statistics." Likewise, Martin and Ross argue that in the industrial relations literature, "that unemployment undermines union bargaining power is axiomatic." Martin and Ross, *Brave New World of European Labor*, 14. See also Kennan, "Economics of Strikes," 2:1091–1137; Soskice, "Strike Waves and Wage Explosions, 1968–1970."

79. Greene and Robertson, "Politics, Justice and the New Russian Strike," 73–95.

80. Greene and Robertson, 76; Teague, "How Did the Russian Population Respond to the Global Financial Crisis?," 423; Kozina, "Zabastovki v sovremennoi Rossii," 13–25; Zainiev, "20 let zabastovok."

81. Greene and Robertson, "Politics, Justice and the New Russian Strike," 76.

82. Greene and Robertson, 74–75.

83. Zainiev, "20 let zabastovok."

84. Kozina, "Zabastovki v sovremennoi Rossii."

85. Vinogradova, Kozina, and Cook, "Russian Labor," 223–24.

86. Olimpieva, *Rossiiskie profsoyuzy v sisteme regulirovaniya sotsial'no-trudovykh otnoshenii.*

87. Hinz and Morris, "Trade Unions in Transnational Automotive Companies in Russia and Slovakia," 97–112.

88. Some viewed this as a broader shift in Russian protests beyond those focused on labor. Comparing overall protests in Russia between 1997 and 2000 and those from 2007 to 2111, Robertson argued that "the nature of protest demands has changed enormously in the intervening decade. In the 1990s, prolonged economic crisis meant that protest demands were first and foremost about economic issues and, most notably, were demands for the payment of wages that were owed but in arrears. By the second half of the 2000s, however, the demands generated by economic crisis had largely (though not entirely) been replaced by demands associated with the growing pains of a rapidly transforming economy and society." Overall he found this "a dramatic shift in Russia from protest that looks very much like the authoritarian model of protest, to one that looks much more like the democratic model." Robertson, "Protesting Putinism," 12, 14.

89. On the severity of the 2008–9 crisis see Remington, *Politics of Inequality in Russia*, 201–15.

90. Crowley, "Monotowns and the Political Economy of Industrial Restructuring in Russia"; Evans, "Protest Patterns in Provincial Russia."

91. Vinogradova, Kozina, and Cook, "Russian Labor," 224. Mass dismissals were as low in 2009 as in 2007, a year of considerable economic growth. Gimpelson and Kapeliushnikov, "Anticipation and Management of Restructuring in Russia," 18–19; Zubarevich, "Sotsial'naya differentsiatsiya regionov i gorodov," 145.

92. Traub-Merz, "Automotive Industry in Russia."

93. Vinogradova, Kozina, and Cook, "Russian Labor," 225.

94. Bizyukov, "Za ves' 2009 god v Rossii utverzhdaet Rosstat proizoshla vsego odna zabastovka." Rosstat can also overcount strikes, for example when teachers in a number of schools go on strike at the same time, and each school is counted as a separate strike. Thus, in 2004, owing to a very brief and symbolic work stoppage at schools around the country, Rosstat recorded 5,933 separate strikes for the year.

95. Bizyukov, "Trudovye protesty." Two publications that refer to this data are Greene, "From Boom to Bust," and Christensen, "Labor under Putin."

96. On the methodology and sources used by the CSLR see "Metodika i informatsionnaia baza monitoringa trudovykh protestov TsSTP."

97. Konfliktologiya (website); TsEPR, "Monitoring sotsial'no-ekonomicheskoi napriazhennosti v trudovoi sfere v 2016 godu."

98. Newspaper accounts can be influenced by editorial policy and other pressures, which in Russia's current media climate might lead to the undercounting or downplaying of protest. Internet reports on the other hand might potentially be influenced by views more sympathetic to protesters, perhaps leading to exaggerated accounts. Theoretically, at least, one might suspect that there would be greater probability of undercounting protests, since certain actions might simply fail to gain media attention. Further, the databases do not report data that would be most useful for comparative purposes, such as the number of participants in each protest, their proportion of a given workforce, and the duration of the protests.

99. However, see the data set compiled by Lankina and colleagues, which aggregates a full range of political and socioeconomic protests and finds a higher level of protest in earlier years. Lankina and Tertytchnaya, "Protest in Electoral Autocracies."

100. Makarov, "Obzor sotsial'no-trudovykh konfliktov v Rossiiskoi Federatsii v pervom kvartale 2017 goda."

101. TsEPR, "Monitoring sotsial'no-ekonomicheskoi napriazhennosti v trudovoi sfere v 2016 godu."

102. Konfliktologiya, "Itogi sotsial'no-trudovykh konfliktov v Rossiiskoi Federatsii i razvitie trudovykh otnoshenii v 2019 godu."

103. Tsentr sotsial'no-trudovykh prav, "Kak protestuiut rossiiane"; "Izmenenie sotsial'no-trudovoi obstanovki."

104. At least according to the CSLR data (which extend far enough into the past) labor protests became significantly greater, and over a more extended period, during the more recent (2014–16) recession than they were in 2009 when the decline in GDP was greater. As we have seen, during the earlier downturn the government mobilized a number of anti-crisis measures but for various reasons did not make the same level of effort during the more recent downturn. But another explanation might be that while real wages declined in 2008–9, they dropped even more, and over a longer period, from 2014 to 2016.

105. The SLC database found that from 2014 to 2106 more than half of all labor protests stemmed from wage arrears, with the proportion growing in 2016, while the CSLR found that 56 percent of all protests did in 2016, rising from 48 percent in 2015, though the CEPR reported that out of 906 reported cases of wage arrears in 2016, only 13 percent led to overt protest. Makarov, "Obzor sotsial'no-trudovykh konfliktov v Rossiiskoi Federatsii v 2016 godu"; Bizyukov, "Trudovye protesty v Rossii v 2008–2016 gg."; TsEPR, "Monitoring sotsial'no-ekonomicheskoi napriazhennosti v trudovoi sfere v 2016 godu."

106. Unfortunately, such actions do not always end in the mere threat of taking one's life, as in the case of the suicide of a Krasnodar farmer and participant in the "tractor march" who failed to rectify what he argued was the unjust seizure of his land. PROVED, "Kubanskii fermer zastrelilsia iz-za reiderskogo zakhvata zemli."

107. TsEPR, "Monitoring sotsial'no-ekonomicheskoi napriazhennosti v trudovoi sfere v 2016 godu"; TsEPR, "Karta Sotsial'no-ekonomisheskikh goriachikh tochek"; Human Rights Watch, "Red Card," June 2017.

108. Tilly, *From Mobilization to Revolution.*

109. Bizyukov, "Trudovye protesty v Rossii v 2008–2016 gg."

110. Konfliktologiya, "Analiz sotsial'no-trudovoi obstanovki i razvitiia trudovykh konfliktov v Rossiiskoi Federatsii (osnovnye itogi 2018 goda)."

111. Makarov, "Konflktologiya 1 kvartale 2015 goda."

112. Konfliktologiya, "Kratkii obzor sotsial'no-trudovykh konfliktov za 2015 god"; Bizyukov, "Labor Protests in Russia, 2008–2011."

113. Wengle and Rasell, "Monetisation of l'goty"; Remington, *Politics of Inequality in Russia*, 64–67.

114. Robertson, *Politics of Protest in Hybrid Regimes*, 176.

115. Petrov, Lipman, and Hale, "Three Dilemmas of Hybrid Regime Governance," 13.

116. Remington, *Politics of Inequality in Russia*, 66.

117. Gimpelson and Kapeliushnikov, "Anticipation and Management of Restructuring in the Russia," 10. See also Kudrin and Gurvich, "New Growth Model for the Russian Economy."

118. World Bank, "Russia: Reshaping Economic Geography," 119.

119. Rosenfeld, "Reevaluating the Middle-Class Protest Paradigm."

120. Matveev and Novkunskaya, "Welfare Restructuring in Russia since 2012."

121. Matveev and Novkunskaya.

122. Holom, "Russian Health-Care Protests Continue despite Putin's Popularity"; *Kommersant*, "Naibolee ostro reforma zdravookhraneniya pochuvstvovalas' v krupnykh gorodakh."

123. openDemocracy, "On the Brink."

124. Budget cuts can also unite employees across traditional work groups: during a May 2015 protest, teachers united with health care workers, while in November 2015, salary cuts in Altai Krai led education, health care, culture, and other budget-sector employees to protest in unison.

125. I am grateful to Irina Olimpieva for this phrase. Crowley and Olimpieva, "Labor Protests and Their Consequences in Putin's Russia."

126. Bizyukov, "Pervye priznaki bol'shogo tsunami."

127. TsEPR, "Monitoring sotsial'no-ekonomicheskoi napriazhennosti v trudovoi sfere v 2016 godu," 4.

128. TsEPR, "Monitoring sotsial'no-ekonomicheskoi napriazhennosti v trudovoi sfere v 2016 godu," 11. As we shall see in the next chapter with Samara's Merkushkin, such conflicts can cost governors their jobs.

6. DOWNSIZING IN "RUSSIA'S DETROIT"

1. Siegelbaum, *Cars for Comrades*, 95.

2. Traub-Merz, "Automotive Industry in Russia," 127.

3. Siegelbaum, *Cars for Comrades*, 96, 105.

4. Horky, *Russian Job—a Documentary Film*, 25:25. The archive of photographs from AvtoVAZ's early days can be seen at the Invisible Cities website, https://monogoroda.com/vot-tebe-rodina-podarok/.

5. Siegelbaum, *Cars for Comrades*.

6. Klebnikov, *Godfather of the Kremlin*.

7. Glazunov, *Business in Post-Communist Russia*, 81; Siegelbaum, *Cars for Comrades*, 117. While addressing AvtoVAZ workers during a visit to the plant during the 2009 economic crisis, Prime Minister Putin acknowledged, "We all know what was happening in the country, in Tolyatti, in the '90s, what kind of owners and criminal plots surrounded AvtoVAZ." Antonova, "Putin Promises."

8. *Moscow Times*, "Slow Death."

9. Glazunov, *Business in Post-Communist Russia*, 81.

10. Kolesnichenko, "Salvage Job."

11. Kolesnichenko.

12. Traub-Merz, "Automotive Industry in Russia," 130.

13. Kozina, "Changes in the Social Organisation of an Industrial Enterprise."

14. Remington, *Politics of Inequality in Russia*, 104.

15. Siegelbaum, *Cars for Comrades*, 122.

16. Remington, *Politics of Inequality in Russia*, 100.

17. Remington, 105.

18. Betting, "System Shaping Its Actors," 28.

19. Hinz and Morris, "Trade Unions in Transnational Automotive Companies in Russia and Slovakia."

20. Traub-Merz, "Automotive Industry in Russia," 130.

21. Traub-Merz, 127.

22. Hinz and Morris, "Trade Unions in Transnational Automotive Companies in Russia and Slovakia."

23. Traub-Merz, "Automotive Industry in Russia," 132.

24. Karliner, "In Russia's Car Industry, Even the Dead Work Overtime."

25. Greene and Robertson, "Politics, Justice and the New Russian Strike."

26. Hinz and Morris, "Trade Unions in Transnational Automotive Companies in Russia and Slovakia." On the theory of working-class power see Wright, "Working-Class Power, Capitalist-Class Interests, and Class Compromise"; Silver, *Forces of Labor*. For an earlier application to Russia see Crowley, "Russia's Labor Legacy."

27. Traub-Merz, "Automotive Industry in Russia."

28. Matveev, "'Two Russias' Culture War," 192.

29. MPRA, "MPRA—Mezhregional'nyy profsoyuz rabochaya assotsiatsiya." As we will explore further in chapter 8, the truckers' protest also led to a form of associational power. See Ob"edinenie perevozchikov, "VSEROSSIISKAIa STAChKA AVTOPEREVOZChIKOV!"

30. Petrova, "Sud likvidiroval odin iz krupneishikh nezavisimykh profsoiuzov Rossii"; Tsentr sotsial'no-trudovykh prav, "Verkhovnyi sud otmenil skandal'noe reshenie o likvidatsii profsoiuza."

31. Traub-Merz, "Automotive Industry in Russia," 132.

32. Traub-Merz, 127, 131.

33. Traub-Merz, 142.

34. Aris, "Russia's Import Substitution Has Not Been a Great Success."

35. Raspopova, "Novye gosprogrammy podderzhki avtoproma zarabotaiut s 1 iiulia."

36. The shuttering of ZIL, the manufacturer of limousines for the Soviet elite, is certainly one example of the closure of a large industrial enterprise, yet the fact that it was located in Moscow, where real estate had become so valuable, may have provided an additional incentive, and the comparatively vibrant labor market there would have cushioned the blow to workers. Kokorin, "ZIL, kotoryi my poteriali."

37. RIA Novosti, "Novyi limuzin prezidenta"; Troianovski, "Putin's Helsinki Showmanship Starts with His Limo."

38. Rahimov, "Eurasian Union"; Lomakin, "'Kortezh' dlia prezidenta sobrali vsem mirom."

39. Traub-Merz, "Automotive Industry in Russia," 135.

40. Traub-Merz, "Automotive Industry in Russia"; Kolesnichenko, "Salvage Job."

41. Kolesnichenko, "Salvage Job."

42. Kozichev, "Istoriia poshlin na inomarki v Rossii."

43. Traub-Merz, "Automotive Industry in Russia," 135.

44. Kolesnichenko, "Salvage Job."

45. Remington, *Politics of Inequality in Russia*, 103.

46. Remington, 209.

47. Siegelbaum, *Cars for Comrades*, 122.

48. Kolesnichenko, "Salvage Job."

49. *Vedomosti*, "Gorod 'AvtoVAZ.'"

50. This was in addition to a $60 million government subsidy to lower interest rates for Lada car loans. Kolesnichenko, "Salvage Job."

51. Levy, "Tariff Protests in Eastern Port Rattle Kremlin"; Stack, "Russians Want U-Turn on Taxing Car Imports."

52. Levy, "Tariff Protests in Eastern Port Rattle Kremlin."

53. Gabowitsch, *Protest in Putin's Russia*, 134.

54. Whitmore, "Thousands Rally across Russia against Government."

55. Gabowitsch, *Protest in Putin's Russia*, 134–35.

56. Levy, "Tariff Protests in Eastern Port Rattle Kremlin"; Kolesnichenko, "Salvage Job."

57. Further, "The protest demonstrations and motorcades continued into 2010, and branches of TIGR were created in a number of regions." Gabowitsch, *Protest in Putin's Russia*, 135.

58. Whitmore, "Thousands Rally across Russia against Government."

59. Whitmore; *Independent*, "Russia's Economic Crisis Leads to Mounting Protests."

60. Gabowitsch, *Protest in Putin's Russia*.

61. Levy, "Tariff Protests in Eastern Port Rattle Kremlin."

62. Stack, "Russians Want U-Turn on Taxing Car Imports."

63. Tooze, *Crashed*.

64. Remington, *Politics of Inequality in Russia*, 210.

65. Antonova, "Putin Promises"; Sudakov, "Putin Buys Russian Car to Save Home Industry from Decline."

66. Gimpelson and Kapeliushnikov, "Anticipation and Management of Restructuring in Russia," 24; Hodouchi, "Car Union Urges State Control"; Clover, "Russian One-Company Towns Face Decline."

67. Remington, *Politics of Inequality in Russia*, 210; Kolesnichenko, "Salvage Job."

68. Kolesnichenko, "Salvage Job."

69. Traub-Merz, "Automotive Industry in Russia," 135.

70. One source puts the number of workers rehired, apparently at full pay, by the two subsidiaries as twenty-four thousand. The number of workers placed on public and temporary work at federal expense in the Samara region as a whole increased by nine times in 2010. Zubarevich, *Regiony Rossii*, 55.

71. Moreover, despite the dire economic situation in Tolyatti, a local housing official explained that people were reluctant to leave since "over the years, people in Tolyatti have acquired comfortable apartments." Tovkailo, Tyomkin, and Nazarova, "AvtoVAZ Workers Offered Chance to Move."

72. Traub-Merz, "Automotive Industry in Russia."

73. Traub-Merz, 137.

74. Asankin and Kir'ian, "Shvedskii menedzhment."

75. Alexandrova, "Massive Sackings at Russia's Largest Carmaker"; Warburton, "AvtoVAZ Hikes Layoffs to 13,000 as Market Falls."

76. Khalaf, "'Le Cost Killer.'"

77. Tsang, "Who Is Carlos Ghosn and Why Is He in Trouble?"

78. Traub-Merz, "Automotive Industry in Russia," 137; Asankin and Kir'ian, "Shvedskii menedzhment."

79. Morzharetto, "Foreigner with No Friends."

80. Remington, *Politics of Inequality in Russia*, 211.

81. Asankin, "Chetyre oshibki Anderssona."

82. Kolesnichenko, "Salvage Job."

83. Horky, *Russian Job—a Documentary Film*, 16:42.

84. Horky, 18:21.

85. Karliner, "In Russia's Car Industry, Even the Dead Work Overtime."

86. Karliner. As someone commented on social media, "Even the dead work over-time at AvtoVAZ."

87. Karliner.

88. Karliner.

89. MacFarquhar, "Trying to Save Russia's Punch Line of a Car"; Betting, "System Shaping Its Actors."

90. Edinstvo's leader Anatolii Ivanov was assaulted twice in 1996, the second time leading to two bullet wounds. Siegelbaum, *Cars for Comrades*, 118–19.

91. Betting, "System Shaping Its Actors," 27.

92. Though Edinstvo means "unity," members are united in their radicalism but not their political ideology. According to Perova, there are leftists, right-wingers, and anarchists in the union. Leonid Emshanov, a twenty-seven-year-old assembly fitter and Edinstvo member, wears a ring with a swastika on it but doesn't seem troubled that his right-wing views might conflict with the revolutionary banners hanging in the union office. Karliner, "In Russia's Car Industry, Even the Dead Work Overtime."

93. Karliner.

94. Betting, "System Shaping Its Actors."

95. Horky, *Russian Job—a Documentary Film*, 42.

96. Tol'iatti Onlain, "V Tol'iatti poiavitsia bol'she 10 tysiach bezrabotnykh"; Raspop-ova, "'AvtoVAZ' vykhodit na pensiiu." Yet this was more than at the end of 2013, when AvtoVAZ stated that Tolyatti's official unemployment rate was 0.6 percent, which it also claimed to be the lowest in Russia. Warburton, "AvtoVAZ Hikes Layoffs to 13,000 as Market Falls."

97. According to the minister of economic development of Samara, there were more job offers than unemployed. The main problem, however, was that most of the unem-ployed were specialized in the automobile industry, and demand for these specialists was low. FederalPress—Samarskaia Oblast', "Bednyi Tol'iatti."

98. TLTReporter, "Tol'iatti stal monogorodom pervoi kategorii."

99. Arkhiv saita Samarskoi Gubernskoi Dumy 5-ogo sozyva, "U 'Zhigulevskoi doliny' shirokie perspektivy. . . .'"

100. Dorozhkina, "Tol'iatti perevodiat v pervuiu gruppu monogorodov."

101. Karliner, "In Russia's Car Industry, Even the Dead Work Overtime."

102. Tol'iatti Onlain, "V Tol'iatti poiavitsia bol'she 10 tysiach bezrabotnykh."

103. Shtanov, "Subsidii dlia 'AvtoVAZa' mogut sokratit'sia bolee chem vtroe do 600 mln rublei."

104. Lankina and Voznaya, "New Data on Protest Trends in Russia's Regions," 334.

105. Horky, *Russian Job—a Documentary Film*.

106. *Russkaya planeta*, "Bez deneg net raboty."

107. TsEPR, "Karta sotsial'no-ekonomisheskikh goriachikh tochek."

108. I am grateful to J. L. F. Betting, who has compiled a comprehensive account of the AVA protests, on which much of the following relies. Betting, "System Shaping Its Actors," 34.

109. Indicative of the challenges in pursuing a legal approach for getting back wages paid, Betting reports that "attempts to move forward in legal processes were slowed down by red tape measures: the court demanded that workers obtain a declaration from the management of AVA, stating that they had not received their salary. However, the man-agement was unwilling to give their workers those declarations." Betting, "System Shap-ing Its Actors."

110. Betting, 134, 140.

111. Betting, 142.

112. As captured by Czech filmmakers making a documentary about Andersson's tenure at the plant. Horky, *Russian Job—a Documentary Film.*

113. MacFarquhar, "Trying to Save Russia's Punch Line of a Car"; Betting, "System Shaping Its Actors," 38, 41.

114. Betting, 38.

115. Horky, *Russian Job—a Documentary Film.*

116. Asankin, "Pikety isportili otnosheniia glavy 'Rostekha' i prezidenta AvtoVAZa."

117. Kalashnikov, "AVTOVAZ eshche mozhno spasti!"; Koltashov and Mamedova, "Leonid Kalashnikov: '"Priekhali, pokatalis' i . . . prokatili AvtoVAZ"'; Betting, "System Shaping Its Actors."

118. Traub-Merz, "Automotive Industry in Russia."

119. Asankin, "Chetyre oshibki Anderssona."

120. Asankin, "Chetyre oshibki Anderssona"; Traub-Merz, "Automotive Industry in Russia," 144.

121. Traub-Merz, "Automotive Industry in Russia," 144.

122. Asankin, "Chetyre oshibki Anderssona."

123. Asankin. Looking and sounding humbled, for his part Andersson complained to a Czech film crew that "in Russia people would like to have a revolution but nothing would change. If I had known half of it I wouldn't have come. . . . In my own mind I failed." As to the reason he was fired, he said, "They had nine different complaints. But most of it was that I did too much, too fast. That I didn't show respect to people, and that I was planning to lay off more people." Horky, *Russian Job—a Documentary Film.*

124. Sivashenkov, "Roboty ne bastuiut."

125. Shtanov, "'AvtoVAZ' prodolzhit optimizatsiiu chislennosti sotrudnikov."

126. Raspopova, "'AvtoVAZ' doplatit sotrudnikam za vykhod na pensiiu."

127. Shtanov, "'AvtoVAZ' prodolzhit optimizatsiiu chislennosti sotrudnikov"; Raspopova, "'AvtoVAZ' doplatit sotrudnikam za vykhod na pensiiu."

128. Sivashenkov, "Roboty ne bastuiut."

129. Shtanov, "Subsidii dlia 'AvtoVAZa' mogut sokratit'sia bolee chem vtroe do 600 mln rublei."

130. Foy and Campbell, "Carmakers Gear Up for Recovery in Russia."

131. Raspopova, "Mashiny podesheveiut po polnoi programme."

132. Betting, "System Shaping Its Actors," 43.

133. Betting, 43.

134. Sapronova, "'V golovakh vse pereputano.'"

135. TsEPR, "Karta sotsial'no-ekonomisheskikh goriachikh tochek," 6.

136. This was not the only conspiratorially minded outburst from Merkushkin. He later continued the allegations, telling Samara citizens that "in April, the U.S. ambassador to Russia—he's the main specialist in organizing Orange Revolutions—came here and he studied the situation," implying that such a "specialist" might have thought that, given the region's tensions, it might be ripe for a revolt. The ambassador went to Tolyatti, Merkushkin said, but "saw that no sparks could come from here in order to spread the conflagration to the whole country." He added, "That is why the CIA decided to go after all of Samara Oblast." Plotnikova and Coalson, "Samara Governor Offers a Stark Choice."

137. Betting, "System Shaping Its Actors," 43.

138. Sapronova, "'V golovakh vse pereputano.'"

139. TsEPR, "Karta sotsial'no-ekonomisheskikh goriachikh tochek."

140. There was in fact one channel for expressing grievances, namely the legal process, but as Betting cogently argues, "Representatives of the local government can plan meetings and then postpone them. The Prosecutor can accept legal cases but let them drag on

for months. The government and the CEO of the plant can promise to have salaries paid within some time, only to break the promise. The purpose of such feet-dragging is to exhaust protestors." "System Shaping Its Actors," 53.

7. THE SPECTER OF A COLOR REVOLUTION

1. Casula and Perovic, *Identities and Politics during the Putin Presidency*; Sakwa, *Putin*.
2. Lukyanov, "Putin's Foreign Policy."
3. Silitski, "Year after the Color Revolutions"; Silitski, "Preempting Democracy."
4. Finkel and Brudny, "Russia and the Colour Revolutions."
5. Clarke, "Development of Industrial Relations."
6. Schreck, "Ten Businesspeople Barred in 2 Years"; *Washington Post*, "Backsliding in Russia."
7. Treisman, "Presidential Popularity in a Hybrid Regime"; Mishler and Rose, "Generation, Age, and Time"; Colton and Hale, "Putin Vote." See the discussion in Smyth and Soboleva, "Looking beyond the Economy."
8. Sakwa added that this was a "pact that could only be sustained, as Gorbachev had discovered to his cost in the late 1980s, as long as the economy could deliver the goods." Sakwa, "Political Leadership," 33.
9. Petrov, Lipman, and Hale, "Three Dilemmas of Hybrid Regime Governance." I am grateful to Evgenia Olimpieva for bringing both quotations to my attention. Olimpieva, "From Performance to Geopolitical Ideology."
10. Gaaze, "Accidental Formation of Russia's War Coalition."
11. Lamberova and Treisman, "Economic Shocks and Authoritarian Responses."
12. Gaaze, "Accidental Formation of Russia's War Coalition."
13. Gaaze.
14. Treisman, "Putin's Popularity since 2010."
15. Chaisty and Whitefield, "Effects of the Global Financial Crisis on Russian Political Attitudes"; Robinson, "Russia's Response to Crisis"; Smyth and Soboleva, "Looking beyond the Economy."
16. For example, see Makarkin, "Protest srednego klassa."
17. Barry, "Tens of Thousands Protest in Moscow, Russia, in Defiance of Putin."
18. Rosenfeld, "Reevaluating the Middle-Class Protest Paradigm." On the question of whether these were "middle-class" protests see Matveev, "'Two Russias' Culture War"; Gabowitsch, *Protest in Putin's Russia*.
19. Krastev and Holmes, "Autopsy of Managed Democracy." As Lamberova and Treisman note, however, "these demonstrations actually mobilized fewer people in total and were more localized than those of 2009–10. But, unlike the economic protests in Pikalyovo and other cities, the Moscow events were explicitly political." Lamberova and Treisman, "Economic Shocks and Authoritarian Responses."
20. Dmitriev and Treisman, "Other Russia," 3; Dmitriev, "Lost in Transition?"
21. Treisman, "Putin's Popularity since 2010."
22. Busygina and Filippov, "Calculus of Non-protest in Russia."
23. Sperling, *Sex, Politics, and Putin*.
24. Walker, "In Search of 'Stability'"; Morris, "Automobile Masculinities and Neoliberal Production Regimes among Russian Blue-Collar Men."
25. Smyth and Soboleva, "Looking beyond the Economy"; Petrov, Lipman, and Hale, "Three Dilemmas of Hybrid Regime Governance."
26. The Kremlin's PR team has certainly worked to cultivate Putin's tough-guy image, partly to appeal to Russia's working-class *muzhik*. See Sperling, *Sex, Politics, and Putin*.
27. Hakvåg, "Russian Defense Spending after 2010," 505.

28. *Putin: Telemost s Nizhnim Tagilom.*

29. ITAR-TASS, "President Appoints Railway Car Building Plant's Workshop Manager Presidental Envoy in Urals."

30. The pundit Aleksei Chadaev, author of *Putin: His Ideology*, also took part in the roundtable, where he claimed that "yes, there are two Russias: one oriented toward consumption and the other oriented toward creation." Curiously, the latter, in Chadaev's definition, includes both the worker and the entrepreneur. They are both "producers," whereas the protesters are only consumers. Chadaev, "Samurai Tagila." See the discussion in Matveev, "'Two Russias' Culture War."

31. *Kommersant*, "Vladimir Putin budet ballotirovat'sia v prezidenty"; *Economist*, "Mr Putin Will Win Next Year despite, Not Because of, the Economy."

32. Guillory, "Whatever Happened to 'Russia without Putin'?"

33. Hakvåg, "Russian Defense Spending after 2010," 505.

34. Interfax.ru. "Al'fa-bank podal isk o priznanii Uralvagonzavoda bankrotom"; *Novaya Gazeta*, "Al'fa-bank podal v Arbitrazhnyi sud."

35. Russian Defense Policy, "Tough Times at UVZ"; Kramer, "Labor Unrest Stirs in Russia as an Economic Chill Sets In"; Titov, "Proizvoditel' tankov 'Armata' poprosit gospodderzhki na 16 mlrd rub."

36. Grove, "Russians in Heartland Sour on Vladimir Putin over Money Woes."

37. Volin, "Oleg Volin."

38. Pavlovskii, "Putin v dni Velikoi russko-ukrainskoi revoliutsii."

39. Ryzhkov, "Russians Feel That Great Power High—Again."

40. Stolyarov, "In Russia's Detroit, Layoffs Are Blamed on Foreign Interlopers."

41. Gontmakher, "Novyi levyi povorot."

42. Smyth and Soboleva, "Looking beyond the Economy," 271.

43. Volkov, "Russian Society Wants Change—But of What Nature?"

44. Chen and Sil, "Communist Legacies, Postcommunist Transformations, and the Fate of Organized Labor in Russia and China." See also Clément, "Social Mobilization and the Question of Social Justice."

45. Rogov, *Osnovnye tendentsii politicheskogo razvitiya Rossii v 2011–2013 gg.*

46. Balmforth, "Paradox of Russia's Left."

47. Vujacic, "Gennadiy Zyuganov and the 'Third Road.'"

48. Holm-Hansen et al., "Welfare Reform, Protest and Stability."

49. Munro, "Predictors of Support for State Social Welfare Provision in Russia and China."

50. Holm-Hansen et al., "Welfare Reform, Protest and Stability."

51. Petrov, Lipman, and Hale, "Three Dilemmas of Hybrid Regime Governance."

52. Yakovlev, "What Is Russia Trying to Defend?"

53. Kudrin and Gurvich, "New Growth Model for the Russian Economy."

54. Lomskaya, "Uchitelia razocharovalis' v ukazakh Putina"; Russian Reader, "Twenty Percent of Russian Schoolteachers Contemplate Quitting."

55. Russian Reader, "Sixty Percent of Russian Doctors Make Less Than 360 Euros a Month."

56. Tsentr sotsial'no-trudovykh prav, "Kak protestuiut rossiiane." For similar findings see TsEPR, "Protestnyi 2017 god."

57. Tsentr ekonomicheskikh i politicheskikh reform, "Protestnaia situatsiia v regionakh."

58. Goble, "Putin's Greatest Fear."

59. *Rossiiskaia Gazeta*, "Voennaia doktrina Rossiiskoi Federatsii," 15; Golts, "Rosgvardiia podminaet Genshtab," translated by the Russian Reader, "Enemy Within Is Everywhere."

60. Russian Reader, "Enemy Within Is Everywhere."

61. Cordesman, "Russia and the 'Color Revolution.'"

62. Defense Intelligence Agency, "Russia Military Power," 70–71.

63. "Russian National Security Strategy, December 2015." The Moscow security conference also discussed the level of corruption in society as a major factor inciting such popular uprisings. Cordesman, "Russia and the 'Color Revolution.'"

64. "Russian National Security Strategy, December 2015."

65. Robertson, *Politics of Protest in Hybrid Regimes*, 179.

66. Østbø, "Between Opportunist Revolutionaries and Mediating Spoilers."

8. RUSSIA'S TRUCKERS AND THE ROAD TO RADICALIZATION

1. I am grateful to Irina Olimpieva on this point. See Crowley and Olimpieva, "Labor Protests and Their Consequences in Putin's Russia."

2. Goodwin, *No Other Way Out*. The phrase is Leon Trotsky's: "People do not make revolution eagerly any more than they do war. . . . A revolution takes place only when there is no other way out." Trotsky, *History of the Russian Revolution*. Thus, while Yeltsin was hugely unpopular during the later years of his presidency, arguably he survived massive protests, such as those over wage arrears, precisely because he was viewed as so ineffectual, and his government was not seen as directly responsible or blameworthy for conditions in a given factory or provincial town. Javeline, *Protest and the Politics of Blame*; Crowley, "Liberal Transformation."

3. Robertson, *Politics of Protest in Hybrid Regimes*, 179.

4. Østbø, "Between Opportunist Revolutionaries and Mediating Spoilers."

5. Volkov, "Russian Society Wants Change—but of What Nature?"

6. Fond bor'by s korruptsiei, *FBK: Don't Call Him "Dimon."*

7. Ioffe, "What Putin Really Wants." By some accounts, despite such populist statements, Navalny's economic views are fairly liberal. See Matveev, "Russia, Inc."; Goble, "Protesters in Russia Today Are Younger, Poorer and Further Left Than a Decade Ago."

8. One reason for the likely trepidation from officials stemming from the truckers' protest has to do with the cultural cachet the drivers have long enjoyed in Russian society. Lewis Siegelbaum posits four different cultural constructions of truck drivers: as heroes, professionals, loners, and wheeler-dealers. More recently the TV series *Dal"noboishchiki*, which ran on NTV from 2001 to 2004, contributed to the popular awareness of long-distance truckers' lifestyles. See Siegelbaum, "'Little Tsars of the Road.'"

9. Østbø, "Between Opportunist Revolutionaries and Mediating Spoilers," 301.

10. Østbø, 280.

11. Østbø, 284.

12. *Novaya Gazeta*, "A. Kotov"; Fomina, "'We Have Plenty of Reasons to Protest apart from Platon.'"

13. Flikke, "Sword of Damocles."

14. Levada Tsentr, "Protesty 'dal'noboishchikov' i gotovnost' protestovat' sredi naseleniia"; Levada Tsentr, "Moskvichi o protestakh dal'noboishchikov."

15. Østbø, "Between Opportunist Revolutionaries and Mediating Spoilers," 279.

16. BBC News Russkaia sluzhba, "Khodorkovskii vidit neizbezhnost' revoliutsii v Rossii," cited in Østbø, "Between Opportunist Revolutionaries and Mediating Spoilers," 280.

17. Gregory, "Has Putin Met His Match in Russia's Truck Drivers?"; Østbø, "Between Opportunist Revolutionaries and Mediating Spoilers."

18. Lomasko, *Other Russias*.

19. Østbø, "Between Opportunist Revolutionaries and Mediating Spoilers."

20. Fomina, "'We Have Plenty of Reasons to Protest apart from Platon.'"

21. Østbø, "Between Opportunist Revolutionaries and Mediating Spoilers," 292.

22. Lomasko, *Other Russias.*

23. Anatrrra, "Dal'noboishchiki."

24. Exclamations in original. Lomasko, *Other Russias.*

25. Østbø, "Between Opportunist Revolutionaries and Mediating Spoilers," 285.

26. Anatrrra, "Dal'noboishchiki."

27. Lomasko, *Other Russias.*

28. Østbø, "Between Opportunist Revolutionaries and Mediating Spoilers," 300, 302.

29. Østbø, "Between Opportunist Revolutionaries and Mediating Spoilers"; Garmonenko, "Dal'noboinyi impichment."

30. Østbø, "Between Opportunist Revolutionaries and Mediating Spoilers."

31. Lomasko, *Other Russias.*

32. Lomasko.

33. Østbø, "Between Opportunist Revolutionaries and Mediating Spoilers."

34. Fomina, "'We Have Plenty of Reasons to Protest apart from Platon.'"

35. Lomasko, *Other Russias.*

36. Fomina, "'We Have Plenty of Reasons to Protest apart from Platon.'"

37. Fomina.

38. Lomasko, *Other Russias.*

39. Babchenko, "Zdes' budet tol'ko bunt." Understandably, political scientists have a lower bar and tend to ask whether such protests will lead to democratization. As Robertson noted about the 2005 protests over benefits, "The first large and radical challenge to Putin melted away almost as quickly as it had begun." Robertson, *Politics of Protest in Hybrid Regimes*, 183. But then the protests were never intended to be a challenge to Putin and were aimed at preserving social benefits, and here they won major concessions. What the protests did demonstrate, however, were limits to authoritarian power, in this case regarding social policy.

40. Babchenko, "Zdes' budet tol'ko bunt." Babchenko received notoriety earlier for dramatically faking his own death in what he claimed was an attempt to foil an assassination plot at the hands of Russian authorities. Harding and Roth, "Arkady Babchenko Reveals He Faked His Death to Thwart Moscow Plot."

41. Lomasko, *Other Russias.*

42. Eidelman, "Lesson in Solidarity."

43. Eidelman.

44. Eidelman.

45. Lomasko, *Other Russias.*

46. Akhmirova, "Glavnyi boi dal'noboishchika Andreia Bazhutina."

47. Petlianova, "Andrei Bazhutin."

48. Akhmirova, "Glavnyi boi dal'noboishchika Andreia Bazhutina."

49. Fomina, "'We Have Plenty of Reasons to Protest apart from Platon.'"

50. Meyer (Olimpieva), "Russian Truck Drivers against the Platon Tax, Round 2."

51. Goble, *Window on Eurasia—New Series*, June 13, 2017.

52. *1 maia 2017 god Miass vystuplenie predsedatelei MPVP i OPR po Cheliabinskoi oblasti.*

53. Ob"edinenie perevozchikov Rossii, "VSEROSSIISKAIa STAChKA AVTO-PEREVOZChIKOV!"; Meyer (Olimpieva), "Russian Truck Drivers against the Platon Tax, Round 2."

54. YouTube, "Novosti OPR s Andreem Bazhutinym. Vypusk #5, 23.06.17."

55. Østbø, "Between Opportunist Revolutionaries and Mediating Spoilers," 300, 302.

56. Griaznevich, "V Peterburge poiavilsia sopernik Vladimira Putina."

57. Griaznevich.

58. Akhmirova, "Glavnyi boi dal'noboishchika Andreia Bazhutina."

59. Balmforth, "Truckers' Leader Rolls On after Russian Election Bid Breaks Down."
60. Vulikh, "'Ia otlip ot televizora i prozrel.'"
61. Ob"edinenie perevozchikov Rossii, "OPR—Regiony"; Balmforth, "Truckers' Leader Rolls On after Russian Election Bid Breaks Down."
62. Rebrov, "Dal'noboishchiki ob"iavili o nachale vserossiiskoi zabastovki."
63. Goble, *Window on Eurasia—New Series*," May 15, 2017.
64. Petrov, Lipman, and Hale, "Three Dilemmas of Hybrid Regime Governance."
65. Oreshkin, "Dal'noboyshchiki kak novyy klass protestuyushchikh."
66. Tilly, *From Mobilization to Revolution.*
67. Østbø, "Between Opportunist Revolutionaries and Mediating Spoilers."
68. TsEPR, "Monitoring 2016."
69. Fantasia, *Cultures of Solidarity.*
70. Fomina, "'We Have Plenty of Reasons to Protest apart from Platon.'"
71. Fomina.
72. Fomina. As Kurbatov relayed earlier to Lomasko, "Our alliance will be like socialism within a democratic society." Lomasko, *Other Russias.*

9. HOW DIFFERENT IS RUSSIA?

1. Bluestone and Harrison, *Deindustrialization of America*; Harvey, *Condition of Postmodernity.* On earlier waves of deindustrialization see Cowie, *Capital Moves.*
2. Gerschenkron, *Economic Backwardness in Historical Perspective.*
3. Green, *Company Town.*
4. Kulikov, "Industrialization and Transformation of the Landscape in the Donbas Region."
5. Collier, *Post-Soviet Social*, 112.
6. World Bank, "Challenge of Russia's Monotowns," 26–27.
7. Japan's past experience with "lifetime employment," though primarily limited to male workers in large enterprises, might be the closest parallel to the Russian case. Takahashi, "Labor Market and Lifetime Employment in Japan."
8. Muro and Whiton, "America Has Two Economies." Somehow global cities "win" economically yet "lose" politically. Coman, "How the Megacities of Europe Stole a Continent's Wealth"; Rodden, *Why Cities Lose.*
9. Streeck, "Trump and the Trumpists." See also Broz, Frieden, and Weymouth, "Populism in Place."
10. Todorova and Gille, *Post-Communist Nostalgia.*
11. Mah, "Devastation but Also Home."
12. Mah, *Industrial Ruination, Community, and Place*; Strangleman and Rhodes, "'New' Sociology of Deindustrialisation?"
13. But see Rodrik, "Premature Deindustrialization."
14. Shleifer and Treisman, "Normal Country"; Doner and Schneider, "Middle-Income Trap."
15. Greskovits, *Political Economy of Protest and Patience.*
16. Crowley and Ost, *Workers after Workers' States*; Kubicek, *Organized Labor in Postcommunist States.*
17. Ost, *Defeat of Solidarity.*
18. Appel and Orenstein, *From Triumph to Crisis.* On variations of neoliberalism within east central Europe see Bohle and Greskovits, *Capitalist Diversity on Europe's Periphery.*
19. Meardi, *Social Failures of EU Enlargement.*
20. Greskovits, "Ten Years of Enlargement and the Forces of Labour in Central and Eastern Europe."

21. Sharma, *Rise and Fall of Nations*; Sharma, "Next Economic Powerhouse?"

22. Rakowski, *Hunters, Gatherers, and Practitioners of Powerlessness*; Morris, *Everyday Post-Socialism*.

23. Meardi, *Social Failures of EU Enlargement*. From 1989 to 2017, Latvia lost 27 percent of its population, Lithuania 22.5 percent, and Bulgaria close to 21 percent. Holmes and Krastev, *Light That Failed*.

24. Nölke and Vliegenthart, "Enlarging the Varieties of Capitalism."

25. Drahokoupil and Myant, "Varieties of Capitalism, Varieties of Vulnerabilities"; Meardi, *Social Failures of EU Enlargement*.

26. Appel and Orenstein, *From Triumph to Crisis*.

27. Tooze, *Crashed*, 227.

28. Appel and Orenstein, *From Triumph to Crisis*.

29. Ost, *Defeat of Solidarity*.

30. Beissinger and Sasse, "End to 'Patience'?"

31. Holmes and Krastev, *Light That Failed*, 14.

32. Interestingly, they find that among citizens with a pro-democracy orientation this "leftist bias" disappears, which corresponds to what we have noted about political liberals in Russia who often fail to connect with those of their fellow citizens seeking greater protection from market forces. Pop-Eleches and Tucker, *Communism's Shadow*.

33. Fabry, "Neoliberalism, Crisis and Authoritarian."

34. One source claims that "111 of the 456 cities in Ukraine are considered monotowns," though the definition of monotown here is unclear. Quintero and Restrepo, "City Decline in an Urbanizing World."

35. Evans and Sil, "Dynamics of Labor Militancy in the Extractive Sector"; Human Rights Watch, "'We Are Not the Enemy'"; Human Rights Watch, "Striking Oil, Striking Workers."

36. Evans and Sil, "Dynamics of Labor Militancy in the Extractive Sector."

37. Way, *Pluralism by Default*.

38. Devyatkov, "Specter of Revolution."

39. Gorbach, "Underground Waterlines." As Mihai Varga notes, only when the economic crisis brought by the transformation recession became so bad as to undermine the enterprises' ability to pay for social benefits would trade unions accept a more militant role. Trade unions would switch back to the model of providing social benefits as soon as the economic situation allowed for enterprises to pay for at least some of these benefits. Varga, *Worker Protests in Post-Communist Romania and Ukraine*, 33.

40. Gorbach, "Underground Waterlines."

41. Guz, "Ukraine."

42. Guillory, "Donbass Miners and the People's Republics"; Gorbach, "Underground Waterlines," 3.

43. Gorbach, "Underground Waterlines," 4; Davis, *Trade Unions in Russia and Ukraine, 1985–95*.

44. Varga, *Worker Protests in Post-Communist Romania and Ukraine*.

45. Dutchak, "Conditions and Sources of Labor Reproduction in Global Supply Chains."

46. Dutchak.

47. Lankina and Libman, "Soviet Legacies of Economic Development, Oligarchic Rule, and Electoral Quality in Eastern Europe's Partial Democracies"; Matsuzato, "Dissimilar Politics in Mariupol and Kramatorsk"; Artiukh and Gorbach, "Workers' Struggles in Ukraine and Belarus."

48. Dutchak, "Conditions and Sources of Labor Reproduction in Global Supply Chains."

49. Dutchak, "Unite or Fall," 152.
50. Artiukh and Gorbach, "Workers' Struggles in Ukraine and Belarus."
51. Gorbach, "Underground Waterlines," 12.
52. Tooze, *Crashed*, 236.
53. Tooze, 237.
54. Tooze, 493.
55. Tooze, 493.
56. Dutchak, "Unite or Fall"; Artiukh and Gorbach, "Workers' Struggles in Ukraine and Belarus."
57. Dutchak, "Unite or Fall."
58. Tooze, *Crashed*, 495.
59. Varga, *Worker Protests in Post-Communist Romania and Ukraine*, 31; Crowley, *Hot Coal, Cold Steel.*
60. Guillory, "Donbass Miners and the People's Republics."
61. Zhukov, "Rust Belt Rising." IMF loans also called for the closing of mines and ending coal subsidies. Guillory, "Donbass Miners and the People's Republics."
62. While Ukraine's divisions certainly contribute to instability, another factor potentially contributes to the dampening of social tensions, namely emigration. Ukraine is by some accounts the leading exporter of labor throughout Europe. Kiryukhin, "Losing Brains and Brawn."
63. Silitski, "Preempting Democracy."
64. Moshes, "Does It Make Sense to Expect a Color Revolution in Belarus?"; EurAsia Daily, "'U belorusskogo obshchestva ischez strakh pered vlast'iu.'"
65. ITUC, "Belarus' Rigged Presidential Election Must Be Re-run and Police Brutality Must Cease, Demands ITUC."
66. Artiukh and Gorbach, "Workers' Struggles in Ukraine and Belarus."
67. Moshes, "Does It Make Sense to Expect a Color Revolution in Belarus?"
68. Artiukh and Gorbach, "Workers' Struggles in Ukraine and Belarus."
69. Artiukh and Gorbach.
70. Aris, "'Italian Strike' Is Hobbling Production at Belarus' Biggest Companies."
71. See Edwards, "Belarusian Workers Support Protesters with Growing Strikes."
72. Artiukh and Gorbach, "Workers' Struggles in Ukraine and Belarus." This presents an interesting parallel with worker protests in east central Europe, despite seemingly different political economies there and in Belarus.
73. Chernyshova, "Very Belarusian Affair"; Nechepurenko and Troianovski, "Workers Join Belarus Protests, as Leader's Base Turns against Him."
74. Kolesnikov, "Dilemma diktatorov: Pochemu Lukashenko ne ukhodit."
75. Chernyshova, "Very Belarusian Affair."
76. Aris, "'Italian Strike' Is Hobbling Production at Belarus' Biggest Companies."
77. Artiukh and Gorbach, "Workers' Struggles in Ukraine and Belarus."
78. Chen, "Elitism and Exclusion in Mass Protest," 908.
79. Hurst, *Chinese Worker after Socialism.*
80. Hurst, 1–2.
81. Lee, *Against the Law*, 8.
82. Hurst, *Chinese Worker after Socialism*, 2, 108.
83. Lee, *Against the Law*, 5.
84. Lee, x.
85. Hurst, *Chinese Worker after Socialism*, 2.
86. Hurst, 1.
87. Chen, "Elitism and Exclusion in Mass Protest," 908.
88. Friedman, *Insurgency Trap.*

89. Gallagher, "China's Older Workers."

90. Blecher and Zipp, "Migrants and Mobilization."

91. Hurst, *Chinese Worker after Socialism.*

92. Elfstrom, "Tale of Two Deltas."

93. Lee, *Against the Law,* 9–11. For a somewhat different interpretation see Blecher, "Hegemony and Workers' Politics in China."

94. Remington, *Politics of Inequality in Russia.*

95. Javeline, *Protest and the Politics of Blame;* Crowley, "Liberal Transformation."

96. Krzywdzinski, *Consent and Control in the Authoritarian Workplace.*

CONCLUSION

1. Greene, "Running to Stand Still."

2. Miller, *Putinomics.*

3. Aron, "Russia's 'Monotowns' Time Bomb"; Gontmakher, "Stenarii': Novocherkassk-2009."

4. Wright, *Classes.*

5. The Russian government did raise the value-added tax and the pension age in 2018, and the pension change certainly led to protests. Yet in neither case was the impact experienced immediately by a concrete group (raising the age for retirement would not be felt by most until some years later).

6. Alexei Navalny, through his protests against corruption and his attempt to create a "union" of budget-sector workers, explicitly sought to break down that divide.

7. Moshes, "Does It Make Sense to Expect a Color Revolution in Belarus?"

8. Nechepurenko and Troianovski, "Workers Join Belarus Protests, as Leader's Base Turns against Him."

9. Artiukh and Gorbach, "Workers' Struggles in Ukraine and Belarus."

10. Goodwin, *No Other Way Out.*

11. Streeck, "Trump and the Trumpists," 5; Broz, Frieden, and Weymouth, "Populism in Place."

12. OECD, *OECD Regional Outlook 2019.*

13. Gaddy and Ickes, *Bear Traps on Russia's Road to Modernization;* Hill and Gaddy, *Siberian Curse.*

14. Bershidsky, "Putin Turns Swathes of Russia."

15. Moore, *Social Origins of Dictatorship and Democracy.*

16. Crowley, *Hot Coal, Cold Steel.*

17. Writing in *Novaya Gazeta,* Mironova argues that the "liberal establishment" views those critical of that period "as either '*sovaks*' or the Putin electorate." Mironova, "Prokliatie devianostykh."

18. Pavel Luzin is only slightly more equivocal about the prospects for political and economic liberalization. As he puts it, "one option would be to attempt democratization while continuing to rely on existing state and quasi-private corporations in order to avoid socio-economic unrest." However, "this scenario would result in an inevitable slowdown to any [economic] reformist plans." The other "option would be to stake it all on deep market reforms." This, however, "would inevitably lead to the collapse of many of Russia's largest companies, spelling shocking consequences for millions of citizens and entire regions." As a consequence, "in order to remain in power while implementing such reforms, the government would be compelled to remain essentially authoritarian." Luzin, "Why Corporations Are the Kremlin's Best Friends."

19. As Matveev argues, Putin's "government settled on a combination of neoliberalism and dirigisme that enhances the political stability of the regime at the expense of

economic growth. However, lack of growth itself undermines stability." Matveev, "State, Capital, and the Transformation of the Neoliberal Policy Paradigm in Putin's Russia," 27.

20. Evans, "Eclipse of the State?"

21. Wood, *Russia without Putin*; Appel and Orenstein, *From Triumph to Crisis*.

22. Regarding Pinochet-type reforms for Russia, Matveev cites the well-regarded poet Timur Kibirov: "I wanted to believe that he [Putin] would be the Russian Pinochet, he'd squeeze and cut freedoms, but quickly carry out liberal economic reforms. Our freedoms are cut down, reforms haven't been carried out." Matveev, "Russia, Inc."

23. Dawisha, *Putin's Kleptocracy*; Åslund, *Russia's Crony Capitalism*.

24. Ledeneva, *Can Russia Modernise?*

25. Christensen, "Russia as Semiperiphery"; Hopf, "Russia's Place in the World."

Bibliography

Acemoglu, Daron, and James A. Robinson. *Economic Origins of Dictatorship and Democracy*. New York: Cambridge University Press, 2006.

Akhmirova, Rimma. "Glavnyi boi dal'noboishchika Andreia Bazhutina." *Sobesednik*, March 12, 2018.

Alasheev, Sergei, and Marina Kiblitskaya. "How to Survive on a Russian's Wage." In *Labour Relations in Transition*, edited by Simon Clarke, 99–118. Cheltenham, UK: Edward Elgar, 1996.

Alexandrova, Lyudmila. "Massive Sackings at Russia's Largest Carmaker." ITAR-TASS, January 27, 2014. http://en.itar-tass.com/opinions/1651.

"Analiz protsessov privatizatsii gosudarstvennoi sobstvennosti v Rossiskoi Federatsii za period 1993–2003 godov." Moscow: Olita, 2004.

Anatrrra. "Dal'noboishchiki." Livejournal, December 26, 2015. https://anatrrra.livejour nal.com/226587.html.

Andrienko, Yuri, and Sergei Guriev. "Determinants of Interregional Mobility in Russia." *Economics of Transition* 12, no. 1 (March 1, 2004): 1–27. https://doi.org/10.1111/j.0967-0750.2004.00170.x.

Anner, Mark, and Xiangmin Liu. "Harmonious Unions and Rebellious Workers: A Study of Wildcat Strikes in Vietnam." *ILR Review* 69, no. 1 (January 1, 2016): 3–28. https://doi.org/10.1177/0019793915594596.

Antonova, Maria. "Putin Promises." *Moscow Times*, March 31, 2009.

AP Archive. "Putin Comments on Iraq, Economy and Other Issues." Accessed August 11, 2018. https://www.youtube.com/watch?v=8ufddW1mpZg.

Appel, Hilary, and Mitchell A. Orenstein. *From Triumph to Crisis: Neoliberal Economic Reform in Postcommunist Countries*. Cambridge: Cambridge University Press, 2018.

Aptekar', Pavel. "Stoit li sudit'sia za zarplatu." *Vedomosti*, November 1, 2017. https://www.vedomosti.ru/opinion/articles/2017/11/02/740260-suditsya-zarplatu.

Aris, Ben. "An 'Italian Strike' Is Hobbling Production at Belarus' Biggest Companies." bne IntelliNews, September 21, 2020. http://www.intellinews.com/an-italian-strike-is-hobbling-production-at-belarus-biggest-companies-192290/.

——. "Russia Is Stuck in the Middle Income Trap." bne IntelliNews (blog), December 21, 2017. http://www.intellinews.com/moscow-blog-russia-is-stuck-in-the-middle-income-trap-134557/.

——. "Russia's Import Substitution Has Not Been a Great Success." bne IntelliNews (blog), October 13, 2017. intellinews.com.

Arkhiv saita Samarskoi Gubernskoi Dumy 5-ogo sozyva. "U 'Zhigulevskoi doliny' shirokie perspektivy. . . ." June 10, 2016. https://archive5.samgd.ru/main/174028/.

Aron, Leon. "Darkness on the Edge of Monotown." *The New York Times*, October 17, 2009, sec. Opinion. http://www.nytimes.com/2009/10/17/opinion/17aron.html.

——. "Russia's 'Monotowns' Time Bomb." *Russian Outlook*, Fall 2009.

Artiukh, Volodymyr, and Denys Gorbach. "Workers' Struggles in Ukraine and Belarus: Comparing Working-Class Self-Activity across the Post-Soviet Uprisings."

Rosa Luxemburg Stiftung, November 4, 2020. https://www.rosalux.de/en/news/id/43290/workers-struggles-in-ukraine-and-belarus?cHash=25197f3015ef2d33cfd619cd5f50e8ce.

Asankin, Roman. "Chetyre oshibki Anderssona: za chto uvol'niaiut prezidenta AvtoVAZa." *RBK*, March 9, 2016. https://www.rbc.ru/business/09/03/2016/56e041989a7947240d410dc4.

——. "Pikety isportili otnosheniia glavy 'Rostekha' i prezidenta AvtoVAZa." *RBK*, November 9, 2015. http://www.rbc.ru/business/09/11/2015/5640b7c09a794768a0cf43aa.

Asankin, Roman, and Petr Kir'ian. "Shvedskii menedzhment i russkii krizis: Pochemu ne edet AvtoVAZ." *Zhurnal RBK*, January 25, 2016. https://www.rbc.ru/magazine/2016/02/56a22e4f9a7947c92b1a15b4.

Ashwin, Sarah. *Russian Workers: The Anatomy of Patience.* Manchester: Manchester University Press, 1999.

Ashwin, Sarah, and Simon Clarke. *Russian Trade Unions and Industrial Relations in Transition.* Houndmills, Basingstoke, Hampshire: Palgrave Macmillan, 2003.

Ashwin, Sarah, and Irina Kozina. "Russia." In *Comparative Employment Relations in the Global Economy,* edited by Carola Frege and John Kelly, 285–304. London: Routledge, 2013.

Åslund, Anders. *Russia's Crony Capitalism: The Path from Market Economy to Kleptocracy.* New Haven, CT: Yale University Press, 2019.

Australian Bureau of Statistics. Accessed October 5, 2018. http://www.abs.gov.au/.

Babchenko, Arkadii. "Zdes' budet tol'ko bunt." *Kasparov.ru*, March 25, 2018. http://www.kasparov.ru/material.php?id=5AB76BF41B808.

Baev, Pavel K. "Russia Is Steered Back toward Petro-Stagnation." Jamestown Foundation (blog), *Eurasia Daily Monitor*, October 10, 2017. https://jamestown.org/program/russia-steered-back-toward-petro-stagnation/.

Balmforth, Tom. "The Paradox of Russia's Left." RadioFreeEurope/RadioLiberty, February 19, 2012, sec. Russia. http://www.rferl.org/content/the_paradox_of_russias_left/24488988.html.

——. "Truckers' Leader Rolls on after Russian Election Bid Breaks Down." *RFE/RL*, January 19, 2018. https://www.rferl.org/a/russia-bazhutin-truckers-protest-election-bid-failed/28984667.html.

Balzer, Harley. "What Have We Learned, and Not Learned, from a Quarter-Century of Transition." *ASEEES NewsNet*, October 2016.

Barenberg, Alan. *Gulag Town, Company Town.* New Haven, CT: Yale University Press, 2014.

Barnes, Andrew Scott. *Owning Russia: The Struggle over Factories, Farms, and Power.* Ithaca, NY: Cornell University Press, 2006.

Baron, Samuel H. *Bloody Saturday in the Soviet Union: Novocherkassk, 1962.* Stanford, CA: Stanford University Press, 2001.

Barry, Ellen. "Tens of Thousands Protest in Moscow, Russia, in Defiance of Putin." *New York Times*, December 10, 2011. World/Europe. http://www.nytimes.com/2011/12/11/world/europe/thousands-protest-in-moscow-russia-in-defiance-of-putin.html.

BBC News Russkaia sluzhba. "Khodorkovskii vidit neizbezhnost' revoliutsii v Rossii." December 9, 2015. https://www.bbc.com/russian/news/2015/12/151209_khodorkovsky_russia_revolution_prognosis.

Bear Market Brief. "Analytical Center Counts 12 Million among Working Poor." October 31, 2017. https://bearmarketbrief.com/.

Beissinger, Mark, and Gwendolyn Sasse. "An End to 'Patience'? The Great Recession and Economic Protest in Eastern Europe." In *Mass Politics in Tough Times: Opinions, Votes and Protest in the Great Recession*, edited by Nancy Bermeo and Larry Bartels, 334–70. New York: Oxford University Press, 2014.

The Bell. "Kto zaplatit za obraz budushchego dlia prezidentskikh vyborov?" September 6, 2017. https://thebell.io/kto-zaplatit-za-obraz-budushchego-dlya-prezidentskih-vyborov/.

Bershidsky, Leonid. "Putin Turns Swathes of Russia into Flyover Country." *Bloomberg*, March 7, 2019. https://www.bloomberg.com/opinion/articles/2019-03-07/putin-s-development-plan-picks-favorites-among-russian-regions.

Betting, J. L. F. "A System Shaping Its Actors." Master's thesis, Leiden University, 2017.

Bizyukov, Petr. "Al'ternativnie profsoyuzi na puti osvoyeniya sotsial'nogo prostranstva." *Sostiologicheskiye Issledovaniya*, no. 5 (2000).

——. "Labor Protests in Russia, 2008–2011." *Russian Analytical Digest*, no. 104 (October 27, 2011): 6–10.

——. "Pervye Priznaki Bol'shogo Tsunami." Gazeta.ru. Accessed April 5, 2016. http://www.gazeta.ru/comments/2016/01/15_a_8023709.shtml.

——. "Trudovye protesty v pervoy polovine 2015 g." Tsentr sotsial'no-trudovykh prav. Accessed September 7, 2015. http://trudprava.ru/expert/analytics/1498.

——. "Trudovye protesty v Rossii v 2008–2016 gg. Analiticheskii otchet po rezul'tatam monitoringa trudovykh protestov TsSTP." 2017. http://trudprava.ru/expert/analytics/protestanalyt/1807/1807.

——. "Underground Miners' Strikes." In *Labour Relations in Transition*, edited by Simon Clarke, 234–74. Cheltenham, UK: Edward Elgar, 1996.

——. "Za ves' 2009 god v Rossii utverzhdaet Rosstat proizoshla vsego odna zabastovka." *gazeta.ru*, February 15, 2010. http://www.gazeta.ru/comments/2010/02/15_a_33 24039.shtml.

Blecher, Marc J. "Hegemony and Workers' Politics in China." *China Quarterly* 170 (June 2002): 283–303. https://doi.org/10.1017/S0009443902000190.

Blecher, Marc J., and Daniel Zipp. "Migrants and Mobilization: Sectoral Patterns in China, 2010–2013." *Global Labour Journal* 6, no. 1 (January 2015). https://mul press.mcmaster.ca/globallabour/article/view/2293.

Bluestone, Barry, and Bennett Harrison. *The Deindustrialization of America: Plant Closings, Community Abandonment, and the Dismantling of Basic Industry*. New York: Basic Books, 1982.

Bohle, Dorothee, and Béla Greskovits. *Capitalist Diversity on Europe's Periphery*. Cornell Studies in Political Economy. Ithaca, NY: Cornell University Press, 2012.

Bolotova, Alla, Anastassia Karaseva, and Valeria Vasilyeva. "Mobility and Sense of Place among Youth in the Russian Arctic." *Sibirica* 16, no. 3 (December 1, 2017): 77–124. https://doi.org/10.3167/sib.2017.160305.

Bolotova, Alla, and Florian Stammler. "How the North Became Home: Attachment to Place among Industrial Migrants in the Murmansk Region of Russia." In *Migration in the Circumpolar North: Issues and Contexts*, edited by Lee Huskey and Chris Southcott, 193–220. Edmonton, Alberta: CCI Press, 2010.

Borisov, Vadim, Veronika Bizyukova, and Konstantin Burnyshev. "Conflict in a Coal-Mining Enterprise: A Case Study of Sudzhenskaya Mine." In *Labour Relations in Transition*, edited by Simon Clarke, 201–33. Cheltenham, UK: Edward Elgar, 1996.

Brancati, Dawn. *Democracy Protests: Origins, Features, and Significance*. Cambridge: Cambridge University Press, 2016.

Broz, J. Lawrence, Jeffry Frieden, and Stephen Weymouth. "Populism in Place: The Economic Geography of the Globalization Backlash." *International Organization*, forthcoming. https://doi.org/10.2139/ssrn.3501263.

Buder, Emily. "The Toxic City of Norilsk, Russia: 'My Deadly Beautiful City.'" *Atlantic*, November 8, 2017. https://www.theatlantic.com/video/index/545228/my-deadly-beautiful-city-norilsk/.

Burawoy, Michael, and Pavel Krotov. "The Soviet Transition from Socialism to Capitalism: Worker Control and Economic Bargaining in the Wood Industry." *American Sociological Review* 57, no. 1 (February 1992): 16–38.

Burmistrova, Svetlana. "Rosatom otsenit protestnye nastroeniia v zakrytykh gorodakh riadom s AES." *RBK*, November 8, 2017. http://www.rbc.ru/business/08/11/2017/5a01c3e89a79479666fc6b63.

Busygina, Irina, and Mikhail Filippov. "The Calculus of Non-protest in Russia: Redistributive Expectations from Political Reforms." *Europe-Asia Studies* 67, no. 2 (February 7, 2015): 209–23. https://doi.org/10.1080/09668136.2014.1002679.

Caraway, Teri L. "Pathways of Dominance and Displacement: The Varying Fates of Legacy Unions in New Democracies." *World Politics* 64, no. 2 (April 20, 2012): 278–305.

Caraway, Teri L., Maria Lorena Cook, and Stephen Crowley, eds. *Working through the Past: Labor and Authoritarian Legacies in Comparative Perspective.* Ithaca, NY: Cornell University Press, 2015.

Casula, Philipp, and Jeronim Perovic. *Identities and Politics during the Putin Presidency: The Foundations of Russia's Stability.* New York: Columbia University Press, 2009.

CEPR. "ZdravoZakhoronenie. Optimizatsiia Rossiiskoi sistemy zdravookhraneniia v deistvii." May 17, 2017. http://cepr.su/2017/05/17/.

Chadaev, Aleksei. "Samurai Tagila." *Izvestiya*, April 15, 2013. https://iz.ru/news/548692.

Chaisty, Paul, and Stephen Whitefield. "The Effects of the Global Financial Crisis on Russian Political Attitudes." *Post-Soviet Affairs*, May 16, 2013. https://www.tandfonline.com/doi/abs/10.2747/1060-586X.28.2.187.

Chang, Ha-Joon. *Bad Samaritans: The Myth of Free Trade and the Secret History of Capitalism.* New York: Bloomsbury, 2008.

Chen, Calvin, and Rudra Sil. "Communist Legacies, Postcommunist Transformations, and the Fate of Organized Labor in Russia and China." *Studies in Comparative International Development* 41, no. 2 (June 2006): 62–87. https://doi.org/10.1007/BF02686311.

Chen, Xi. "Elitism and Exclusion in Mass Protest: Privatization, Resistance, and State Domination in China." *Comparative Political Studies* 50, no. 7 (June 1, 2017): 908–34. https://doi.org/10.1177/0010414016655532.

Chernyshova, Natalya. "A Very Belarusian Affair: What Sets the Current Anti-Lukashenka Protests Apart?" PONARS Euarasia, Policy Memo 671, September 17, 2020. https://www.ponarseurasia.org/memo/very-belarusian-affair-what-sets-current-anti-lukashenka-protests-apart.

Christensen, Paul T. "Labor under Putin: The State of the Russian Working Class." *New Labor Forum* 26, no. 1 (January 1, 2017): 64–73. https://doi.org/10.1177/1095796016682019.

——. "Russia as Semiperiphery: Political Economy, the State and Society in the Contemporary World System." In *The Political Economy of Russia*, edited by Neil Robinson, 169–89. Lanham, MD: Rowman & Littlefield, 2013.

City Population—Population Statistics of All Countries of the World. "City Population." https://www.citypopulation.de/.

Clarke, Simon, ed. *Conflict and Change in the Russian Industrial Enterprise*. Cheltenham, UK: Edward Elgar, 1996.

——. "Labor Relations and Class Formation." In *Labor Relations in Transition*, edited by Simon Clarke, 1–40. Cheltenham, UK: Edward Elgar, 1996.

——, ed. *Structural Adjustment without Mass Unemployment? Lessons from Russia*. Cheltenham, UK: Edward Elgar, 1998.

Clément, Karine. "Social Mobilizations and the Question of Social Justice in Contemporary Russia." *Globalizations* 16, no. 2 (February 23, 2019): 155–69. https://doi.org/10.1080/14747731.2018.1479014.

Clover, Charles. "Russian One-Company Towns Face Decline." *Financial Times*, October 27, 2009.

Clover, Joshua. *Riot. Strike. Riot: The New Era of Uprisings*. London: New York: Verso, 2016.

Coletta, Claudio, Leighton Evans, Liam Heaphy, and Rob Kitchin. *Creating Smart Cities: Regions and Cities*. New York: Routledge, 2019.

Collier, Ruth Berins. *Paths toward Democracy: The Working Class and Elites in Western Europe and South America*. Cambridge: Cambridge University Press, 1999.

Collier, Stephen J. *Post-Soviet Social: Neoliberalism, Social Modernity, Biopolitics*. Princeton, NJ: Princeton University Press, 2011.

Colton, Timothy, and Henry E. Hale. "The Putin Vote: Presidential Electorates in a Hybrid Regime." *Slavic Review* 68 (September 1, 2009): 473–503, viii. https://doi.org/10.1017/S0037677900019690.

Coman, Julian. "How the Megacities of Europe Stole a Continent's Wealth." *Guardian*, November 10, 2019, sec. Cities. https://www.theguardian.com/cities/2019/nov/10/how-europes-cities-stole-continents-wealth.

Commander, Simon, Zlatko Nikoloski, and Alexander Plekhanov. "Employment Concentration and Resource Allocation: One-Company Towns in Russia." IZA Discussion Paper no. 6034 (October 2011).

Connor, Walter D. *The Accidental Proletariat: Workers, Politics, and Crisis in Gorbachev's Russia*. Princeton, NJ: Princeton University Press, 1991.

Cook, Linda J. *Postcommunist Welfare States: Reform Politics in Russia and Eastern Europe*. Ithaca, NY: Cornell University Press, 2007.

——. "Russian Labour." In *Routledge Handbook of Russian Politics and Society*, 318–28. New York: Routledge, 2011.

——. "Trade Unions, Management, and the State in Contemporary Russia." In *Business and the State in Contemporary Russia*, edited by Peter Rutland, 151–72. Boulder, CO: Westview, 2001.

Cooper, Julian. "The Military Dimension of a More Militant Russia." *Russian Journal of Economics* 2, no. 2 (June 1, 2016): 129–45. https://doi.org/10.1016/j.ruje.2016.06.002.

Cooper, William H. "The Russian Financial Crisis of 1998: An Analysis of Trends, Causes, and Implications." Washington, DC: Congressional Research Service, Library of Congress, February 18, 1999. http://congressionalresearch.com/98-578/document.php?study=The+Russian+Financial+Crisis+of+1998+An+Analysis+of+Trends+Causes+and+Implications.

Cordesman, Anthony. "Russia and the 'Color Revolution': A Russian Military View of a World Destabilized by the US and the West." Center for Strategic & International Studies, May 28, 2014. https://www.csis.org/analysis/russia-and-%E2%80%9Ccolor-revolution%E2%80%9D.

Cowie, Jefferson. *Capital Moves: RCA's Seventy-Year Quest for Cheap Labor*. New York: New Press, 2001.

Crawford, Beverly. "Post-Communist Political Economy: A Framework for the Analysis of Reform." In *Markets, States and Democracy: The Political Economy of Post-Communist Transformations*, edited by Beverly Crawford, 3–42. Boulder, CO: Westview, 1995.

Crowley, Stephen. "Explaining Labor Weakness in Post-Communist Europe: Historical Legacies and Comparative Perspective." *East European Politics and Societies* 18, no. 3 (August 1, 2004): 394–429. https://doi.org/10.1177/0888325404267395.

——. *Hot Coal, Cold Steel: Russian and Ukrainian Workers from the End of the Soviet Union to the Post-Communist Transformations*. Ann Arbor: University of Michigan Press, 1997.

——. "Liberal Transformation: Labor and the Russian State." In *Building the Russian State*, edited by Valerie Sperling, 157–76. Boulder, CO: Westview, 2000.

——. "Monotowns and the Political Economy of Industrial Restructuring in Russia." *Post-Soviet Affairs* 32, no. 5 (2016): 397–422. https://doi.org/10.1080/10605 86X.2015.1054103.

——. "Russia's Labor Legacy: Making Use of the Past." In *Working through the Past: Labor and Authoritarian Legacies in Comparative Perspective*, edited by Teri L. Caraway, Maria Lorena Cook, and Stephen Crowley, 122–41. Ithaca, NY: Cornell University Press, 2015.

——. "The Social Explosion That Wasn't: Labor Quiescence in Postcommunist Russia." In *Workers after Workers' States: Labor and Politics in Postcommunist Eastern Europe*, edited by Stephen Crowley and David Ost, 199–218. Lanham, MD: Rowman & Littlefield, 2001.

Crowley, Stephen, and Irina Olimpieva. "Labor Protests and Their Consequences in Putin's Russia." *Problems of Post-Communism* 65, no. 5 (2018): 344–58. https://doi.org/10.1080/10758216.2017.1364135.

Crowley, Stephen, and David Ost, eds. *Workers after Workers' States: Labor and Politics in Postcommunist Eastern Europe*. Lanham, MD: Rowman & Littlefield, 2001.

Davis, Sue. *Trade Unions in Russia and Ukraine, 1985–95*. New York: Palgrave, 2001.

Dawisha, Karen. *Putin's Kleptocracy: Who Owns Russia?* New York: Simon & Schuster, 2014.

Defense Intelligence Agency. "Russia Military Power: Building a Military to Support Great Power Aspirations." 2017.

Department of State. Office of Website Management, Bureau of Public Affairs. *Russia*. Report. February 25, 2009. http://www.state.gov/j/drl/rls/hrrpt/2008/eur/1191 01.htm.

Desai, Padma, and Todd Idson. *Work without Wages: Russia's Nonpayment Crisis*. Cambridge, MA: MIT Press, 2000.

Devyatkov, Andrey. "The Specter of Revolution: Moldova's Future Hangs on Protests." Carnegie Moscow Center, July 5, 2018. https://carnegie.ru/commentary/76741.

Deyo, Frederic C. *Beneath the Miracle: Labor Subordination in the New Asian Industrialism*. Berkeley: University of California Press, 1989.

Dixon, Megan, and Jessica Graybill. "Uncertainty in the Urban Form: Post-Soviet Cities Today." In *Questioning Post-Soviet*, edited by Edward C. Holland and Matthew Derrick, 19–38. Washington, DC: Kennan Institute, Wilson Center, 2016.

Dmitriev, Mikhail. "Lost in Transition? The Geography of Protests and Attitude Change in Russia." *Europe-Asia Studies* 67, no. 2 (February 7, 2015): 224–43.

Dmitriev, Mikhail, and Daniel Treisman. "Other Russia: Discontent Grows in the Hinterlands." *Foreign Affairs* 91 (2012): 59.

Doner, Richard F., and Ben Ross Schneider. "The Middle-Income Trap: More Politics Than Economics." *World Politics* 68, no. 4 (October 2016): 608–44. https://doi.org/10.1017/S0043887116000095.

Dorozhkina, Dar'ia. "Tol'iatti perevodiat v pervuiu gruppu monogorodov." *Volga N'ius*, November 5, 2015. https://volga.news/article/396489.html.

Drahokoupil, Jan, and Martin Myant. "Varieties of Capitalism, Varieties of Vulnerabilities: Financial Crisis and Its Impact on Welfare States in Eastern Europe and the Commonwealth of Independent States." *Historical Social Research / Historische Sozialforschung* 35, no. 2 (132) (2010): 266–95.

Dutchak, Oksana. "Conditions and Sources of Labor Reproduction in Global Supply Chains: The Case of Ukrainian Garment Sector." *Bulletin of Taras Shevchenko National University of Kyiv: Sociology* 1, no. 9 (2018): 17–23.

———. "Unite or Fall: Labor Protests in Ukraine in the Face of the Crises." *Intersections: East European Journal of Society and Politics* 1, no. 3 (September 2015): 140–57. https://intersections.tk.mta.hu/index.php/intersections/article/view/95.

Dyakina, Oksana. "Esli monogorod deshevle razrushit', to vyvod naprashivaetsia sam soboi." *FederalPress*, November 11, 2019. https://fedpress.ru/interview/2362198.

Earle, John S., and Klara Sabirianova Peter. "Equilibrium Wage Arrears: A Theoretical and Empirical Analysis of Institutional Lock-In." *SSRN ELibrary*, September 2000. http://papers.ssrn.com/sol3/papers.cfm?abstract_id=251999.

Ebel, Francesca. "In World Cup's Shadow, Layoffs and Anger at Russian Factory." *US News & World Report*, June 5, 2018. https://www.usnews.com/news/world/articles/2018-06-15/in-world-cups-shadow-layoffs-and-anger-at-russian-factory.

Economist. "Mr Putin Will Win Next Year Despite, Not Because of, the Economy." December 19, 2017. https://www.economist.com/europe/2017/12/19/mr-putin-will-win-next-year-despite-not-because-of-the-economy.

Economy Times. "Ol'ga Golodets: Bednost' Rossiian—Osnovnoe prepiatstvie dlia rosta ekonomiki." February 7, 2018. http://economytimes.ru/novosti/olga-golodec-bednost-rossiyan-osnovnoe-prepyatstvie-dlya-rosta-ekonomiki.

Edwards, Maxim. "Belarusian Workers Support Protesters with Growing Strikes." Global Voices (blog), August 13, 2020. https://globalvoices.org/2020/08/13/belarusian-workers-support-protesters-with-a-general-strike/.

Eidelman, Tamara. "A Lesson in Solidarity: With the Striking Truckers in Khimki." Russian Reader, December 26, 2015. https://therussianreader.com/2016/01/02/solidarity-lesson-khimki-striking-truckers/.

Elder, Miriam. "Vladimir Putin Takes Oleg Deripaska to Task." *Telegraph*, June 4, 2009, sec. World. http://www.telegraph.co.uk/news/worldnews/europe/russia/5446293/Vladimir-Putin-takes-Oleg-Deripaska-to-task.html.

Elfstrom, Manfred. "A Tale of Two Deltas: Labour Politics in Jiangsu and Guangdong." *British Journal of Industrial Relations* 57, no. 2 (2019): 247–74. https://doi.org/10.1111/bjir.12467.

Erlanger, Steven. "Serbian Strikers, Joined by 20,000, Face Down Police." *New York Times*, October 5, 2000, sec. World. https://www.nytimes.com/2000/10/05/world/serbian-strikers-joined-by-20000-face-down-police.html.

EurAsia Daily. "'U belorusskogo obshchestva ischez strakh pered vlast'iu.'" March 7, 2017. https://eadaily.com/ru/news/2017/03/07/u-belorusskogo-obshchestva-ischez-strah-pered-vlastyu.

Evans, Allison D. "Local Democracy in a Hybrid State: Pluralism and Protest in Volzhskiy, Russia." *Post-Soviet Affairs* 30, no. 4 (July 4, 2014): 298–323. https://doi.org/10.1080/1060586X.2013.862971.

———. "Protest Patterns in Provincial Russia: A Paired Comparison of Company Towns." *Studies in Comparative International Development*, July 19, 2015, 1–26. https://doi.org/10.1007/s12116-015-9191-5.

Evans, Allison D., and Rudra Sil. "The Dynamics of Labor Militancy in the Extractive Sector: Kazakhstan's Oilfields and South Africa's Platinum Mines in

Comparative Perspective." *Comparative Political Studies*, October 16, 2019, 0010414019879715. https://doi.org/10.1177/0010414019879715.

Evans, Peter B. "The Eclipse of the State? Reflections on Stateness in an Era of Globalization." *World Politics* 50, no. 1 (October 1997): 62–87. https://doi.org/10.1017/S0043887100014726.

——. *Embedded Autonomy: States and Industrial Transformation*. Princeton Paperbacks. Princeton, NJ: Princeton University Press, 1995.

Fabry, Adam. "Neoliberalism, Crisis and Authoritarian—Ethnicist Reaction: The Ascendancy of the Orbán Regime." *Competition & Change* 23, no. 2 (April 1, 2019): 165–91. https://doi.org/10.1177/1024529418813834.

Fantasia, Rick. *Cultures of Solidarity: Consciousness, Action, and Contemporary American Workers*. Berkeley: University of California Press, 1989.

FAS Russia. "Report on Competition Policy in Russian Federation in 2016 to OECD." Moscow: Federal Antimonopoly Service of the Russian Federation, 2016.

Federal'naia sluzhba gosudarstvennoi statistiki. "Chislennost' naseleniia Rossiiskoi Federatsii po munitsipal'nym obrazovaniiam." Accessed August 21, 2018. http://www.gks.ru/wps/wcm/connect/rosstat_main/rosstat/ru/statistics/publications/catalog/afc8ea004d56a39ab251f2bafc3a6fce.

——. "Itogi Vserossiiskoi perepisi naseleniia 2010 goda." Accessed August 21, 2018. http://www.gks.ru/free_doc/new_site/perepis2010/croc/perepis_itogi1612.htm.

FederalPress—Samarskaia Oblast'. "Bednyi Tol'iatti: Problemy goroda vsplyli na federal'nom urovne." January 20, 2015. http://fedpress.ru/news/econom/reviews/1421767582-bednyi-tolyatti-problemy-goroda-vsplyli-na-federalnom-urovne.

Fedorinova, Yuliya, and Andrey Lemeshko. "Russia Steel Mills Become World Beaters after Ruble's Slide." Bloomberg.com, March 3, 2015. https://www.bloomberg.com/news/articles/2015-03-03/russia-s-steel-mills-become-world-beaters-after-ruble-s-slide.

Finkel, Evgeny, and Yitzhak M. Brudny. "Russia and the Colour Revolutions." *Democratization* 19, no. 1 (February 1, 2012): 15–36. https://doi.org/10.1080/13510347.2012.641297.

Flikke, Geir. "The Sword of Damocles: State Governability in Putin's Third Term." *Problems of Post-Communism* 65, no. 6 (2018): 434–46. https://www.tandfonline.com/doi/abs/10.1080/10758216.2017.1291308?journalCode=mppc20.

Florida, Richard L. *The Rise of the Creative Class: And How It's Transforming Work, Leisure, Community and Everyday Life*. New York: Basic Books, 2004.

FNPR. "Federatsiia Nezavisimykh Profsoiuzov Rossii—ofitsial'nyi sait." Accessed September 4, 2018. http://www.fnpr.ru/n/55/7219.html.

Fomina, Yekaterina. "'We Have Plenty of Reasons to Protest Apart from Platon.'" openDemocracy, December 14, 2017. https://www.opendemocracy.net/en/odr/russia-truck-driver-protest/.

Fond bor'by s korruptsiei. *FBK: Don't Call Him "Dimon."* March 2, 2017. https://fbk.info/english/english/post/304/.

Fond razvitiia monogorodov. "Strategiia razvitiia nekommercheskoi organizatsii' do 2020 g." N.d.

Fortescue, Stephen. "The Russian Economy and Business—Government Relations." In *Routledge Handbook of Russian Politics and Society*, edited by Graeme J. Gill, 274–87. New York: Routledge, 2011.

——. "The Russian Steel Industry, 1990–2009." *Eurasian Geography and Economics* 50, no. 3 (May 1, 2009): 252–74. https://doi.org/10.2747/1539-7216.50.3.252.

Foy, Henry, and Peter Campbell. "Carmakers Gear Up for Recovery in Russia." *Financial Times*, September 28, 2017.

Franzosi, Roberto. "One Hundred Years of Strike Statistics: Methodological and Theoretical Issues in Quantitative Strike Research." *Industrial and Labor Relations Review* 42, no. 3 (1989): 348–62. https://doi.org/10.2307/2523393.

Friedman, Eli. *Insurgency Trap: Labor Politics in Postsocialist China.* Ithaca, NY: Cornell University Press, 2014.

Frye, Timothy, Israel Marques, Eugeniia Nazrullaeva, Denis Ivanov, and Andrei Yakovlev. "Through Thick and through Thin: Economic Shocks, Transfers and Strategic Priorities in Russia." NRU, HSE preprints, December 16, 2015.

Frye, Timothy, Ora John Reuter, and David Szakonyi. "Hitting Them with Carrots: Voter Intimidation and Vote Buying in Russia." *British Journal of Political Science* 49, no. 3 (February 2018): 1–25. https://doi.org/10.1017/S0007123416000752.

——. "Political Machines at Work: Voter Mobilization and Electoral Subversion in the Workplace." *World Politics* 66, no. 02 (2014): 195–228.

Gaaze, Konstantin. "The Accidental Formation of Russia's War Coalition." Carnegie Moscow Center. Accessed October 31, 2017. http://carnegie.ru/commentary/71340.

Gabowitsch, Mischa. *Protest in Putin's Russia.* Malden, MA: Polity, 2017.

Gabriel, P. E., and S. Schmitz. "A Longitudinal Analysis of the Union Wage Premium for US Workers." *Applied Economics Letters* 21, no. 7 (May 3, 2014): 487–89. https://doi.org/10.1080/13504851.2013.868583.

Gaddy, Clifford G. *The Price of the Past: Russia's Struggle with the Legacy of a Militarized Economy.* Washington, DC: Brookings Institution, 1996.

Gaddy, Clifford, and Barry W. Ickes. *Bear Traps on Russia's Road to Modernization.* Abingdon, Oxon, UK: Routledge, 2013.

——. "The Russian Economy through 2020: The Challenge of Managing Rent Addiction." In *Russia in 2020: Scenarios for the Future*, edited by Maria Lipman and Nikolay Petrov, 165–86. Washington, DC: Carnegie Endowment for International Peace, 2011.

——. *Russia's Virtual Economy.* Washington, DC: Brookings Institution Press, 2002.

Gallagher, Mary. "China's Older Workers: Between Law and Policy, between Laid-Off and Unemployed." In *Laid-Off Workers in a Workers' State: Unemployment with Chinese Characteristics*, edited by T. Gold, W. Hurst, J. Won, and Q. Li, 135–58. New York: Palgrave Macmillan, 2009.

Gandhi, Jennifer, and Adam Przeworski. "Cooperation, Cooptation, and Rebellion under Dictatorships." *Economics & Politics* 18, no. 1 (2006): 1–26. https://doi.org/10.1111/j.1468-0343.2006.00160.x.

Garmonenko, Dar'ia. "Dal'noboinyi impichment." *Nezavisimaya Gazeta*, March 28, 2016. http://www.ng.ru/politics/2016-03-28/1_impichment.html.

Gazeta.ru. "Kudrin: Moskva i Sankt-Peterburg k 2035 godu sostaviat 40% VVP Rossii." July 17, 2018. https://www.gazeta.ru/business/news/2018/07/17/n_11800609.shtml.

Gerber, Theodore P., and Michael Hout. "Tightening Up: Declining Class Mobility during Russia's Market Transition." *American Sociological Review* 69, no. 5 (October 1, 2004): 677–703. https://doi.org/10.1177/000312240406900504.

Gerschenkron, Alexander. *Economic Backwardness in Historical Perspective.* Cambridge, MA: Harvard University Press, 1962.

Gimpelson, Vladimir, and Rostislav Kapeliushnikov. "Anticipation and Management of Restructuring in Russia." European Commission: DG Employment, Social Affairs and Inclusion. October 2011.

——. "Labor Market Adjustment: Is Russia Different?" In *The Oxford Handbook of the Russian Economy*, edited by Michael Alexeev and Shlomo Weber, 693–724. Oxford: Oxford University Press, 2013.

Gimpelson, Vladimir, Rostislav Kapeliushnikov, and S. Iu. Roshchin, eds. *Rossiiskii rynok truda: Tendentsii, instituty, strukturnye izmeneniia*. Moscow: Tsentra trudovykh issledovaniĭ NIU VShE, 2017. https://publications.hse.ru/books/204342588.

Gimpelson, Vladimir, and Douglas Lippoldt. *The Russian Labour Market: Between Transition and Turmoil*. Lanham, MD: Rowman & Littlefield, 2001.

Gimpelson, Vladimir, and Galina Monusova. "Strakh bezrabotitsi: Mezhstranovikh sopastovlenii." *Voprosy Ekonomiki*, no. 2 (2010): 117–38.

Gimpelson, Vladimir, and Aleksey Oshchepkov. "Does More Unemployment Cause More Fear of Unemployment?" *IZA Journal of Labor & Development* 1, no. 1 (December 31, 2012): 6. https://doi.org/10.1186/2193-9020-1-6.

Glazunov, Mikhail. *Business in Post-Communist Russia: Privatisation and the Limits of Transformation*. Milton Park, Abingdon, Oxon; New York: Routledge, 2013.

Goble, Paul. "Like Other 'Local' Protests, Truckers Strike Greatest Often Where Participation in Elections Was Lowest, New Study Finds." *Window on Eurasia—New Series* (blog), May 15, 2017. http://windowoneurasia2.blogspot.com/2017/06/russias-striking-long-haul-truckers.html.

——. "Moscow Can't Afford to Support Russia's Villages or to Shut Them Down." *Window on Eurasia—New Series* (blog), January 17, 2017. http://windowoneurasia2.blogspot.com/2017/01/moscow-cant-afford-to-support-russias.html.

——. "Protesters in Russia Today Are Younger, Poorer and Further Left Than a Decade Ago." *Moscow Times*, March 26, 2019. https://www.themoscowtimes.com/2019/03/26/protesters-in-russia-today-are-younger-poorer-and-further-left-than-a-decade-ago-a64958.

——. "Putin's Greatest Fear Is the FSB Refusing to Fire on the Russian People, Golts Says." *Window on Eurasia—New Series* (blog), July 6, 2017. http://windowoneurasia2.blogspot.com/2017/07/putins-greatest-fear-is-fsb-refusing-to.

——. "Russia's Striking Long Haul Truckers Take Active Part in Navalny Anti-corruption Protest." *Window on Eurasia—New Series* (blog), June 13, 2017. http://windowoneurasia2.blogspot.com/2017/06/russias-striking-long-haul-truckers.html.

Golikova, V., K. Gonchar, and B. Kuznetsov. "Rossiiskaia promyshlennost' na pereput'e. Chto meshaet nashim firmam stat' konkurentosposobnymi." Moscow: GU—VSE, 2007. http://window.edu.ru/resource/069/52069.

Golts, Aleksandr. "Militarizm i konkurentosposobnost' Rossii." 2017. Unpublished manuscript.

——. "Rosgvardiia podminaet Genshtab." *New Times*, June 5, 2017. https://newtimes.ru/articles/detail/116432.

Golubkova, Katya. "Kremlin Tells Companies to Deliver Good News." Reuters, November 14, 2017. https://www.reuters.com/article/us-russia-kremlin-pr/exclusive-kremlin-tells-companies-to-deliver-good-news-idUSKBN1DE0MP.

Gontmakher, Evgenii'. "Novyi levyi povorot." *Vedomosti*, October 3, 2017. https://www.vedomosti.ru/opinion/articles/2017/10/03/736227-novii-levii-povorot.

——. "Stenarii': Novocherkassk-2009." *Vedomosti*, November 6, 2008, no. 210 edition.

Goodwin, Jeff. *No Other Way Out: States and Revolutionary Movements, 1945–1991*. Cambridge Studies in Comparative Politics. New York: Cambridge University Press, 2001.

Gorbach, Denys. "Underground Waterlines: Explaining Political Quiescence of Ukrainian Labor Unions." *Focaal: Journal of Global and Historical Anthropology* 2019, no. 84 (July 1, 2019): 33–46. https://doi.org/10.3167/fcl.2019.840103.

Gorbachev, Mikhail Sergeevich. *Zhizn' i reformy*. Moskva: Novosti, 1995.

Gordon, Leonid Abramovich, and Eduard Viktorovich Klopov. *Poteri i obreteniia v Rossii devianostykh: Istoriko-sotsiologicheskie ocherki ekonomicheskogo polozheniia narodnogo bolshinstva*. Moscow: Editorial URSS, 2000.

Granovetter, Mark. "Economic Action and Social Structure: The Problem of Embeddedness." *American Journal of Sociology* 91, no. 3 (November 1985): 481–510.

Green, Hardy. *The Company Town: The Industrial Edens and Satanic Mills That Shaped the American Economy*. New York: Basic Books, 2010.

Greene, Samuel A. "From Boom to Bust: Hardship, Mobilization and Russia's Social Contract." *Daedalus*, March 27, 2017. https://doi.org/10.1162/DAED_a_00439.

——. *Moscow in Movement: Power and Opposition in Putin's Russia*. Stanford, CA: Stanford University Press, 2014.

——. "Running to Stand Still: Aggressive Immobility and the Limits of Power in Russia." *Post-Soviet Affairs* 34, no. 5 (September 3, 2018): 333–47. https://doi.org/10.1080/1060586X.2018.1500095.

Greene, Samuel A., and Graeme B. Robertson. "Politics, Justice and the New Russian Strike." *Communist and Post-Communist Studies* 43, no. 1 (March 2010): 73–95.

——. *Putin v. the People: The Perilous Politics of a Divided Russia*. New Haven, CT: Yale University Press, 2019.

Gregory, Paul. "Has Putin Met His Match in Russia's Truck Drivers?" Forbes.com, November 30, 2015. https://www.forbes.com/sites/paulroderickgregory/2015/11/30/has-putin-met-his-match-in-russias-truck-drivers/#3d09b137741c.

Greskovits, Béla. *The Political Economy of Protest and Patience: East European and Latin American Transformations Compared*. New York: Central European University Press, 1998.

——. "Ten Years of Enlargement and the Forces of Labour in Central and Eastern Europe." *Transfer: European Review of Labour and Research* 21, no. 3 (August 1, 2015): 269–84. https://doi.org/10.1177/1024258915585932.

Griaznevich, Vladimir. "V Peterburge poiavilsia sopernik Vladimira Putina." *RBK*, June 16, 2017. https://www.rbc.ru/spb_sz/16/06/2017/5943aec59a7947a3293db891.

Grigoriev, Ivan S. "Labor Reform in Putin's Russia: Could Modernization be Democratic?" In *Authoritarian Modernization in Russia: Ideas, Institutions, and Policies*, edited by Vladimir Gel'man, 183–99. New York: Routledge, 2016.

Grigoriev, Ivan S., and Anna A. Dekalchuk. "Collective Learning and Regime Dynamics under Uncertainty: Labour Reform and the Way to Autocracy in Russia." *Democratization* 24, no. 3 (April 16, 2017): 481–97. https://doi.org/10.1080/13510347.2016.1223629.

Grove, Thomas. "Russians in Heartland Sour on Vladimir Putin over Money Woes." *Wall Street Journal*, March 22, 2019, sec. World. https://www.wsj.com/articles/russians-in-heartland-sour-on-vladimir-putin-over-money-woes-11553252400.

Guillory, Sean. "Donbass Miners and the People's Republics." *Warscapes*, July 15, 2014. http://www.warscapes.com/opinion/donbass-miners-and-peoples-republics.

——. "Whatever Happened to 'Russia without Putin'?" *New Eastern Europe*, no. 1 (2017). http://www.neweasterneurope.eu/articles-and-commentary/2235-whatever-happened-to-russia-without-putin.

Guriev, Sergei, and Daniel Treisman. "The Popularity of Authoritarian Leaders: A Cross-National Investigation." *World Politics* 72, no. 4 (October 2020): 601–38. https://doi.org/10.1017/S0043887120000167.

Guz, Serhiy. "Ukraine: The International Workers' Day That We Lost." openDemocracy, May 1, 2019. https://www.opendemocracy.net/en/odr/ukraine-the-international-workers-day-that-we-lost/.

Haggard, Stephan, and Robert R. Kaufman. *Dictators and Democrats: Masses, Elites, and Regime Change*. Princeton, NJ: Princeton University Press, 2016.

———. "Introduction: Institutions and Economic Adjustment." In *The Politics of Economic Adjustment: International Constraints, Distributive Conflicts and the State*, edited by Stephan Haggard and Robert Kaufman, 3–40. Princeton, NJ: Princeton University Press, 1992.

———. *The Political Economy of Democratic Transitions*. Princeton, NJ: University Press, 1995.

Hakvåg, Una. "Russian Defense Spending after 2010: The Interplay of Personal, Domestic, and Foreign Policy Interests." *Post-Soviet Affairs* 33, no. 6 (November 2, 2017): 496–510. https://doi.org/10.1080/1060586X.2017.1388472.

Hale, Henry E. *Patronal Politics: Eurasian Regime Dynamics in Comparative Perspective*. Problems of International Politics. New York: Cambridge University Press, 2014.

Harding, Luke, and Andrew Roth. "Arkady Babchenko Reveals He Faked His Death to Thwart Moscow Plot." *Guardian*, May 30, 2018, sec. World News. https://www.theguardian.com/world/2018/may/30/arkady-babchenko-reveals-he-faked-his-death-to-thwart-moscow-plot.

Harvey, David. *The Condition of Postmodernity: An Enquiry into the Origins of Cultural Change*. Oxford: Blackwell, 1989.

———. *Cosmopolitanism and the Geographies of Freedom*. Wellek Library Lectures. New York: Columbia University Press, 2009.

———. "From Managerialism to Entrepreneurialism: The Transformation in Urban Governance in Late Capitalism." *Geografiska Annaler. Series B, Human Geography* 71, no. 1 (1989): 3–17. https://doi.org/10.2307/490503.

———. *The Limits to Capital*. New and fully updated ed. New York: Verso, 2006.

Hauslohner, Peter. "Gorbachev's Social Contract." *Soviet Economy* 3, no. 1 (January 1, 1987): 54–89. https://doi.org/10.1080/08826994.1987.10641271.

Hedlund, Stefan. "Russia's Monotowns—Evidence of an Increasingly Obsolete Economy." *World Review* (blog), February 4, 2014.

Heleniak, Timothy. "International Comparisons of Population Mobility in Russia." *International Journal of Population Research*, 2012. https://doi.org/10.1155/2012/361497.

———. "Out-Migration and Depopulation of the Russian North during the 1990s." *Post-Soviet Geography and Economics* 40, no. 3 (April 1, 1999): 155–205. https://doi.org/10.1080/10889388.1999.10641111.

Helmer, John. "Kremlin Loses Fear of Regional Demonstrations—the Steel Oligarchs Issue 'Production Release' Pink Slips." *Dances with Bears* (blog), June 9, 2014. http://johnhelmer.net/?p=10930.

Henry, Laura A. "Complaint-Making as Political Participation in Contemporary Russia." *Communist and Post-Communist Studies* 45, no. 3–4 (2012): 243–54.

Hill, Fiona, and Clifford Gaddy. *The Siberian Curse: How Communist Planners Left Russia Out in the Cold*. Washington, DC: Brookings Institution, 2003.

Hille, Kathrin, and Henry Foy. "Russia's Next Revolution: How Technology Came to the Mines." *Financial Times*, October 26, 2017.

Hinz, Sarah, and Jeremy Morris. "Trade Unions in Transnational Automotive Companies in Russia and Slovakia: Prospects for Working-Class Power." *European Journal of Industrial Relations* 23, no. 1 (March 1, 2017): 97–112. https://doi.org/10.1177/0959680116676718.

Hirschman, Albert O. *Exit, Voice, and Loyalty: Responses to Decline in Firms, Organizations, and States*. Cambridge, MA: Harvard University Press, 1970.

Hodouchi, Ayano. "Car Union Urges State Control." *Moscow News*, August 4, 2009, no. 29 edition.

Holmes, Stephen, and Ivan Krastev. *The Light That Failed: Why the West Is Losing the Fight for Democracy*. New York: Pegasus Books, 2020.

Holm-Hansen, Jørn, Mikkel Berg-Nordlie, Aadne Aasland, and Linda Cook. "Welfare Reform, Protest and Stability in the Light of Reforms of Old-Age Pensions, Housing and Primary Education." *Russian Politics* 4, no. 3 (September 27, 2019): 354–74. https://doi.org/10.1163/2451-8921-00403004.

Holom, Brittany. "Russian Health-Care Protests Continue Despite Putin's Popularity." *Washington Post* (blog), January 1, 2015. http://www.washingtonpost.com/blogs/monkey-cage/wp/2015/01/01/russian-health-care-protests-continue-despite-putins-popularity/.

Hopf, Ted. "Russia's Place in the World: An Exit Option?" PONARS Eurasia, Policy Memo 79, September 2009. https://www.ponarseurasia.org/memo/russias-place-world-exit-option.

Horky, Petr, dir. *The Russian Job—a Documentary Film*. Krutart, 2017.

Human Rights Watch. "Red Card: Exploitation of Construction Workers on World Cup Sites in Russia." Human Rights Watch, June 2017.

——. "Striking Oil, Striking Workers." Human Rights Watch, 2012. https://www.hrw.org/report/2012/09/10/striking-oil-striking-workers/violations-labor-rights-kazakhstans-oil-sector.

——. "'We Are Not the Enemy': Violations of Workers' Rights in Kazakhstan." November 23, 2016. https://www.hrw.org/report/2016/11/23/we-are-not-enemy/violations-workers-rights-kazakhstan.

Hurst, William. *The Chinese Worker after Socialism*. New York: Cambridge University Press, 2009.

ICEM. "Russia Campaign: Strikes and Protests," *ICEM*, May 18, 2000. http://www.icem.org/campaign/no_pay_cc/protests_0001a.html. (Webpage no longer available.)

Il'ina, I. I. "Strategiya modernizatsii monogorodov Rossii." In *Razvitie monoprofil'nykh naselennykh punktov v Rossiyskoy Federatsii*, edited by A. V. Turkov, 4–11. Moscow: Finansovyy universitet, 2012.

Independent. "Russia's Economic Crisis Leads to Mounting Protests." HuffPost, March 5, 2009. https://www.huffpost.com/entry/russias-economic-crisis-l_n_163056.

Inozemtsev, Vladislav. "Chto tyanet nas obratno v SSSR? Ne FSB i ne 'Edinaya Rossiya.'" *Slon*, May 20, 2015. https://slon.ru.

——. "Nas malo, no eto ne vazhno." Gazeta.ru, September 7, 2016. https://www.gazeta.ru/column/vladislav_inozemcev/10177625.shtml.

——. "Russia's Economic Modernization: The Causes of a Failure." *Russie.Nei.Visions*, no. 96 (September 2016). Ifri.org.

——. "Russia Shouldn't Work but It Does." *Le Monde Diplomatique*, November 1, 2010. http://mondediplo.com/2010/11/09russia.

——. "The Sources of Putin's Regime: Traces That Lead into the 1990s." Center for Transatlantic Relations. Accessed August 10, 2018. https://archive.transatlanticrelations.org/publication/sources-putins-regime-traces-lead-1990s-vladislav-inozemtsev/.

Interfax.ru. "Al'fa-bank podal isk o priznanii Uralvagonzavoda bankrotom." June 10, 2016. http://www.interfax.ru/business/512862.

International Labour Office. *Year-Book of Labour Statistics*. Geneva: International Labour Office, 2000.

International Monetary Fund and Organisation for Economic Co-operation and Development, eds. *A Study of the Soviet Economy*. Paris: OECD, 1991.

Ioffe, Julia. "What Putin Really Wants." *Atlantic*, January/February 2018. https://www.theatlantic.com/magazine/archive/2018/01/putins-game/546548/.

ITAR-TASS. "President Appoints Railway Car Building Plant's Workshop Manager Presidential Envoy in Urals." May 21, 2012. http://en.itar-tass.com/russianpress/675842.

ITUC (International Trade Union Confederation). "Belarus' Rigged Presidential Election Must Be Re-run and Police Brutality Must Cease, Demands ITUC." November 8, 2020. https://www.ituc-csi.org/belarus-rigged-presidential.

Izvestiya. "Putin ozhidaet znachitel'nogo snizheniya urovnya bezrabotitsy k godu 2015." January 12, 2011. http://izvestia.ru/news/483926.

Jarmas, Christopher. "Yes, the Kremlin Is Worried—about Russia's Own Presidential Elections." *Washington Post*, December 16, 2017. https://www.washingtonpost.com/news/monkey-cage/wp/2017/12/06/yes-the-kremlin-is-worried-about-russias-own-presidential-elections/.

Javeline, Debra. "Labor Challenges and the Problem of Quiescence." In *Russia's Policy Challenges: Security, Stability, and Development*, edited by Stephen K. Wegren, 179–99. Armonk, NY: M. E. Sharpe, 2003.

——. *Protest and the Politics of Blame: The Russian Response to Unpaid Wages.* Ann Arbor: University of Michigan Press, 2003.

Kabalina, Veronika. "Privatisation and Restructuring of Enterprises: Under 'Insider' or 'Outsider' Control?" In *Conflict and Change in the Russian Industrial Enterprise*, edited by Simon Clarke, 241–88. Cheltenham, UK: Edward Elgar, 1995.

Kagarlitsky, Boris. "A Labor Code in Bad Need of Revision." *Moscow Times*, April 3, 2008, no. 3875 edition.

Kalashnikov, Konstantin Nikolaevich, and Vladimir Vasil'evich Shrov. "Trudovye otnosheniia v Rossii: Mezhdu partnerstvom i konfrontatsiei." *Sotsiologicheskie issledovaniia*, no. 4 (2017): 73–81.

Kalashnikov, Leonid. "AVTOVAZ eshche mozhno spasti! Otkrytoe pis'mo deputata Gosdumy Predsedateliu Pravitel'stva RF D.A. Medvedevu." Ofitsial'nyi internet-sait TsK KPRF, February 17, 2016. https://kprf.ru/dep/gosduma/activities/151883.html.

Karelina, Marina. "Tendentsii izmeneniya chislennosti professional'nykh soyuzov." *Sostiologicheskiye Issledovaniya*, no. 5 (2000).

Karliner, Diana. "In Russia's Car Industry, Even the Dead Work Overtime." openDemocracy, February 5, 2018. https://www.opendemocracy.net/od-russia/diana-karliner/russia-car-industry-avtovaz.

Katsva, A.M. "Kollektivnye deistviya v konste 90-kh godov: Radikalizatsiya metodov stachechnoi bor'by." In *Trudovie otnosheniya i kollektivnye deistviya v sovremenoi Rossii*, edited by A. M. Katsva, 159–90. Moscow: Editorial URSS, 1999.

Kennan, John. "The Economics of Strikes." In *Handbook of Labor Economics*, edited by Orley Ashenfelter and P. R. G. Layard, 2:1091–1137. Amsterdam: North-Holland, 1986.

Khalaf, Roula. "'Le Cost Killer': The Relentless Drive of Carlos Ghosn." *Financial Times*, June 15, 2018. https://www.ft.com/content/e3acccf2-6e20-11e8-92d3-6c13e5c92914.

Kiryukhin, Denys. "Losing Brains and Brawn: Outmigration from Ukraine." *Focus Ukraine* (blog), May 14, 2019. https://www.wilsoncenter.org/blog-post/losing-brains-and-brawn-outmigration-ukraine-0.

Klebnikov, Paul. *Godfather of the Kremlin: The Decline of Russia in the Age of Gangster Capitalism.* New York: Houghton Mifflin Harcourt, 2001.

Klintsov, Vitaly, Irene Shvakman, and Yermolai Solzhenitsyn. "How Russia Could Be More Productive." McKinsey and Co., September 2009. https://www.mckinsey.com/featured-insights/europe/how-russia-could-be-more-productive.

Knutsen, Carl Henrik, and Magnus Rasmussen. "The Autocratic Welfare State: Old-Age Pensions, Credible Commitments, and Regime Survival." *Comparative Political Studies* 51, no. 5 (April 1, 2018): 659–95. https://doi.org/10.1177/00104140 17710265.

Kokorin, Aleksei. "ZIL, kotoryi my poteriali: Rastsvet, upadok, agoniia i smert' velikogo zavoda." Kolesa.ru. Accessed August 17, 2019. https://www.kolesa.ru/article/zil-koto ryj-my-poterjali-rascvet-upadok-agonija-i-smert-velikogo-zavoda-2015-03-11.

Kolesnichenko, Aleksandr. "Salvage Job." Transitions Online, May 27, 2009. http:// www.tol.org/client/article/20606-salvage-job.html.

Kolesnikov, Andrei. "By Bread Alone: Why Poor Russians Aren't Protesting." Carnegie Moscow Center, 2016. http://carnegie.ru/commentary/2016/01/18/by-bread-alone-why-poor-russians-aren-t-protesting/ist2.

———. "Dilemma diktatorov: Pochemu Lukashenko ne ukhodit." Carnegie Moscow Center, August 21, 2020. https://carnegie.ru/commentary/82543.

Koltashov, Vasilii, and Mariia Mamedova. "Leonid Kalashnikov: 'Priekhali, pokatalis' i . . . prokatili AvtoVAZ.'" Svobodnaia Pressa, February 19, 2016. https://svpressa.ru/online/sptv/142778/.

Kommersant. "Naibolee ostro reforma zdravookhraneniya pochuvstvovalas' v krupnykh gorodakh." November 21, 2014. http://www.kommersant.ru/doc/2615484?9f476940.

———. "Vladimir Putin budet ballotirovat'sia v prezidenty." December 6, 2017. https://www.kommersant.ru/doc/3488438.

Konfliktologiya. "Izmenenie sotsial'no-trudovoi obstanovki i rost sotsial'no-trudovykh konfliktov v Rossiiskoi Federatsii v pervom polugodii 2020," July 10, 2020. http://industrialconflicts.ru/lib/74/izmenenie_sotsialyno-trudow.

———. "Analiz sotsial'no-trudovoi obstanovki i razvitiia trudovykh konfliktov v Rossiiskoi Federatsii (osnovnye itogi 2018 goda)." Accessed July 19, 2019. http://industrialcon flicts.ru/lib/63/analiz_sotsialyno-trudowoy_obstanowki_i_razwitiya_trudo.html.

———. "Itogi sotsial'no-trudovykh konfliktov v Rossiiskoi Federatsii i razvitie trudovykh otnoshenii v 2019 godu." January 24, 2020. http://industrialconflicts.ru/lib/71/ itogi_sotsialyno-trudowyh_konfliktow_w_rossiyskoy_fede.html.

———. "Kratkii obzor sotsial'no-trudovykh konfliktov za 2015 god." Accessed November 3, 2016. http://industrialconflicts.ru/lib/20/kratkiy_obzor_sotsialyno-trudowyh_kon fliktow_za_2015_god.html.

Kornai, János. Economics of Shortage. Amsterdam: North-Holland, 1980.

Kotkin, Stephen. Magnetic Mountain: Stalinism as a Civilization. Berkeley: University of California Press, 1997.

Kotz, David M., and Fred Weir. Russia's Path from Gorbachev to Putin: The Demise of the Soviet System and the New Russia. London: Routledge, 2007.

Kozichev, Evgenii. "Istoriia poshlin na inomarki v Rossii." Kommersant Vlast', February 2, 2009. https://www.kommersant.ru/doc/1111783.

Kozina, Irina. "Changes in the Social Organisation of an Industrial Enterprise." In Labour Relations in Transition: Wages, Employment and Industrial Conflict in Russia, edited by Simon Clarke, 146–59. Cheltenham, UK: Edward Elgar, 1996.

———. "Profsoyuzy v kollektivnykh trudovykh konfliktakh." Sostiologicheskiye Issledo-vaniya, no. 5 (2000): 49–56.

———. "Zabastovki v sovremennoi Rossii." Sostiologicheskiye Issledovaniya, no. 9 (September 2009): 13–25.

Kozlov, Petr. "Kreml' nachal monitoring ekonomicheskikh sobytii, vliiaiushchikh na regional'nye nastroeniia." Vedomosti, February 27, 2017. https://www.vedomosti.ru/politics/articles/2017/02/27/679036-kreml-monitoring.

Kramer, Andrew E. "Labor Unrest Stirs in Russia as an Economic Chill Sets In." New York Times, February 24, 2016, sec. World. https://www.nytimes.com/2016/02/25/world/europe/stirrings-of-labor-unrest-awaken-as-russias-economic-chill-sets-in.html.

Krastev, Ivan, and Stephen Holmes. "An Autopsy of Managed Democracy." Journal of Democracy 23, no. 3 (2012): 33–45.

Krichevskii, Nikita. "PostPikalevskaia Rossiia: Novaia poltiko-ekonomicheskaia real'nost'." August 31, 2009. http://www.profile.ru/politics/item/57383-postpi kalevskaya-rossiya-novaya-politiko-ekonomicheskaya-realnost-57383.

Krugman, Paul R. *The Age of Diminished Expectations: U.S. Economic Policy in the 1990s.* Cambridge, MA: MIT Press, 1990.

Krzywdzinski, Martin. *Consent and Control in the Authoritarian Workplace: Russia and China Compared.* Oxford: Oxford University Press, 2018.

Kubicek, Paul. *Organized Labor in Postcommunist States: From Solidarity to Infirmity.* Pittsburgh: University of Pittsburgh Press, 2004.

Kudrin, Aleksei. "Goroda vmesto nefti." *Vedomosti*, July 20, 2017. https://www.vedo mosti.ru/opinion/articles/2017/07/20/724744-goroda-nefti.

Kudrin, Alexey, and Evsey Gurvich. "A New Growth Model for the Russian Economy." Institute for Economies in Transition Policy Brief, 2015. https://helda.helsinki. fi/bof/handle/123456789/13571.

———. "Novaia model' rosta dlia rossiiskoi ekonomiki." *Voprosy Ekonomiki*, no. 12 (2014).

Kulikov, Volodymyr. "Industrialization and Transformation of the Landscape in the Donbas Region." In *Migration and Landscape Transformation: Changes in Central and Eastern Europe in the 19th and 20th Century*, edited by Hedi Hein-Kircher and Martin Zuckert, 57–82. Göttingen, Germany: Vandenhoeck & Ruprecht, 2016.

Kuromiya, Hiroaki. *Freedom and Terror in the Donbas: A Ukrainian-Russian Border-land, 1870s–1990s.* Cambridge Russian, Soviet and Post-Soviet Studies 104. Cambridge: Cambridge University Press, 1998.

Kuvshinova, Ol'ga. "Rabota bez zarabotka: Za chertoi bednosti—kazhdyi chetvertyi rabotnik v Rossii." *Vedomosti*, March 15, 2017. https://www.vedomosti.ru/ economics/articles/2017/03/15/681200-rabota-bez-zarabotka.

Lamberova, Natalia, and Daniel Treisman. "Economic Shocks and Authoritarian Responses: Putin's Strategy after the Global Financial Crisis of 2008–9." In *Economic Shocks and Authoritarian Stability*, edited by Victor C. Shih, 97–118. Ann Arbor: University of Michigan Press, 2020.

Lankina, Tomila, and Alexander Libman. "Soviet Legacies of Economic Development, Oligarchic Rule, and Electoral Quality in Eastern Europe's Partial Democracies: The Case of Ukraine." *Comparative Politics* 52, no. 1 (October 2019).

Lankina, Tomila, and Katerina Tertytchnaya. "Protest in Electoral Autocracies: A New Dataset." *Post-Soviet Affairs*, August 2, 2019. http://eprints.lse.ac.uk/101301/.

Lankina, Tomila, and Alisa Voznaya. "New Data on Protest Trends in Russia's Regions." *Europe-Asia Studies* 67, no. 2 (February 7, 2015): 327–42. https://doi.org/10.1080/ 09668136.2014.1002696.

Laruelle, Marlene, and Sophie Hohmann. "Biography of a Polar City: Population Flows and Urban Identity in Norilsk." *Polar Geography* 40, no. 4 (October 2, 2017): 306–23. https://doi.org/10.1080/1088937X.2017.1387822.

Latukhina, Kira. "Putin obeshchal prodolzhit' podderzhku monogorodov." *Rossiiskaia Gazeta*, December 13, 2019. https://rg.ru/2019/12/13/reg-pfo/putin-obeshchal-prodolzhit-podderzhku-monogorodov.html.

Ledeneva, Alena V. *Can Russia Modernise? Sistema, Power Networks and Informal Governance.* Cambridge: Cambridge University Press, 2014.

Lee, Ching Kwan. *Against the Law: Labor Protests in China's Rustbelt and Sunbelt.* Berkeley: University of California Press, 2007.

Leonard, Carol. "Spatial Development and Innovation in Russia." *Foresight and STI Governance* 10, no. 3 (September 28, 2016): 30–33. https://doi.org/10.17323/ 1995-459X.2016.3.30.33.

Leutert, Wendy. "China's State Enterprise Reform: Bigger, Yes, but Better?" *Brookings* (blog), April 23, 2015. https://www.brookings.edu/opinions/chinas-state-enterprise-reform-bigger-yes-but-better/.

Levada Tsentr. "Moskvichi o protestakh dal'noboishchikov." *Levada Tsentr* (blog), December 9, 2105. https://www.levada.ru/2015/12/09/moskvichi-o-protestah-dalnobojshhikov/.

———. "Protesty 'dal'noboishchikov' i gotovnost' protestovat' sredi naseleniia." *Levada Tsentr* (blog), December 30, 2015. https://www.levada.ru/2015/12/30/protesty-dalnobojshhikov-i-gotovnost-protestovat-sredi-naseleniya/.

Levy, Clifford J. "Tariff Protests in Eastern Port Rattle Kremlin." *New York Times*, February 15, 2009, sec. Europe. https://www.nytimes.com/2009/02/16/world/europe/16russia.html.

Lichbach, Mark Irving. "Will Rational People Rebel against Inequality? Samson's Choice." *American Journal of Political Science* 34, no. 4 (1990): 1049–76. https://doi.org/10.2307/2111471.

Linz, Susan J., and Anastasia Semykina. "How Do Workers Fare during Transition? Perceptions of Job Insecurity among Russian Workers, 1995–2004." *Labour Economics* 15, no. 3 (June 1, 2008): 442–58. https://doi.org/10.1016/j.labeco.2007.05.003.

Litovkin, Viktor. "S 'bulavoi' napereves." *Nezavisimaya Gazeta*, August 31, 2018. http://nvo.ng.ru/realty/2011-07-08/1_bulava.html.

Lomakin, Daniil. "'Kortezh' dlia prezidenta sobrali vsem mirom." Gazeta.ru, November 3, 2016. https://www.gazeta.ru/auto/2016/11/01_a_10297055.shtml.

Lomasko, Viktoriia. *Other Russias*. New York: n+1, 2017.

Lomskaya, Tat'yana. "Uchitelia razocharovalis' v ukazakh Putina." *Vedomosti*, August 8, 2017. https://www.vedomosti.ru/economics/articles/2017/08/08/728387-uchitelya-razocharovalis-putina.

Lukyanov, Fyodor. "Putin's Foreign Policy." *Foreign Affairs*, April 18, 2016. https://www.foreignaffairs.com/articles/russia-fsu/2016-04-18/putins-foreign-policy.

Lussier, Danielle N. "Contacting and Complaining: Political Participation and the Failure of Democracy in Russia." *Post-Soviet Affairs* 27, no. 3 (July 1, 2011): 289–325.

Luzin, Pavel. "Why Corporations Are the Kremlin's Best Friends." *Moscow Times*, September 2, 2019. https://www.themoscowtimes.com/2019/09/02/why-corporations-are-the-kremlins-best-friends-a67106.

Lyashok, Viktor. "Povyshenie MROT: Pliusy i minusy." *Ekonomicheskoe Razvitie Rossii* 24, no. 6 (July 2017): 68–70.

MacFarquhar, Neil. "Trying to Save Russia's Punch Line of a Car." *New York Times*, December 21, 2014, sec. World. https://www.nytimes.com/2014/12/22/world/trying-to-save-russias-punch-line-of-a-car.html.

Mah, Alice. "Devastation but Also Home: Place Attachment in Areas of Industrial Decline." *Home Cultures* 6, no. 3 (November 1, 2009): 287–310. https://doi.org/10.2752/174063109X12462745321462.

———. *Industrial Ruination, Community, and Place: Landscapes and Legacies of Urban Decline*. Toronto: University of Toronto Press, 2012.

Makarkin, Aleksey. "Protest srednego klassa." Politcom.ru, December 12, 2011. http://www.politcom.ru/13024.html.

Makarov, E. "Analiz sotsial'no-trudovoy obstanovki v Rossiyskoy Federatsii v 1 kvartale 2015 goda." Publikatsii Tsentra monitoringa i analiza sotsial'notrudovykh konfliktov, SanktPeterburgskogo Gumanitarnogo universiteta profsoyuzov, April 29, 2015. http://www.gup.ru/uni/science/industrialconflicts/detail.php?ID=180823.

———. "Obzor sotsial'no-trudovykh konfliktov v Rossiiskoi Federatsii v 2016 godu." Konfliktologiya. Accessed July 18, 2017. http://industrialconflicts.ru/lib/27/obzor__sotsialyno-trudowyh.

Maksimov, Boris Ivanovich. "Yavlenie Rossii v Pikalyovo." *Sostiologicheskiye Issledo-vaniya*, no. 4 (2010): 42–53.

Malysheva, Elena. "Krizis okhvatil monogoroda." Gazeta.ru, May 18, 2017. https://www.gazeta.ru/business/2017/05/18/10679105.shtml.

Mandel, David. "'Why Is There No Revolt?' The Russian Working-Class and Labor Movement." In *Working Classes, Global Realities: Socialist Register 2001*, edited by Leo Panitch and Colin Leys, 171–95. New York: Monthy Review, 2000. https://monthlyreview.org/product/socialist_register_2001/.

Markus, Stanislav. "Secure Property as a Bottom-Up Process: Firms, Stakeholders, and Predators in Weak States." *World Politics* 64, no. 2 (April 2012): 242–77. https://doi.org/10.1017/S0043887112000044.

Martin, Andrew, and George Ross, eds. *The Brave New World of European Labor: European Trade Unions at the Millennium*. New York: Berghahn Books, 1999.

Matsuzato, Kimitaka. "Dissimilar Politics in Mariupol and Kramatorsk: Two Ukrainian Cities on the Eastern Front." PONARS Euarasia, Policy Memo 532, June 4, 2018. http://www.ponarseurasia.org/memo/dissimilar-politics-mariupol-kramatorsk-two-ukrainian-cities-eastern-front.

Matveev, Ilya. "Russia, Inc." openDemocracy, March 16, 2016. https://www.opendemocracy.net/en/odr/russia-inc/.

——. "The 'Two Russias' Culture War: Constructions of the 'People' during the 2011–2013 Protests." *South Atlantic Quarterly* 113, no. 1 (January 1, 2014): 186–95. https://doi.org/10.1215/00382876-2390482.

Matveev, Ilya, and Anastasiya Novkunskaya. "State, Capital, and the Transformation of the Neoliberal Policy Paradigm in Putin's Russia." *International Review of Modern Sociology* 45, no. 1 (Spring 2019): 27–48.

——. "Welfare Restructuring in Russia since 2012: National Trends and Evidence from the Regions." *Europe-Asia Studies*, October 21, 2020: 1–22. https://doi.org/10.1080/09668136.2020.1826907.

Meardi, Guglielmo. *Social Failures of EU Enlargement: A Case of Workers Voting with Their Feet*. London: Routledge, 2012.

Meduza. "At 39 Percent of GDP, Russia's Shadow Economy Is the Fourth Largest in the World, according to a New Report." June 30, 2017. https://meduza.io/en.

Mellander, Charlotta, Richard L. Florida, Bjørn Terje Asheim, Meric S. Gertler, and Regional Studies Association (Seaford, England), eds. *The Creative Class Goes Global*. London: Routledge, 2014.

Mereminskaia, Ekaterina. "Konkurentsii ne stalo bol'she." *Vedomosti*, April 16, 2017. https://www.vedomosti.ru/economics/articles/2017/04/17/685866-konkurentsii-ne-bolshe.

"Metodika i informatsionnaia baza monitoringa trudovykh protestov TsSTP." Accessed March 10, 2017. http://trudprava.ru/expert/analytics/protestanalyt/1360.

Meyer (Olimpieva), Irina. "Russian Truck Drivers against the Platon Tax, Round 2." *Russia File: A Blog of the Kennan Institute*, May 17, 2017. http://www.kennan-russiafile.org/2017/05/17/russian-truck-drivers-against-the-platon-tax-round-2/.

——. "The Tragedy of the Working Poor and the Populism of Russia's Presidential Campaign." *Russia File: A Blog of the Kennan Institute*, February 21, 2018. https://www.wilsoncenter.org/blog-post/the-tragedy-the-working-poor-and-the-populism-russias-presidential-campaign.

Mikhailova, Tatiana. "Gulag, WWII and the Long-Run Patterns of Soviet City Growth." MPRA paper, September 9, 2012. https://mpra.ub.uni-muenchen.de/41758/.

——. "Where Russians Should Live: A Counterfactual Alternative to Soviet Location Policy." MPRA paper, January 13, 2012. https://mpra.ub.uni-muenchen.de/36157/.

Milanovic, Branko. *Income, Inequality, and Poverty during the Transition: From Planned to Market Economy*. World Bank Regional and Sectoral Studies. Washington, DC: World Bank, 1998.

Miles, Tom. "Russia Was Most Protectionist Nation in 2013—Study." Reuters, December 30, 2013. https://www.reuters.com/article/trade-protectionism/russia-was-most-protectionist-nation-in-2013-study-idUSL6N0K927X20131230.

Miliukova, Iana. "FSO zafiksirovala ukhudshenie situatsii v monogorodakh." *RBK*, May 17, 2016. http://www.rbc.ru/economics/17/05/2016/573b493e9a7947a4eefec46b.

Miller, Chris. *Putinomics: Power and Money in Resurgent Russia*. Chapel Hill: University of North Carolina Press, 2018.

Miller, Liza, and Maksim Ivanov. "Regiony vstupili v bor'bu za iavku." *Kommersant*, January 25, 2018.

Mironova, Anastasia. "Prokliatie devianostykh: Pochemu narod ottorgaet liberalov." Novayagazeta.ru, October 7, 2019, 112 edition. https://www.novayagazeta.ru/.

Mishler, William, and Richard Rose. "Generation, Age, and Time: The Dynamics of Political Learning during Russia's Transformation." *American Journal of Political Science* 51, no. 4 (2007): 822–34. https://doi.org/10.1111/j.1540-5907.2007.00283.x.

Mitchell, Timothy. *Carbon Democracy: Political Power in the Age of Oil*. London: Verso, 2013.

"Monogoroda.rf." Accessed August 16, 2018. http://xn--80afd4affbbat.xn--p1ai/.

Moore, Barrington. *Social Origins of Dictatorship and Democracy: Lord and Peasant in the Making of the Modern World*. Boston: Beacon, 1966.

Morris, Jeremy. "Automobile Masculinities and Neoliberal Production Regimes among Russian Blue-Collar Men." In *Masculinity, Labour, and Neoliberalism: Working-Class Men in International Perspective*, edited by Charlie Walker and Steven Roberts, 171–93. Cham, Switzerland: Springer, 2017.

——. *Everyday Post-Socialism: Working-Class Communities in the Russian Margins*. Cham, Switzerland: Springer International, 2016.

Morzharetto, Igor. "A Foreigner with No Friends: Bo Andersson Pushed from Russia's AvtoVAZ." *Moscow Times*, March 10, 2016. http://themoscowtimes.com/articles/a-foreigner-with-no-friends-bo-andersson-pushed-from-russias-avtovaz-52120.

Moscow News. "Weak Trade Unions Suit Business, but Might Hit Back in a Crisis." December 5, 2008, no. 48 edition.

Moscow Times. "Slow Death." Accessed September 25, 2017. http://old.themoscowtimes.com/news/article/tmt/289213.html.

Moshes, Arkady. "Does It Make Sense to Expect a Color Revolution in Belarus?" PONARS Euarasia, Policy Memo 485, October 6, 2017. http://www.ponarseurasia.org/memo/does-it-make-sense-expect-color-revolution-belarus.

Moskovskii Tsentr Karnegi. "Stenogramma osnovnykh vystuplenii na seminare 'Reforma trugodovo zakonodatel'stva: Novyi Trudovoi Kodeks.'" Moskovskii Tsentr Karnegi, November 11, 2001. http://carnegie.ru/russian/pr/2001/inf01-122-steno.htm.

MPRA. "MPRA—Mezhregional'nyy Profsoyuz Rabochaya Assotsiatsiya." Accessed September 7, 2015. http://mpra.info/.

Mukhametshina, Elena. "Piataia chast' rossiiskikh uchitelei dumaiut ob ukhode iz shkoly." *Vedomosti*, June 27, 2018. https://www.vedomosti.ru/politics/articles/2018/06/27/773990-uchitelei-uhode.

Mukhametshina, Elena, Svetlana Bocharova, and Ol'ga Churakova. "Protesty profsoiuzov protiv pensionnoi reformy vygodny dlia Kremlia." *Vedomosti*, June 22, 2018. https://www.vedomosti.ru/politics/articles/2018/06/22/773488-protesti-profsoyuzov.

Munro, Neil. "Predictors of Support for State Social Welfare Provision in Russia and China." *Europe-Asia Studies* 69, no. 1 (January 2, 2017): 53–75. https://doi.org/10.1080/09668136.2016.1265643.

Murillo, M. Victoria. "From Populism to Neoliberalism: Labor Unions and Market Reforms in Latin America." *World Politics* 52, no. 2 (January 2000): 135–68. https://doi.org/10.1017/S0043887100002586.

Muro, Mark, and Jacob Whiton. "America Has Two Economies—and They're Diverging Fast." *Brookings* (blog), September 10, 2019. https://www.brookings.edu/blog/the-avenue/2019/09/10/america-has-two-economies-and-theyre-diverging-fast/.

Nagornykh, Irina. "Na vyborakh zadeistvuiut korporativnyi resurs." *Kommersant*, February 26, 2017. https://www.kommersant.ru/doc/3227902.

Narodnoe televidenie Asbesta. "'Iazev, gde zarplata za 3 mesiatsa?' Rabotniki Kirpichnogo zavoda vstretilis' s ministrom Bidon'ko." 2016. https://www.youtube.com/watch?v=saEO29_ejA8.

——. "Obrashchenie rabotnikov Kirpichnogo zavoda k Iazevu, Kuivashevu o vyplate dolgov po zarabotnoi plate!!!" 2016. https://www.youtube.com/watch?v=qi2RvjYKVC0.

——. "Rabotnikam Kirpichnogo zavoda chastichno pogasili zadolzhennost' po zarabotnoi plate." 2016. https://www.youtube.com/watch?v=MFE21ThgHXU.

Nechepurenko, Ivan, and Anton Troianovski. "Workers Join Belarus Protests, as Leader's Base Turns against Him." *New York Times*, August 14, 2020, sec. World. https://www.nytimes.com/2020/08/14/world/europe/Belarus-strike-Aleksandr-Lukashenko.html.

Nedoseka, Elena, and Nikolay Karbainov. "Sotsial'noe samochuvstvie zhitelei postsovetskogo monogoroda." *Sotsial'noe prostranstvo*, no. 5 (22) (2019). https://doi.org/10.15838/sa.2019.5.22.2.

Nelson, Joan M. "The Politics of Economic Transformation: Is Third World Experience Relevant in Eastern Europe?" *World Politics* 45, no. 3 (April 1993): 433–63. https://doi.org/10.2307/2950725.

Nemtsova, Anna. "On the Edge of Siberia's Dark Blue Heart." Pulitzer Center, November 4, 2013. http://pulitzercenter.org/reporting/europe-russia-siberia-largest-lake-baikal-workers-labor-job-loss-poverty-politics.

Nevidimye goroda. "Asbest the Best." Accessed August 21, 2018. http://monogoroda.com/asbest-the-best/.

Nölke, Andreas, and Arjan Vliegenthart. "Enlarging the Varieties of Capitalism: The Emergence of Dependent Market Economies in East Central Europe." *World Politics* 61, no. 4 (October 2009): 670–702. https://doi.org/10.1017/S0043887109990098.

Novaya Gazeta. "A. Kotov: 'Sistema "Platon" grabit ne tol'ko dal'noboishchikov, no i vse naselenie Rossii'." 2015. https://www.youtube.com/watch?v=gelxWOhL5N8.

——. "Al'fa-bank podal v Arbitrazhnyi sud Sverdlovskoi oblasti zaiavlenie o priznanii bankrotom 'Uralvagonzavod,'" June 10, 2016. https://www.novayagazeta.ru/news/2016/06/10/122397-alfa-bank-poprosil-priznat-uralvagonzavod-bankrotom.

Novokmet, Filip, Thomas Piketty, and Gabriel Zucman. "From Soviets to Oligarchs: Inequality and Property in Russia 1905–2016." National Bureau of Economic Research, working paper 23712, July 29, 2017.

Ob"edinenie perevozchikov Rossii (OPR). "OPR—regiony." Accessed August 18, 2019. https://opr.com.ru/regiony/?%20chita.ru/news/101622/%20gazetayakutia.ru/kilometryproblem/.

——. "VSEROSSIISKAIa STAChKA AVTOPEREVOZChIKOV!" Accessed July 20, 2017. https://opr.com.ru/info/news/vserossiyskaya-stachka-avtoperevozchikov/.

OECD (Organisation for Economic Co-operation and Development). *OECD Regional Outlook 2019: Leveraging Megatrends for Cities and Rural Areas, 2019*. https://www.oecd-ilibrary.org/content/publication/9789264312838-en.

——. *Russia: Modernising the Economy. Better Policies.* OECD, 2013. https://doi. org/10.1787/9789264207998-en.

Offe, Claus. *Contradictions of the Welfare State.* Edited by John Keane. Cambridge, MA: MIT Press, 1984.

Olimpieva, Evgenia. "From Performance to Geopolitical Ideology: Collective Memory of WWII and Legitimacy in Putin's Russia." Master's thesis, University of Chicago, 2015.

Olimpieva, Irina. "'Free' and 'Official' Labor Unions in Russia: Different Modes of Labor Interest Representation." *Russian Analytical Digest*, no. 104 (October 27, 2011): 2–6.

——. "Labor Unions in Contemporary Russia: An Assessment of Contrasting Forms of Organization and Representation." *WorkingUSA* 15 (June 2012): 267–83. https://doi.org/10.1111/j.1743-4580.2012.00387.x.

——. *Rossiiskie profsoyuzy v sisteme regulirovaniya sotsial'no-trudovykh otnoshenii: Osobennosti, problemy i perspektivy issledovaniya.* Moscow: Moscow Social Science Fund, 2010.

——. "The Tragedy of the Working Poor and the Populism of Russia's Presidential Campaign." Wilson Center, February 21, 2018. https://www.wilsoncenter.org/blog-post/ the-tragedy-the-working-poor-and-the-populism-russias-presidential-campaign.

1 maia 2017 god Miass vystuplenie predsedatelei MPVP i OPR po Cheliabinskoi oblasti. Accessed July 20, 2017. https://ok.ru/video/296219840839.

openDemocracy. "On the Brink: Why Russia's Healthcare Workers Are Organising." Accessed August 19, 2019. https://www.opendemocracy.net/en/odr/on-the-brink-why-russias-healthcare-workers-are-organising/.

Oreshkin, Dmitry. "Dal'noboyshchiki kak novyy klass protestuyushchikh." Svop.ru, November 24, 2015. http://svop.ru/main/17820/.

——. "The 2nd-Largest Potemkin Village in History." *Moscow Times*, December 17, 2008.

Ost, David. *The Defeat of Solidarity: Anger and Politics in Postcommunist Europe.* Ithaca, NY: Cornell University Press, 2005.

Østbø, Jardar. "Between Opportunist Revolutionaries and Mediating Spoilers: Failed Politicization of the Russian Truck Drivers' Protest, 2015–2016." *Demokratizatsiya: The Journal of Post-Soviet Democratization* 25, no. 3 (July 21, 2017): 279–303.

Panitch, Leo. "The Development of Corporatism in Liberal Democracies." *Comparative Political Studies* 10, no. 1 (April 1, 1977): 61–90. https://doi.org/10.1177/0010414 07701000104.

Pavlovskii, Gleb. "Putin v dni Velikoi russko-ukrainskoi revoliutsii." *Gefter* (blog), March 14, 2014. http://gefter.ru/archive/11640.

Pertsev, Andrey, and Maxim Solopov. "What Putin Reads: Vital Policymaking in Russian Relies on Sociological Research Conducted by the Secret Service." Meduza, July 16, 2020. https://meduza.io/en/feature/2020/07/17/what-putin-reads.

Petkov, Radoslav K., and Natan M. Shklyar. "Russian Regions after the Crisis: Coping with Economic Troubles Governors Reap Political Rewards." *Demokratizatsiya* 7, no. 4 (September 22, 1999): 527.

Petlevoy, Vitaliy. "Metallurgicheskie kompanii uvolili v proshlom godu 33,500 chelovek." Vedomosti.ru, June 4, 2014. http://www.vedomosti.ru/companies/ news/27349431/metallurgam-razreshili-uvolnyat.

Petlianova, Nina. "Andrei Bazhutin: 'Po vsei strane stoit bolee milliona mashin.' Pochemu silovymi metodami protest dal'noboishchikov ne podavit'." *Novaya Gazeta*, April 6, 2017. https://www.novayagazeta.ru/articles/2017/04/07/72058-andrey-bazhutin-po-vsey-strane-stoit-bolee-milliona-mashin.

Petrov, Nikolay, Maria Lipman, and Henry E. Hale. "Three Dilemmas of Hybrid Regime Governance: Russia from Putin to Putin." *Post-Soviet Affairs* 30, no. 1 (January 2, 2014): 1–26. https://doi.org/10.1080/1060586X.2013.825140.

Petrova, Yuliana. "Sud likvidiroval odin iz krupneishikh nezavisimykh profsoiuzov Rossii." *Vedomosti*, January 11, 2019. https://www.vedomosti.ru/management/articles/2018/01/11/747429-likvidirovan-organizator-zabastovok.

Plotnikova, Yelena, and Robert Coalson. "Samara Governor Offers a Stark Choice: United Russia or the CIA." RadioFreeEurope/RadioLiberty, September 10, 2016. https://www.rferl.org/a/russia-samara-governor-merkushkin-united-russia-cia/27978955.html.

Plusnin, Juri, Yana Zausaeva, Natalia Zhidkevich, and Artemy Pozanenko. *Wandering Workers: Mores, Behavior, Way of Life, and Political Status of Domestic Russian Labor Migrants.* New York: Columbia University Press, 2014.

Podtserob, Mariia. "Pochemu v Rossii vygodno byt' 'rabotaiushchim bednym.'" *Vedomosti*, March 29, 2017. https://www.vedomosti.ru/economics/articles/2017/03/29/683161-rossii-rabotayuschim-bednim.

Polinkevich, Roman. "Zachem predlagaiut sokratit' monogoroda?" *Argumenty i Fakty*, November 7, 2019. https://aif.ru/politics/opinion/zachem_predlagayut_sokratit_monogoroda.

Pop-Eleches, Grigore, and Joshua A. Tucker. *Communism's Shadow: Historical Legacies and Contemporary Political Attitudes.* Princeton, NJ: Princeton University Press, 2017.

Pravitel'stvo Rossii. "Ob utverzhdenii perechnya monogorodov." July 31, 2014. http://m.government.ru/docs/14051.

——. "O kriteriyakh otneseniya munitsipal'nykh obrazovaniy k monogorodam i o kategoriyakh monogorodov v zavisimosti ot riskov ukhudsheniya ikh sotsial'noekonomicheskogo polozheniya." July 31, 2014. http://m.government.ru/docs/14049.

Pravitel'svo Rossiiskoi Federatsii. "Kompleksnogo plana modernizatsii i rasshireniia magistral'noi infrastruktury na period do 2024 goda." September 30, 2018. http://government.ru/docs/34297/.

——. "Stratagiia prostranstvennogo razvitiia Rossiiskoi Federatsii na period do 2025 goda." February 13, 2019. http://government.ru/docs/35733/.

President of Russia. "Presidential Address to the Federal Assembly." January 15, 2020. http://en.kremlin.ru/events/president/news/56957.

——. "Vladimir Putin's Annual News Conference." Official Website of the President of Russia. Accessed December 23, 2019. http://en.kremlin.ru/events/president/news/62366.

Prezident Rossii. "Soveshchanie po voprosam stabil'nogo razvitiia monogorodov." April 28, 2014. http://kremlin.ru/events/president/news/20873.

PROVED. "Kubanskii fermer zastrelilsia iz-za reiderskogo zakhvata zemli." October 1, 2016. http://xn--b1ae2adf4f.xn--p1ai/society/incidents/37535-kubanskiy-fep mep-zastpelilsya-iz-za-peydepskogo-zahvata-zemli.html.

Przeworski, Adam. *Democracy and the Market: Political and Economic Reforms in Eastern Europe and Latin America.* New York: Cambridge University Press, 1991.

Putin: Telemost s Nizhnim Tagilom. RT Na Russkom, 2012. https://www.youtube.com/watch?v=4atPDPKyz2I.

Pye, Oliver. "A Plantation Precariat: Fragmentation and Organizing Potential in the Palm Oil Global Production Network." *Development and Change* 48, no. 5 (2017): 942–64. https://doi.org/10.1111/dech.12334.

Quintero, Luis E., and Paula Restrepo. "City Decline in an Urbanizing World." October 23, 2019. http://pubdocs.worldbank.org/en/302391572287457633/CityDecline-in-a-urbanizing-world-Quintero-Restrepo.pdf.

Rahimov, Rahim. "The Eurasian Union: A Political Project in an Economic Guise." *Russia File* (blog), April 13, 2017. https://www.wilsoncenter.org/blog-post/the-eurasian-union-political-project-economic-guise.

Rakowski, Tomasz. *Hunters, Gatherers, and Practitioners of Powerlessness: An Ethnography of the Degraded in Postsocialist Poland.* New York: Berghahn Books, 2016.

Rambler. "Golodets o roste bednosti v RF: Zhit' na prozhitochnyi minimum nevozmozhno." December 16, 2016. https://finance.rambler.ru/economics/35604105-golodets-o-roste-bednosti-v-rf-zhit-na-prozhitochnyy-minimum-nevozmozhno/.

Raspopova, Alina. "'AvtoVAZ' doplatit sotrudnikam za vykhod na pensiiu." Gazeta.ru, October 6, 2016. https://www.gazeta.ru/auto/2016/10/05_a_10231763.shtml.

———. "Mashiny podesheveiut po polnoi programme." Gazeta.ru, June 7, 2017. https://www.gazeta.ru/auto/2017/06/07_a_10712495.shtml.

———. "Novye gosprogrammy podderzhki avtoproma zarabotaiut s 1 iiulia." Gazeta.ru, June 7, 2017. https://www.gazeta.ru/auto/2017/06/07_a_10712495.shtml.

RBC. "Putin poruchil uravniat' MROT i prozhitochnyi minimum k nachalu 2019 goda." *RBK*, September 11, 2017. http://www.rbc.ru/rbcfreenews/59b68ec99a79474ba3be5364.

Rebrov, Dmitry. "Dal'noboishchiki ob"iavili o nachale vserossiiskoi zabastovki." *Novaya Gazeta*, December 15, 2017. https://www.novayagazeta.ru/news/2017/12/15/137936-dalnoboyschiki-ob-yavili-o-nachale-vserossiyskoy-zabastovke.

Remington, Thomas F. "Business-Government Cooperation in VET: A Russian Experiment with Dual Education." *Post-Soviet Affairs* 33, no. 4 (July 4, 2017): 313–33. https://doi.org/10.1080/1060586X.2017.1296730.

———. *The Politics of Inequality in Russia.* New York: Cambridge University Press, 2011.

———. *Presidential Decrees in Russia: A Comparative Perspective.* New York: Cambridge University Press, 2014.

RF Human Rights Commissioner. "The 1999 Report of RF Human Rights Commissioner." *Rossiyskaya Gazeta*, April 4, 2000.

RFE/RL. "Dual Rallies over Baikal Paper Mill." RadioFreeEurope/RadioLiberty, February 13, 2010. https://www.rferl.org/a/Siberians_Hold_Competing_Rallies_Over_Baikal_Paper_Mill/1957064.html.

RIA Novosti. "Novyi limuzin prezidenta." July 16, 2018. https://ria.ru/20180716/1524666652.html.

———. "Razvitie gorodov dolzhno stat' dvizhushchei siloi dlia strany, zaiavil Putin." March 1, 2018. https://ria.ru/economy/20180301/1515514425.html.

RIAPO. "Na podderzhku monogorodov budet ezhegodno vydeliat'sia 5,5 mlrd rublei." December 16, 2019. https://riapo.ru/penza/obshchestvo/na-podderzhku-monogorodov-budet-ezhegodno-vydelyatsya-5-5-mlrd-rublej.

Robertson, Graeme B. *The Politics of Protest in Hybrid Regimes: Managing Dissent in Post-Communist Russia.* New York: Cambridge University Press, 2011.

———. "Protesting Putinism." *Problems of Post-Communism* 60, no. 2 (March 1, 2013): 11–23. https://doi.org/10.2753/PPC1075-8216600202.

———. "Strikes and Labor Organization in Hybrid Regimes." *American Political Science Review* 101, no. 04 (2007): 781–98. https://doi.org/10.1017/S0003055407070475.

Robinson, Neil. "Russia's Response to Crisis: The Paradox of Success." *Europe-Asia Studies* 65, no. 3 (May 1, 2013): 450–72. https://doi.org/10.1080/09668136.2013.779462.

Rochlitz, Michael. "Political Loyalty vs Economic Performance: Evidence from Machine Politics in Russia's Regions." 2016. https://publications.hse.ru/en/preprints/182403707.

Rochlitz, Michael, Vera Kulpina, Thomas Remington, and Andrei Yakovlev. "Performance Incentives and Economic Growth: Regional Officials in Russia and China." *Eurasian Geography and Economics* 56, no. 4 (July 4, 2015): 421–45. https://doi.org/10.1080/15387216.2015.1089411.

Rodden, Jonathan. *Why Cities Lose: The Deep Roots of the Urban-Rural Political Divide.* New York: Basic Books, 2019.

Rodrik, Dani. "Premature Deindustrialization." National Bureau of Economic Research working paper. February 2015. https://doi.org/10.3386/w20935.

Rogers, Douglas. *The Depths of Russia: Oil, Power, and Culture after Socialism.* Ithaca, NY: Cornell University Press, 2015.

Rogov, Kirill, ed. *Osnovnye tendentsii politicheskogo razvitiya Rossii v 2011–2013 gg.* Moscow: Doklad Fonda Liberal'naya Missiya, 2014. http://www.liberal.ru/articles/6537.

Romanov, Pavel. "The Regional Elite in the Epoch of Bankruptcy." In *Conflict and Change in the Russian Industrial Enterprise,* edited by Simon Clarke, 210–40. Cheltenham, UK: Edward Elgar, 1996.

Rosbalt. "Analitik: Sredniaia zarplata v Rossii stala nizhe, chem v Kitae i Pol'she." Rosbalt, May 19, 2016. http://www.rosbalt.ru/russia/2016/05/19/1515681.html.

Rosenfeld, Bryn. "The Popularity Costs of Economic Crisis under Electoral Authoritarianism: Evidence from Russia." *American Journal of Political Science* 62, no. 2 (2018): 382–97. https://doi.org/10.1111/ajps.12338.

——. "Reevaluating the Middle-Class Protest Paradigm: A Case-Control Study of Democratic Protest Coalitions in Russia." *American Political Science Review,* September 2017, 1–16. https://doi.org/10.1017/S000305541700034X.

Rossi, Ugo. *Cities in Global Capitalism.* Urban Futures Series. Malden, MA: Polity, 2017.

Rossiiskaya Gazeta. "Trudovoi kodeks Rossiiskoi Federatsii ot 30 Dekabrya 2001 g. n 197-F3." Dokumenti, December 31, 2001. http://www.rg.ru/2001/12/31/trud-dok.html.

——. "Voennaia doktrina Rossiiskoi Federatsii." December 30, 2014. https://rg.ru/2014/12/30/doktrina-dok.html.

Rossiiskaya Federatsiya. "Federal'naya sluzhba gosudarstvennoi statistiki." Accessed August 2, 2010. http://www.gks.ru/.

Rosstat. "Federal'naia sluzhba gosudarstvennoi statistiki. Chislennost' naseleniia Rossiiskoi Federatsii po munitsipal'nym obrazovaniiam na 1 ianvaria 2020 goda," January 2020.

——. "Finansy Rossii—2018 g.: Statisticheskii sbornik." Federal'naia sluzhba gosudarstvennoi statistiki, 2018. https://gks.ru/bgd/regl/b18_51/Main.htm.

Rueschemeyer, Dietrich, Evelyne Huber, and John D. Stephens. *Capitalist Development and Democracy.* Chicago: University of Chicago Press, 1992.

Russian Defense Policy. "Tough Times at UVZ." August 15, 2016. https://russiandefpolicy.blog/2016/08/15/tough-times-at-uvz/.

"Russian National Security Strategy, December 2015—Full-Text Translation." December 2015.

Russian Reader. "The Enemy Within Is Everywhere." June 10, 2017. https://therussianreader.com/2017/06/10/the-enemy-within-is-everywhere/.

——. "Sixty Percent of Russian Doctors Make Less Than 360 Euros a Month." December 16, 2017. https://therussianreader.com/2017/12/16/sixty-percent-of-russian-doctors-make-less-than-360-euros-a-month/.

——. "Twenty Percent of Russian Schoolteachers Contemplate Quitting." June 30, 2018. https://therussianreader.com/2018/06/30/twenty-percent-of-russian-school teachers-contemplate-quitting/.

Russkaya Planeta. "Bez deneg net raboty." March 1, 2015. https://rusplt.ru/society/ zavod-zabastovka-8439.html.

Rutland, Peter. "Russia: Entrenched Elites Ride Out the Crisis." In *The Political Economy of International Financial Crisis: Interest Groups, Ideologies, and Institutions,* edited by Shale Asher Horowitz and Uk Heo, 243–64. Lanham, MD: Rowman & Littlefield, 2001.

Ryzhkov, Vladimir. "Russians Feel That Great Power High—Again." *Moscow Times,* May 12, 2014. https://www.themoscowtimes.com/2014/05/12/russians-feel-that-great-power-high-again-a35359.

Sadovskaya, Yulia. "Pod Shmakovym zashatalos' kreslo." *Nezavisimaya Gazeta,* January 11, 2011.

Sakwa, Richard. "Political Leadership." In *Return to Putin's Russia: Past Imperfect, Future Uncertain,* edited by Stephen K. Wegren, 25–44. Lanham, MD: Rowman & Littlefield, 2013.

——. *Putin: Russia's Choice.* 2nd ed. London: Routledge, 2008.

Sapronova, Yulia. "'V golovakh vse pereputano': Chem zapomnitsia eks-gubernator Merkushkin." *RBK,* September 25, 2017. http://www.rbc.ru/politics/25/09/2017/ 59c90d8d9a7947313b4c918c?from=right_1.

Sassen, Saskia. *The Global City: New York, London, Tokyo.* Princeton, NJ: Princeton University Press, 1991.

——. *Globalization and Its Discontents.* New York: New Press, 1998.

Schenk, Caress. *Why Control Immigration? Strategic Uses of Migration Management in Russia.* Toronto: University of Toronto Press, 2018.

Schreck, Carl. "Ten Businesspeople Barred in 2 Years." *Moscow Times,* August 1, 2006.

Schumpeter, Joseph Alois. *Capitalism, Socialism and Democracy.* 6th ed., with a new introduction by Tom Bottomore. Boston: Unwin Paperbacks, 1987.

Schwartz, Gregory. "Employment Restructuring in Russian Industrial Enterprises." *Work, Employment & Society* 17, no. 1 (March 1, 2003): 49–72. https://doi.org/1 0.1177/0950017003017001252.

Scott, James C. *Seeing Like a State: How Certain Schemes to Improve the Human Condition Have Failed.* New Haven, CT: Yale University Press, 1998.

Sharma, Ruchir. "The Next Economic Powerhouse? Poland." *New York Times,* January 20, 2018, sec. Opinion. https://www.nytimes.com/2017/07/05/opinion/poland-economy-trump-russia.html.

——. *The Rise and Fall of Nations: Forces of Change in the Post-Crisis World.* New York: W. W. Norton, 2016.

Shih, Victor C. *Economic Shocks and Authoritarian Stability: Duration, Financial Control, and Institutions.* Ann Arbor: University of Michigan Press, 2020.

Shiklomanov, Nikolay, Dmitry Streletskiy, Luis Suter, Robert Orttung, and Nadezhda Zamyatina. "Dealing with the Bust in Vorkuta, Russia." *Land Use Policy,* July 31, 2019, 103908. https://doi.org/10.1016/j.landusepol.2019.03.021.

Shiklomanov, Nikolay I., and Marlene Laruelle. "A Truly Arctic City: An Introduction to the Special Issue on the City of Norilsk, Russia." *Polar Geography* 40, no. 4 (October 2, 2017): 251–56. https://doi.org/10.1080/1088937X.2017.1387823.

Shleifer, Andrei, and Daniel Treisman. "A Normal Country." National Bureau of Economic Research Working Paper Series, no. 10057 (November 2003). http:// www.nber.org/papers/w10057.

Shmakov, Mikhail. "Press Conference with Independent Trade Unions Federation Chairman Mikhail Shmakov." Federal News Service, December 3, 2001.

Shorrocks, Anthony, James B. Davies, Rodrigo Lluberas, and Antonios Koutsoukis. "Global Wealth Report 2016." Zurich: Credit Suisse AG, November 2016.

Shorrocks, Anthony, and Stanislav Kolenikov. "Poverty Trends in Russia during the Transition." January 1, 2001. Unpublished manuscript.

Shtanov, Vladimir. "'AvtoVAZ' prodolzhit optimizatsiiu chislennosti sotrud-nikov." *Vedomosti*, October 2, 2016. https://www.vedomosti.ru/newspaper/articles/2016/10/03/659316-avtovaz-optimizatsiyu.

——. "Subsidii dlia 'AvtoVAZa' mogut sokratit'sia bolee chem vtroe do 600 mln rublei." *Vedomosti*, July 10, 2017. https://www.vedomosti.ru/auto/articles/2017/07/10/717264-subsidii-avtovaza.

Siberian Times. "'There Is No Way Back,' Prime Minister Medvedev Says as the Main Polluter of Lake Baikal Is to Close." June 19, 2013.

Siegelbaum, Lewis H. *Cars for Comrades: The Life of the Soviet Automobile*. Ithaca, NY: Cornell University Press, 2008.

——. "'Little Tsars of the Road': Soviet Truck Drivers and Automobility, 1920s–1980s." In *The Socialist Car: Automobility in the Eastern Bloc*, edited by Lewis H. Siegelbaum. Ithaca, NY: Cornell University Press, 2011.

Sil, Rudra. "The Fluidity of Labor Politics in Postcommunist Transitions: Rethinking the Narrative of Russian Labor Quiescence." In *Political Creativity: Reconfiguring Institutional Order and Change*, edited by Gerald Berk, Dennis Galvan, and Victoria Hattam, 188–208. Philadelphia: University of Pennsylvania Press, 2013.

——. "Privatization, Labor Politics, and the Firm in Post-Soviet Russia: Non-market Norms, Market Institutions and the Soviet Legacy." In *The Politics of Labor in a Global Age: Continuity and Change in Late-Industrializing and Post-Socialist Economies*, edited by Christopher Candland and Rudra Sil, 205–32. Oxford: Oxford University Press, 2001.

Silitski, Vitali. "Preempting Democracy: The Case of Belarus." *Journal of Democracy* 16, no. 4 (October 2005): 83–97.

——. "A Year after the Color Revolutions: Preemptive Authoritarianism and Challenges for Democratization in the Former Soviet Union." PONARS Euarasia, Policy Memo 376, December 2005. http://www.ponarseurasia.org/memo/year-after-color-revolutions-preemptive-authoritarianism-and-challenges-democratization-former.

Silver, Beverly J. *Forces of Labor: Workers' Movements and Globalization since 1870*. Cambridge: Cambridge University Press, 2003.

Sinelschikova, Yekaterina. "'Putin's People': The Mysterious Agency That Guards the President's Life." Russia beyond the Headlines, June 1, 2016. https://www.rbth.com/politics_and_society/2016/06/01/putins-people-the-mysterious-agency-that-guards-the-presidents-life_599181.

Sivashenkov, Aleksei. "Roboty ne bastuiut: Chto izvestno o novom prezidente 'AvtoVAZa.'" Lenta.ru, March 16, 2016. https://lenta.ru/articles/2016/03/15/avtovaz/.

Smyth, Regina, and Irina Soboleva. "Looking beyond the Economy: Pussy Riot and the Kremlin's Voting Coalition." *Post-Soviet Affairs* 30, no. 4 (July 4, 2014): 257–75. https://doi.org/10.1080/1060586X.2013.865940.

Sobesednik. "'Sindrom' Pikalevo." June 16, 2009. https://sobesednik.ru/politics/pikalevo.

Solovenko, Igor S., and Tatiana S. Kust. "Social Attitudes to Miners' Protests during the Transition to Market Relations (1992–1999)." *Procedia—Social and Behavioral Sciences, Proceedings of the International Conference on Research Paradigms Transformation in Social Sciences 2014* (RPTSS-2014), 166 (January 7, 2015): 660–65. https://doi.org/10.1016/j.sbspro.2014.12.592.

Solov'eva, Ol'ga. "FSO i profsoiuzy pomogaiut sledit' za sotsial'nym dinamitom." *Nezavisimaya Gazeta*, December 16, 2015. http://www.ng.ru/economics/2015-12-16/4_fso.html.

——. "Zhitelei monogorodov prevratiat v predprinimatelei." *Nezavisimaya Gazeta*, March 2, 2017. http://www.ng.ru/economics/2017-03-01/1_6939_shuvalov.html.

Song, Houbing, Ravi Srinivasan, Tamim Sookoor, and Sabina Jeschke. *Smart Cities: Foundations, Principles, and Applications*. Hoboken, NJ: John Wiley & Sons, 2017.

Soskice, David. "Strike Waves and Wage Explosions, 1968–1970: An Economic Interpretation." In *The Resurgence of Class Conflict in Western Europe since 1968*, edited by Colin Crouch and Alessandro Pizzorno, 221–46. New York: Holmes & Meier, 1978.

Sperling, Valerie. *Sex, Politics, and Putin: Political Legitimacy in Russia*. New York: Oxford University Press, 2015.

Stack, Megan K. "Russians Want U-Turn on Taxing Car Imports." *Los Angeles Times*, December 23, 2008. http://articles.latimes.com/2008/dec/23/world/fg-russia-autos23.

Standing, Guy. "Reviving Dead Souls." In *Structural Adjustment without Mass Unemployment*, edited by Simon Clarke, 147–85. Cheltenham, UK: Edward Elgar, 1998.

Statistics Canada. "Statistics Canada: Canada's National Statistical Agency." February 1, 1995. https://www.statcan.gc.ca/eng/start.

Stoliarova, Viktoriia. "'Oni prakticheski pustye': Pochemu v Rossii umiraiut monogoroda." TVK6.ru. Accessed January 22, 2020. https://www.tvk6.ru/publications/sunday-news/46592/.

Stolyarov, Gleb. "In Russia's Detroit, Layoffs Are Blamed on Foreign Interlopers." Reuters, April 27, 2016. https://www.reuters.com/article/us-russia-avtovaz/in-russias-detroit-layoffs-are-blamed-on-foreign-interlopers-idUSKCN0XO0EE.

Strange, Clayton. *Monotown: Urban Dreams Brutal Imperatives*. San Francisco: Oro Editions, 2019.

Strangleman, Tim, and James Rhodes. "The 'New' Sociology of Deindustrialisation? Understanding Industrial Change." *Sociology Compass* 8, no. 4 (2014): 411–21. https://doi.org/10.1111/soc4.12143.

Streeck, Wolfgang. "Trump and the Trumpists." *Inference: International Review of Science* 3, no. 1 (April 2017). http://inference-review.com/article/trump-and-the-trumpists.

Stubbs, Jack. "Prospects Brighten for Russian Steelmakers as Economy Improves." Reuters, January 27, 2017. https://in.reuters.com/article/russia-steel-2017-idINL5N1FH21R.

Sudakov, Dmitry. "Putin Buys Russian Car to Save Home Industry from Decline." PravdaReport, March 30, 2009. http://www.pravdareport.com/society/107326-putin_russian_car/.

Svolik, Milan W. *The Politics of Authoritarian Rule*. Cambridge: Cambridge University Press, 2012.

Szakonyi, David. "Monopolies Rising: Consolidation in the Russian Economy." PONARS Euarasia, Policy Memo 491, November 2, 2017. http://www.ponarseurasia.org/memo/monopolies-rising-consolidation-russian-economy.

Takahashi, Yukichi. "The Labor Market and Lifetime Employment in Japan." *Economic and Industrial Democracy* 18, no. 1 (February 1, 1997): 55–66. https://doi.org/10.1177/0143831X97181003.

TASS. "Putin Signs Law on Minimum Wage Hike to $195 Starting 2020." Accessed January 21, 2020. https://tass.com/economy/1104553.

——. "Schetnaia Palata: Depressivnye monogoroda ne poluchali subsidii ot gosprogrammy s 2016 goda." July 29, 2019. https://tass.ru/ekonomika/6713799.

——. "Spisok monogorodov v Rossii 'zamorozhen' do kontsa 2018 goda." January 16, 2017. https://tass.ru/ekonomika/3944436.

Taubman, William. *Governing Soviet Cities: Bureaucratic Politics and Urban Development in the USSR*. New York: Praeger, 1973.

Teague, Elizabeth. "How Did the Russian Population Respond to the Global Financial Crisis?" *Journal of Communist Studies and Transition Politics* 27, no. 3–4 (December 1, 2011): 420–33. https://doi.org/10.1080/13523279.2011.596118.

Tepliakov, Sergei. "Sergei Mukhortov: 'Ia ne ponimal, naskol'ko eto neprosto—sovmeshchat' biznes i politiku.'" *Kapitalist: Zhurnal o biznese*, February 5, 2016. http://kapitalist.tv/2016/02/05/sergey-mukhortov-ya-ne-ponimal-naskol/.

Tilly, Charles. *From Mobilization to Revolution*. New York: McGraw-Hill, 1978.

Titov, Sergei. "Proizvoditel' tankov 'Armata' poprosit gospodderzhki na 16 mlrd rub." *RBK*, July 12, 2016. https://www.rbc.ru/business/12/07/2016/5784cf7b9a7947a2 3a3f7818.

Tkachev, Ivan. "Issledovanie RBK: Skol'ko v Rossii chinovnikov i mnogo li oni zarabatyvaiut." *RBK*, October 15, 2014. http://top.rbc.ru/economics/15/10/2014/543 cfe56cbb20f8c4e0b98f2.

Tkachev, Ivan, and Anton Feinberg. "Zerkalo zastoia: Chto nuzhno znat' o novom reitinge RBK 500." *RBK*, September 21, 2017. http://www.rbc.ru/economics/21/ 09/2017/59c061fd9a7947581a01ed0c.

TLTReporter. "Tol'iatti stal monogorodom pervoi kategorii." November 6, 2015. http:// tltreporter.ru/tolyatti-stal-monogorodom-pervoj-kategorii/.

Todorova, Maria, and Zsuzsa Gille. *Post-Communist Nostalgia*. New York: Berghahn Books, 2012.

Tol'iatti Onlain. "V Tol'iatti poiavitsia bol'she 10 tysiach bezrabotnykh." March 18, 2016.

Tooze, J. Adam. *Crashed: How a Decade of Financial Crises Changed the World*. New York: Viking, 2018.

Tovkailo, Maksim, Anatoly Tyomkin, and Katya Nazarova. "AvtoVAZ Workers Offered Chance to Move." *Moscow Times*, January 29, 2010.

Townsend, Anthony M. *Smart Cities: Big Data, Civic Hackers, and the Quest for a New Utopia*. New York: W. W. Norton, 2013.

Traub-Merz, Rudolf. "Automotive Industry in Russia: Between Growth and Decline." In *The Automotive Sector in Emerging Economies: Industrial Policies, Market Dynamics and Trade Unions; Trends & Perspectives in Brazil, China, India, Mexico and Russia*, edited by Rudolf Traub-Merz, 127–47. Berlin: Friedrich-Ebert-Stiftung, 2017.

Treisman, Daniel. "Presidential Popularity in a Hybrid Regime: Russia under Yeltsin and Putin." *American Journal of Political Science* 55, no. 3 (2011): 590–609. https://doi.org/10.1111/j.1540-5907.2010.00500.x.

Tribuna. "FNPR proshla nezavisimuiu e'kspertizu." April 8, 2010, no. 13 edition.

Troianovski, Anton. "Putin's Helsinki Showmanship Starts with His Limo." *Washington Post*, July 16, 2018. https://www.washingtonpost.com/news/worldviews/ wp/2018/07/16/putins-helsinki-showmanship-starts-with-his-limo/.

Trotsky, Leon. *The History of the Russian Revolution*. Translated by Max Eastman. 1st paperback ed. New York: Anchor Foundation, 1980.

Tsang, Amie. "Who Is Carlos Ghosn and Why Is He in Trouble?" *New York Times*, November 21, 2018, sec. Business. https://www.nytimes.com/2018/11/21/busi ness/who-is-carlos-ghosn.html.

Tsentr sotsial'no-trudovykh prav. "Kak protestuiut rossiiane: Rezul'taty monitoringa protestnoi aktivnosti v pervom kvartale 2019 goda." 2019. trudprava.ru.

—— "Verkhovnyi sud otmenil skandal'noe reshenie o likvidatsii profsoiuza." Accessed August 17, 2019. http://trudprava.ru/news/unionnews/2022/2022.

Tsentr strategicheskikh razrabotok. "Tekhnologii umnogo goroda v rossiiskikh gorodakh: Prioritetnye napravleniia vnedreniia." Moscow: Tsentr strategicheskikh razrabotok, June 2018.

TsEPR. "Karta sotsial'no-ekonomisheskikh goriachikh tochek: Rezul'taty monitoringa za pervyi kvartal 2016 goda." Tsentr ekonomicheskikh i politicheskikh reform, 2017. cepr.su/.

——. "Monitoring sotsial'no-ekonomicheskoi napriazhennosti v trudovoi sfere v 2016 godu: Itogi." May 17, 2017.

——. "Protestnaia situatsiia v regionakh." February 1, 2016. cepr.su/wp-content/uploads/2016/02/Протестная-ситуация.pdf.

——. "Protestnyi 2017 god: Rost chisla protestov vo II kvartale goda." July 10, 2017. http://cepr.su/2017/07/10/.

Turovsky, Daniil. "The Novocherkassk Massacre: How the Soviet Authorities Murdered Peaceful Demonstrators in 1962 and Kept It a Secret for Decades, until the Victims Fought Back." Meduza, November 22, 2017. https://meduza.io/en/feature/2017/11/23/the-novocherkassk-massacre.

United Nations. "World Urbanization Prospects." World Urbanization Prospects—Population Division—United Nations. Accessed October 5, 2018. https://population.un.org/wup/.

US Census Bureau. "American FactFinder—Results." Accessed October 5, 2018. https://factfinder.census.gov/faces/tableservices/jsf/pages/productview.xhtml?pid=PEP_2017_PEPANNRES&prodType=table.

Ushakin, S. The Patriotism of Despair: Nation, War, and Loss in Russia. Culture and Society after Socialism. Ithaca, NY: Cornell University Press, 2009.

US News & World Report. "In World Cup's Shadow, Layoffs and Anger at Russian Factory." June 15, 2018. https://www.usnews.com/news/world/articles/2018-06-15/in-world-cups-shadow-layoffs-and-anger-at-russian-factory.

Varga, Mihai. Worker Protests in Post-Communist Romania and Ukraine: Striking with Tied Hands. Manchester: Manchester University Press, 2014.

Varsegov, Nikolai, Elena Blaginina, and Oleg Adamovich. "V glubinku dorogu prolozhim, sozhzhem milliardy rublei." Komsomolskaya Pravda, January 17, 2017. https://www.kp.ru/daily/26630/3649576/.

Vedomosti. "Freedom from Labor." April 15, 2010.

——. "Gorod 'AvtoVAZ.'" July 17, 2009. https://www.vedomosti.ru/opinion/articles/2009/07/17/ot-redakcii-gorod-avtovaz.

——. "Vladimir Gimpel'son: Gde vziat' 25 mln rabochikh mest." February 19, 2013. https://www.vedomosti.ru/opinion/articles/2013/02/19/v_poiskah_25_millionov.

Vesti.ru. "Dying Soviet 'Monotowns' to Be Repurposed! The Era of Bleak Industrial Rust Cities Is Over!" August 9, 2019. https://www.vesti.ru/doc.html?id=3176985&cid=4441.

Vinogradova, Elena, Irina Kozina, and Linda Cook. "Russian Labor: Quiescence and Conflict." Communist and Post-Communist Studies 45, no. 3–4 (2012): 219–31.

Volin, Oleg. "How Capitalism Kills in Nizhny Tagil." Russian Reader (blog), March 1, 2019. https://therussianreader.com/2019/03/01/oleg-volin-how-capitalism-kills-in-nizhny-tagil/.

Volkov, Denis. "Russian Society Wants Change—but of What Nature?" Carnegie Moscow Center, August 29, 2017. https://carnegie.ru/commentary/?fa=72933&mkt_tok=eyJpIjoiWm1FeU1UY3haVGd.

Volkov, Vadim. *Violent Entrepreneurs: The Use of Force in the Making of Russian Capitalism*. Ithaca, NY: Cornell University Press, 2002.

Voskoboynikov, Ilya B. "Structural Change, Expanding Informality and Labor Productivity Growth in Russia." *Review of Income and Wealth* 66, no. 2 (2020): 394–417. https://doi.org/10.1111/roiw.12417.

Vujacic, Veljko. "Gennadiy Zyuganov and the 'Third Road.'" *Post-Soviet Affairs* 12, no. 2 (1996): 118–54.

Vulikh, Yekaterina. "'Ia otlip ot televizora i prozrel.' Pochemu Riazanskie perevozchiki sobiraiutsia na vserossiiskuiu stachku." 7x7, March 22, 2017. https://7x7-jour nal.ru/articles/2017/03/22/ya-otlip-ot-televizora-i-prozrel-pochemu-ryazan skie-perevozchiki-sobirayutsya-na-vserossijskuyu-stachku.

Walker, Charlie. "In Search of 'Stability': Working-Class Men, Masculinity and Wellbeing in Contemporary Russia." In *Masculinities under Neoliberalism*, edited by Andrea Cornwall, Frank G. Karioris, and Nancy Lindisfarne, 51–65. London: Zed Books, 2016.

Wallace, Jeremy. "Cities, Redistribution, and Authoritarian Regime Survival." *Journal of Politics* 75, no. 3 (July 1, 2013): 632–45. https://doi.org/10.1017/S0022381613000340.

Walsh, Bryan. "Urban Wastelands: The World's 10 Most Polluted Places." *Time*, November 4, 2013. http://science.time.com/2013/11/04/ urban-wastelands-the-worlds-10-most-polluted-places/slide/norilsk-russia/.

Warburton, Simon. "AvtoVAZ Hikes Layoffs to 13,000 as Market Falls." *Just Auto*, June 10, 2014. http://www.just-auto.com/news/more-avtovaz-pruning-sees-job-losses-accel erate-to-13000_id146970.aspx.

Washington Post. "Backsliding in Russia." January 11, 2003. https://www.washingtonpost. com/archive/opinions/2003/01/11/backsliding-in-russia/57159167-fc45-4cce-a7ec-a05626a6b670/.

Way, Lucan. *Pluralism by Default: Weak Autocrats and the Rise of Competitive Politics*. Baltimore: Johns Hopkins University Press, 2015.

Wengle, Susanne A. *Post-Soviet Power: State-Led Development and Russia's Marketization*. New York: Cambridge University Press, 2015.

Wengle, Susanne A., and Michael Rasell. "The Monetisation of l'goty: Changing Patterns of Welfare Politics and Provision in Russia." *Europe-Asia Studies* 60, no. 5 (July 1, 2008): 739–56. https://doi.org/10.1080/09668130802085125.

White, Stephen, Ian McAllister, and Neil Munro. "Economic Inequality and Political Stability in Russia and China." *Europe-Asia Studies* 69, no. 1 (January 2, 2017): 1–7. https://doi.org/10.1080/09668136.2016.1270580.

Whitmore, Brian. "Thousands Rally across Russia against Government." RadioFreeEurope/RadioLiberty, March 20, 2010. https://www.rferl.org/a/At_Least_1500_ Rally_Against_Putin_In_Vladivostok/1989060.html.

Wines, Michael. "The World; O.K., the Ruble's Junk. Not to Worry. Russians Get By." *New York Times*, September 6, 1998, sec. Week in Review. https://www.nytimes. com/1998/09/06/weekinreview/the-world-ok-the-ruble-s-junk-not-to-worry-russians-get-by.html.

W.M. Mercer Consulting. "Worldwide Benefit and Employment Guidelines 2001/2002." November 5, 2001.

Wood, Tony. *Russia without Putin: Money, Power and the Myths of the New Cold War*. London: Verso, 2018.

Woodruff, David. *Money Unmade: Barter and the Fate of Russian Capitalism*. Ithaca, NY: Cornell University Press, 1999.

Working, Russell. "Russia's Patchwork Economy; Korean Companies, Chinese Workers and U.S. Entrée." *New York Times*, March 18, 1999, sec. Business. https://www.

nytimes.com/1999/03/18/business/russia-s-patchwork-economy-korean-com
   panies-chinese-workers-and-us-entree.html?searchResultPosition=1.
World Bank. "The Challenge of Russia's Monotowns." Russian Economic Report, no. 22
   (June 2010).
———. "Reducing Poverty through Growth and Social Policy Reform in Russia." Wash-
   ington, DC: World Bank, 2006.
———. "Russia: Reshaping Economic Geography." Washington, DC: World Bank, 2011.
———. "Russia's Recovery: How Strong Are Its Shoots?" November 1, 2017. http://docum
   ents.worldbank.org/curated/en/526851512129359061/Russia-s-recovery-How-
   strong-are-its-shoots.
World Bank Group. "Rolling Back Russia's Spatial Disparities: Re-assembling the
   Soviet Jigsaw under a Market Economy." World Bank Publications, 2018. http://
   www.worldbank.org/en/country/russia/publication/rolling-back-russias-
   spatial-disparities.
Wright, Erik Olin. Classes. 2nd ed. New York: Verso, 1998.
———. "Working-Class Power, Capitalist-Class Interests, and Class Compromise."
   American Journal of Sociology 105, no. 4 (January 2000): 957–1002.
Wynn, Charters. Workers, Strikes, and Pogroms: The Donbass-Dnepr Bend in Late Impe-
   rial Russia, 1870–1905. Princeton, NJ: Princeton University Press, 1992.
Yakovlev, Andrei. "What Is Russia Trying to Defend?" Russian Journal of Economics 2,
   no. 2 (May 31, 2016): 146–61. https://doi.org/10.1016/j.ruje.2016.06.003.
Yakutin, E. M., and N. A. Matern. "'Sindrom Pikalievo' v ekonomike Rossii." EKO.
   Vserossiiskii ekonomicheskii zhurnal, no. 7 (July 2010): 127–34.
Yankov, Kirill. "Monogoroda s problemami i bez." Vedomosti, November 19, 2019.
   https://www.vedomosti.ru/opinion/articles/2019/11/20/816677-monogoroda-
   problemami.
YouTube. "Novosti OPR s Andreem Bazhutinym. Vypusk #5, 23.06.17." Accessed July 20,
   2017. https://www.youtube.com/watch?v=VPi89TWRybA.
Zainiev, Anton. "20 let zabastovok." Trud, September 30, 2009, no. 182 edition.
Zamyatina, N., and A. Pilyasov. Innovatsionnyi poisk v monoprofil'nykh gorodakh:
   Blokirovki razvitiia, novaia promyshlennaia politika i dorozhnaia karta peremen.
   Moscow: URSS, 2015.
———. "Single-Industry Towns of Russia: Lock-In and Drivers of Innovative Search."
   Foresight and STI Governance 10, no. 3 (2016): 53–64.
Zheleznova, Maria. "Bezalabernost' protiv terrorizma." Vedomosti, January 9, 2019. https://
   www.vedomosti.ru/opinion/articles/2019/01/09/790940-bezalabernost-protiv-
   terrorizma.
Zhukov, Yuri M. "Rust Belt Rising." Foreign Affairs, June 11, 2014. https://www.for
   eignaffairs.com/articles/eastern-europe-caucasus/2014-06-11/rust-belt-rising.
"Zipf's Law for Cities—a Simple Explanation for Urban Populations." Networks course
   blog for INFO 2040/CS 2850/Econ 2040/SOC 2090. Accessed June 25, 2019. https://
   blogs.cornell.edu/info2040/2016/11/13/zipfs-law-for-cities-a-simple-explanation-
   for-urban-populations/.
Zubarevich, Natalia. "Chetyre Rossii." Vedomosti.ru, December 30, 2011. http://www.
   vedomosti.ru/opinion/news/1467059/chetyre_rossii.
———. "Four Russias: Rethinking the Post-Soviet Map." openDemocracy. Accessed
   August 28, 2014. https://www.opendemocracy.net/od-russia/natalia-zubarevich/
   four-russias-rethinking-post-soviet-map.
———. "Geopolitical Priorities in Russia's Regional Policies." Russian Politics & Law 53,
   no. 5–6 (November 2, 2015): 44–62. https://doi.org/10.1080/10611940.2015.11
   46060.

——. "Gubernatoropad: K chemu privedet nyneshniaia volna otstavok glav regionov." Carnegie Moscow Center. Accessed August 15, 2018. https://carnegie.ru/commentary/73299.

——. *Regiony Rossii: Neravenstvo, krizis, modernizatsiya.* Moscow: Nezavisimyi institut sotsial'noi politiki, 2010.

——. "Sotsial'naya differentsiatsiya regionov i gorodov." *Pro et Contra*, October 2012, 135–52.

——. "Strana gotova szhimat'sya i vyzhivat'." Rosbalt, January 8, 2016. http://www.rosbalt.ru/business/2016/01/08/1476897.html.

Zvezdina, Polina. "Eksperty rasskazali o stavke nizhe 25 tys. rub. u poloviny vrachei." *RBK*, December 11, 2017. https://www.rbc.ru/society/08/12/2017/5a2a74c29a79476a18384ffd.

Index

Page numbers in italic refer to figures.

Alasheev, Sergei, 35
Albats, Yevgenia, 159
Aleshin, Boris, 136
alternative unions, 106, 108, 120–21, 123, 132–33, 153, 172, 203. *See also* trade unions
Andersson, Bo Inge, 141–43, 145, 147–50, 152–54, 238n123
Appel, Hilary, 190–91
Arab Spring uprisings, 160, 176, 208
Aris, Ben, 198, 214n51
Armenia, 193
Artiakov, Vladimir, 131, 138, 151
Artiukh, Volodymyr, 196–98
Asbest, 94
Ashwin, Sarah, 105
Åslund, Anders, 35, 217n59
attachment to place, 91–94, 98, 189, 203, 227n144, 236n71. *See also* immobility; rootedness
Audit Chamber, 88, 96
austerity, 104, 123, 186
Australia, 60, 75
authoritarian regimes, 2–11, 16–18, 44, 156, 173, 210, 213n8, 242n39. *See also* state control over economy
automobile industry: in China, 200; import substitution in, 131–32, 134–37; protectionism and, 134–35; strikes, 132–33, 137, 143–44, 149–50; trade unions, 115, 132–33, 142–44, 146, 153, 204. *See also* MPRA (Interregional Trade Union of Autoworkers); subsidies
AvtoVAZ (auto factory), 22, 82, 158, 166; economic crisis in, 135–42; labor productivity, 149, *150*; labor protests and, 145–54; layoffs, 142–45, 148–49, 152–54, 164, 227n118, 237n96; social services provided by, 136, 139–40; in Soviet era, 127–31, 200
AvtoVAZagregat (AVA), 145–53, 237n109

Babchenko, Arkady, 179, 210, 242n40
Baikalsk pulp and paper mill, 81, 83–84

Baltic states, 90–91
Balzer, Harley, 66
bankruptcies, 28, 31, 33, 62, 137, 139, 141, 149, 152–53, 163, 182, 199, 217n44
barter, 35–36
Bazhutin, Andrei, 177–78, 180–82
Belarus: deindustrialization, 187, 192, 201; labor protest and color revolution, 5, 16, 22, 155, 169–70, 195–98, 204, 207–8; protectionism, 59
Benteler Automotive, 132–33
Berezovsky, Boris, 129
Bershidsky, Leonid, 89, 98, 209
Betting, J. L. F., 238n140
Bizyukov, Petr, 116, 120
Bolotova, Alla, 93, 227n144
Brancati, Dawn, 8
Brazil, 75, 224n23
Brexit, 189
Brezhnev era, 105, 215n61
BRIC countries (Brazil, Russia, India, China), 10, 189, 201
budget-sector workers, 122–23, 167, 203, 229n18, 234n124
Bulgaria, 216n27
Bulldozer Revolution, 156, 213n7
bunt (spontaneous protest), 9, 11, 120

Canada, 75–76
capitalism, 10–11, 17, 22, 27, 54, 102, 190, 215n61; accumulation and, 6, 70, 174, 210, 212; advanced capitalist economies, 6, 11, 56–58, 95, 101, 128, 187–201; global, 10, 210; "state capitalism," 197, 207. *See also* postcommunism
"catness" (categories), 19, 119–24, 183, 206
Center for Economic and Political Reforms (CEPR), 116–18, 124–25
Center for Strategic Research, 71, 160
Chelyabinsk, 95
Chemezov, Sergei, 148–49, 152–54
Chen, Xi, 165, 198–99
Cherepovets, 96

Shmakov, Mikhail, 102–3, 106–7, 109
shortage economy, 25–26, 28, 46, 54, 101–2
Shuvalov, Igor, 87–88
Siberia, 44, 76, 85, 90
Siegelbaum, Lewis, 128, 136, 241n8
Sil, Rudra, 165, 214n31, 215n56, 221n68
Silitski, Vitali, 18
single-industry towns. *See* monotowns
sitsevaia revolution, 121
skills training, 56–57
SLC database, 116–17, 120, 233n105
Slovakia, 37, 131, 191, 216n27
slowdowns ("Italian strikes"), 116, 197
Smyth, Regina, 165
Soboleva, Irina, 165
social explosion, fear of, 12–13, 23, 27, 39, 46,
    69, 202; auto industry and, 152–54; labor
    relations and, 125–26; military industry
    and, 64–65; monotowns and, 80–84, 97–99;
    regional leaders and, 34–37. *See also* unrest,
    social and political
social mobility, 35–36
social sphere, 2, 25–26, 160, 165–68, 203;
    cuts to benefits, 20, 121–23, 186, 204, 206,
    242n39; services provided by industrial
    enterprises, 12–13, 25, 32, 34, 44, 73, 77–78,
    83, 136, 139, 215n5, 217n30. *See also*
    unemployment benefits; welfare state
Solidarity (Poland), 10, 26, 190
South Korea, 7, 58
Soviet Union: collapse of, 10, 12, 24, 34, 50,
    129, 205, 216n14; former Soviet republics,
    201 (*see also individual countries*);
    industrialization, 12, 22, 24, 40, 69, 73–77,
    188, 201 (*see also* monotowns); military
    industry, 63; *nomenklatura*, 215n61;
    Novocherkassk uprising, 9, 26, 78, 97;
    unions in, 101–2
special economic zones (TORs), 85–87, 144
spontaneous protests, 9, 11, 109, 120–22, 175,
    180, 203, 205
SPU, 118, 124
stability, 40, 42–46, 156–65, 205; economic
    conditions and, 7–8, 22, 201, 246n19;
    foreign investment and, 191; labor protest
    and, 2–3, 17; labor relations and, 125–26;
    large industrial enterprises and, 12–15;
    monotowns and, 73; stagnation and, 20.
    See also social explosion, fear of; vertical of
    power
stagnation, 3, 20–21, 163–64, 211
Stalinism, 9, 24, 69
Stammler, Florian, 93, 227n144

standards of living, 20–21, 36, 164. *See also*
    poverty
Standing, Guy, 36, 217n56
state control over economy, 18, 44–46, 58–59,
    127, 135, 153, 155, 208, 210–11; economic
    crises and, 159, 173; labor productivity
    and, 65–68; monotowns and, 91 (*see also*
    monotowns); state-owned banks, 221n70;
    state-owned enterprises, 61, 67, 207. *See also*
    authoritarian regimes; reforms; subsidies
steel industry, 11, 95–96, 215n2, 215n5,
    228n151
Stepashin, Sergei, 37, 104
Stephenson, Irene, 157
St. Petersburg, 14, 71–72, 74–75, 90, 132, 202
Streeck, Wolfgang, 189
strikes, 9, 46; in 1990s, 35, 103–5, 172;
    alternative unions and, 108; auto industry,
    132–33, 137, 143–44, 149–50; in Belarus,
    196–98; in budget sector, 229n18; coal
    miners, 9, 11–12, 26–27, 103–4, 157, 193,
    195, 205, 209; economic conditions and,
    13, 114–16; health care workers, 123;
    laws against (*see* labor laws); numbers of,
    232n94; pre-strike procedures, 231n60;
    truckers, 176, 180–81; in Ukraine, 193–95;
    wildcat, 16, 109. *See also* hunger strikes;
    labor protest
subsidies, 20, 44, 60–62, 80, 209; auto industry,
    129–31, 139–41, 150, 152–55, 158, 203–4,
    236n50; for monotowns, 84–85, 88, 91, 95,
    97; votes and, 66–67. *See also* state control
    over economy
suicide, 36, 104–5, 118, 163, 218n71, 233n106
Sverdlovsk, 95
Svolik, Milan, 7
Sweden, 48, 56
Szakonyi, David, 62, 66

Taiwan, 7, 58
taxes, 20, 31, 175–78, 180–83, 185, 246n5
teachers, 123, 218n65, 229n18, 234n124
technology, 56–57, 64
Thatcher, Margaret, 39
TIGR, 138, 236n57
Tikhvin, 139–40
Tilly, Charles, 16, 19, 119, 121, 183
Titov, Konstantin, 130–31, 141
Togliatti, Palmiro, 128
Tolyatti (city), 22, 82, 126, 236n71;
    establishment of, 188; protests in, 121,
    145–54; state support for, 154, 203–4;
    support for Putin in, 164; unemployment

CPSIA information can be obtained
at www.ICGtesting.com
Printed in the USA
LVHW011934230322
714108LV00012BA/607